The Artist as Economist

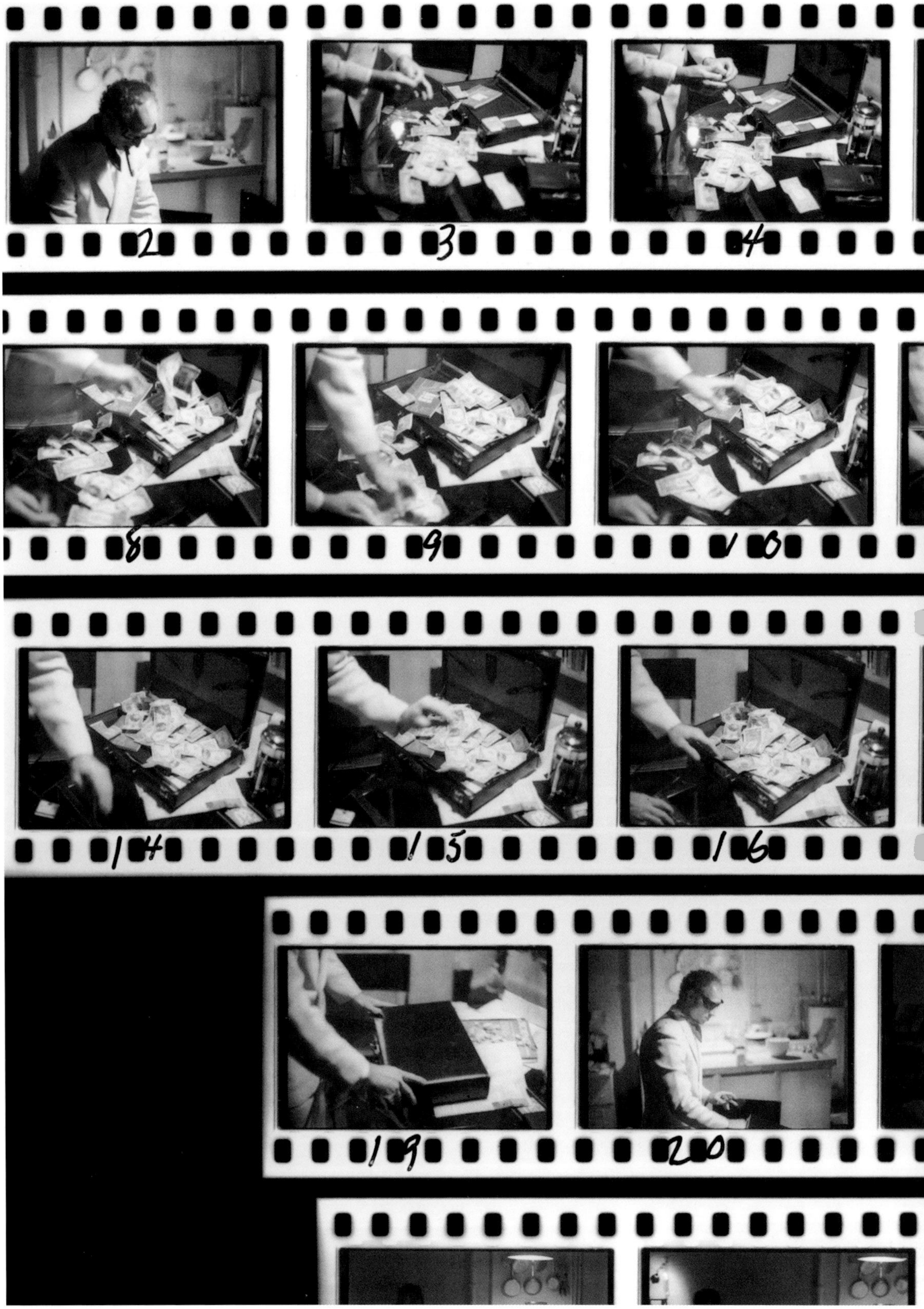
2
3
4
8
9
10
14
15
16
19
20

The Artist as Economist

Art and Capitalism in the 1960s

Sophie Cras

Translated from the French by Malcolm DeBevoise

Yale University Press
New Haven and London

This publication has been made possible through support from the Terra Foundation for American Art International Publication Program of CAA.

Cet ouvrage a bénéficié du soutien des Programmes d'aide à la publication de l'Institut français.

This work received the French Voices Award for excellence in publication and translation. French Voices is a program created and funded by the French Embassy in the United States and FACE Foundation (French American Cultural Exchange).

Avec le concours de l'Ecole doctorale 441 Histoire de l'art, Université Paris 1 Panthéon-Sorbonne. Avec le concours de l'HiCSA, Université Paris 1 Panthéon-Sorbonne.

The present volume is a translation, with revisions, of *L'économie à l'épreuve de l'art: Art et capitalisme dans les années 1960* (Les presses du réel, 2018).

yalebooks.com/art

Designed by Jeff Wincapaw and Jo Ellen Ackerman
Cover designed by Jo Ellen Ackerman
Set in Akagi Pro and Adobe Text Pro type
Printed in China through Asia Pacific Offset

Library of Congress Control Number: 2018967999
ISBN 978-0-300-23270-7

A catalogue record for this book is available from the British Library.

This paper meets the requirements of ANSI/NISO Z39.48-1992 (Permanence of Paper).

10 9 8 7 6 5 4 3 2 1

Jacket illustrations: (front) fig. 27; (back) detail of fig. 66
Frontispiece: detail of fig. 56

Contents

Foreword

Just like the artist Robert Filliou, who plays a key role in her book, art historian Sophie Cras has professional training as an economist. While undertaking her advanced work in art history at the École Normale Supérieure (ENS), she completed a master's degree in finance from the Paris Institute d'études politiques (Sciences Po), where she graduated summa cum laude. Her rigorous academic background in both art history and economics has enabled her to author the present book, in which she examines with keen nuance the ways in which money and financial systems became a central focus of artistic practice in the 1960s.

The Artist as Economist: Art and Capitalism in the 1960s (expertly translated from the French by Malcolm DeBevoise) considers how artists in both the United States and Europe—most of whom did not have Filliou's expertise even as they shared his interest in economics—engaged with issues of monetary exchange between 1955 and 1975. Cras develops not parallel tales but overlapping stories as she traces the practices of artists who traveled among New York, Paris, and other European capitals. In so doing she pays careful attention to the regional varieties of capitalist economics, while also tracing overarching commonalities such as anxieties about financial stability, the development of a neoliberal economic discourse, and the international economic crisis at the beginning of the 1970s.

In the pages that follow, Cras presents a complex and historically specific analysis of how art participated in economic systems in the 1960s. She discusses the manifold ways in which artists tried to come to grips with the financial market, whether representing paper money or stock charts directly, turning the act of investing into a work of art, or critiquing economic systems themselves. She also brings to light the ambiguous and intriguing interrelationships between economic and aesthetic valuation. The text is attentive to the specifics of local financial context, the emergence of economic expertise and the debates among economists in the 1960s, the particularities of the work of art, and the cross-Atlantic dialogue among artists within the Western economic bloc during the Cold War.

But as it deepens our understanding of the era, this book also raises issues that remain pressing today, from the tensions over finances in the European Union to the extremes of financial speculation in the art market. It invites us to consider how artists of our time can reimagine the agency of the individual—and of art—within our economy.

CÉCILE WHITING

Acknowledgments

This book has benefited from the support and goodwill of so many people and institutions that it would be futile to even try to name them all.

I feel very lucky that this book, initially published in French by Les presses du réel in partnership with the German Center for Art History, is now accessible to a wider English-speaking audience in this new, revised and expanded edition. For this, I thank very warmly my publisher, Yale University Press, and especially Amy Canonico for her trust, and for accompanying me at every step of this project. Malcolm DeBevoise proved to be the most dedicated, meticulous, and talented translator any writer could hope to have. None of this would have been possible without the financial support of the Terra Foundation for American Art (Translation Grant), the Cultural Services of the French Embassy (Acquisition of Right Grant and French Voices Award, in partnership with the PEN American Center, with the support of the Florence Gould Foundation and the Andrew W. Mellon Foundation), as well as of the Doctoral School of Art History at the Université Paris 1–Panthéon-Sorbonne.

I would like to express my gratitude to the artists, or representatives from their estates, who agreed to meet with me, gave me access to documentation and artworks, graciously permitted the images in this book to be reproduced, and facilitated my research and publication: Mara Devereux, Maria Gilissen, Dan Graham, Les Levine, Larry Miller, Robert Morris, Peter Saul, Klaus Staeck, Ben Vautier, Bernar Venet and his studio, William Wilson, the Robert Filliou Estate (Peter Freeman, Inc.), Ray Johnson Estate (Richard L. Feigen and Co. and president Frances F. L. Beatty), Edward Kienholz Estate (L.A. Louver), Archives Yves Klein, Yayoi Kusama Studio, and Lee Lozano Estate (Hauser and Wirth). I owe special thanks to Liliana Dematteis (Archivio Gallizio) and Amy Plumb Oppenheim (Oppenheim Estate and Studio/Archive) for their time and generosity.

This study would not have been possible without the allowances, scholarships, and residencies I received, which allowed me to travel and work under exceptional conditions. I would therefore especially like to thank the institutions that have offered me their support: the Université Paris 1–Panthéon-Sorbonne, École Normale Supérieure, Remarque Institute at New York University, Terra Foundation for American Art, Smithsonian American Art Museum, Alliance Franco-Néerlandaise, École française de Rome, and German Center for Art History.

I am deeply indebted to the museum curators, librarians, archivists, collectors, and dealers who have generously given me access to works or archives and shared their knowledge and experiences in their field. I would particularly like to thank: Tobias Bäumer (Michael Werner Gallery), Claire Cauchy (Musée d'art moderne de Saint-Étienne), Anita Duquette (Whitney Museum of American Art), Baptiste Essevaz-Roulet, the late Joni Gordon (Newspace Gallery), Nicholas Martin (Fales Library, New York University), Mirjam Meisen (Bonnefantenmuseum), Ghislain Mollet-Viéville, Chiara Parisi, Claudia Pasko (Konrad Fischer Gallery), Michael Sampson (Secret Services, Washington, D.C.), Arturo Schwarz, Aimee Soubier (Hirshhorn Museum and Sculpture Garden), Gonçalo Sousa Pinto and Ursula Trieloff (Kunsthalle Hamburg), Franco Stella (Biblioteca d'arte della Fondazione Torino musei), Hana Streicher and Maik Schult (Staatliche Museen, Neue Nationalgalerie, Berlin), Matt Wrbican (Andy Warhol Museum), Michael Zakian (Frederick R. Weisman Museum of Art), the teams at the Archives of American Art, the Kandinsky Library, the Prints Department of the Bibliothèque nationale de France, the Nelson-Freeman Gallery, the Philadelphia Museum of Art, the Stedelijk Museum and its library, and the Getty Research Institute.

I would like to thank very warmly the colleagues and research groups who followed and supported this work as it developed. My gratitude goes to Philippe Dagen, my PhD advisor, as well as to the members of my jury, Laurence Bertrand Dorléac, Luc Boltanski, Evelyne Toussaint, and Jean-Marie Schaeffer. I also thank Ken Allan, Julia Bryan-Wilson, Benoît Buquet, Maggie Cao, Cathleen Chaffee, Loïc Charles and Yann Giraud (and the "History of Economics as Culture" group), Pauline Chevalier, Tony Côme, Larisa Dryansky, Vincent Duchaussoy (and the Historical Mission of the Banque de France), Jacopo Galimberti, Anne Goodyear, Charlotte Guichard, Arthur Jatteau and Simon Bittman (and the seminar "Multidisciplinary Approaches to the Economy"), Étienne Jollet, Déborah Laks, Patrice Maniglier (and all the participants of the "Art/Value" seminar), Julien Pénasse, Denys Riout, Rachel Stella, Alex Taylor, Erik Verhagen, all the fellows of the Smithsonian American Art Museum, of the Terra Foundation Summer Residency in Giverny, of the École française de Rome, and of the German Center for Art History, as well as my colleagues and students from the Université Paris 1-Panthéon-Sorbonne. My special thanks go to Trevor Merrill, Kaira Cabañas, Emmanuel Guy (and the participants of the "Sixties" seminar), Béatrice Joyeux-Prunel (and the Artlas team), Veerle Thielemans (and the entire team of the Terra Foundation in Paris), Cécile Whiting, Natalie Adamson, and the colleagues and friends who gave their time to review various stages of this work: Laurine Célarier, Charles Davoine, Morgan Labar, Maxime Morel, Constance Moréteau, Camille Paulhan, and Hélène Valance.

Finally, I would like to thank all my family and friends, as well as Eric and Noé.

Parts of this book have appeared in somewhat different form in journals in several countries. My discussion of Yves Klein in chapter 1 draws on my article "De la valeur de l'œuvre au prix du marché: Yves Klein à l'épreuve de la pensée économique," in *Marges*, no. 11 (November 2011): 30–45; in chapter 2, concerning Larry Rivers, see "Larry Rivers, de la Banque française," in *Les cahiers du Musée national d'art moderne*, no. 133 (Autumn 2015): 52–63; in chapter 3, with regard to Dennis Oppenheim, see "Dennis Oppenheim und das Ende des ticker tapes," in *Archiv fuer Mediengeschichte* 17 (2017): 126–39; also in chapter 3, my treatment of the financial aspects of art draws on "Art as an Investment and Artistic Shareholding Experiments," in *American Art* 37, no. 1 (Spring 2013): 2–23.

Additionally, the opening section of chapter 2 devoted to Andy Warhol is based on a translation of the original French text by Trevor Merrill, corrected and extensively revised by Malcolm DeBevoise.

Introduction

In 1966, in a short manifesto published in New York, the Franco-American artist Robert Filliou issued the following order to himself: "A *Principles of Poetical Economy* must be written. Write it."[1] This work was meant to reconcile two phases of Filliou's career. Before devoting himself to literature and the plastic arts, he had worked for a few years as a professional economist. Raised in France, he earned a master's degree in economics at the University of California in Los Angeles in June 1951, and then traveled in East Asia before being recruited by the United Nations as an advisor on the reconstruction of Korea in February 1953. A witness to the end of the war, he helped to draw up a five-year plan for the reconstruction and development of the country, published the following year.[2] American pressure soon made life increasingly uncomfortable for Filliou, a former Communist, and in March 1954 he suddenly resigned his position and began a new life as an artist, living in Denmark, France, the United States, and Germany.[3] He led a marginal existence, often in extreme poverty as a result of his refusal to produce collectible works of art, preferring instead to collaborate on projects in a variety of media as a member of the international avant-garde collective Fluxus.

Despite having dropped out of mainstream society, the artist never ceased to think as an economist. "Of course my own experience is limited," Filliou conceded some years later. "I have lived only in capitalist countries." Nevertheless the strikingly different forms of capitalism he had observed in a world shaped by the Cold War convinced him that one could not be satisfied with a "debate of capitalism vs socialism."[4] Seeking to go beyond class divisions and political dogmas, Filliou drew upon the practical lessons of his life as an artist to devise solutions to the problems created by what he called an "economics of prostitution." Looking back on his search for a third way between the two dominant systems, he recalled thinking that "it would be interesting to know how artists make money, and how they spend it. It is from this modest beginning that some of the ideas I expressed . . . were developed. I have a hunch that a new theory of value, upon which to build a much-needed new economic model, might come out of these investigations."[5]

Filliou's aim, in other words, was to make artistic practice, and the economy of which it was a part, into a laboratory where economics could

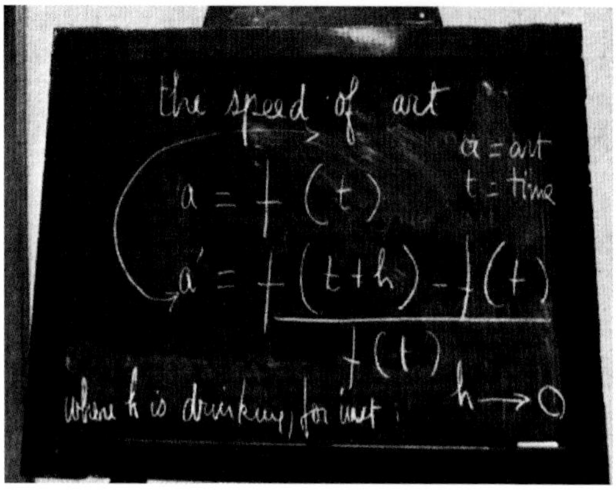

Fig. 1 View of the installation by Robert Filliou, *Research at the Stedelijk*, Stedelijk Museum, Amsterdam (November 5–December 5, 1971). Published in *Research at the Stedelijk*, exhibition catalogue (Amsterdam: Stedelijk Museum, 1971), n.p.

be reconstructed from first principles. Art, he believed, need not merely be the passive object of economic constraints exerted upon it; art could be an active force, the generative source of a more meaningful way of thinking about economic life itself. Over a period of years, through writings, lectures, experimental videos, and deliberately primitive and makeshift works, Filliou produced bits and pieces of his promised treatise on poetical economy. Often he exploited the technical vocabulary of mathematical economics in order to subvert it, most memorably in the case of the blackboard covered with formulas that he exhibited at the Stedelijk Museum in the autumn of 1971 (fig. 1).

The case of Robert Filliou is, in many respects, emblematic of what I examine in this book—namely, the way in which certain artists in the capitalist world of the 1960s put the economic life of their time to the test of artistic creativity. Their works reveal them to have been perceptive observers, not only of current events, but also of the profound structural changes that capitalist economies were undergoing throughout the decade. They showed that capitalism during the Cold War cannot be reduced to a particular combination of economic, institutional, and political circumstances, for it was shaped also by a set of complementary, competing, and sometimes conflictual cultural representations—what we may call "the spirit of capitalism," borrowing Max Weber's famous expression, later justified and given a critical basis by the sociologists Luc Boltanski and Ève Chiapello.[6] This spirit has a visual and plastic dimension that artists can exploit and enrich. Far from being uniform throughout the capitalist bloc, it was deeply affected by local perspectives and power relations that developed in response to American domination, as these cosmopolitan artists, many of whom had transatlantic careers, were well aware from personal experience.

AESTHETICS AND POLITICAL ECONOMY

That artists should have taken an interest in economic questions is all the more striking, as it meant breaking with a tradition that dated back to at least the eighteenth century.[7] When Stéphane Mallarmé remarked, in 1889, that "[t]o seek to assign a work of art its real price, in money, is to insult it," he was echoing a widespread idea, that art and economics were utterly separate, indeed opposed, spheres of human activity.[8] His celebrated aphorism, "Everything is summed up between aesthetics and political economy," assumed that the two domains are fundamentally incomensurable.[9] Throughout the nineteenth century and during the first half of the twentieth, economists themselves helped to set art and the artist apart from economic life. For David Ricardo, as for Karl Marx after him, works of art escaped classical economic analysis, for "their value is wholly independent of the quantity of labor originally necessary to produce them," and depends only on "the varying wealth and inclinations of those who are desirous to possess them."[10] Because each work of art is unique and because "[w]hat [artists] do can hardly be called work," as Gustave Flaubert put it, the arts theoretically constitute an exception, lying outside the economy.[11] For later thinkers, such as Theodor Adorno, this position of exteriority in relation to the capitalist market system is precisely what endowed art with a capacity for critical resistence.[12]

In the 1960s, the mutual exclusiveness—in principle, if not in fact—of art and economics was unmistakably called into question. In the case of pop art, of course, mass culture and the market became favored iconographic themes. Throughout the decade and continuing into the next, money, monetary signs, and even financial statistics found a prominent place in works by artists such as Andy Warhol (see fig. 19), Larry Rivers (see figs. 30–31), Bernar Venet (see fig. 43), and Marcel Broodthaers (see fig. 70). These artists were not content simply to mimic the visual vocabulary of the economic world; they created works that laid bare the mechanisms of economic activity itself. The problem of attaching a price to works of art and offering them for sale, traditionally considered to be external to creation in this domain, was now incorporated in artistic practice. In the late 1950s, when Yves Klein was asking a few grams of pure gold for his so-called immaterial works in Paris (see fig. 5), Giuseppe Gallizio was selling his abstract industrial painting in Turin by the meter (see fig. 15). A decade later, Edward Kienholz's watercolors (see fig. 9) were exchanged at their face value—the price in dollars indicated on the work of art itself.

In many respects, however, the economy was hardly a new theme in the history of European and American art. Painting since the Renaissance has been filled with representations of merchants, bankers, money changers, and various kinds of commercial and financial transactions.[13] Genre scenes and allegorical paintings, in denouncing the lure of lucre, undoubtedly helped to popularize the opposition between a world of commerce obsessed with the base and contemptible search for profit and an artistic sphere absorbed in a quest for spiritual values. But other genres, such as portrait painting, also testified to the economic ties that bound artists to their patrons and to collectors; indeed, many patrons and collectors were themselves members of the commercial and financial elite. What is more, the materials they used sometimes made the dynamics of economic value and exchange a physical part of their works.[14] Svetlana Alpers, in her study of Rembrandt, has persuasively shown that the artist's sensitivity to market conditions influenced his art, not only from the iconographic point of view but also in helping to fashion a distinctive style amounting almost to a commercial brand.[15]

From the eighteenth century, the development of paper money—in the form of bills of exchange, promissory notes, and later banknotes—gave a new dimension to the dialogue between artistic production and monetary creation. As art historians and numismatists have pointed out, artists were hired to assist in the design of coins and banknotes, and the motifs and images they devised were adopted as embellishments.[16] The historian Jennifer Roberts, in particular, has shown that trade in printing machinery and related technology was a decisive factor in the growing circulation of money and the development of the decorative arts.[17] Moreover, the transition from metal currency to fiduciary currency fundamentally transformed the representation of money in art. Monetary values, like artistic values, became mere "face values." Deprived of their precious material substrate, they now had value only by virtue of the trust that was placed in them. The formal integrity and authenticity of a person's signature, and the credit granted to it, were an essential aspect of works of art and money alike, as artists did not fail to emphasize, especially in periods of crisis when precisely this trust had been undermined.[18] The preoccupation with the trompe-l'oeil depiction of paper money was unusually pronounced in the work of an original school of nineteenth-century American painting that included William Michael Harnett, John Haberle, and John Frederick Peto, to the point that the dollar bills they re-created seemed almost to be detached from the canvas, arousing at once avarice and frustration (fig. 2). The plastic and iconographic treatment of these objects captured the ambivalence of American attitudes toward paper money. In the aftermath of the Civil War, fierce debates over bimetallism and rampant counterfeiting made it suspect on all sides. The harassment of Harnett, Haberle, and Peto by agents of the Secret Service Division of the Department of the Treasury, established in 1865 and charged with rooting out forgery, shows how serious a threat their hyperrealistic productions were imagined to pose.[19]

The history of abstraction in modern art, however much it may seem, at least at first sight, to be opposed to mimetic representation, is also closely related to the evolution of economic thought. Already in 1878, the famous libel suit brought by the painter James McNeill Whistler against the critic and part-time economist John Ruskin, who had accused him of asking "two hundred guineas for flinging a pot of paint in the public's face," had cast the artistic debate in economic terms, by calling into question a conception of value founded on the labor embodied by a meaningful pictorial statement and its social repercussions.[20] A century later, in his groundbreaking work *Les monnayeurs du langage* [*The Coiners of Language*], the philosopher

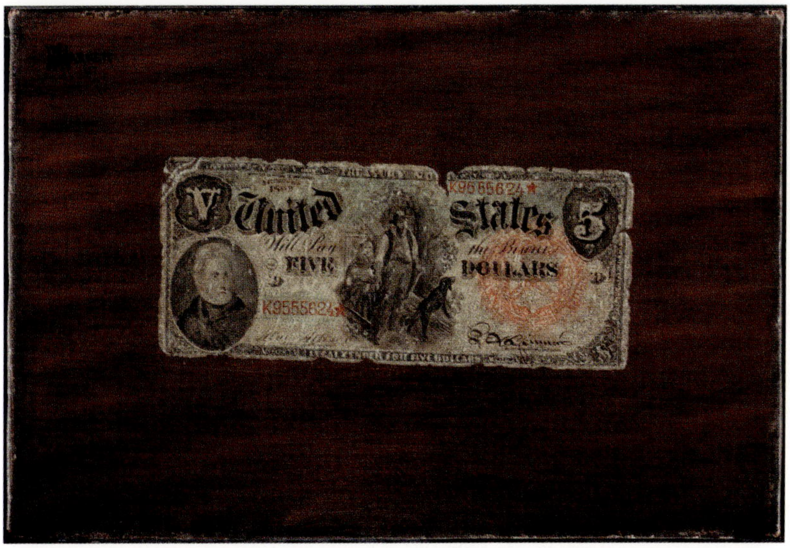

Fig. 2 William Michael Harnett, *Still Life—Five-Dollar Bill*, 1877. Oil on canvas, 8 × 12⅛ in. (20.3 × 30.8 cm). Philadelphia Museum of Art, The Alex Simpson Jr. Collection, 1943.

Jean-Joseph Goux argued that the crisis of classical economics and the gold standard at the turn of the twentieth century was mirrored by the crisis of novelistic realism. Goux considered the two phenomena to have been part of a rupture between the sign and the thing signified: whereas the weakening attachment to strict convertibility between legal tender and precious metal opened the way to "floating" currencies whose value varied with the whims of financial markets, poetic language slipped its old moorings in the faithful description of reality and became its own master.[21] Goux's thesis opened up fresh perspectives on the history of pictorial representation in relation to economic history. The art historian T. J. Clark, for example, has reinterpreted Kazimir Malevich's attempt to devise a new kind of pictorial abstraction as the symptom of a dissolution of "trust in the sign," just when the Russian monetary system was on the verge of collapse—a situation regarded by the revolutionaries as a reason for hope rather than a catastrophe.[22] And yet, as Rosalind Krauss has argued, it is not a question simply of equating abandonment of the gold standard with the rise of abstraction. Explicitly following Goux, she analyzes Pablo Picasso's transition from the prewar *papiers collés* to his Ingres-esque period not as a return to the gold standard of mimetic representation, as it were, but as the amplification of an inflationary process meant to completely disconnect sign from referent, so that the pastiche image could now be seen to be a deliberately inauthentic counterfeit currency.[23]

ART AND THE ECONOMY IN THE 1960S

More than twenty years ago, the interpenetration of the history of art and economic life suggested to the comparativist Marc Shell the need for a transhistorical study that would establish the consubstantiality of art and money.[24] In the present work, I have chosen to adopt a narrow chronological approach, on the ground that the decade of the 1960s constitutes a special chapter of this history, standing out in stark relief from all that came before. The distinctive character of this period is due to three factors, acting in combination at three interdependent levels: the general economy, the economy of the art market, and the controversies peculiar to the art world of the time.

First, the 1960s were a decisive moment of the Cold War, when capitalism asserted itself all the more forcefully as Soviet Communism presented a quite real and threatening alternative. I am interested in both the visual instruments of capitalist propaganda and the hopes of certain artists, Filliou among them, that capitalism would soon be overthrown in favor of a new system, yet to be invented. The roughly fifteen years on which I concentrate, from the late 1950s to the early 1970s, correspond to the second half of what the French economist Jean Fourastié called "les Trente Glorieuses" (the thirty years after the war known in German as the "Wirtschaftswunder," in Italian as the "miracolo economico," and in English as the "Golden Age of Growth").[25] In Europe, this period was marked not only by a strong and sustained expansion of commerce among the six founding countries of the Common Market but also by profound currency exchange imbalances, aggravated by widespread fears of inflation and shocks to the international monetary system. It culminated in a grave economic and monetary crisis and the collapse of the system of fixed exchange rates instituted by the Bretton Woods agreement in 1944, which provided for the convertibility of paper currencies into gold while at the same time granting a preponderant role to the dollar. This was front-page news, printed everywhere in the mainstream press and broadcast on network television. Journalistic coverage, rooted in common perceptions on both sides of the Atlantic, reflected the economic orthodoxy of the day.

Second, the predicament of capitalist countries impressed artists all the more strongly as it assumed the form of a very specific economic cycle in the art world. In both Europe and the United States, the second half of the 1950s inaugurated an unprecedented era of growth in the display and purchase of art.[26] The art market only began to really feel the effects of the general crisis that gripped the global economy in 1973–74. Throughout this period, not only the specialist press but also the financial columns of major newspapers and magazines reported the escalating prices being achieved at public sales, the brisk business being done in galleries, and the increasing interest of business corporations in sponsoring and collecting art. As one observer remarked about the feverish financial atmosphere of the time, "no discussion of the fine arts is possible today without mention of the fantastic prices that paintings and sculpture are bringing at auction."[27] The consequences of this situation for the art world were not simply material. The boom helped to modify the very nature of the viewer's encounter with the work. Meyer Schapiro, writing in 1960, expressed alarm at the extent to which both the creation and appreciation of art were affected by such publicity: "The knowledge of prices and possible gain through art enters into the common perception of art. It also makes artists keenly aware of sales price as a measure of value."[28] Speaking of paintings as "giant banknotes" or as "an investment" became a commonplace of critical discourse. Not even Marcel Duchamp was averse to thinking in terms of economic metaphors. As he explained in a 1963 interview, "We have so many standards. The gold standard, the platinum standard, and now the burlap standard. It's surprising that a piece of cloth, a piece of burlap on a stretcher with a few nails, can bring such prices. . . . Between 1946 and now, the thing has become a crazy machine of money. . . . It seems today that the artist couldn't survive if he didn't swear allegiance to the good old mighty dollar."[29]

Outside the world of art, economists and sociologists saw this likening of works of art to financial instruments as something much more than a disparaging analogy; for them, it was actually a working hypothesis. Once the artist was regarded as a professional, and the work of art as a commodity, the art market itself was no longer understood as a separate domain but as a specific segment of the larger economy on which more general phenomena such as growth, inflation, international trade, and monetary uncertainty had a measurable impact.[30]

Finally, these macroeconomic developments had a special resonance in the dynamics peculiar to artistic production in the 1960s. The central themes of the decade, manifest in how artists made their pieces and how they thought about them—conventional versus intrinsic value, dematerialization, exchange, the relation of a work's price to the artist's labor—directly echoed the economic and monetary transformations of the period, and this in an atmosphere of intense political involvement.[31] The artists I consider in this book were not content to sit back and passively illustrate the economic problems of their time. They took hold of the economy with both hands and used it as a social material to reinvent artistic forms.

THE ECONOMY AT WORK

A new way of studying these artists is needed if we are to properly assess the nature and scope of their contribution. I do not follow the approach adopted by many valuable works on the sociology, economics, and cultural history of the art market, which interpret variations in price by analyzing the economic constraints exerted on the creation and sale of objects and describe the career strategies of the various actors involved, while holding the works of art themselves, which appear only by way of illustration, at arm's length.[32] Nor do I have any intention of developing a critical and theoretical examination, as many authors have tried to do with regard to the current art scene.[33] What I want to do is consider the economy, and the economics of art, on the basis of artistic practice. Note that this does not imply a purely iconographic orientation of the sort favored recently by a number of monographs and expositions dealing with subjects such as gold or money in contemporary art, as a consequence of artists' renewed interest in these themes in recent years.[34] I am not concerned here with a material, such as gold, or even money in its role as currency, whether it functions as artifact or as medium ("specialized technology," to recall Marshall McLuhan's term).[35] I am concerned instead with the complex notion of an economy, that is, a dynamic system in which material and immaterial resources circulate, acquire value, and are allocated for various purposes.[36] Still more specifically, I am interested in a set of economic institutions and a state of economic thought peculiar to a particular historical period: postwar capitalism.

In her study of the Byzantine debate over iconoclasm, the philosopher Marie-José Mondzain retraced the semantic evolution of the word *economy* (Greek *oikonomia*) in ancient texts. She showed how, from its origins in Xenophon and Aristotle as a word denoting the principles of sound household administration, *economy* eventually came to be understood as "an art of enlightened flexibility," the ordering of available means subject to external constraints in such a manner that their organization approaches some higher end as closely as possible.[37] Extending Mondzain's argument about the medieval icon to contemporary art, an artistic economy may be defined on three levels: first of all, as the "*living* articulation" of plastic means internal to a work of art; second, as that which governs the production and circulation of this work; finally, as the general mode of administration of public affairs, which includes the production and circulation of works of art. These three levels are concurrently and consciously addressed by the works I look at in the pages that follow, and, by virtue of exactly this, their status as works of art, they scrutinize the capitalist economy of their time as well as the economy of art of which they are a part. The makers of these works did not limit themselves to representing the economy; they also articulated in a critical and vital way their own position within it.

In this sense the so-called fiduciary works of Marcel Duchamp offered an important precedent, and often an inspiration, for later experiments. They were exemplary not least for putting the aspects of money, sale, price, and investment at the heart of the work of art itself, and for investigating its place in a larger artistic economy. The *Chèque Tzanck* [*Tzanck Check*] (1919), for example, is a check in the amount of $115, carefully drawn by hand and impressed with a stamp, that Duchamp had made out to his dentist Daniel Tzanck in payment for his services (fig. 3). In transforming a drawing into a form of direct payment, Duchamp called into question the artistic and economic value of the artist's signature, and the monetary nature of art in general. At the same time, by reproducing the visual codes of an official banking document, he inquired into the validity of paper money, and suggested that art and money both depend on a shared trust.[38]

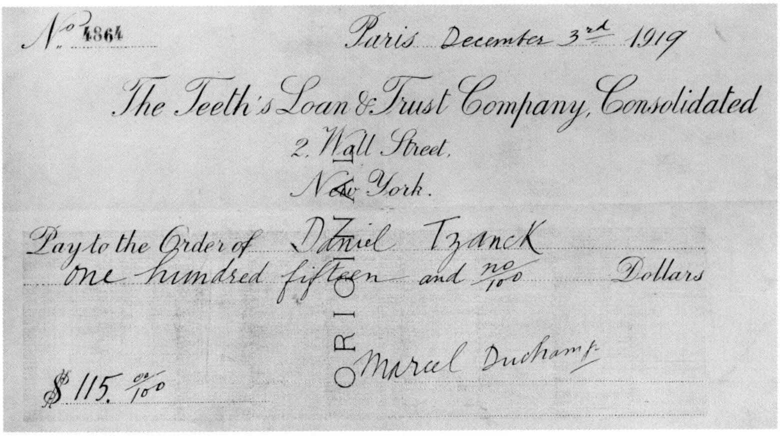

Fig. 3 Marcel Duchamp, *Chèque Tzanck* [*Tzanck Check*], 1919. Ink on paper, 8¼ × 15 in. (21 × 38.2 cm). Private collection.

Beginning in the late 1950s, in a climate of rapid economic growth, artists worked out several different strategies. Certain works—taking up where the *Chèque Tzanck* left off—exploited the signs and instruments of economic activity: money itself was sometimes represented, as in the case of Warhol and Rivers, or directly included in collages, as with Ray Johnson (see fig. 59); tables and charts of stock price movements were reproduced by Venet (see fig. 43), and reinterpreted by Broodthaers (see fig. 70). In other works, economic transactions were depicted in a performative manner: exchanging gold for immaterial goods, in Klein; producing and selling on an industrial scale, in the case of Gallizio. Still other artists parasitically encroached on certain kinds of economic activity, as in the case of Lee Lozano and Les Levine, who made the act of investing in stocks a work of art (see figs. 51 and 53). Like Duchamp before them, these artists refused to limit themselves to treating the economy as a fixed iconographic theme, external to a work of art, whose various elements the work more or less directly expresses. All of the works I examine consider the economy not as a set of signs, but as an active process in which art—as a commercial object—fully participates. Warhol was not content merely to represent dollar bills; he likened his artistic production instead to a perverse sort of Bureau of Engraving and Printing that, in creating banknotes whose value was a matter of dispute, worked to stimulate inflation. Similarly, Johnson did not use the dollar bill as a motif; he sought to capture both the circulation and the immobilization of currency through the dual practice of mail art and collage.

The case studies I have selected share neither a common medium nor a common style, nor membership in a particular artistic movement, nor a common political tendency. They are united, however, in suggesting that the tension between aesthetic and economic values may be taken as a point of departure for a broader study of the artistic economy, whose foundations they explore in a dynamic and reflexive manner. In frankly recognizing their own status as tradable commodities, they remind us that the art market, notwithstanding its many contradictions, is only a microcosm of economic life in general.

Unlike authors who bring a broader focus to bear on art and the economy, I am interested in looking at these things less in general terms than as a state of affairs specifically situated in the postwar capitalist system. The fruitfulness of this perspective is connected with two arguments, one historical, the other geographical.

Works surveying the artistic landscape of the 1960s as an outgrowth of the capitalist economy are typically oriented along one of two main axes: consumption and production. The first approach studies the way in which artistic practices—here one thinks particularly of the controversies surrounding pop art and Nouveau Réalisme—welcomed the advent of a full-fledged consumer society, with its auction rooms, its marketing and publicity techniques, and its rules governing the purchase and transfer of merchandise.[39] The second approach stresses the interest shown by artists in the nature and value of labor in an era marked by new methods of industrial production and bureaucratic organization.[40] The preeminence of these two approaches, which are not restricted to the history of art but extend more generally to research on the history and culture of capitalism, is readily explained by the privileged status accorded by scholars in the humanities and social sciences to the critique of the consumer society, on the one hand, and to the Marxist analysis of labor and value, on the other.

Marxist theorists of art, and the social historians who have come after them, treat works of art as the expression of an ideology and seek to explore the underlying socioeconomic power relations. Since the early 1970s, and the celebrated warning issued by T. J. Clark, this approach has abandoned both the view of art as a mirror or reflection of economic conditions and the reliance on analogies between economic structures and modes of representation.[41] Social historians of art nonetheless continue to favor structural interpretations in adopting the theoretical perspectives elaborated by Marx and Georg Simmel, rather than anchoring their analysis in the context of a specific period of economic history. Often they do so with an explicitly critical objective, praising the progressivism of the artist vis-à-vis the status quo or, to the contrary, condemning his perpetuation of a dominant ideology.[42] Deirdre McCloskey, an economist well known for her impatience with neoclassical orthodoxy, recently deplored the fact that the familiarity of most scholars in the humanities with economics begins and ends with Marx: "I beseech you, dear reader, think it possible that economists, even Chicago School economists, even Samuelsonian economists, have some important things to say about the economy."[43]

This is why I refer to prominent conservative voices in the economic debate of the 1960s, such as Jacques Rueff in France and Milton Friedman in the United States, while also drawing from recent works of economic sociology and anthropology. In this way I hope to promote a new way of looking at postwar capitalism. Although the present work does take up questions of consumption and production from time to time (mainly in the first chapter), on the whole it puts forward a different view of the history of capitalism during the 1960s, laying emphasis primarily on its financial and monetary aspects. In this I join with authors as different as the economist Geoffrey M. Hodgson and the philosopher Joseph Vogl, both of whom have insisted on the essential and still poorly understood role of the development of financial institutions in contemporary capitalism.[44] I hope to show, following their example, the importance in shaping the capitalist spirit of the 1960s of phenomena that are more commonly associated with succeeding decades, not only the financialization of markets for goods and services but also the fear of inflation and monetary imbalance. It will be evident that the financial crisis of 2007–8, and its cruel aftermath in the rest of the economy, have added to the plausibility of this new way of looking at the period. As Walter Benjamin famously argued in his essay on the philosophy of history, our consciousness of the present summons and informs our sense of the past.[45]

The second position I argue for in this book is geographical. The binary view of a world divided by the Cold War into a Communist sphere and a capitalist sphere has encouraged the false idea that each was homogeneous and monolithic. Even though as early as the mid-1960s scholars such as Andrew Shonfield had identified numerous forms of capitalism, contrasting the United States and Great Britain with France, West Germany, and Japan, the history of capitalism has been written on the whole from an Anglo-American perspective.[46] One of my purposes in this book is to expose capitalism for what it was during this period—a set of localized institutional and cultural forms that gave rise to debates that were no less national than international. Although the United States did unquestionably remain a central point of reference for artists in all countries, the iconic themes of American capitalism were reappropriated and reinterpreted far beyond its borders. As the incarnation of capitalism for the rest of the world, the American model aroused fascination, particularly in the emblematic form of the New York Stock Exchange (chapter 3), but also disappointment and disenchantment, in response to the sudden and dramatic decline of the "almighty dollar" (chapters 2 and 4), and even outright rejection, with the emergence of anticapitalist countermodels and alternative free trade areas (chapters 1 and 4 respectively). In calling attention to socioeconomic phenomena—monetary uncertainty, the rise of neoliberal and anticapitalistic challenges to the existing order, and the international economic crisis of the early 1970s—whose effects were felt everywhere, but especially in the United States and Europe, it will be possible to illuminate common artistic interests on both sides of the Atlantic as well as divergent local responses.

The artists I discuss in this book testify by their national origin and the range of their interests to the diversity of capitalist democracies in the 1960s. Many of them are American, but an equal or greater number are European—French, Italian, Danish, German, and Belgian—and for this reason all the more able to appreciate the plural character of the political economy of the time, as most of them had international careers within the Western capitalist world. This means, among other things, that the works by these artists should not be considered successively, in isolation from one another, but in parallel and with due regard for the transatlantic experience of their creators. Thus, for example, the American Larry Rivers painted a deeply subversive picture of the new French franc in Paris, while in New York the Frenchman Bernar Venet helped create a new way of looking at Wall Street. The present work is therefore part of a recent tendency that regards the internationalization of American art not as a mechanical process of domination, imposed on one side and submitted to on the other, but as a phenomenon jointly constructed by the active collaboration and confrontation of local art scenes around the world.[47] On this view, the impact of American art abroad is to be understood, as the historian Hiroko Ikegami puts it, "as a reciprocal, cross-cultural, and yet necessarily conflicted process rather than as a result of unilateral cultural imperialism."[48]

It needs to be kept in mind, too, that the minor presence of women among these artists is not only a reflection of the canon of postwar art, from which they are still largely excluded; it points to a larger problem, the exclusion of women—and members of other groups subject to discrimination—from positions of responsibility in the economy as a whole, occupied by the agents of a dominant class. I take up this phenomenon of exclusion in chapters 1 and 3.

The historical and geographical focus of the four chapters that make up this work shifts over the course of what needs to be seen as a long decade: from Paris and Turin in the late 1950s to New York and Paris around 1962 (with a brief detour through Los Angeles); again to New York in 1968–69 and 1970–71; and then finally to Cologne and Düsseldorf in the years immediately following. These four moments are connected in turn with four fundamental economic concepts: value, currency, financial markets, and commerce.

The first chapter examines the challenge to the notion of value mounted by artists in Western Europe in the late 1950s, a period of rapid economic growth accompanied by high inflation. I study the ambivalent critique of French postwar capitalism formulated by Yves Klein, who, in his own way, argued against a return to the gold standard, and I review its impact on a series of works by the American artist Edward Kienholz. Whereas Klein expounded a theory of intrinsic value based on scarcity, Giuseppe Gallizio, a member of the Situationist International, proposed what he called "industrial painting" as an antidote to the spiraling prices in the market for abstract art. His campaign on behalf, not of a gold standard, but of a luxury standard (in the sense that luxury should be a standard feature of a democratic society, accessible to all) through the sale of painting by the meter, was inspired both by the assembly-line production of the postwar period and by developments in the Italian fashion industry. Both Gallizio and Klein conceived of their creations as a laboratory for a revolutionary program that could be applied to society as a whole.

The second chapter is concerned with currency as an instrument of exchange. In 1962, Larry Rivers and Andy Warhol, the one working in Paris and the other in New York, simultaneously adopted banknotes as the principal subject of their pictorial work. They were interested above all in the notion of a "face value," common to both works of art and banknotes: just as a painter makes a work of art out of a piece of canvas, a central bank transforms a valueless piece of paper into money. In reconceiving monetary iconography, they questioned the institutional, religious, and political values on which public confidence rests and the nature of the credit on which works of art and currency both depend. Rivers painted a profoundly ironic portrait of the new French franc, situating it somewhere between patriotism, monetary uncertainty, and decolonization; Warhol's famous dollar bill paintings reproduced a form of legal tender at a moment when it was at the center of public controversy in the United States, aggravated by fears of anti-Communism and inflation.

The third chapter concentrates on the growing interest among artists in the 1960s in the stock exchange as an institution. Whereas economists were pleased to treat art as an investment, the market where securities are traded became an object of fascination for conceptual artists such as Bernar Venet and Dennis Oppenheim. In contrast to the work of these artists—which ran the risk of spectacularizing speculation, of transforming financial activity into an entertainment, a spectacle that was both mesmerizing and out of reach—the exercises in "artistic shareholding" conceived by Dan Graham, Les Levine, Lee Lozano, and Robert Morris broke the spell by intervening directly in the speculative process and raising investment to the rank of a work of art.

The fourth and final chapter takes up the notion of commerce, in both an informal and a formal sense, as it was understood by artists at the beginning of the 1970s, the dawn of a worldwide economic crisis and the collapse of the international monetary system. With the New York Correspondence School, Ray Johnson devised an original method for exchanging art—by mail, on the basis of friendship and completely free of charge—that offered a communitarian alternative to the traditional market for art. Less optimistically, Marcel Broodthaers added a Financial Section to his conceptual work *Museum of Modern Art, Department of Eagles*, at a time of mounting protest against the financialization of the West German art market. Comparing the anarchic rates of exchange among currencies to failed translations among poetical languages, Broodthaers saw the growth of international trade among the original members of the nascent European Economic Community as a source of economic warfare rather than a way to bring about a more peaceful world.

My purpose in surveying the course of art and the capitalist economy during the long decade of the 1960s is twofold. First, looking at the art of the period contributes to the pluridisciplinary reinterpretation of the history of capitalism that is now being undertaken in the humanities and social sciences on both sides of the Atlantic, and all the more urgently in view of the most recent crisis of capitalism, whose effects are still being felt today.[49] In this, I hope to do my own small part in answering Thomas Piketty's plea that the study of economic facts not be left to economists,[50] by submitting them to the clear-sighted, ironic, and stimulating scrutiny of artists. Second, I want to understand how capitalism became a social material for artists in the 1960s, bringing into existence new plastic forms and theoretical perspectives, which in turn exerted a profound influence on the economic status of artistic production. The question arises, then, whether a radical critique of economy can be developed on the basis of artistic practice, when this is embedded in a particularly sophisticated economic system of its own.

CHAPTER 1

Valuing the Invaluable

The notion of value is at the heart of the relationship between art and economy. Determining the aesthetic value of artistic works and the economic value of goods runs up against difficulties that have long been of theoretical and practical interest in both fields. In each case, the chief question posed by value has to do with its origin and its nature: is value intrinsic to an object, normative and absolute, or is it contingent, the accidental result of an object encountering an evaluating subject? The term *value,* from the Latin word meaning to "be well, to have strength," was originally used to denote bravery, particularly martial valor.[1] To begin with, then, it was a quality peculiar to an individual; only later did it gradually come to signify something that is worthy of another's esteem and moral approval. If value figures in the act of evaluation, on the occasion of an object being contemplated by an observer, does the observer do anything more than notice qualities objectively present in the object? Or is value instead conferred subjectively by the observer himself, according to his personal preferences, his psychological disposition, and, as we would say today, his own values? In the field of economics, this question was customarily translated by a pair of terms, *value* and *price.* In the *Encyclopédie* of Denis Diderot and Jean d'Alembert, for example, one finds this definition: "The worth of things in themselves determines their *value,* and estimation determines their *price. Value* is the rule of *price,* but a rather uncertain rule and one that is not always followed. That one of two things that is of greater *value,* is better, and that which is of greater *price,* is worth more."[2]

Here a value is understood to be an intrinsic property of a thing, its inherent worth. Nonetheless, a variable price can be attached to it. Passing from value to price involves substituting subjectivity ("estimation") for objectivity (inherent "worth"), and quantity ("more") for quality ("better"). Later, in the nineteenth century, the expressions "use value" and "exchange value" were generally employed to characterize this opposition between value and price. As the latter expression changed in meaning over time, value came to incorporate the notion of price. The problematic richness of our term *value* derives from precisely this semantic shift. In ordinary speech today, *value* signifies either a recorded market price or what a moral subject reckons it should be, whether on the basis of normative or psychological criteria. One may speak of the value of a work of art, referring to the price it commanded at auction, and at the same time regret that it was not sold for its "true" value.

By the 1960s, though it had been a central issue of debate when economics first came to be established as a discipline in the late eighteenth and early nineteenth centuries, the notion of value seemed almost to have disappeared from economic theory. Adam Smith and David Ricardo saw the value of a commodity as the reflection of the "quantity of labour originally necessary to produce [it]."[3] They conceived of value, in other words, as something objective, intrinsic. The human labor embedded in the commodity justified and measured its exchange value, and therefore represented its "real" or "natural" price, as Smith called it, which could differ from the "market" price established by "higgling and bargaining."[4] While Smith admitted that current prices fluctuate, depending on market supply and demand at a given moment, he held that there nonetheless exists an absolute natural price, peculiar to a given commodity, which the economist must seek to determine. For Jean-Baptiste Say, however, the idea of distinguishing a natural price, that is, the price a commodity ought to have, from a current price, the one that is, in fact, observed in the market, was "altogether chimerical." "There are only current prices in political economy," Say insisted. "There is no natural price, no common and fixed rate in anything having to do with values."[5] To accept that there are only current prices, that there is no such thing as intrinsic value, only the price that a commodity will fetch at a given moment, amounted to renouncing the normative character of classical economic thought—as Adam Smith's French translator, the economist Germain Garnier, rather anxiously pointed out: "With such doctrines, there are no longer any laws of political economy, and values circulate blindly, like the matter of chaos in the confusion of anarchy. If the value of a thing has no measure other than its current price . . . , it is no longer prices that vary, but values themselves. . . . Value is no longer a quality that exists in the subject, a quality inherent in the thing itself and independent of the contingent exchanges to which a commodity may be liable."[6]

With the so-called marginalist revolution of the late nineteenth century, decades of debate came to an end and the era of neoclassical economic thought began. The theory of general equilibrium developed by Léon Walras and Vilfredo Pareto reconciled the chief factors of value—production costs, which determine the relative scarcity of goods supplied, and marginal utility, which determines demand—in a system in which "there is nothing real, apart from [the] price [of a commodity], which is its 'value,' "[7] and in which value is created by the act of exchange alone. Little by little, as the new tradition took root, the question of value all but vanished from monographs and textbooks alike.[8]

European artists in the late 1950s, in reviving the notion of value and setting it once more in opposition to price, ventured to dispute one of the main articles of modern economic orthodoxy. The timing was auspicious in two ways. First, with the advent of the post-Stalin era, the European left devoted itself to a critical reinterpretation of Marxist thought, which once more became a major source of inspiration for the critique of contemporary capitalist society. The writings of Lucien Goldmann and Henri Lefebvre, following on from those of György Lukács and Herbert Marcuse, had a particularly strong influence on the artists of this generation. In addition to Marx, whose analysis of forms of value and the fetishism of commodities was the object of sustained and productive attention, unfashionable economists of the nineteenth century were rehabilitated in artistic circles as part of an attempt to develop a freer and more wide-ranging style of economic thought. Thus Charles Fourier was rediscovered by André Breton before being taken up by Robert Filliou, and John Ruskin was read in a new light by Asger Jorn.

Second, the changing nature of the art market during this period helped draw attention to the analysis of price and value. By the late 1950s, the price of works of art had risen to unprecedented levels.[9] At least for works by some of the most collected artists of the period, there was a growing suspicion that prices had become detached from real artistic value. It is important to keep in mind that this feeling was due as much to the vagaries of an inflationary economy on both sides of the Atlantic as to the actual functioning of the market for art. As Geneviève Bonnefoi put it, writing in *Les Lettres nouvelles* in 1959:

> Faced with currency instability, which leads them to look for new speculative investments, the bourgeoisie has perceived the possibilities that works of art present in this connection. The biannual tournaments at the Galerie Charpentier where ship owners and diamond merchants fork out millions for the least of Cézanne's apples or Renoir's nudes, the hidden war between Paris, London, and New York for preeminence in this new stock market, are revelatory. . . . Caught up in a general inflationary process, art cannot escape the conditions of a society governed by money. Having been handed over to dealers, publicity, and speculators, it is a commercial commodity (this is true not only for painting but for all other artistic activities).[10]

This opinion, though expressed here in the pages of a politically left-wing review, is typical of a way of thinking that was common in artistic circles of the period. Value and price in art were no longer discussed in isolation from the economy as a whole. Currency instability, inflation, and the idea that collectors constituted an economic elite constantly recurred as topics of conversation and themes of newspaper accounts now that the art market was understood not as a separate domain, a world of its own, but as a microcosm of the capitalist world, one that, more clearly than any other, exposed its excesses to public view.

That artists in the late 1950s should have sought to make their work a kind of laboratory for an economic critique of value therefore seems unsurprising. Two figures stand out: Yves Klein and Giuseppe Gallizio. Neither one was concerned with treating the economy or value as an iconographic theme. In each case the economic critique entered in through the conception, exhibition, and circulation of works of art—through their own internal economy, so to speak. To borrow an idea developed for several decades by the sociologist Luc Boltanski, and recently extended in collaboration with Arnaud Esquerre, one may say that value operates in the work of these artists as a device for justifying or objecting to the price of things.[11] Klein and Gallizio pose the question of value and price in terms of the one and the many, that is, the place occupied by a unique work of art at a time when standardization and automatization made possible the productivity gains underlying the postwar boom. Harking back to the theoretical tradition of the nineteenth century, they seek to create a new theory of value that will allow the economic system once more to be seen in its entirety. Klein's so-called blue revolution and Gallizio's manifesto—inspired by Jorn's pamphlet *Critique de la politique économique* [*Critique of Economic Policy*]—sketched the outlines of an alternative economic system in which art, as a standard of value, and the artist, as producer of value, play a central role. The writings and practices of both Klein and Gallizio were riddled with contradictions, however, and haunted by a premonition of failure.

THE ECONOMIC THOUGHT OF YVES KLEIN

"I am neither a philosopher, nor an economist, nor anything else," Klein confessed in one of his earliest essays. "I limit myself to expressing my ideas only as *utopias*."[12] Throughout his entire career, if the artist himself is to be believed, he was "searching for the real value of a painting."[13] Are we to understand value here as the relative intensity of a color, determined by its degree of saturation—and the quest for "real" value as culminating in the chemical isolation of a very famous blue pigment, International Klein Blue (IKB), his signature color? Or as the true artistic merit of a work, whose creator, longing for it to be considered "a classic," may himself hope to be assured one day of "universal" and "eternal" recognition?[14] Or else as a definitive commercial value, the price governing the sale of a painting—and this in the case of a painter who was one of the first to make selling an integral part of his artistic practice? The evidence suggests that all these things figure in Klein's work, a wide-ranging inquiry into the relative importance of the objective and the subjective, the weight of strictly individual judgment in the balance of collective reckonings, and the tension between the volatility of stock prices and the universal permanence of Kantian aesthetic values.

The importance of the problem of value in Klein's work has been remarked on by many authors. The historian Nan Rosenthal was perhaps the first to consider it a "central theme."[15] Two later writers treated it in considerable detail, and in quite different ways. The art theorist Thierry de Duve explored Klein's notion of value in a 1989 article, "Yves Klein, or the Dead Dealer." The analysis is thorough, the judgment implacable. In proclaiming his right to sell "immaterial" works having no physical existence at arbitrarily fixed prices, de Duve maintains, Klein nullified labor value while at the same time glorifying exchange value; and in daring to appropriate a color for himself, indeed to make it a personal trademark—"Klein blue"—he "systematically acted as the owner of the means of artistic production," solely for the benefit of the buyer, who was reserved a "monopoly over aesthetic pleasure."[16] De Duve thus sees Klein as a fetishistic gravedigger of avant-garde ideals, incapable of choosing between sincerity and cynicism, who accelerated the "artist's identification with the capitalist, the dealer."[17] This essentially theoretical argument, which condemned Klein on ethical grounds, provoked several attempts at ideological rehabilitation.[18] The historian Denys Riout, by contrast, in an important monograph on Klein published in 2004, and subsequently in various articles and lectures, has addressed the economic question with great subtlety on the basis of a very careful study of the artist's writings and personal papers. Riout was able to reconstruct the course of events that produced the monochrome paintings as well as the celebrated *Zones de sensibilité picturale immatérielle* [*Zones of Immaterial Pictorial Sensibility*], settling many disputed matters of fact and correcting a number of common misconceptions, among them the belief that Klein took out a patent to assert intellectual ownership of the blue pigment he had created.[19]

Building on the work of de Duve and Riout, it will be possible to place the ideas animating Klein's writings and artistic practices in the context of contemporary economic history, including developments not only in the international monetary economy but also in European art markets. But rather than adopt a rigid definition of value—in de Duve's case, a Marxist definition—it will be more illuminating, I believe, to take a longer view of this problematic concept, from the medieval period until the 1960s. If the historian Sylvère Lotringer is right in supposing that "[w]hat Klein, in fact, had been doing was recapitulating step by step the genealogy of value, returning to its mystical essence,"[20] this genealogy nonetheless remains to be retraced.

The Just Price of a Painting

On January 2, 1957, at the Galleria Apollinaire in Milan, the young painter Yves Klein entered upon a new period in his career. The solo exhibit, *Proposte monochrome, epoca blu* [*Monochrome Propositions, Blue Period*], featured eleven canvases in an identical rectangular format (30¾ × 22 in. [78 × 56 cm]) with rounded corners, entirely covered with the same ultramarine blue and hung by metal brackets at a distance of 7⅞ inches (20 centimeters) from the walls of the gallery. Here is how Klein described the event two years later in a lecture at the Sorbonne:

> All of these blue monochrome propositions, wholly similar in appearance, were recognized by the public as being quite different from one another. The connoisseur duly passed from one to the next and entered into an instantaneous state of contemplation in a world of blue. [*Laughter*] The most sensational observation concerns the buyers. Each one chose a painting from among the eleven exhibited and each one paid the price asked for. And the prices were all different, of course. [*Laughter*] This serves to demonstrate that the pictorial quality of each painting is perceptible by something other than the material and physical appearance. Those who [bought a painting] recognized this state of affairs, which I call pictorial sensibility.[21]

This striking anecdote, of an artist who had managed to sell identical paintings at different prices, kept the legend of Yves Klein alive long after his death. And yet, as Riout has shown and as several articles of the period testify, it was untrue, a fiction that Klein had circulated after the fact in order to make the point of his work more easily understood. In a review published shortly after the show's opening, for example, Dino Buzzati noted that the asking price was "modest"—25,000 lire per painting.[22] The existence of a uniform price was confirmed by a notice in the local paper, *Il Corriere lombardo*, and by an article in the German magazine *Neue Illustrierte*; indeed, it was given in francs by Klein himself—"15,000 francs apiece" (equivalent in 1957 to 25,000 lire), as he was quoted as saying in an article in *L'espoir de Nice et du Sud-Est*.[23] Yet the exceptional influence of the artist's fable, which became a key element of his reputation in the years to come, began to make itself felt only a few weeks after the Italian exhibition. On February 15, *Le Monde* reported that Klein "not long ago asked different prices for strictly monochromatic canvases in the same format."[24] Retold many times, the anecdote was frequently modified to suit the occasion, but always with the same didactic intent. Thus, for example, in response to a sarcastic question from a *New York Herald Tribune* reporter in 1961, "Have your all-blue paintings changed over the years?," Klein responded, "Very much. They may look the same, just all blue. But those done a few years ago showed no quality at all. I'm terribly ashamed of them." Here it was no longer the work displayed in a single gallery show, but over a whole phase of his career, that was alleged to exhibit different degrees of artistic quality, despite its apparent uniformity.[25]

In Klein's painting, value—artistic quality—is bound up with the tension between uniqueness and reproducibility. To exhibit identical works, and to insist on a different value for each one, permitted Klein to demonstrate that discerning the true value of a painting depends on something other than its material and physical appearance. Differences in quality are therefore invisible, for they cannot be perceived by visual inspection; nor are they somehow external to works of art, as a result of the judgments brought to bear on them by collectors or critics. The quality of a painting is intrinsic to it. To clarify his thinking on this point, Klein resorted more than once to a parable involving the forger and his copy. In an essay from 1959, he explains: "I am therefore searching for the painting's real value, owing to which two paintings that are identical in every visible and legible respect, such as lines, colors, drawing, forms, format, thickness of the paint, and technique in general, except that one of them is painted by a 'painter' and the other by a capable 'technician,' an 'artisan,' though both are officially recognized as 'painters' by the community; owing to this invisible real value, one of the two objects is a 'painting,' but not the other."[26]

By insisting on the insufficiency of appearance and formal properties as justification for asserting a difference between the true and the false, the good and the bad, Klein was saved (or so he imagined, at any rate) from falling into relativism. Far from affirming the subjective nature of value and its dependence on a social or institutional context (public acclaim, the approval of expert opinion, and so on), he held that true painters, and true paintings having genuine value in and of themselves, do actually exist. The problem is how to go about identifying them. In the particular sense that Klein gives to the term *sensibility* in his writings, so that it becomes a property of the painting, independent of any attribution by the critic or collector, Riout sees proof of Klein's "substantialism."[27] The story invented about the Galleria Apollinaire show in Milan therefore made it possible to insist on the intrinsic character of the value of works of art as something that only artists and true connoisseurs are capable of perceiving.

One detail of this account needs to be emphasized. Not only are apparently identical canvases recognized by true connoisseurs as being different, but variable prices confirm and support this difference. The lesson is both simple and of great theoretical import: to an intrinsic difference in quality there necessarily corresponds a difference in price, which reflects it. If value is inherent in the object itself, if value is part of its substance, unaffected by the judgment of any spectator, then this object naturally has a "just" price, a straightforward monetary translation of this proper value. The price, in other words, defined without reference to the relation between supply and demand, is only a derivative aspect of valuation. This conception recalls the manner in which works of art were charged for until the Renaissance, when the artist's production costs contractually determined the sale price. In a 1958 letter addressed to the secretary general of the International Conference for the Detection of Nuclear Explosions, offering his services for "painting [French] A and H bombs blue," Klein referred directly to this type of contract. The work would be performed in exchange for:

> a payment to be discussed but that must in any case cover:
> —The cost of coloring agents;
> —My own artistic contribution. . . .
> It is quite obvious that we will rule out cobalt blue as ignominiously

radioactive and that we will use only the Klein blue for which I am famous, as you know.[28]

This arrangement parodies an archaic method for establishing the price of artistic works as a function of raw materials and labor. Thus Fra Filippo Lippi, for painting a triptych for Cosimo de' Medici, was paid "sixty florins to include materials, gold, gilding and painting," to which was added "labour costs," according to the contract cited by the historian Michael Baxandall.[29] As with Klein's paintings, the content of the work, in terms of the materials and artistic effort physically incorporated in the painting—even though these things go beyond what is immediately visible—determines its value, and not the play of market forces. When Klein maintained that variable prices are a recognition of differences in intrinsic quality, with the result that an artistic contract serves to objectify the price of a work, he was, in effect, reintroducing the notion of "just price" in an age no longer familiar with it. Borrowed from ancient philosophy, it dominated medieval economic thought and survived at least as late as the Renaissance. It rests on the principle, as the historian Jean Ibanès put it, that economic analysis "is not, strictly speaking, separable from a theological and philosophical conception of man and the world, from which it draws the 'problem' to be studied, as well as a system of values conferring a normative character on its conclusions."[30] There exists, in other words, a realm of values conferred on things by God, and the aim of economic analysis must be to make price, the human instrument of exchange, agree with the divine norm. This is why, as Simmel had pointed out earlier, the economic study of value and price long emphasized that the proportion between two values must be "seen as proper, in moral as well as in objective terms."[31]

This moral dimension is a fundamental part of Klein's thinking, for he saw both artistic inquiry and economic thought as coming under the head of "ethics."[32] On this view of the matter, price cannot be determined by the free operation of the market, which is subject to no higher authority and whose outcomes are not merely contingent, but arrived at without the least consideration of what is just and unjust. For Klein, as for medieval thinkers, the just price must be (in the words of the historian Philippe Contamine), a "response to market instability [that] manifests the extension to the economic domain of the requirement of justice, the virtue par excellence of kings."[33] In setting different prices for seemingly identical canvases, Klein invoked exactly this sovereign power to unilaterally demand a price that reflects the real value of works, which the artist alone is worthy to judge; a power that, for want of actually possessing it himself, Klein could at least imagine himself possessing in the fictive account he publicized. To adopt Hannah Arendt's terminology, we may say that he tried to reverse a course of events that saw values in the modern age lose their traditional status as "ideas," or "transcendent unities"; having become "commodities," and therefore dependent on social relations, they were now the proper object of the social sciences.[34]

What accounts for Klein's obstinacy in holding that the price of a work of art is independent of the "fortuitous combinations" that Marx believed it to be governed by, appealing instead to the archaic notion of a just price? It was only in the course of the 1950s that developments in the art market had suggested to many people that the price of a work could, in fact, be entirely disconnected from its artistic value. In France, a debate on the topic of art and commercial value sponsored by the newspaper *Combat* in March 1962, on the eve of the great crisis in the Paris art market, addressed this increasingly widespread perception. Its central question—"[W]hether the price of a work of art is due to its speculative value or whether it is due to its real value, to its intrinsic value, which will remain its eternal value"—linked up directly with Klein's preoccupations. For the writer and critic Alain Bosquet, it was clear that "painting has become a security."[35] Works of art, like financial investments, were now regarded as interchangeable. As the critic Catherine Valogne, writing in *Les Lettres françaises* two years earlier, had put it:

> In the world of the arts, where trading is king, one hears it said too often: I've got to have a Rouault, a Matisse, a Klee, a Braque, a Picasso, a Buffet, a Bazaine, I have a bidder. It seems unthinkable that one can demand to have a Braque the way one would demand a packet of butter. Two packets may have identical qualities if they are from the same source, and even then, the weather, the grass, the mood of the cows can influence the state of the butter! But are there two identical paintings, two identical sculptures?[36]

In affirming the irreducible uniqueness of even the most similar works, the tale Klein related of the Galleria Apollinaire show seems to have anticipated this criticism of the emerging "market for name artists."[37]

Klein had a particularly keen appreciation of the price-setting mechanisms that regulated the artistic economy of his time, and by depicting them, by experimenting with them, he sought to gain greater control over them. Scarcity and the monopoly of supply constituted by the artist's production, as he well knew, were guarantees of commercial recognition.[38] "The blue," the American critic Harold Rosenberg noted, "served Klein as a trademark."[39] In taking measures, though they were more symbolic than anything else, to protect his invention of the paint formula by registering the date of its invention with the National Institute of Industrial Property as proof of priority, Klein helped to create the mistaken impression that he had, in fact, obtained a trademark reserved for his exclusive use. Following the example of photographers who deliberately limit the number of prints of an image in order to push up its price, Klein managed to contrive an artificial scarcity for his immaterial works, whose number was otherwise potentially unlimited. By carefully arranging the *Zones de sensibilité picturale immatérielle* by series and numbering them individually in separate receipt books, at different prices per series, it became possible to incorporate these novel creations in

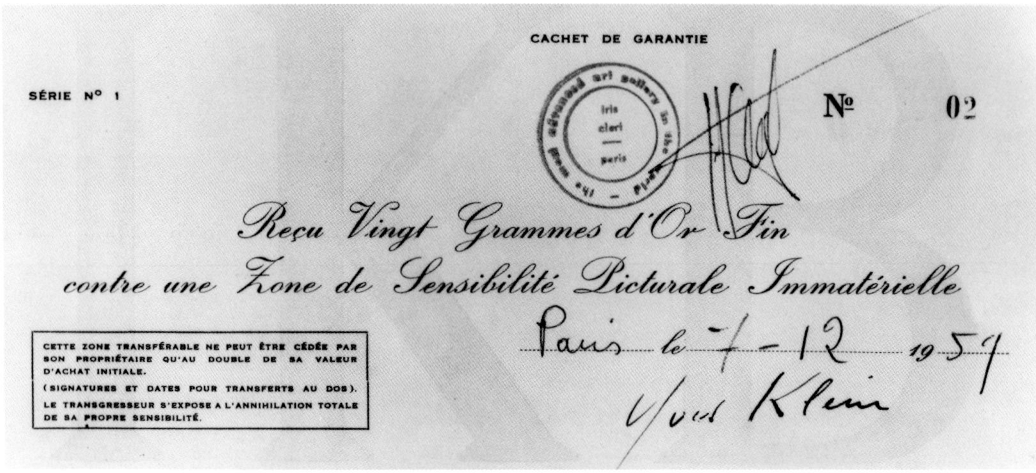
CACHET DE GARANTIE

SÉRIE N° 1

№ 02

Reçu Vingt Grammes d'Or Fin
contre une Zone de Sensibilité Picturale Immatérielle

CETTE ZONE TRANSFÉRABLE NE PEUT ÊTRE CÉDÉE PAR SON PROPRIÉTAIRE QU'AU DOUBLE DE SA VALEUR D'ACHAT INITIALE.
(SIGNATURES ET DATES POUR TRANSFERTS AU DOS).
LE TRANSGRESSEUR S'EXPOSE A L'ANNIHILATION TOTALE DE SA PROPRE SENSIBILITÉ.

Paris le 7-12 1959
Yves Klein

Fig. 4 Yves Klein, receipt given to Jacques Kugel for purchase of *Zone de sensibilité picturale immatérielle* [*Zone of Immaterial Pictorial Sensibility*] no. 2, series no. 1 (December 7, 1959). Private collection.

the classical regime for selling a scarce good (fig. 4). Klein had also given considerable thought to the effects of speculation, which caused the price for a work suddenly to rise or fall. He thus introduced a clause, appearing in a box at the bottom left of receipts for the *Zones*, providing that "this transferable zone may be sold by its owner only at twice the amount of its initial purchase price." Klein was under no illusion that more than a very few buyers would adhere to the complete set of "ritual rules of transfer"—which included the destruction of the receipt signed by the artist himself, the sole proof of original purchase; to the contrary, he expected that his works would change hands many times, and that future sales would be accompanied by a steady rise in price. He was perfectly conversant with the mechanisms of a market of supply and demand. Far from denying the reality of their operation, or somehow seeking to prevent it, he chose instead to manage them himself according to his own rules.

Klein's Gold and the Monetary Policy of the Fifth Republic

The experiments Klein conducted with regard to the sale of his art are best known perhaps for the requirement that payment be made in gold. In March 1957, he made it the condition for acquiring his immaterial works. "I no longer want them to be bought for money at present," he explained. "For my three pictorial states on exhibit I have asked for pure gold. A kilo of GOLD per work."[40] The series of *Zones de sensibilité picturale immatérielle* conceived from 1959 onward were offered on a graduated scale of prices, expressed as a quantity of precious metal: 20 grams (¾ ounce) of pure gold for the *Zones* of series no. 1, the least expensive, to 1,280 grams (2⅞ pounds) for those of series no. 7, the most expensive. According to the ritual rules governing these transactions, a buyer who wished to possess "the full authentic immaterial value of the work" had to burn his receipt in the presence of witnesses, while the artist threw half of the gold received into the water (fig. 5).[41] During this same period, Klein used gold as the material for

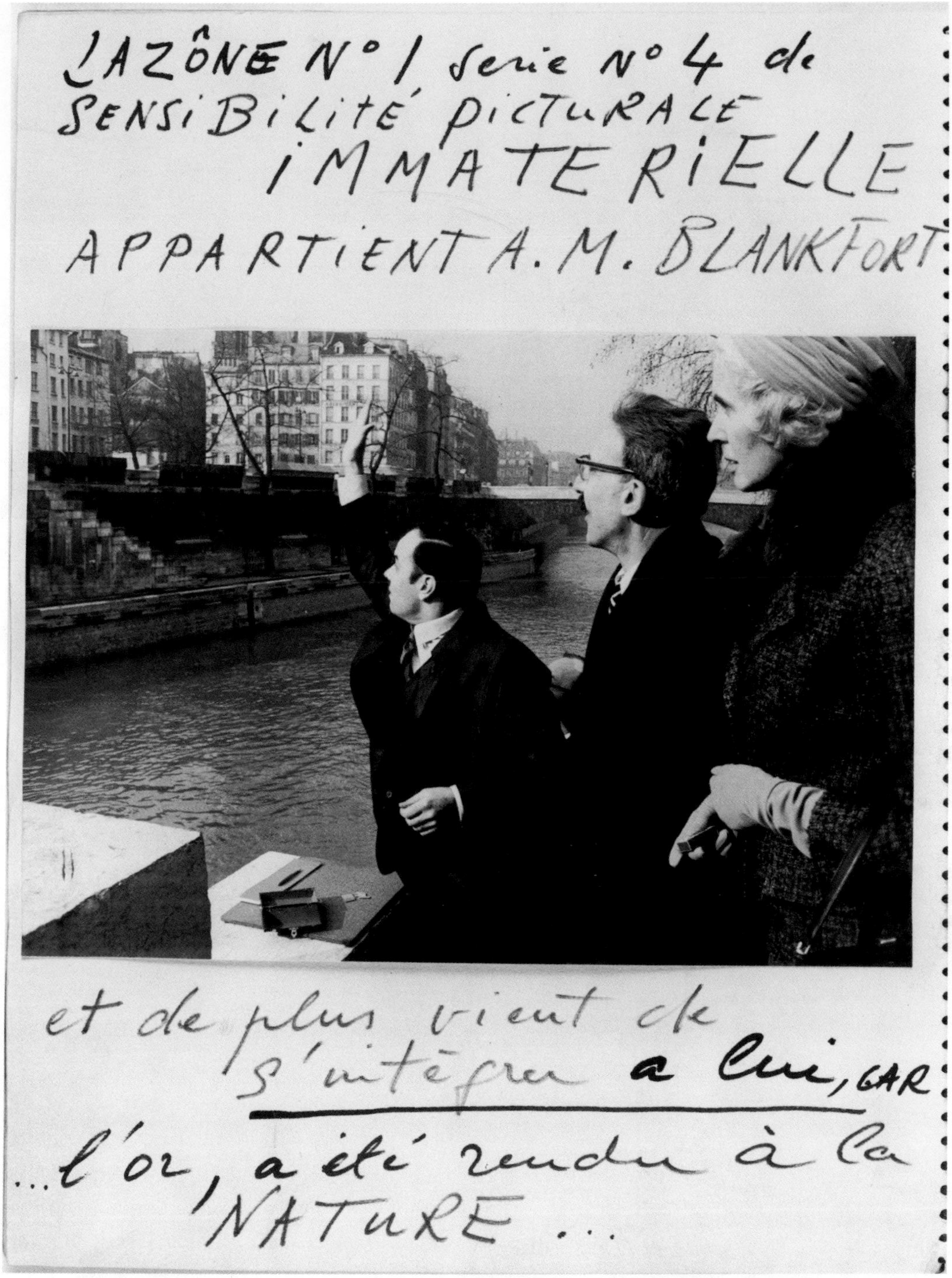

Fig. 5 Yves Klein selling *Zone de sensibilité picturale immatérielle* [*Zone of Immaterial Pictorial Sensibility*] no. 1, series no. 4 (February 10, 1962) to Michael Blankfort. Authenticated by François Mathey. Photograph, Archives Klein, Paris.

Fig. 6 Yves Klein, *Valeur or* [*Value Gold*] (*Monogold* 22), 1960. Gold leaf on panel, 23¼ × 17½ in. (59 × 44.5 cm). Kaiser Wilhelm Museum, Krefeld, Germany.

his works in the *Monogold* series, panels covered with gold leaf (fig. 6).[42] Between the idea of gold as a material for realizing his designs (gold as use value) and gold as a means of payment for these realizations (gold as exchange value) there is no contradiction. Indeed, in demanding to be paid in gold for his works, Klein saw it as a material possessing a certain intrinsic value, which therefore was amenable to barter.[43] Commentators on Klein's work have tended to underestimate the monetary motivations of this form of exchange by laying emphasis on its symbolic or poetic character.[44] And yet Klein's correspondence with his dealer, Iris Clert, makes it clear that pricing in gold was indeed thought of in terms of its equivalent in legal tender. In an undated note to Klein, conserved in the artist's archives, Clert wrote: "For gold I've got an idea. . . . When something worth 1 kg of gold has been sold, for example. A kg will be displayed at the Gallery, we'll get the bank to loan it for the opening (I've got an idea), which will allow you in the meantime to live on the zones you sell, without having to buy the gold, since first one has to make a living."[45]

That Klein should have sought to live off of the sale of his *Zones* is hardly surprising, for his income was always limited and uncertain. More than this, taking into account the strictly monetary dimension of gold will allow us to look at his immaterial works in the light of the debates over economic policy that attended the birth of the Fifth Republic in the late 1950s. As Riout was the first to point out, this larger economic context formed the background against which Klein worked out his ideas about gold.[46] On coming to power in May 1958, Charles de Gaulle had inherited not only a political and military crisis with the war in Algeria, but also a state of monetary disorder that had persisted since the end of World War II. After six successive devaluations in little more than twenty years, the franc was still under assault from speculators, and inflation had become no less a preoccupation of the general press, forever alerting readers to the latest rise in prices, than it was a matter of concern for experts at the Banque de France.[47] De Gaulle's immediate response was to turn once more to what throughout the nineteenth century had been the ultimate guarantor of French currency: gold. In July 1958, only weeks after taking up his duties as finance minister, Antoine Pinay floated a public loan at 3.5 percent, guaranteed by gold and accompanied by a massive purchase of this metal by the Banque de France (fig. 7). The aim was both to avoid an immediate liquidity crisis and to encourage French citizens to relinquish a part of the gold hoarded during the postwar years of monetary uncertainty, reckoned at some 3,000 billion francs.[48]

Several months later, in November 1958, a sweeping monetary reform was undertaken with the objective of restoring lasting confidence in the franc and bringing inflation under control. The architect of this reform was Jacques Rueff, an economist known for his devotion to free-market principles (liberalism, in the French sense), his anti-Keynesianism, and his conservatism in monetary matters. Some years earlier, in a 1952 lecture entitled "Tomorrow, the Gold Franc?," he had advocated a return to strict

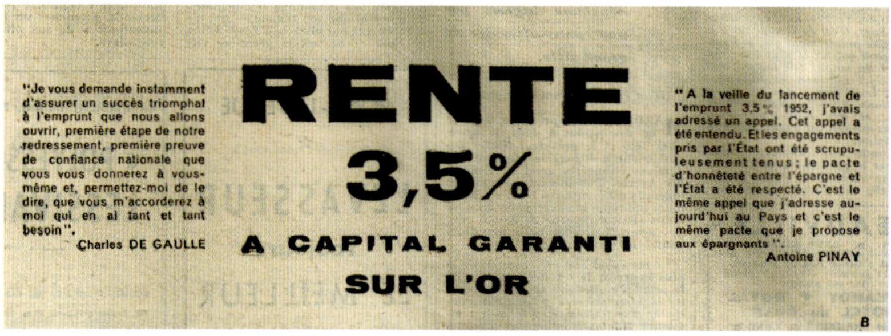

Fig. 7 Advertisement ("Rente 3,5% à capital garanti sur l'or") for the de Gaulle–Pinay public loan. Published in *L'Express*, July 10, 1958, p. 12.

convertibility of the franc into gold and, more generally, again as a result of his dissatisfaction with the Bretton Woods agreement, the adoption of an international monetary system based on a gold standard.[49] In his many publications and interviews given to the press, Rueff habitually cloaked the question of the materiality or immateriality of currency in a rhetoric of truth and falsehood, reality and unreality. Trust, he held, can be placed only in what is solid, genuine; immateriality is the realm of the artificial, the inauthentic. From this it followed that "the truthfulness of currency is the condition of human liberty," whereas inflation "respects appearances, but destroys realities."[50] Similarly, Pinay's official remarks in January 1959, after the new economic measures had been put in place, exhorted the public to "renounce the lie that was smuggled into the heart of our economy," and pleaded for a "return to truth," which is to say to the metal value of the franc.[51] For Rueff, the "tutelage of gold" was nothing less than "the condition of maintaining Western civilization."[52] For the general public, the most tangible result of the monetary reform of 1958–59 was the introduction of a new franc, scheduled for January 1, 1960. Worth one hundred times the old one, it was based on a certain weight in gold: 180 milligrams (less than 1⁄100 ounce) for one franc. The value of this new currency, commonly called the "heavy franc" (*franc lourd*), was once again ensured by its materiality, its palpable solidity, and, more specifically, its weight.

This measure—wholly symbolic, since it consisted simply in dividing all prices and wages by one hundred—provoked a withering response from the opposition press. "The 'heavy franc,' despite the efforts of the [Gaullist press], makes its future users contemptuous or indignant, depending on the person," Claude Bourdet retorted in *France Observateur* in December 1958. "The franc, alas, is once again a bit lighter; it is the regime and its leader that begin to weigh upon the country."[53] The government's adversaries mockingly accused it of believing that it could pass off an arbitrary change in the unit of measurement as a thoroughgoing reform. One critic, writing in the weekly magazine *L'Express*, ridiculed the revaluation as a pure charade: "To really appreciate the impact of the economic 'revolution' that has just been proposed to us, one has only to apply this revolutionary principle to daily life. Take the thermometer. One day physicians decided that any temperature higher than 37 degrees centigrade signaled a feverish state in human beings. Nothing could be more arbitrary. They might just as well have decided that this temperature was 3.7 degrees (heavy). What prevents us then from doing the same thing in order to eliminate fever, and therefore illness, once and for all?"[54]

Although Rueff was seen in many quarters as a prisoner of the past, and widely reproached for his technocratic liberalism, the press attacked him chiefly by turning his own rhetoric of truth and falsehood against him, accusing him of abusing the French people by a form of monetary manipulation that had more to do with magical incantation than economics:

> A certain lingering technocratic odor, an impression of falsification and insincerity (the expression "hypocrite" [*faux jeton*] is, if one may say so, worth its weight in gold), are not alone enough to explain the public's aversion to all forms of "manipulation." The monetary experience of a millennium also makes its weight felt. Liberalism, victorious in the nineteenth century, tied currencies to gold, to the detriment of everything else. With the franc *germinal*, our fathers believed, there opened up for all eternity a new era, an era of stability. In fact, the nineteenth century of the triumphant financial bourgeoisie appears today as nothing more than an isolated episode, interrupting a long series of monetary degradations. But did tying the currency to gold really signify a golden age? One may doubt it. For evidence one has only to point to the strange shocks that unsettle prices. . . . The pride of being able to read in the stock exchange quotations that the French franc is [now] worth ten Belgian francs and almost a mark is certainly understandable. In a single stroke one theatrically erases the failings of one's predecessors. There is an element of magic in such an action. The spirit of evil is driven out.[55]

Within this context Klein devised his rules of transfer for the *Zones de sensibilité*, mimicking the terms of the monetary debate over the weight of the franc, that is, its convertibility into a certain number of milligrams of fine gold. At a moment when the so-called heavy franc was supposed by its inventors to have restored confidence in the truthfulness of exchange through the backing of a precious metal, Klein made gold the guarantee of his invisible works, which otherwise might arouse skepticism and doubt as to the veracity of their status as works of art. As he put it in his Chelsea Hotel Manifesto in April 1961: "I demanded in exchange for the highest quality of the immaterial the highest quality of material payment: an ingot of pure gold."[56] In the event, the nominal devaluation of wages and prices brought about by the new monetary regime had mechanically entailed a very appreciable rise in nonmonetary values, gold foremost among them. In February 1959, slightly before the first mention of gold by Klein at Anvers in March, one financial columnist made a list of "assets that a reasonable person urgently needs to acquire and can afford" in order to take

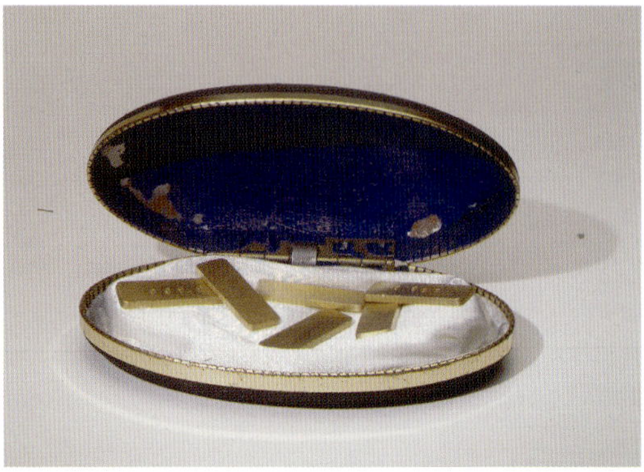

Fig. 8 Yves Klein, *Boîte à lingots* [*Ingot Box*], c. 1959. 1⅜ × 4⅜ × 2⅛ in. (3.5 × 11 × 5.5 cm). Private collection.

advantage of the devaluation. In the first place: "Fine gold whose price per gram has increased in the following fashion: November 520 francs; 31 December 562 francs; 22 January 573 francs. Still, one must be wary of the interventions in gold sometimes secretly carried out by the Banque de France to push down prices."[57] His article was illustrated by a photograph showing a line of people in front of the "Exchange" and "Gold" windows of a "registered financial institution" above the caption: "They didn't waste any time. . . ." Are we to conclude from this that Klein, in agreement with the position taken by de Gaulle and his ministers and advisors, saw the materiality of a precious, "heavy" metal as the only possible guarantee of trustworthy exchange? In that case, the artist would stand to profit from the rising price of gold at the turn of the decade, while at the same time basing his argument on one of the basic principles of medieval economics, which considered the use of gold as an instrument of exchange and a unit of account to reflect its intrinsic value as a material.[58] His highly fetishistic work *Boîte à lingots* [*Ingot Box*] (c. 1959) seems to lend itself to this interpretation, halfway between a chest containing ingots of raw gold and a box painted in blue containing precious jewels (fig. 8).

And yet, once again, Klein's position is more complex than it may seem at first sight. As we have noted, he takes "real" value to be immaterial and primary. As he prophesied in his 1959 Sorbonne lecture, immaterialism "will make us rediscover a true love of matter in opposition to the quantitativism, the mummifying materialism that makes us slaves—of this matter—and transforms it into a tyrant."[59] Turning the rhetoric of Pinay and Rueff inside out, he holds that all that is true and genuine is immaterial, whereas all that is false and inauthentic is material. With these words, he unambiguously took the side of the opponents of the heavy franc, who likewise saw gold as a "tyrant," a weight dragging down the French economy and threatening to sink it. Thus a cartoon in the year-end issue of *L'Express* in 1959, showing a man about to throw himself into the water, a piece of the new franc tied around his neck as a millstone, expressed the wish for 1960: "May the heavy franc not be too heavy!"[60] Klein's use of the term *mummifying* also recalls the charge to which Rueff made himself vulnerable by calling for a return to the gold standard, namely, that he had an unreasonable fixation on the past. The new monetary reform held out the startling prospect, as one journalist put it in January 1959, that "[t]hese entities—the queen currency, the gold standard—which were thought to be mummified, would be splendidly alive once more."[61]

Klein emphasized the materiality of precious metal in order to bring out more clearly the superiority of the immaterial. His method was paradoxical: the choice of gold, perceived at the time as the preeminent physical embodiment of legal tender, as an equivalent value for his immaterial works had the result less of giving his art a material basis than of casting doubt on the material worth of gold itself. If gold could be used as payment for the "void"—as critics at the time characterized Klein's art—what then was the true value of gold?[62] If, moreover, the same void could be sold for different amounts of pure gold, from 20 to 1,280 grams (¾ ounce to 2¾ pounds) for the different series of the *Zones de sensibilité*, then weight in gold turned out to be a measure altogether as arbitrary as any other. Finally, the capacity of gold-backed currency to contain price inflation seems to have been very much doubted by Klein himself, who, as we have seen, anticipated a geometric progression in the price of his *Zones* as they circulated from one owner to another. The *Monogolds* had exactly this aim, of demonstrating that the value of gold cannot be reduced to the weight of a precious metal; the true value of these paintings had to do with their status as works of art. This is the problem posed in particular by the one titled *Valeur or* [*Value Gold*] (1960; see fig. 6), at once a standard of monetary value in a system where convertibility is threatened and a standard of aesthetic value for an artist then searching for a way to establish an equivalence in his work between blue, pink, and gold that would make it possible to go back, once and for all, to a barter system.

The Economic System of the Blue Revolution

Substituting "quality" for "quantity" and abandoning a monetary standard for an artistic standard in a system without money—these were the two fundamental principles of the economic plank of Klein's program, the blue revolution, expounded in a 1959 manuscript titled "Esquisse et grandes lignes du système économique de la révolution bleue" ["Main Features of the Economic System of the Blue Revolution"].[63] If the thrust of the argument was deliberately utopian, it was nonetheless anchored not only in current events but also in the history of economic thought. Klein begins by noticing the failure of various "schools" to come to terms with "the economic matter." The physiocrats of the mid-eighteenth century, he says, were "down to earth" in the sense that they made agriculture the origin of wealth. A cursory review of the ideas of their successors follows, from the neoclassical (or marginalist) school of Walras, identified by little more than an allusion to marginal utility, to the Keynesian school, whose theory of full employment and the related concept of a multiplier are found wanting. A single error is held to vitiate all these approaches: the futile quest for a purely quantitative description of economic life. Klein, by contrast, argues on behalf of "a qualitative perception of the energy field of the economy" that would make it possible to "direct the fundamental inertia of the 'living world' toward a dynamic conception of the created thing." The rejection of mathematical methods, the metaphorical reliance on the notion of an "energy field" borrowed from physics, and the admiring regard for the dynamic character of economic activity are all typical of a certain literature challenging the claim of economics to be an independent discipline, whose authors include not only Georges Bataille and Asger Jorn, but also the poet and visual artist Isidore Isou.[64]

The rest of Klein's brief sketch is sprinkled with references to current events that amount to a compendium of journalistic clichés current in the late 1950s. A sentence such as "[E]verything [today] is analyzed in terms of bankruptcy, and the balance sheet of mixed economies today shows only a large deficit" must be read in the context of the widely publicized deficit in the balance of trade recorded for 1958. The problem of France's "cumulative deficit" was a daily preoccupation of the major papers and magazines, which fretted over the prospect of a national "bankruptcy."[65] Expressions such as "short-term variations," "cyclical fluctuations," and "inflationary spiral" were commonly applied to the financial crisis France experienced in 1957–58 as a result of rapid economic growth; on the trade side, talk of a "customs war" and "commercial Malthusianism" was frequently heard in the debates surrounding the opening of the Common Market of the six-member European Economic Community, effective in 1958.

Exasperated by the unremitting failure of economic theories and alarmed by the current international situation, Klein urged the necessity of bringing forth a "new era" that would redefine the quantitative instrument par excellence, the thing chiefly responsible for mummification—money. In the 1959 manuscript, he rejected both "reserves and currencies" and demanded the "elimination of fiduciary currency," that is, paper money, which he accused of being a "costly intermediary," a "pure system of representation" that interposes itself between real things and masks "the very meaning of value." The abolition of money was the foremost task of the new economy needing to be built, a system that would reinstate the moral principle of a just price—a system, finally, that would reconcile "intellectual aspirations and universal moral principles with the most urgent economic imperatives," in which "the rich man will necessarily be an authentic genius," and in which justice rules the economy. This system was to be founded on the invention of a new standard of value. Like Rueff, Klein could not conceive of equitable exchange without reference to a standard, and dismissed out of hand a monetary system subject to the contingencies of supply and demand. Nevertheless he managed to free himself from the "tutelage of gold" and advocated a new standard that would make it possible to "stick to reality," to turn "toward an acceptance of the intrinsic value of matter." This standard, artistic and immaterial, consists in the peculiar aura that works of art have—what he called their "latent power." In the 1959 manuscript, Klein went on to imagine a world in which, "[o]n this structurally qualitative basis, every corporation will be required to hand over for safekeeping in the vaults of the central bank, previously emptied of all metal deposits, the masterpiece of [its] profession. These masterpieces, thus gathered together, will materialize the basic spiritual guidance of the country. . . . This permanent example, catalyzer of latent power, representing a stable—though not closed—sampling, will make it possible finally to lay the foundations of a fundamentally sound barter system protected from short-term quantitative variations."[66]

At a historic transitional moment, then, when Rueff was waging a futile battle in defense of the gold standard, considered by its opponents to be obsolete and doomed to disappear once and for all from the world economy, Klein chose neither to embrace a modern system of floating rates, unconstrained by any higher moral rule, nor to take refuge in an obstinate conservatism. He insisted on keeping a standard. This could not be a contemptibly material "metal deposit," however; it had to be a "quasi-spiritual value"—a work of art. Like gold, a work of art is an inalterable and sterile good, which has worth only as a store of its own value, producing no income; from the point of view of investment, it is a safe haven and an instrument of speculation. Nevertheless, the masterpieces that Klein envisioned taking the place of gold ingots in central bank vaults were not to be considered as reserves of material value, but as aesthetic and spiritual points of reference, defining an ethics—a "guide for living," as he put it in the Sorbonne lecture.[67] Unlike currency, which is characterized by an absence of quality, owing to its purely quantitative nature, a work of art is invested with a spiritual quality that makes it incomparable to any other, however great the degree of formal resemblance may be. This was one of the chief lessons of the Galleria Apollinaire show.

Klein's economic system, harnessed to an archaic conception of value, dismissed Communist and capitalist alternatives alike, regarding them as equally responsible for the development of a quantitative and technocratic economics.[68] In defending quality against quantity, and calling for a return to barter, the artist combined a certain elitism with the sort of French patriotism that was typical of this period. This is where one runs up against the limits of his position: asserting the normativity of values committed him to a hierarchical conception of social relations; elevating a unique work of art to the rank of a standard obliged him to confer an exceptional status on the artist; considering materials to be transformed by immaterial creation rather than by material production canceled all hope of reassigning ownership of the means of production and redistributing surplus value. One is bound nonetheless to admire the workings of an original and stimulating mind, whose influence may be measured by the further experiments of one artist, in particular, who sought to tease out the implications of what Klein had been the first to do.

The Economic Experiments of Edward Kienholz

Artists, more than anyone else, were able to appreciate how fundamental the economic aspect of Klein's work was. And no artist was more receptive to it than the American assemblage sculptor and painter Edward Kienholz, who met Klein in June 1961, during his stay in Los Angeles, where he started work on a new series of *Zones de sensibilité picturale immatérielle*, this one unnumbered and reserved for his friends as gifts.[69] In the years that followed, Kienholz likewise undertook to investigate the economic forms of existence and exchange available to his creations. At the time, he was creating large-scale, often brutally realistic installations called *Tableaux*, which the viewer could enter and walk around in, containing sculptures, found objects, and painted elements, sometimes accompanied by a soundtrack.[70] Between 1963 and 1965 Kienholz began to look for a new way of financing such works, which had become costly to produce and whose prospects of sale remained uncertain.[71] Thus were born the *Concept Tableaux*: instead of creating a work and offering it to prospective buyers, he reversed the process and sold the concept of a work that had yet to be realized, along with an exclusive option to purchase the executed idea. This novel payment arrangement at once calls to mind Klein's imaginary contracts for painting atomic and hydrogen bombs. Kienholz dissociated the purchase price of the concept, which is to say the strictly artistic and creative contribution (an arbitrary and usually high price), from the cost of actually producing the tableau itself, limited to the cost of materials and labor, which in turn was calculated on the basis of "the combined hourly wage scale for plumbers, electricians, and carpenters then prevailing in the Los Angeles area."[72]

The impact of Klein's thinking is more evident still in the series of *Watercolors* that Kienholz exhibited in 1969. These were aquarelles on paper of fixed dimensions that appeared almost untouched except for two streaks of color applied horizontally to the watercolor wash and, stenciled in the center, the price at which they were to be exchanged. They were displayed in metal frames designed by the artist, and, as in the case of the *Concept Tableaux*, authenticated by his thumbprint. Paintings of a first type mentioned a sum in dollars: "For $25.00," "For $77.00," and so on, with prices ranging from $1.00 to $10,000.00 (fig. 9). The different colors of paint, distributed according to the principle of a mathematical series, were intended to divide the whole set into subseries.[73] Paintings of a second type specified, in lieu of a dollar price, an object or service for which they were to be exchanged, thus establishing a barter system: a suit donated by Monte Factor (an art collector and clothier to Hollywood stars), for example, or a Rockwell portable electric saw; sometimes a particular person or thing was designated ("For Anything I Want from Maurice Tuchman," "For a Baldessari Painting," and so on), other times a generic object ("For a Fur Coat"). The range of monetary value for these goods and services, as for the prices denominated in dollars, was extremely large.

Fig. 9 Edward Kienholz, *For $77.00*, 1969. Watercolor and ink on paper, 12¼ × 16¼ in. (31.1 × 41.3 cm). Collection of Nancy Reddin Kienholz.

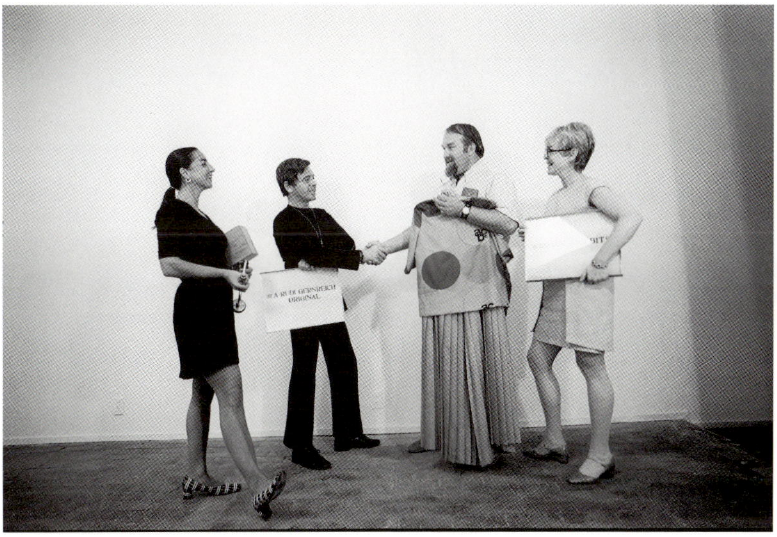

Fig. 10 The opening of the exhibition *Ed Kienholz: Watercolors* at the Eugenia Butler Gallery, Los Angeles, 1969 (from left to right): an unidentified buyer, Rudi Gernreich, Edward Kienholz, Eugenia Butler. Photograph by Malcolm Lubliner.

Exhibited for the first time at the Eugenia Butler Gallery in Los Angeles in 1969, Kienholz's *Watercolors* met with much greater enthusiasm than the *Concept Tableaux*. If the artist's own recollection can be trusted, "there were literally lines of people waiting to buy the 'cheap' ones opening night."[74] A certain number of the works were sold for only a few dollars, and many for prices considerably lower than what an artist of Kienholz's reputation might have expected to command. The show was remarkable, as the museum curator Jane Livingston noted, for "the dauntlessly cheerful willingness of his public to barter."[75] This playful spirit is captured in photographs of the opening taken by Malcolm Lubliner (fig. 10), which show a buyer presenting a brace (a tool for drilling holes in wood) and a box of bits in exchange for a work by Kienholz asking for just these things, and the fashion designer Rudi Gernreich himself offering one of his dresses in exchange for a work asking for "a Rudi Gernreich Original." Kienholz envisaged these works not only as a practical attempt to rethink how the art market and, more generally, the monetary economy operate (by virtue of the experience it provided in interacting with individual collectors), but also as a theoretical innovation. "What I have done, in effect," he explained, "is to issue a kind of currency which is not dependent on the normal monetary system. As inflation goes up, it sweeps my 'money' along, and in a peculiar way appreciates it while devaluing the dollar/pound/mark/franc."[76]

The idea of selling virtually identical works at very different prices, fixed in advance by the artist, arbitrarily it would appear, cannot fail to recall the story of the sale of Klein's monochromes at the Galleria Apollinaire in 1957. More generally, the whole of Kienholz's economic experimentation, from the *Concept Tableaux* to *Watercolors*, can be seen as extending and deepening the questions posed earlier by Klein concerning the opposition between barter and monetary exchange, between intrinsic value and market value, between uniqueness and multiplicity. Like Klein, Kienholz adamantly affirmed the individuality of each aquarelle: "They are all different and unique and should not be confused in any way with an edition";[77] at the same time, and as with Klein's works once more, only differences in price served to physically differentiate them. Finally, yet again like Klein, thinking about the economy led Kienholz both to search for an archaic origin of value and to examine how value was understood in the present day. As Larry Rivers (whose *French Money* paintings I study in the second chapter) noted in connection with Kienholz's *Watercolors*, the market tends to value all the works of a given series—comparable in respect of dimensions, concept, material, and period—at the highest price achieved by any single piece; indeed, this is the very principle underlying an assessment of artistic worth.[78] Accordingly, Rivers continued, as the going price continues to rise, all those who purchased a painting in the series at a lower price may expect to see their asset increase in value. Kienholz himself made much the same argument in a 1974 essay: "Anyone buying a piece in series only risks one dollar as the previous buyer has just paid the same price minus $1.00, the buyer before him the same price minus $2.00, etc. The series has a respectably broad base and does well in practice as well as in theory."[79] Kienholz therefore devised one final theoretical flourish: he decided that the first and last works of the series—*For $1.00* and *For $10,000.00*—could only be sold together. "This," he observed, "permits the purchaser of *[For] $10,000.00* to immediately double his or her money," since the canvas acquired for $1.00 will henceforth be worth $10,000.00 as well. In principle, then, such a sale should "elevate all of the money watercolors to the same price regardless of the printed face value."[80] It was on account of the particular interest shown by collectors in the first and last pieces of a series, which led Kienholz to impose the restrictive condition just mentioned, that he was able explore the economic psychology of offering limited editions for sale and the sources of artistic worth more fully than Klein had done. Like Klein, Kienholz had a shrewd intuitive understanding of how the art market worked. The idea of substituting for it a new system, fully under the artist's control, came from this very insight.

In 1972, Kienholz reinterpreted the themes he had developed up to this point in a work that summarized his thinking about the relation between art and speculation on financial markets. *The Commercial No. 3, Sort of a Commercial for "Watercolors"* (fig. 11) took the form, as its title suggests, of

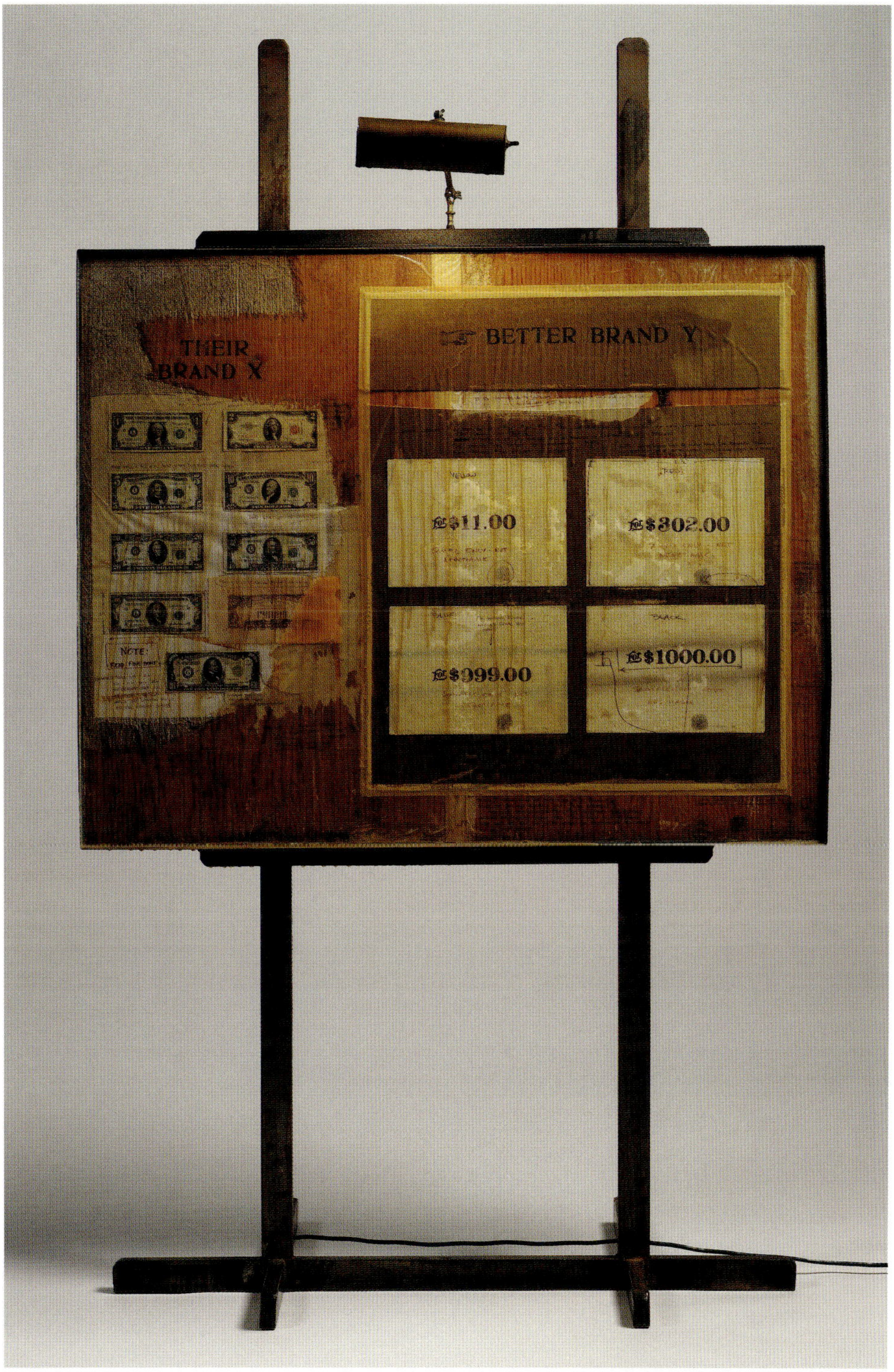

Fig. 11 Edward Kienholz, *The Commercial No. 3, Sort of a Commercial for "Watercolors,"* 1972. Steel, zinc, wood, paper, cardboard, plastic, and electrical device, 79 × 27½ in. (200.5 × 70 cm). Kunsthalle, Hamburg.

a miniature billboard advertising his earlier paintings. A framed wooden picture, mounted on an easel and illuminated from above by a lamp connected to an electrical device built into the work, presents the viewer with a comparison between two products. To the left, "Their Brand X" is shown by banknotes: each of the nine denominations of dollar bills is represented, eight of them by actual notes (a handwritten note explains that they have been "withdrawn from circulation") and one—a $500 bill—by a reddish-brown reproduction of inferior quality. To the right, "Better Brand Y" is illustrated by four of the watercolors: *For $11.00*, *For $302.00*, *For $999.00*, and *For $1000.00*. Each one bears the disclaimer "Sample Only—Not Negotiable." Mimicking the techniques employed by manufacturers in promoting their products, the "Better Brand Y" is set off by its own frame and a manicule (the hand with pointing finger). Handwritten annotations cover the bills and the aquarelles, commenting on their size, color, and composition; the signatures and the thumbprints of the *Watercolors* are circled and remarked upon, as if to emphasize a major advantage of Brand Y over Brand X. Above the watercolors appears this legend: "It is impossible to compute percentage of increase on this issue (in use all over the world)." The *Watercolors* are recommended, in other words, as a sounder and much more remunerative investment, in both aesthetic and financial terms, than the degraded American currency of the early 1970s (a point I discuss further in chapter 4). And yet, a certain uneasiness hangs over Kienholz's advertisement for art as a monetary instrument. The billboard itself shows unmistakable signs of willful neglect: the surface of the wood is damaged, the paper is torn in places, and the documents exhibited are covered with splashes of paint and drips of varnish; the frame around the watercolors is built up from ordinary masking tape. If, in 1969, Kienholz appeared to regard the enthusiasm for art as a tradable financial asset with humor and good cheer, three years later it filled him with a bitter sense of foreboding. In the interval, the effects of the economic crisis had begun to make themselves felt, causing the prices paid for works of art to seem more and more indecent, if not actually obscene, and doomed themselves soon to collapse.

THE INDUSTRIAL PAINTING OF GIUSEPPE GALLIZIO

On May 31, 1958, a month after the exhibition by Yves Klein known as *Le vide* [*The Void*] opened in Paris, the Italian artist Giuseppe Gallizio (he had recently made the nickname "Pinot" part of his professional identity, and is still today frequently referred to as "Pinot Gallizio," with or without a faux-aristocratic hyphen),[81] inaugurated his *Primi esperimenti di pittura industriale* [*First Experiments in Industrial Painting*]. Whereas the only thing to see in Iris Clert's empty gallery had been the freshly painted white walls, Luciano Pistoi's Galleria Notizie in Turin was a riot of color, in vast quantities: three rolls of canvas—twelve meters (about thirty-nine feet), fourteen meters (about forty-six feet), and seventy meters (about 230 feet) long, according to press accounts—painted with thermostable resin-based oils and partly unrolled, were stretched along the walls and on a table. Gallizio, both artist and producer, was present at the opening: armed with a pair of scissors and a wooden measuring stick, he sold his painting by the meter.

Industrial painting was then, in the spring of 1958, one of the most important initiatives of the Situationist International (SI), a revolutionary group of artists and intellectuals. Gallizio had been a member since its founding the year before, in July 1957 at Cosio di Arroscia in Italy. As Guy Debord, also a cofounder and the movement's chief theoretician, wrote a few months later, the Turin exhibition marked "a decisive turning point in the ongoing disappearance of the old plastic arts, an outcome that contains at the same time the premises of their transformation into a new force."[82] The exhibition was immediately remounted in Milan, at the Galleria Montenapoleone (July 1958), and then in Munich at the Galerie van de Loo (April–May 1959). Gallizio then went on to present his production in Paris, at the Galerie René Drouin (May 1959), as part of an installation that was re-created the following year at the Stedelijk Museum in Amsterdam (May–June 1960). Over a period of two years, then, thanks to the combined efforts of SI members to bring his work to the attention of the major capitals of European avant-garde painting of the period, industrial painting came to enjoy a growing notoriety. On May 31, 1960, however, it abruptly came to an end, with the banishment of Gallizio and the whole "Italian section" around him. An admiring monograph of the artist was published by the SI little more than a month later, in July—"on the occasion," as a footnote on the last page quietly acknowledged, "of his expulsion from the Situationist International."[83]

What accounts for the sudden abandonment of industrial painting by Debord and his allies, who, until then, had placed such great hopes in it? The literature on the movement, which for the most part treats Gallizio as a rather marginal figure, typically speaks of a transition in the early 1960s from an original artistic phase to a later political phase.[84] Several recent scholarly works have sought to reevaluate Gallizio's place in the group and his role in elaborating Situationist doctrines. Nevertheless, they throw little light on the unmet expectations that seem to have led to the split.[85] In the meantime, however, improved access to archival documents has given us a more precise idea of Gallizio's activities between 1957 and 1960,[86] and makes it possible to reconstruct the power struggles and divergent interests within the SI, as well as the group's relationship to the contemporary artistic scene.

The revolutionary force claimed for industrial painting arose from its perceived promise to upset not only the economy of traditional art, but also, as a consequence, the economy as a whole—and this on two levels: first, production, by combining artisanal quality with large-scale output; and second, consumption, by emphasizing the popular appeal of a new kind of art committed to increasing social welfare. The ambition of this challenge to the established order extended beyond the fine arts to the worlds of design and fashion, whose economics were likewise seen to contain an alternative to industrial production and commercial distribution. The new "theory of value and its application to culture," to recall the phrase of Asger Jorn, another founding member of the SI, was therefore not the result of a retreat into the supposed radical purity of avant-garde art. To the contrary, it directly confronted all the contradictions inherent in a cultural economy obliged to satisfy elitist tastes while at the same time reaching a mass commercial audience.

Producing Industrial Painting

As the historian Giorgina Bertolino has pointed out, industrial painting underwent "a theoretical gestation prior to its actual production."[87] The first mention of it occurs in December 1956 in a leaflet announcing a "Demonstration in Favor of Unitary Urbanism" that took place over six days, December 10–15, 1956, in Turin. "Of every three people who take the bus," the authors informed an ignorant public, "two are unaware of Gallizio's industrial painting!"[88] In fact, it did not yet exist: Gallizio himself noted that the first samples were completed only at the end of 1957. A year earlier, when Gallizio, Jorn, and Debord met for the first time in Italy, industrial painting was no more than an idea, a topic of discussion.

Like all of the activities sponsored by the Situationist International, industrial painting has often been looked at through the prism of Debord's view of the group's purpose. To his mind, it was bound up with a more general interest in the place of automation in revolutionary artistic practices. In the mid-1950s, Debord was intent on declaring his independence from the Surrealist movement, having begun his career as a member of the Letterist International. Insisting on the Surrealists' inability to play a positive role in an industrialized future—even though he had to exaggerate their rejection of the machine in order to condemn them for clinging to a sterile occultism having no radical consequence—he was able to cast one of the distinctive features of his own movement in a more favorable light.[89] In opposition to the "reactionary side of Surrealism that was part of it from the beginning (magic, belief in a golden age that could be somewhere other than ahead in history)," as he wrote in the group's journal, *International situationniste*, in June 1958, Debord set about devising ways to take "control of new conditioning techniques."[90] This embrace of the machine—understood here to mean the most advanced tools of capitalist technology—came at a moment when Debord and his colleagues had resolved for the first time to make a serious study of Marxist concepts, with the aim of rethinking Letterist principles in the broader context of society and the modern economy.[91]

Nevertheless, within the SI, Jorn's influence on Gallizio was at least as important as that of Debord. For Jorn, the notion of industrial painting was closely connected with the struggle he had been waging for several years against the rational and functional aesthetics of the architect and artist Max

Bill, founder of the Ulm School of Design in Germany, which saw itself as the successor to the Bauhaus. In direct opposition to this "imaginary" Bauhaus, Jorn and Gallizio joined to create an "imaginist" counterpart through the Mouvement international pour un Bauhaus imaginiste [MIBI] in 1953.[92] The strictly functionalist teaching of the Ulm School was based on scientific and technological training, the promotion of a cold and refined aesthetic, and the integration of the artist in an automatized process of serial production; Jorn's aspirations as a founder of CoBrA, as an artist who celebrated naive painting and folk arts, spontaneity in pictorial creation, and training through free experimentation, pointed in an entirely different direction. As against the industrial production of standardized objects, intended solely to fulfill a definite social function, Jorn urged the necessity of an art having no predetermined use, an art in which, though it retained a social function, form preceded—and, indeed, invented—function.[93]

In 1956, then, Jorn and Debord agreed that Gallizio's painting held out the promise of becoming a truly industrial form of art. Nevertheless they insisted on a demanding set of requirements that were not easily reconciled with one another. For Jorn, painting in this style should use machines in a purely ludic way, assigning to the artist the social role of a creative coordinator who could stimulate research in other fields, science in particular; standardization and serial production for the purpose of carrying out a definite function were ruled out. For Debord, by contrast, industrial painting had to combat "Surrealist automatism" on its own terms.[94] Taking automation in its most materialistic and least metaphorical sense, he insisted that the new style reject the sterile, repetitive, and individualistic glorification of the unconscious, and put forward in its place an "applicable" art, collective and revolutionary in spirit, that would appropriate the methods of capitalist technology in order to subvert capitalism itself.

The first experiments in industrial painting, performed at the Alba Laboratory (named for the town outside Turin where Gallizio lived, and later, in July 1957, officially renamed the Experimental Laboratory of the Situationist International), grew out of the artist's attempt to find a practical means of satisfying these theoretical conditions. In keeping with Debord's wishes, Gallizio sought to imitate the methods of automatized production. He worked according to a "quantitative principle" on immense canvases, several dozen meters in length.[95] To cover these increasingly vast surfaces—at one point reaching a length of seventy-four meters (about 240 feet)—he employed a variety of techniques. Semimechanical or iterative methods, such as monotype printing, held particular appeal because they reduced the direct impact of the painter's hand and made it possible to create the impression of assembly-line production. Other techniques involved the use of nontraditional tools ("machines") to apply materials, often rather violently. Colors were deposited in thick sheets, sometimes atomized with the aid of a spray gun, sometimes slathered directly on the canvas. Another technique, applied in the works exhibited at the Galerie René Drouin in

Paris in May 1959, involved exploding a small packet filled with paint and a firecracker on a canvas, anticipating the method made famous by Niki de Saint Phalle in her shooting pictures, *Tirs*.[96] Like factory production, industrial painting was a collective undertaking: Gallizio's son Giorgio (who took the pseudonym of Giors Melanotte on joining the SI) worked with him, assisted occasionally by his friend Glauco Wuerlich. Visitors to the Alba Laboratory were sometimes encouraged to contribute as well, as part of what Gallizio called "group painting."[97] Gallizio seems nonetheless temperamentally to have been drawn more to Jorn's vision, for he did not really go any further than this in adapting an industrial model to artistic creation: his new synthetic resins were more the product of recreational chemistry than a result of scientific innovation in the service of industry; his mechanized techniques were deliberately haphazard, and gave a preponderant place to the manual application of paint and ink with brushes, a sort of spontaneous action painting that created an abstract or quasiabstract effect in which animal or anthropomorphic figures could sometimes be discerned. Furthermore, the informally collective nature of the effort was plainly incompatible, not only with any rational division or organization of labor, but also with any systematic use of technology in the production process itself. The only thing "industrial" about this painting, finally, was its name.

This implicit tension between the proclaimed advent of industrial production in art and the privately acknowledged reliance on artisanal methods is perhaps the outstanding fact of Gallizio's work during this period. At the opening of his exhibition in Turin, he grossly exaggerated what industrial production on demand was capable of guaranteeing: "You ask me for three meters, or twenty-five, or a kilometer," he told *La Gazzetta del popolo*, "and your order is fulfilled at once. Orders for more than a kilometer must be placed a few days in advance."[98] Gallizio's correspondence with Debord, however, tells another story. It reveals a slow and exhausting process of creation, the difficulty of which was substantially increased by problems encountered in drying the canvases without inhaling the toxic fumes emitted by the chemicals used in decorating them.[99] The same tension is manifest in the photographs that the SI chose to distribute of the Alba Laboratory and of Gallizio himself. In the monograph published by the group, a picture of the studio bears the caption: "The industrial painting assembly line, at the dessication stage" (fig. 12). This last, apparently technical, term, borrowed (or so it was meant to seem) from the vocabulary of industrial chemistry, refers to nothing more than the drying of a solid material by the evaporation of liquid, which is to say the drying out of painted canvases exposed to hot air. The photograph itself clearly belies any industrial pretension: it shows Gallizio's studio, the vaulted basement of a seventeenth-century monastery, in which an improvised installation of boards lying across trestles serves as makeshift scaffolding for drying the long canvases. There are only two workers on this so-called assembly line, Gallizio himself and his son Giorgio (seen from behind). The only machine actually present,

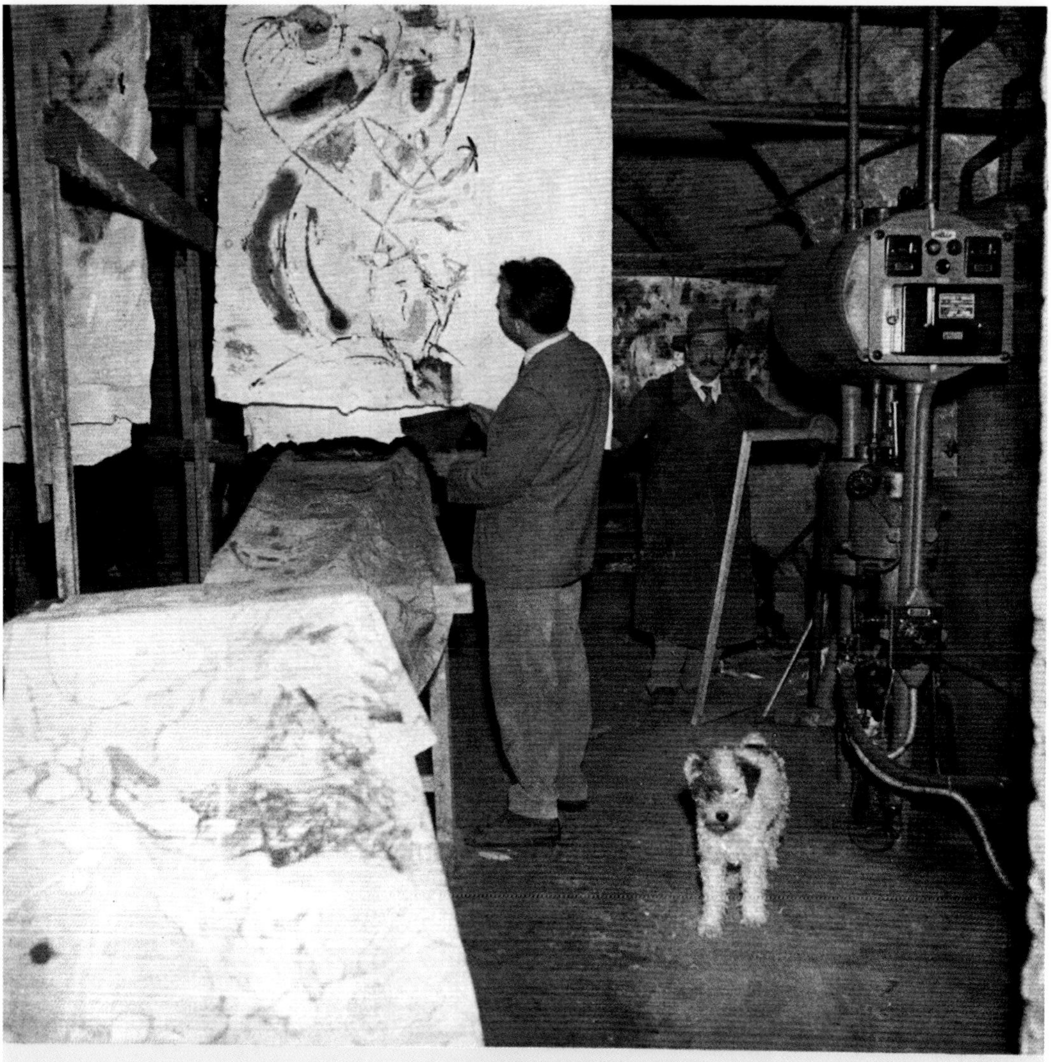

La chaine de peinture industrielle, au stade de la dessication. Au premier plan, le chien de Pinot-Gallizio qui, après avoir soudainement viré au bleu, sera la première victime des émanations qui constituent le principal danger de la peinture industrielle pendant sa production.

Fig. 12 Picture with caption from the monograph *Pinot-Gallizio* (Paris: Internationale situationniste, 1960), n.p.

probably used for heating air and water, appears to be a household appliance having nothing to do with the creative process of painting.

A few pages later, there is a picture of a rather more sophisticated apparatus: a long metal flatbed printing table equipped with three hand-operated cylinders and brush (fig. 13). Some historians consider this to be a faithful illustration of a machine that Gallizio actually used.[100] No surviving photograph of Gallizio's studio confirms the use of such a device (elaborate by comparison with an air heater, but relatively rudimentary nonetheless), and study of the works themselves has identified nothing that constitutes evidence of a technique for superimposing coats of paint applied by successive rollings. Gallizio's archives contain the source of this image: far from

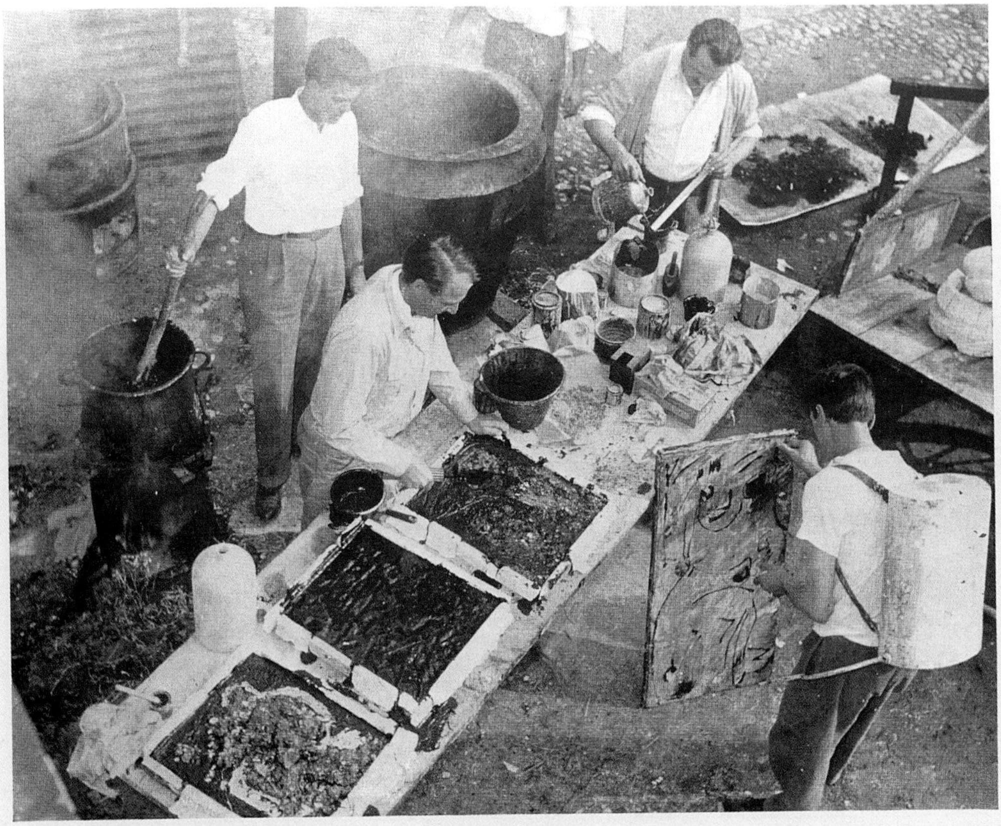

Les premières installations rudimentaires du Laboratoire Expérimental d'Alba, en 1956.

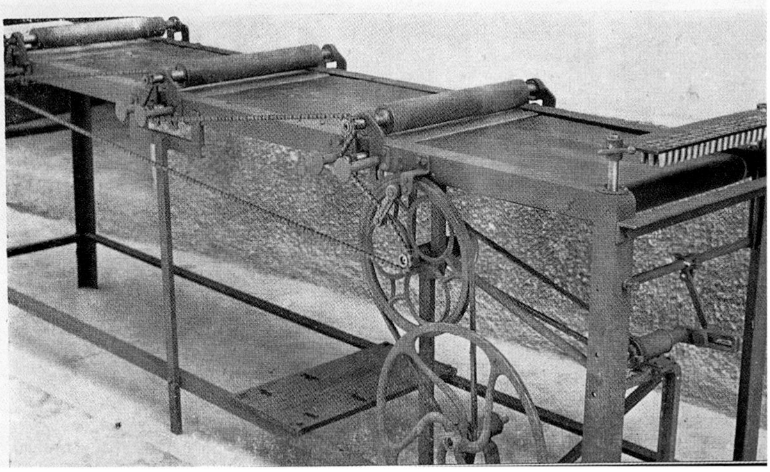

Fig. 13 Pictures from the monograph *Pinot-Gallizio* (Paris: Internationale situationniste, 1960), n.p.

being a photograph of a piece of equipment used at Alba, it was, in fact, taken from a series of images, probably distributed for publicity purposes by the machine's manufacturer, showing a worker demonstrating its use.[101] Its association with industrial painting came about as a result of a Situationist *détournement*, as it was called—in this case, a way of using ridicule and satire to suggest a new use for the rhetoric, vocabulary, and images of the world of industry.[102]

In his 1958 year-end report on "The Activity of the Italian Section," Debord described the "hand-made" character of industrial painting as a defect of the current production process, and recommended the "improvement of working techniques, which must pass from a yet artisanal stage to truly industrial efficiency."[103] Operating in a truly industrial manner would contradict the principles upheld by Jorn, however. If what was really at issue was "finding a justified place for the artist in the machine age," as Jorn had argued, then it would be necessary above all "to avoid a total automatism, a transformation of our intelligence into an instinctive and standardized reflex."[104] It may be for this reason that Debord quotes Jorn's own words in the same December 1958 article, aimed at ensuring that Gallizio's industrial painting would not be misinterpreted: "It would be a mistake to imagine that Pinot-Gallizio's industrial painting can be regarded as an example of industrial design. It is not a matter of reproducing models, but of realizing a unique creation, [one that is] perfectly useless except for Situationist-style experiments."[105] Similarly, Giorgio Gallizio sought to eliminate an ambiguity sustained by the SI itself that made it possible to mask disagreements within the group concerning the proper place of automation in industrial painting:

> We would also like to dispel any other doubts that surface at the sight of the term *industrial*. By using this word we don't mean to say that artistic production is constrained by the criteria of industrial production (working times, production costs, etc.), or by the intrinsic qualities of the machine, but we wish to establish a "quantitative" concept of production. And we mustn't fall into the easy mistake of thinking that the term *industrial* implies the concept of "mass-production," as each meter of *industrial* painting represents a unique experience and result.[106]

Indeed, an examination of the rolls on which this sort of painting was done shows not only that the canvases differ from one another, but that each of the rolls displays great variety over its entire length, which makes each meter of industrial painting wholly original.[107] Giorgio Gallizio's clarification was nonetheless necessary, for the image of standardized and repetitive painting rapidly came to dominate press accounts, influenced by the expression "industrial painting." Thus, for example, a cartoon appeared in a German newspaper on the occasion of the Munich exhibition, conserved by Giuseppe Gallizio in his personal archives (fig. 14), showing the artist as

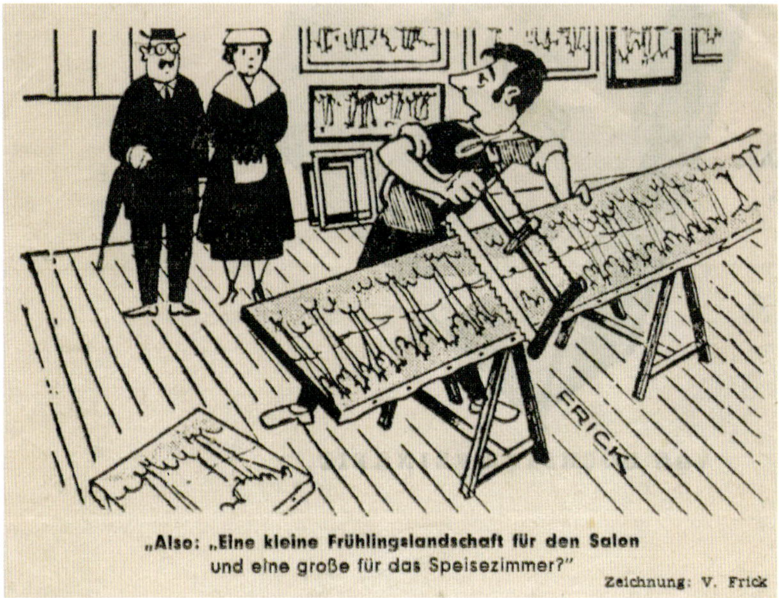

Fig. 14 Cartoon published on the occasion of Giuseppe Gallizio's exhibit at the Galerie van de Loo, Munich, April–May 1959. Press clipping, source unknown. Folder "Documenti—Mostre—Eventi (1956–1964)," Archivio Gallizio, Turin.

a stereotypical Italian worker, sleeves rolled up, sawing off part of a decorative panel for two buyers, a bourgeois couple. "A small landscape for the living room," he casually inquires, "and a large one for the dining room?" The entire length of the panel is covered with a strange frieze verging on abstraction, in which one can make out a series of trees whose repeated trunks recall the mechanical recordings of an electrogram. On the wall, different lengths of the same motif, individually framed, confirm that this painting is the sole model available, with only the format left to the buyer's choosing. This cartoon, which shows how badly the principles upheld by Jorn and Gallizio could be misinterpreted on the basis of Situationist rhetoric itself, is revelatory of the contradictions inherent in the economic role that industrial painting claimed for itself.

Selling Industrial Painting

The idea of making industrial painting a laboratory for criticizing the capitalist economy was explicit in the very first theoretical statement of its aims, the "Éloge de Pinot-Gallizio" ["In Praise of Pinot-Gallizio"], composed on the occasion of the Turin exhibition in May 1958 by Michèle Bernstein, Debord's companion and herself a founding member of the SI. Bernstein presented Gallizio's work as a critique of the existing market for art, which was understood to constitute a microcosm of the economy as a whole. The first sentences of her essay in the exhibition catalogue refer to the difficult period of economic reconstruction in Italy in the late 1950s: "In today's Italy, which is incapable of resolving the problem of unemployment, there is at least one [job needing to be filled]: the social function of paint[ing]."[108] At bottom, Bernstein's argument is an exposition and defense of Gallizio's "quantitative principle," which she contrasts with the operation of a traditional market based on scarcity. The availability of industrial painting in unlimited quantities can only have the effect of discouraging speculative investment: since any increase in demand is now promptly balanced by a corresponding increase in supply, prices will remain stable. There would be no more speculation on painting, Bernstein warned. "If you have money to invest, settle for shares in the Suez Canal."[109]

In denouncing "overproduction and monotony," as well as the rampant speculation responsible for the current crisis in abstract art, a victim of its own success, she deliberately echoed the terms of a polemic that was then very much alive on the Parisian—not the Italian—scene in order to divert them for Situationist purposes.[110] Debord and the cosigners of the *Potlatch* Manifesto four years earlier had already inveighed against the "formal repetitions" of abstract art and the "inflation of imitators."[111] By the spring of 1958, this idea had become a commonplace of art criticism. But if Bernstein was determined to carry on the argument, she was ready now to reverse its implication: far from deploring the decline of the spontaneous creative gesture as a result of the abstract artist's obsession with mechanical repetition, she rejoiced in this depreciation and looked to automated production as a way of making it complete. And if speculation and rising prices led to more and more standardized and repetitive production, as "bourgeois" art critics such as Michel Ragon and Pierre Restany maintained, then it was necessary to push the economic cycle to its breaking point: only a drastic increase in production would make it possible to put an end to speculation through total artistic and commercial devaluation. This would have the consequence of causing the "problem" of painting to disappear, and, with it, painters themselves. "We have now reached a stage of experimentation with new collective constructions and new syntheses," Bernstein concluded, "and there is no longer any point in combating the values of the old world by a neodadaist refusal. Whether these values are ideological, artistic, or even financial, the proper thing is to unleash inflation everywhere. Gallizio is in the forefront."[112] Bernstein saw artistic creation, in other words, as a vehicle for upsetting the established order. Degrading bourgeois painting ("this giant banknote called a picture," as Debord put it, paraphrasing Gallizio)[113] was a first step toward undermining the capitalist economy from within.

The devaluation of painting proceeded by means of a novel sales model: industrial painting was to be sold "by the meter" at an unbeatable price.[114] As in the case of Klein, however, mass distribution made it necessary to protect intellectual and artistic property in such a way that the management of scarcity could be regarded as a matter, not of the work itself, but of the technique used to produce it. In her introduction to the Turin show, Bernstein baldly asserted that the style of "painting by the meter is original, its reproduction is forbidden, its process patented."[115] Gallizio's archives reveal that in 1957 the artist did, in fact, make inquiries with the

International Patent Research Corporation about existing patents in the domain of chemical products—though not, of course, about techniques of production.[116] It is, therefore, possible that he did contemplate, as Klein had done for the binder medium of International Klein Blue, patenting the formula for one of his synthetic resins. But no attempt to secure intellectual property protection seems subsequently to have been made. The claim that a patent had actually been obtained is probably a result of Bernstein's resolve to anchor Gallizio's practice more firmly in the industrial imagination. Besides, applying for a patent would hardly have been consistent with the outlook of an artist who in the fall of 1956, not even two years before the Turin show, had proclaimed the need for an "antipatent"—a guarantee of "shared task" that would be both subversive and "antieconomic."[117] A few years later, he stated still more clearly his opposition to the "patented society" that artists such as Klein were thought to have helped to create, "conceived and based on simple ideas, on the elementary gestures of artists and scientists reduced to captivity like fleas by ants."[118]

In the event, sales of industrial painting did not fulfill the hopes that Bernstein had aroused. The SI put a brave face on the matter, claiming that the first exhibition of industrial painting in Turin, in May 1958, was an "unexpected commercial success."[119] And yet Jorn could not help but notice that "no one had come to buy a piece of a painting at a cheap price; the whole lot was sold by the roll to some of the most intelligent collectors from Europe and America."[120] The tendency to buy industrial painting in bulk, rather than in unit lengths of a meter, is attested by the catalogue raisonné: very few rolls were cut up in pieces.[121] Debord, for his part, suspected that this refusal to buy by the meter was due to the conformism of the public: "It is a primary defensive reaction of commerce in paintings, which, while hesitating to declare the whole of such painting outside the real world of the arts, has preferred until now to incorporate it into its system of values by treating each roll as a one big picture, amenable to the usual criteria of taste and talent."[122]

In response, privately, the SI recommended increasing prices and producing longer rolls—in order to discourage bulk purchasing—as well as more innovative methods of exhibition. As Debord's correspondence with Gallizio makes clear, the rise in prices urged in the wake of the Turin exhibition was also seen as a way of limiting the quantity sold: contrary to the impression that the SI was at pains to create, industrial painting was produced haltingly and only with great difficulty.[123] A list of prices for Gallizio's second show, at the Galleria Montenapoleone in Milan in July 1958, conserved among the artist's personal papers, helps explain the continuing appeal of buying by the roll rather than by the meter: the greater the quantity purchased, the lower the price (and sharply lower at the upper end).[124] It seems probable that gallery owners had pressed for a graduated pricing scale to encourage the view that large expanses of canvas were works of art in their own right, while contenting themselves with smaller sales by the

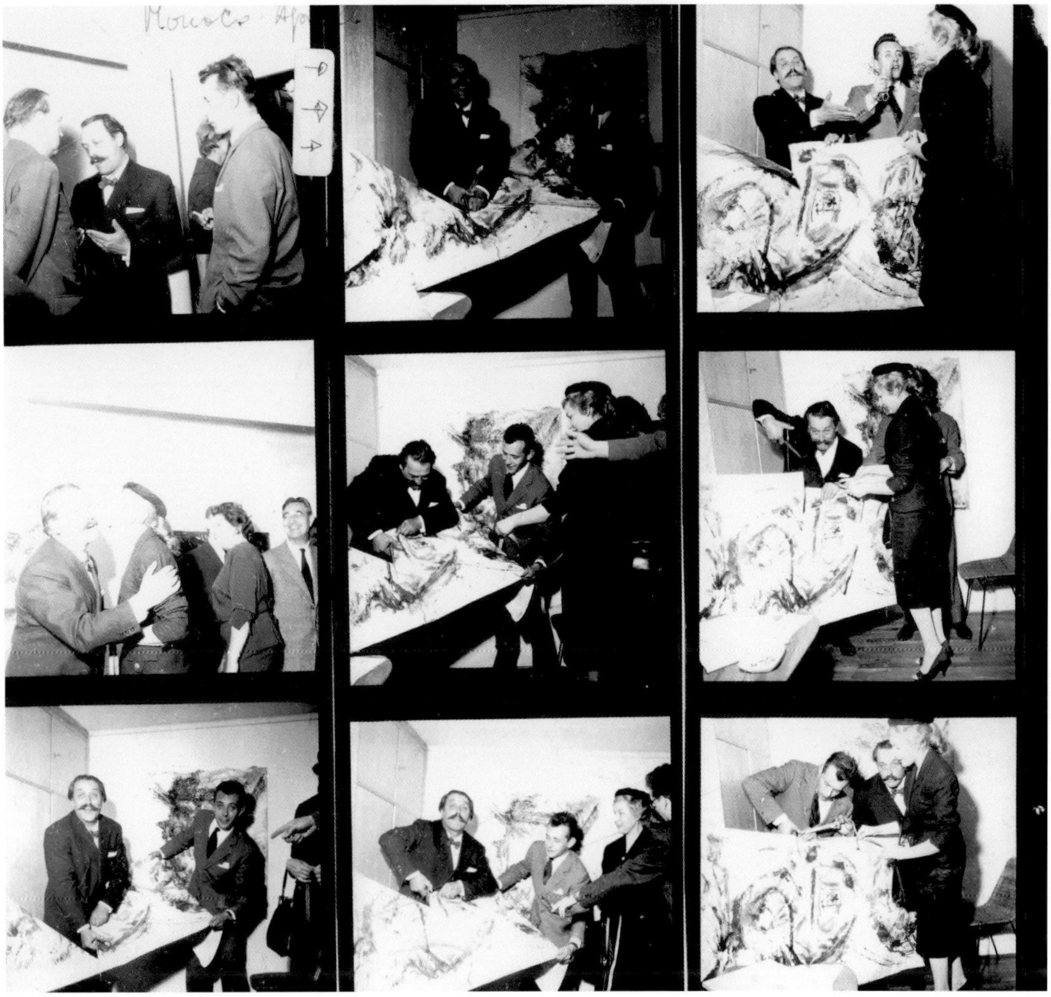

meter on the day of the opening in order to profit from the publicity it could be counted on to generate. The series of photographs taken of the opening at the Galerie van de Loo in Munich, in the spring of 1959, shows how carefully the event was staged: here Gallizio is seen brandishing his scissors, there wielding his measuring stick—obviously posed pictures with the same segment of canvas, meant to immortalize the act of satisfying consumer demand on a customized basis (fig. 15).

Fig. 15 Giuseppe Gallizio selling painting "by the meter" at the opening of his show at the Galerie van de Loo, Munich, April 1959. Contact sheet. Folder "Fotografie III," Archivio Gallizio, Turin.

Another, no less unconventional sale, this time by correspondence, is attested in Gallizio's archives. In May 1959, an American named Wilfred Weiss wrote to the artist after reading an article about him in *Time* entitled "Art by the Yard."[125] "I've long been curious about this kind of contemporary painting," Weiss wrote, "but usually do not have the means to indulge my curiosity. I am enclosing a check for $10, would you send me as much as that will buy?"[126] A few months later Gallizio replied that he had granted Weiss's request, but with a caveat: "Let me make it clear that, exceptionally, I have sent a meter of my industrial painting, but for any future requests by you or your friends, the price is set by my dealers at 70,000 Italian lire."[127] Although the prospect of selling directly to persons unknown to him, beyond the usual circles of art collectors and outside traditional distribution channels, seems to have appealed to Gallizio, he nonetheless had not forgotten his commercial commitments to gallery owners, and the need to protect his own interests by quoting a high rate. Ten dollars at that time was worth only about 6,200 lire, far below the unit price of a single meter. Unsurprisingly, the American had made a further request: "I'd appreciate it if you'd sign [the painting], as I anticipate I will have difficulty convincing some people that this is legitimate."[128] This practice—transforming a fragment of industrial painting into a picture by inscribing the artist's signature—was one that Gallizio consistently observed. All the sold pieces inventoried in the catalogue raisonné were signed, and in some cases dated as well. The inscription was made on the back, or else on a corner that then, by virtue of the left-to-right direction of the writing, automatically became the lower-right corner—causing a ninety-degree shift in viewing position, from the verticality of the roll to the horizontality of the traditional picture.

The selling of industrial painting throws into relief the whole problem of constructing a viable alternative economic model once the artist is part of a gallery system. An alternative model was perhaps all the more difficult to devise in this case as the SI was counting on the group's painters not only to provide it with a platform for public recognition, but also to assure its economic subsistence: Jorn's financial contribution in helping to finance the SI's publications and seeing to it that his colleagues had enough to live on is attested by multiple sources; and there is every reason to suppose that Gallizio likewise paid over to the group at least a part of the proceeds from the sale of his works.[129]

From Critique of Economic Policy to Luxury Standard and Haute Couture

Gallizio's experiments had gotten underway at a time when the capitalist economy represented, for Debord and the other Situationists, a central topic of theoretical investigation. Jorn's landmark essay, announced in June 1959 as a study "on 'The Theory of Value and Its Application to Culture,'" was published by the SI the following year as *Critique de la politique économique*. In its main thrust it is a reinterpretation (due, in part, to the writings of Goldmann and Lukács) of the theory of commodity exchange value developed by Marx in *Das Kapital*.[130] The influence of Bataille's *La part maudite* is also evident in its style of economic analysis, which relies on many of the same analogies with concepts in anthropology and the natural sciences, particularly physics.[131] In Jorn's interpretation, value is not to be considered as a state, whether qualitative or quantitative, but as a process, either of appreciation through production or depreciation through consumption. Drawing on the physical principle of potential energy, Jorn defines value as available, latent energy that permits an object to pass from one form to another, but that is used up in the course of being converted into actual energy, which is to say realized as a fixed value. Accordingly, the real enemy of value, as Goldmann maintained, is "reification." In Jorn's words, "The fixing of value in an object as identical reproduction is its neutralization, its transformation into quality."[132] Machine-based industrial society, in both its dominant forms, capitalist and socialist, therefore leads to the destruction of value by giving it a stable form. Indeed, both capitalism and socialism are founded on the ideal of a regime in which standardized mass low-cost production makes it possible to satisfy a standardized demand through a "socialization" of useful things, which now become commodities—the most perfect example of a socialized, universal commodity being a currency. The constant rhythm of the machine is accompanied by a uniform and rationalized process of directed consumption, as well as by the control and subjugation of workers' spare time, freed up through automation. This situation of permanent economic equilibrium, in which there is no longer either appreciation or depreciation, is for Jorn a nightmare, not an ideal.

In order to remedy this state of affairs, the *Critique de la politique économique* pleads for a return to the idea of value as discrepancy, variation, and surplus in relation to a measurable norm. The importance of the nonfunctional and the irrational must once more be recognized, both in production, through aimless experimentation, and in consumption, through a taste for luxury and lavish expenditure—in a word, potlatch (the title, not coincidentally, of the "information bulletin" of the French section of the Letterist International that Debord helped edit between June 1954 and November 1957). In this sense, it was believed, art could serve as a model for reconceiving economic relations: "The value of art is thus a countervalue by comparison with practical values, and is measured in the opposite way to them. Art is an invitation to expend energy, with no specific purpose other than the one that the viewer can bring to it."[133] Because art is inherently "extravagant," it must adopt an antieconomic (that is, a nonfunctional) attitude toward both its production and its reception. What is more, because artistic value is the only use value that is not used up the moment it is consumed, which strengthens its capacity to do away with the established order, not only does art promise to bring about the overthrow of the capitalist economy, but "the end of the economy will also lead to the realization of art."[134]

Gallizio appears to have been strongly influenced by Jorn's thinking, at least to judge from his own brief statement, "Il manifesto della pittura industriale" ["Manifesto of Industrial Painting"]. Written in August 1959 and published in an Italian art journal two months later, it was followed almost at once by Debord's French translation. Elaborating on the theme of value as variation, Gallizio celebrates dynamism and all that is new while condemning the concept of eternity: "Value," he says, "will become identical to change."[135] Speaking of the monetary system, the artist makes it clear that what he is working toward is "the melting down of *gold value*, [understood] as the frozen energy [of] the ignoble banking system that is now decomposing."[136] He proposes substituting for it "a new currency of *shock*," founded on variations in emotional intensity meant to combat the boredom of a rationalized industrial society. Corresponding to this mode of production is a mode of consumption by excess—once again, potlatch, which he describes as an exchange of "gifts that can only be paid for by other poetic experiences."[137] The replacement of currency by works of art cannot fail to recall the artistic standard Klein put forward in his "economic system of the blue revolution." Additionally, the poetical and mystical interpretation that Gallizio gives of Situationist rhetoric and the argument made by Jorn in his essay resemble some of the ideas that Klein was developing at the same time, first in his June 1959 Sorbonne lecture and then in his work *Le dépassement de la problématique de l'art* [*Overcoming the Problems of Art*], published toward the end of the same year.

Gallizio nonetheless set himself apart from Klein by endorsing a basic principle originally formulated by Jorn: depreciation and appreciation go hand in hand and must be jointly encouraged. If so-called inflationary industrial art entails aesthetic depreciation, it is in order to produce a new and superior social value: this is the essence of "applicable" art. Applicable art, he says, must take care not to become merely an applied art, as in the case of industrial design, scorned by Jorn and MIBI as the sterile spawn of economic rationality. Gallizio followed Bataille in promoting a cult of destruction, of useless expenditure and idleness. Like Debord, he approved Bataille's rehabilitation of the notion of luxury, particularly the dictum in *La part maudite*: "It is not necessity but its contrary, 'luxury,' that presents living things and human beings with their most basic problems."[138] Once the enemy is understood to be parsimony, the frugal habit of a rationalist bourgeoisie, luxury can take on a positive value as gratuitous, extraeconomic expenditure. In Debord's summary, it is necessary to "create a revolutionary conception of luxury, enemy both of the old false luxury and the absence of luxury (the comfortable functionalist void of houses and of life)."[139] Nevertheless, when it came to saying exactly how painting might make this new way of life available to the poor, Gallizio stumbled over the patently self-contradictory notion of a "luxury standard."[140] For in the same way that industrial painting paradoxically rejected standardization, it had to be accessible to everyone without thereby losing the unique character that its luxury value confers on it. Whereas Jorn saw the industrial design of the Ulm School as the countermodel of his creation, the model (and countermodel) in relation to which Gallizio positioned himself was altogether unexpected—fashion.

As the historian Nancy J. Troy has noted, the alliance of avant-garde art and fashion that took shape during this period was looked down upon by most art historians. For authors such as T. J. Clark and Thomas Crow, the intrusion of fashion into the space of art—and, correspondingly, the deterioration of art into mere accessories of fashion and design—signaled the end of any political ambitions the avant-garde might have had, having now been hijacked and neutralized by the bourgeois cultural industry.[141] Nevertheless, Troy contends, it was precisely this permeability that enabled works of art not only to attract the attention of a sophisticated public, but also to win support among ordinary working people, whom avant-garde artists, Gallizio foremost among them, hoped most of all to reach. What seems to have interested Gallizio in the domain of fashion, to the point that he treated it as a laboratory for working out what a luxury standard might look like in practice, is directly connected exactly with the situation Troy described in an earlier book, *Couture Culture*. By its very nature, she observes, fashion is caught in a vise-like grip between, on the one hand, the requirement that masterpieces custom-tailored for a small number of wealthy clients be unique and, on the other, the inevitable degeneration of unique designs into a series of identical copies for a mass market—a commercial twist of fate that paradoxically is indispensable in creating the mystique that leading designers must seek to cultivate.[142] The world of avant-garde art, forced to confront the same tensions—between individuality and conformity, between authenticity and accessibility in an industrial society—as the world of haute couture, faces a similar predicament. Moreover, Gallizio himself may have had a taste for the ephemeral and the ludic, which, after all, were reasons for the Ulm School's firm rejection of fashion.[143]

Gallizio's interest in haute couture, as a specific economic model combining the luxury of uniqueness with the standardization of ready-to-wear clothing, must be understood in the particular context of the development of the Italian fashion industry after the war. In the 1950s, Northern Italy—and particularly the region formed by the triangle of Turin, Milan, and Florence—succeeded in creating an international market for a style of haute couture that both exploited and consolidated the comparative economic advantage of its textile industry, to the benefit of the leading houses of the day, Ferragamo, Gucci, and Pucci.[144] The American magazine *Life* welcomed the success of "Italy's fledgling fashion industry," noting that "Americans liked the beautiful fabrics and half-Paris prices"; and although Italian designs were, no doubt, simpler and less imaginative than their French competitors, they featured quality materials and inexpensive patterns that could be reproduced in great quantity.[145] The town of Alba in Piedmont, near Turin, where Gallizio lived and worked, was the seat of the textile firm Miroglio, one of the chief suppliers of the booming fashion industry, from haute couture to ready-to-wear. It was precisely this firm that furnished Gallizio with the rolls of canvas and fabric that he used for his industrial painting.[146]

In his manifesto, Gallizio expressed the hope of being able to use machines "to make the most [strikingly] unique fabrics, which joyous crowds will wear with [great] artistic sense."[147] His earliest experiments were displayed at the first exhibitions of industrial art in Turin and Milan. Thus, the headline in the newspaper *Il Popolo nuovo* following the opening at Galleria Notizie in May 1958 read: "Painting and Fashion."[148] Reporters

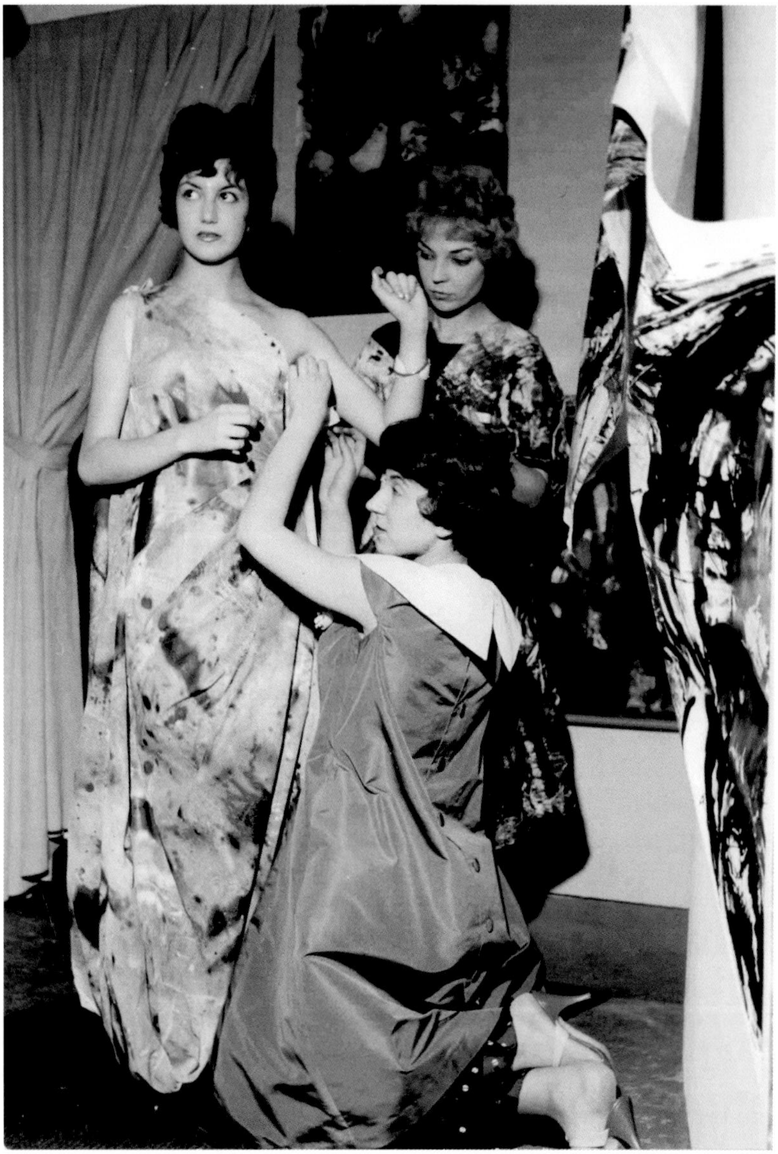

Fig. 16 Models being fitted for painted dresses at Galleria Notizie in Turin, May 1958. Folder "Fotografie III," Archivio Gallizio, Turin.

agreed that "unlike a usual show, the gallery took on the appearance of a fabric shop whose window displays arranged the materials with singular skill," among them "several pieces of fabric with abstract patterns in bright or subdued colors."[149] But more than anything else it was the young women wearing dresses made from painted fabrics who created the impression that the relationship between art and fashion was the subject of the exhibition (fig. 16). "Two pretty young women, one blonde, the other brunette, walked with the characteristic rhythm of models at a fashion show," noted one journalist.[150] Three months later, Gallizio was the subject of a full-page profile in the Italian edition of *Marie Claire*. Industrial painting was an "indisputably profitable" innovation, the writer assured his readers, "to be sold by the meter to women who wish to create extravagant and original clothes." The painter is seen here as a supremely self-assured couturier: "Gallizio strutted about, scissors and measuring stick in hand, saying to the ladies present: 'Ninety high, ten thousand [lire] per meter; seventy high, seven thousand [lire].'" The article claimed that the exhibition pieces offered for sale in Turin "serve only for making clothes and aprons," and even that for his next show, in Paris, the artist would use "special washable resins." In reality, this was quite untrue: the designs worn by the models were executed on fabric, a soft, supple nylon also used for the curtains that decorated the exhibition space in both Munich and Paris (fig. 17); the painting sold by the meter was done on canvas, much too stiff a material to be used for clothes. Gallizio, for his part, appears to have been prepared to accept this deliberate misrepresentation as the price of demonstrating the "applicable" character of his work. The applicability to haute couture seems in any case to have been taken for granted by the Italian press, which was delighted to discover a unique, authentic, and original way of creating custom-tailored fashions. The *Marie Claire* writer made a point of saying that clients demanded different widths of canvas depending on their figure, obligingly "cut out and wrapped up" by the artist himself in the desired quantities.[151]

Asserting a direct connection between artistic creation and fashion, under the aegis of a luxury standard, nonetheless put the SI in a delicate position. Several dangers had to be avoided. On the one hand, it was important

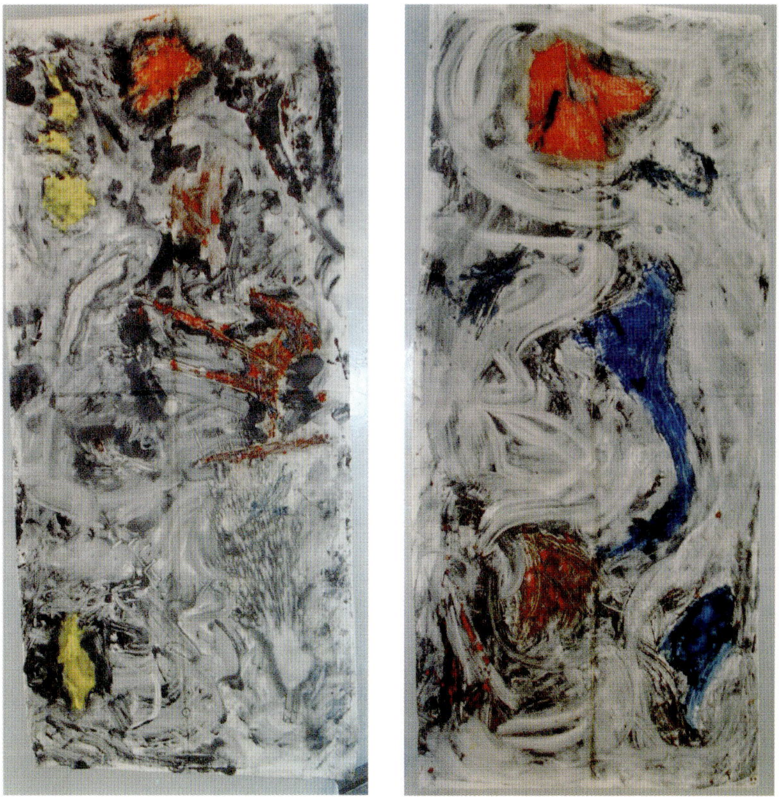

Fig. 17 Curtains used for Giuseppe Gallizio's exhibition *Une Caverne de l'anti-matière* [*A Cavern of Antimatter*] at the Galerie René Drouin, Paris, in May 1959. Mixed-media technique (with ink on watercolor) on nylon, 118⅛ × 53¾ in. (300 × 136.5 cm) each. Archivio Gallizio, Turin.

not to present painting as a luxury product created for a select clientele: thus Bernstein, in her essay introducing the exhibition, contrasted industrial painting to the "hand-sewn in every domain."[152] On the other hand, the functional character of such painting, and the need to make it more widely accessible, could not be allowed to open the way to deadening standardization through the degeneration of an artistic design into a mass-market commodity: Jorn gave the example of a picture by Mondrian, which, when repeated, yields the clichéd pattern of a Scottish tartan.[153] Finally, in addition to these two pitfalls, there was the vogue, already widespread in the late 1950s, for bringing artists together with designers and couturiers in order to create objects and clothes in more or less limited editions. The *Marie Claire* article, unsurprisingly, likened Gallizio's industrial painting to the bathing suits designed by Picasso, Bernard Buffet's creations for Yves Saint Laurent, and the scarves bearing the autograph of the illustrator Raymond Peynet.[154] Preemptively, the SI spoke out strongly against what it saw as the cooptation of art by capitalist commerce, holding up Salvador Dalí—famously versed in every manner of collaboration with the worlds of fashion, jewelry, publicity, and design—as Gallizio's official countermodel. Bernstein, in her Turin essay, contrasted the unlimited production of industrial painting with the "successively numbered editions of [this or that work] by Salvador Dalí"; Jorn, two years later, was still maintaining that Gallizio had toppled the "sacred cuckold" Dalí from his pedestal.[155]

The chance that Gallizio could have invoked a luxury standard without falling into at least one of these three traps seems unavoidably small in retrospect. His 1957 painting *La haute couture: Alla memoria di Christian Dior e del mondo borghese* [*Haute Couture: In Memory of Christian Dior and the Bourgeois World*], more commonly known as *Hommage à Dior* and exhibited in Turin, Milan, and Munich at the same time as his industrial painting, strikingly illustrates the difficulties Gallizio had created for himself (fig. 18). A skeletal figure, crowned by a whitish skull pitted with black cavities, is shown clothed in an elaborate dress and holding a fan. Its hair is a tangle of thick white, yellow, and orange threads encrusted in the paint, apparently fastened to the skull by a black button. The face, in gilded paper, stands out at the end of an inordinately elongated neck drawn with the aid of a blackish plastic resin. Through the clothing, one can make out a bust with broad shoulders, and a tight skirt—in painted aluminum foil—the lower part of which suddenly opens up at the ankles into a diaphanous train. The quality of the fabric is suggested by the use of yellow paint and red and brown resins, combined in layers to form abscesses and craters of remarkable relief and texture. Green and red sewing threads, stuck in the paint and the resins, further deepen the contrasts of materials and colors. A number of accessories indicate the sophistication of the costume: a fan made of painted aluminum foil and set off by black lace; a long fringed ribbon marks out the right-hand contour and meanders down to the bottom of the dress; several other ribbons, some painted and tied, are overlaid on the material. Buttons,

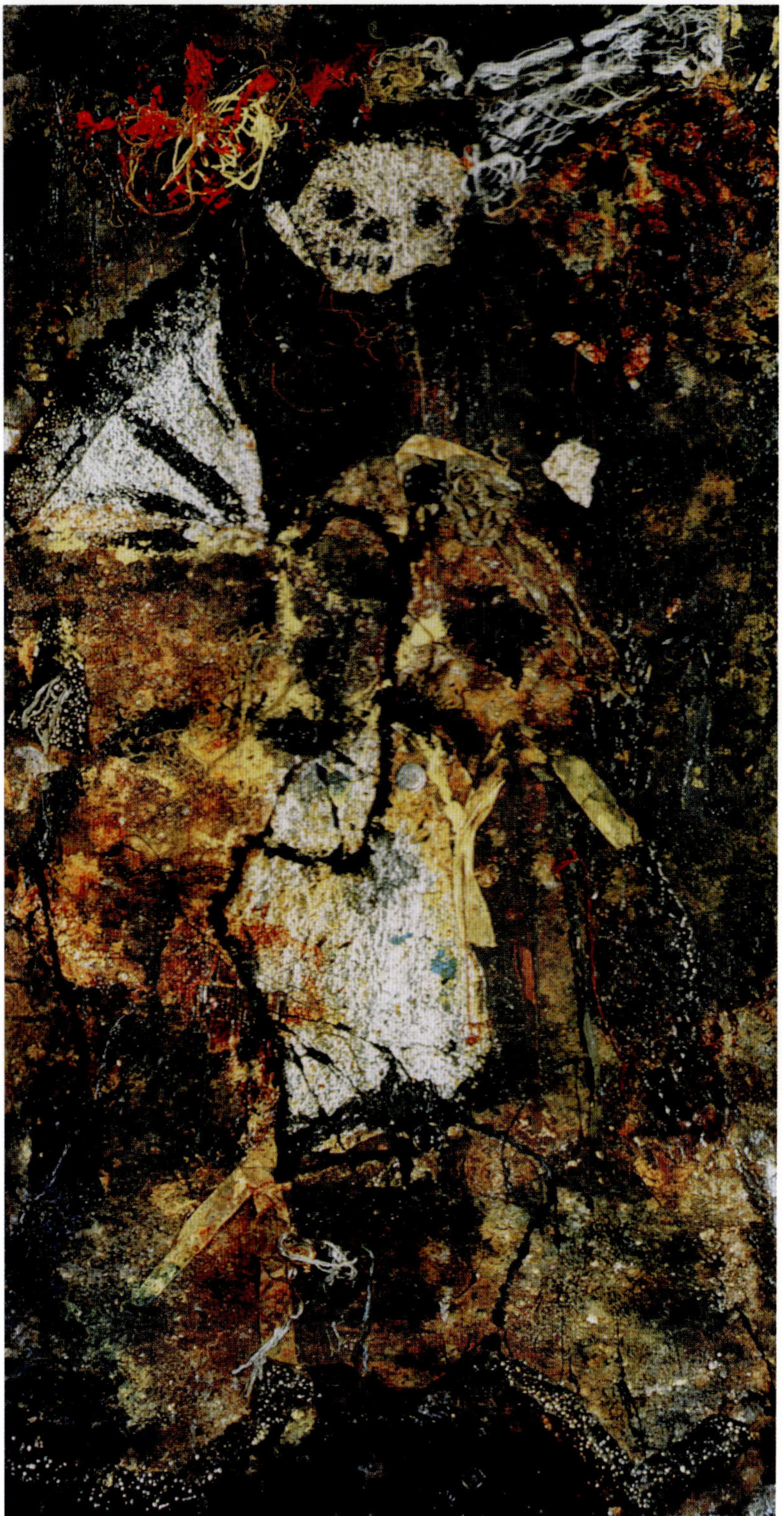

Fig. 18 Giuseppe Gallizio, *La haute couture: Alla memoria di Christian Dior e del mondo borghese* [*Haute Couture: In Memory of Christian Dior and the Bourgeois World*], 1957. Mixed-media collage technique (plastic resin, natural resin, aluminum foil, buttons, lace, thread) on linen, 82⅝ × 42½ in. (210 × 108 cm). Neue Nationalgalerie, Staatliche Museen, Berlin.

bits of fabric and lace, and fragments of a belt complete the ensemble. The surface throughout is broken up by patches of bright or light-reflective materials, such as paper covered with gold leaf or silver leaf, fabric coated with paste, and gilded metal buckles.

Created on the occasion of Christian Dior's sudden death while on vacation in Italy, in October 1957, Gallizio's picture is a morbid memorial. The wedding gown was no doubt meant to echo the design that traditionally concluded the presentation of a new collection by Dior, and the work itself to proclaim the imminent disappearance of the bourgeois world Dior represented. And yet the painstaking attention to detail apparent in this painting makes it a memorial that goes beyond mere derision. With Gallizio's enthusiastic approval, it was exhibited at the Maison Joséphine in Munich, a fashion house run by Josephine Platschek (née Gastinau, wife of Hans Platschek, a friend of Jorn and briefly a member of the SI), the first buyer of industrial painting in Munich.[156] Christian Dior, himself a former art dealer and a friend of Dalí, with whom in 1950 he had created a weirdly futuristic dress ("Costume de l'année 2045"), declared shortly before his death that his creations were a protest against an "impoverished, stingy era, obsessed with ration coupons and stitched fabrics," which he contrasted with the extravagant luxury of "long, pleated, immensely full dresses."[157] At a time "when one pretends to despise luxury," Dior, an enthusiast of lavish social entertainments, praised them as "veritable works of art." He conceded that some might find festive gatherings of this kind objectionable by reason of "their very splendor," but they are, he insisted, "desirable, necessary, and important if they restore the taste and the meaning of authentic popular celebrations."[158] In Gallizio's homage to Dior, the buttons, ribbons, and lace pay tribute to a designer who loved precious materials and embroidered work, trinkets and accessories, and what Dior called "fripperies" (*frivolités*).

Debord, for his part, seems to have been well aware of the risk that such a work might give rise to conflicting interpretations of the SI's new initiative, beginning with the first show in Turin. Even though he affected to pay no attention to the "silly newspaper commentaries—struck above all by the presence of two cover girls dressed in industrial painting,"[159] these models, invariably attractive young women, were plainly an integral part of the original plan: they were present at all four of the industrial painting exhibitions held in 1958 and 1959. In Munich, as one local journalist noted, it was actually the "charming wife of the director of the Galerie van de Loo" who played this role, which led another to say that her "action-painting charm . . . was the thing that worked most in Pino[t]-Gallizio's favor."[160] For the exhibition in Paris, at the Galerie René Drouin, Gallizio wrote at least twice to Debord beforehand, urging him to select not only a model but also a seamstress who could make a dress for her to wear using the yellow and brown nylon fabric he had prepared.[161] The artist himself appears to have encouraged a gendered reading of his art, both in making "pretty young girls" the main attraction of his openings and in promoting the idea, largely accepted by both the German and the Italian press, that he was a "painter for ladies."[162] His public, he told journalists, was "any housewife used to doing her own shopping" as well as "the high society woman who sends out her maid."[163] The *Marie Claire* article seized on this last remark as evidence of an affluent clientele that was as snobbish as it was ridiculous, quoting a stylish "long-limbed lady" as exclaiming, "Finally, a real use for abstract painting! I would never hang a picture like that on the wall, but for a *palloncino soirè* [evening party with balloons] that would look *très chic*, don't you think? A bit psychointellectual."[164] In Munich, the magazine *Madame* covered the exhibition at the Galerie van de Loo in a similar vein.[165]

This instrumentalization of women, both as consumers and as fashion models displaying the "applicable" character of industrial painting, may also be seen in the profound male chauvinism that animates Jorn's 1960 essay on Gallizio. There the Italian artist is described as a man's man, "driven by the permanent provocation of heterosexuality." The creative act is designated as a "mental rape," the exclusive prerogative of (heterosexual) males, since females are too close to nature to escape being prisoners of matter, and, therefore, can only be the receptacles of creation.[166] In a letter of March 1959, moreover, Gallizio informed Debord that "one of the next activities of the Experimental Laboratory . . . will be to dress so-called call girls *only* in love."[167]

The sexist use of women in redefining the creative economy reached its height at Gallizio's Paris exhibition, *Une caverne de l'antimatière* [*A Cavern of Antimatter*], in May 1959, where the walls, ceiling, floor, and window of the Galerie René Drouin were completely filled with industrial painting. The presence of a model "dressed in paint" at the center of the show was no longer intended, as at the Italian and German exhibitions, to demonstrate the applicable character of industrial art through the display of fashion. There was now a deeper ambition: according to the printed invitation, the young woman represented the "provisional reality" produced by "the attempt to create a [Situationist] atmosphere."[168] Indeed, the true function of artistic methods, for the SI, was to contrive a special sort of ambiance that, by producing a new, alternative reality, would favor the emergence of novel behaviors through "the further clarification of . . . simple basic desires, and the confused emergence of new desires"—which in turn would arouse new creative and revolutionary impulses.[169] Noting the great many buxom, scantily clad women appearing in Debord's films and pictured in his articles, the historian Emmanuel Guy argues that these images served, on the one hand, to demonstrate the transformation of the female body into a fetishized commodity in capitalist society, the tool of a "separation" dispossessing individuals of their authentic desires, and, on the other, to evoke the persistent possibility of a "passionate life" outside the society of the spectacle.[170] For Gallizio, however, the "pretty young girls" seem to have had little dialectical function. The failure of the *Caverne* exhibition, in the eyes of the critic Georges Limbour, had to do precisely with the cheerlessness, the triteness, the sheer vacuousness of the model's behavior, to which he devoted a considerable part of his May 1959 review:

> At the back of this cave, a young lady, in a skimpy tight-fitting dress, of an ugly color, that left her back bare, a girl with rather nice curves, certainly a very respectable girl, who gave the impression, as children of street performers frequently do, of having been soundly thrashed in order to go on playing her very provisional role of reality, did not know what countenance to adopt or what to do with her slender arms. The poor little thing . . . apparently did not know how to do much of anything, neither to walk on her hands nor to do the splits nor to do modeling, not even to do a bit of striptease, which in any case wasn't at all her sort of thing. Fortunately her friends from Saint-Germain came to see her, and she laughed, thoroughly embarrassed by her stupid role. She even deserted her post and went out for a quick chat into the rue Visconti, where a few people [from the opening] could be heard saying how charming they found this little dump.[171]

The author of this rather condescending account was offended not so much by the erotic role that women were bound to play in the clarification of men's primitive desires in the cave of industrial painting as by the fact that this role was not effectively played—that the atmosphere was not overwhelming enough to bring about the shedding of inhibitions that would lead to "mental rape" (to recall the term used by Jorn in describing Gallizio's creative process).[172] Even though she wore a clinging dress that left her back exposed, the shapely young woman did not perform what might have been expected of her if everything had gone as planned: a striptease.

In effect, then, the Situationists had unwittingly betrayed their own principles in making women the experimental objects of an economic critique of value. The Marxist theorist Lucien Goldmann, in a widely noticed essay on reification that appeared shortly before the Paris exhibition, deplored just this sort of ideological and gendered understanding of the economy. Goldmann held that with the expansion of capitalism a preeminent place came to be assigned to the presumptively masculine faculty of rational, quantitative, and abstract analysis, relegating "human comprehension of the qualitative and sensible elements of the natural world" to a position of very minor importance. These elements now formed the private domain "of poets, children, and women, that is, of persons *on the periphery of economic life*."[173] Gallizio, through his methods of exhibition and sale, encouraged exactly this marginalizing of women, henceforth condemned either to play the role of the alienated consumer—never the role of the autonomous producer, which remained a masculine prerogative—or to be the antieconomic embodiment of primitive human urges and impulses.

Industrial painting nonetheless stands out as a fascinating attempt to recast conventional economic models of value, on both a theoretical and a practical level. Unlike Klein's blue revolution, Gallizio's challenge to the status quo proceeded not by affirming the exteriority and superiority of "pure" art in comparison with other domains of the economy and culture, but by regarding the practice of painting as part of a continuum extending from the uniquely individual work of art to the standardized mass-consumption commodity in order to examine the luxury goods, limited-edition objects, derivative products, and useless gadgets that fall between these two extremes. More than this, the hope that art might play a social role gave rise to an original style of thinking inspired by models and countermodels in industrial design and haute couture. Gallizio's experiment failed because it was unable to free itself from the pull of the art market and world of galleries, on which it depended for its existence. It was strangely conservative as well. Incapable of seeing that cultural forms, once decompartmentalized and stripped of their old hierarchical character, might point the way to a genuinely progressive conception of the economy and social life, it was bound to fall back on traditional sexist stereotypes and role playing.

CHAPTER 2

Currency as Convention

Long before Andy Warhol created his *Dollar Bill* series and Larry Rivers his *French Money* paintings, Walter Benjamin had perceived the importance of such works, albeit in a different form. "A descriptive analysis of banknotes is needed," Benjamin wrote in 1928. "The unlimited satirical force of such a book would be equaled only by its objectivity. For nowhere more naively than in these documents does capitalism display itself in solemn earnest. The innocent cupids frolicking about numbers, the goddesses holding tablets of the law, the stalwart heroes sheathing their swords before monetary units, are a world of their own: ornamenting the facade of hell."[1]

Apart from Warhol's own *Campbell's Soup Cans* and Roy Lichtenstein's DC Comics–inspired paintings, few works managed to acquire the iconic status of Warhol's money portraits (fig. 19). The earliest critics and historians of the movement, led by Lawrence Alloway and Lucy Lippard, considered his subject to be the very embodiment of the pop sensibility.[2] The iconography of the dollar bill, already explored by nineteenth-century American trompe-l'oeil painters such as William Michael Harnett, John Frederick Peto, and John Haberle, was seen to have something authentically American about it, something banal, even vulgar, that sprang from popular imagery associated specifically with the world of business and the consumer society to which it gave rise. And yet, even though Warhol's *Dollar Bill* paintings were a landmark in the history of pop art, enjoying exceptional notoriety, they were only the best-known representatives of a vogue for paper-money iconography that lasted in America for almost an entire decade. In the first months of 1962, nearly simultaneously and often independently of one another, Rivers, then working in France, along with artists as different as Robert Watts and Yayoi Kusama, in New York, and Robert Dowd and Phillip Hefferton, in Los Angeles, helped to make the dollar bill arguably the outstanding motif of American art in the 1960s. Kusama's *Untitled* collage of c. 1962–63 perhaps best embodies the spirit of such appropriations (fig. 20). The hand-drawn bill, copies of which are arranged on a grid, playfully displays a series of impertinent puns: "One Dollar" becoming "One Rollar" (also "Won Hollar") and "The United States of America" turning into "The Untied Skates of Arnica."

This craze for the representation of money in painting is apt to seem paradoxical in light of a whole tradition of socioeconomic thought. From the point of view of classical and neoclassical economics, the history of monetary currency is bound up with the gradual recognition of money as something fundamentally abstract, and therefore inaccessible to sensory perception. In the early nineteenth century, economists followed Jean-Baptiste Say in describing money as a transparent "veil" superimposed on the real sphere of exchange, and looked forward to the day when the function of a currency would be reduced to a single sign.[3] As precious metals gave way to paper money, the idea of an abstract currency, divested of all physical substance, was advanced by authors such as Georg Simmel. If, as Marx held, money is a "universal equivalent," that is, the only commodity capable of serving as the equivalent of any other, then for Simmel it followed that money itself must be devoid of any specific form. "As a purely arithmetical addition of value units," he wrote in *Philosophie des Geldes* [*The Philosophy of Money*, 1900], "money can be characterized as absolutely formless"—indeed, as "the most terrible destroyer of form" there

Fig. 19 Andy Warhol, *200 One Dollar Bills*, 1962. Silkscreen ink and pencil on linen, 80¼ × 92¼ in. (203.8 × 234.3 cm). Private collection.

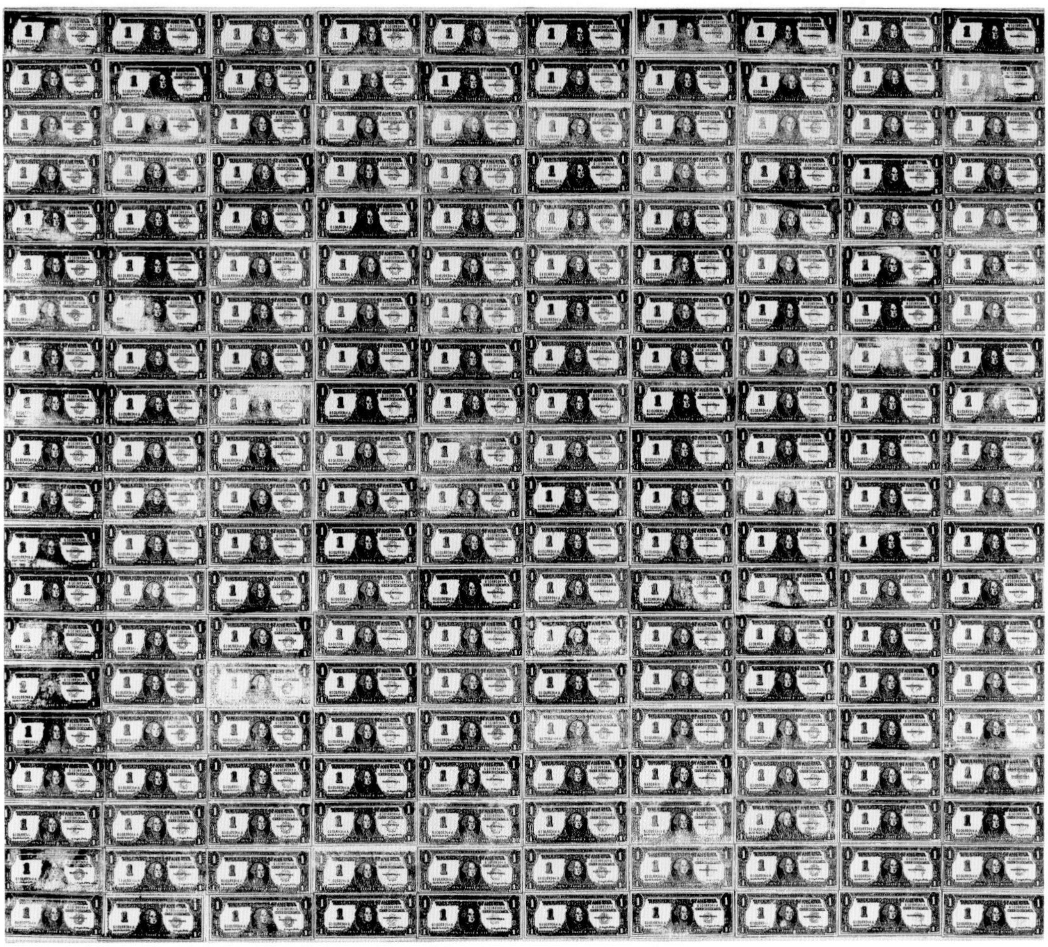

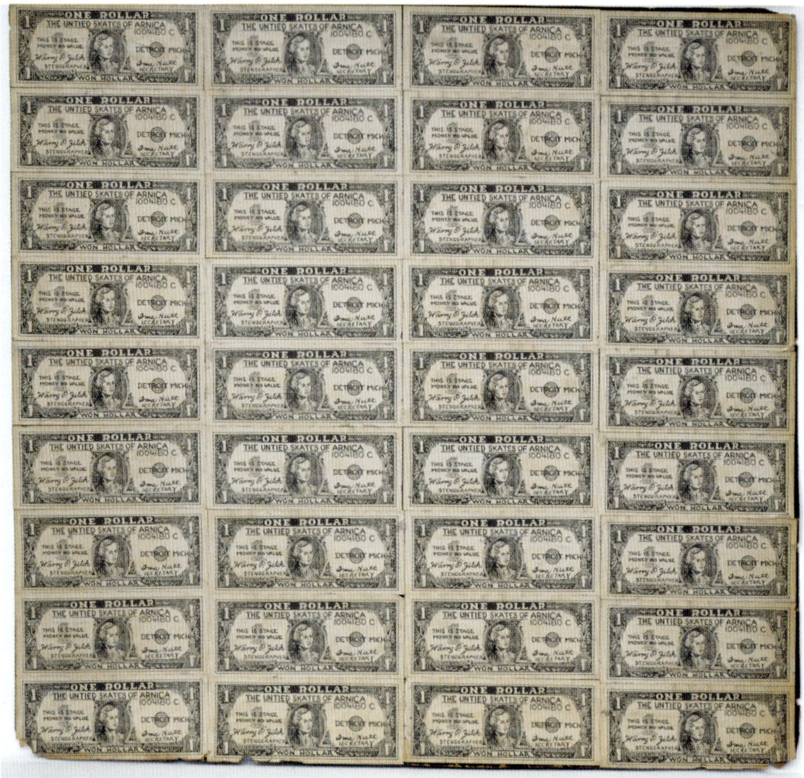

Fig. 20 Yayoi Kusama, *Untitled*, c. 1962–63. Collage on paper, 25 × 23⅞ in. (63.5 × 60.5 cm).

is.[4] Why should a transparent, amorphous, and neutral veil have become the subject of so many works of art in the 1960s? Why did so many artists attempt to give substance to what was usually supposed to be an abstraction, to impose form on a destroyer of form, to restore to the domain of pictorial art—the visual domain par excellence—what was imagined to belong to the realm of the invisible, the numerary, and the technical? What one encounters in these works is not the immateriality, the impersonal abstraction of money; to the contrary, the vivid green of Warhol's silkscreens and the expressive brushstrokes of Rivers's paintings succeed in anchoring banknotes in the physical materiality of an artifact having a complex and richly meaningful iconography.

Already by the beginning of the 1960s, in the midst of a booming art market, it was common to compare works of art and legal tender. "In our time, paintings have become banknotes," wrote one French critic in the fall of 1960. "But these 'notes' are of a new denomination and have no value unless a 'bank' stabilizes them. The bank in this case is the art dealer."[5] The comparison rested not only on a common material characteristic—a dollar bill and a painting both present images displayed on a flat rectangular surface—but also on a shared relationship to a certain value. Their exchange value is distinct from their intrinsic value—not only with regard to the materials they are made of, but also the use value that they directly underwrite. This dissociation presupposes a relationship of trust: confidence in the value of paper money despite the risks of counterfeiting and inflation, on the one hand, and confidence in the value of the work of art despite the threats of forgeries and changing tastes, on the other.

The intricate design of banknotes, combining text, graphic elements, and images, is intended to ensure their authenticity and to instill the confidence on which a dematerialized monetary system depends. It gives visual expression to a set of values that are endorsed by the members of a given exchange community as the result of a mass-marketing effort undertaken by the monetary authorities. Paper money is an instrument of propaganda, in effect, part of a patriotic campaign with strong religious and moral overtones.[6] By more or less faithfully reproducing the image of the banknote, sometimes in a manner bordering on parody, artists attracted attention not only to currency as a ubiquitous and yet invisible artifact, but also to the tripartite convention—monetary, institutional, and sociocultural—on which it rests.

Close study of two emblematic examples, Warhol's *Dollar Bill* series and Rivers's *French Money* paintings, will make it possible to show how the banknote came to be seen as just this, a convention. Inflation, devaluations, and the first important challenge to the Bretton Woods system of currency convertibility, which together cast doubt on monetary value; the extraordinary rise in prices paid for art, which had a profound effect on the work of artists themselves; the Cold War and wars of decolonization, which unsettled political opinion and inflamed patriotic sentiment on both sides of the Atlantic—all these things form the background against which Warhol and Rivers made their works in the early 1960s.

With these paintings, the banknote lost its authority as a pure abstraction and became an object of belief, a matter of personal conviction about which there was bound to be disagreement. What is more, as a mirror image of the uncertainty that now attached to paper money, the value and authority of art itself came to be questioned. If paintings had, in fact, become banknotes, and banknotes had become paintings, which of the two things was more trustworthy? We shall see, too, that an element of humor and mockery, even self-mockery, was never absent from the attack artists mounted on monetary conventions—perhaps because, as Benjamin had seen more than thirty years earlier, the awful solemnity of capitalism, its almost papal seriousness, would one day have to be opposed with all the weapons that satire can marshal.

ANDY WARHOL AND THE SOCIAL MEANING OF MONEY

The *Dollar Bill* paintings that Warhol created in 1962 quickly came to occupy the special place in the history of art reserved for veritable icons. This status was inseparable, of course, from pop art's commercial destiny: in retrospect, the dollar bill motif can be seen as a prophetic declaration. The paintings themselves took on new meaning in the 1970s, when Warhol proclaimed himself a "business artist,"[7] and even more so in the decade that followed, when a booming market propelled prices for pop works to unprecedented

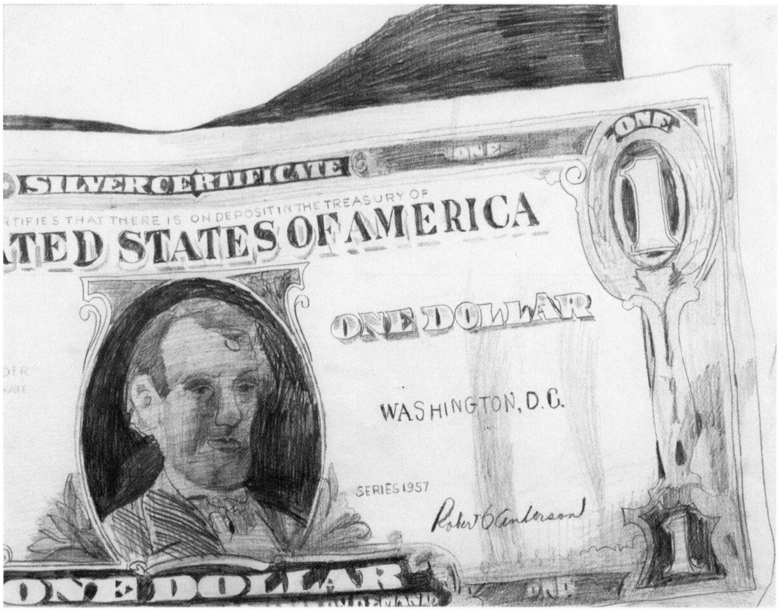

Fig. 21 Andy Warhol, *One Dollar Bill*, 1962. Pencil and watercolor on paper, $16\frac{1}{8} \times 23\frac{5}{8}$ in. (41.1×60 cm).

heights. Surely, the most striking example is Warhol's painting *200 One Dollar Bills* (see fig. 19), bought at the Green Gallery in New York by Ethel and Robert Scull in 1962. Legend has it (though the legend is almost certainly mistaken) that the purchase was made at face value, which is to say $200. The artist thought that the value of his works would "just stay at the same level" after his death, and advised prospective buyers to think twice: "Say you were going to buy a $200,000 painting. I think you should take that money, tie it up, and hang it on the wall."[8] History ended up proving Warhol wrong. The painting was resold at Sotheby's in 1985 for $385,000; in 2009, on being offered for sale by the same auction house, it fetched $43,000,000.[9] In this case painted money turned out to be a better investment than printed money.

Money recurs as a theme throughout Warhol's career, beginning with his personal drawings and commercial illustrations in the 1950s. In 1961–62 he made a systematic exploration of this theme using a variety of supports and mediums: pencil drawings with watercolor (fig. 21), ink on paper, and, finally, silkscreen prints (see fig. 19). The same motif appears in works of several kinds during the 1960s and 1970s, culminating in the more abstract treatment of the famous *Dollar Signs* (fig. 22), a group of drawings, paintings, and silkscreen prints on canvas and paper that was first exhibited in 1982 at the Leo Castelli Gallery in New York. The show was very poorly received. Writing in *Artforum*, Thomas Lawson spoke for many disillusioned observers: "That nothingness [which has always characterized Warhol's work] has now developed into something banal, unfortunately proving right all those critics who always hated pop art."[10]

The frequent recurrence of money as a motif in Warhol's work, along with intense media exposure and the prestige this conferred, stands in sharp contrast to its relative absence from the abundant critical and historical

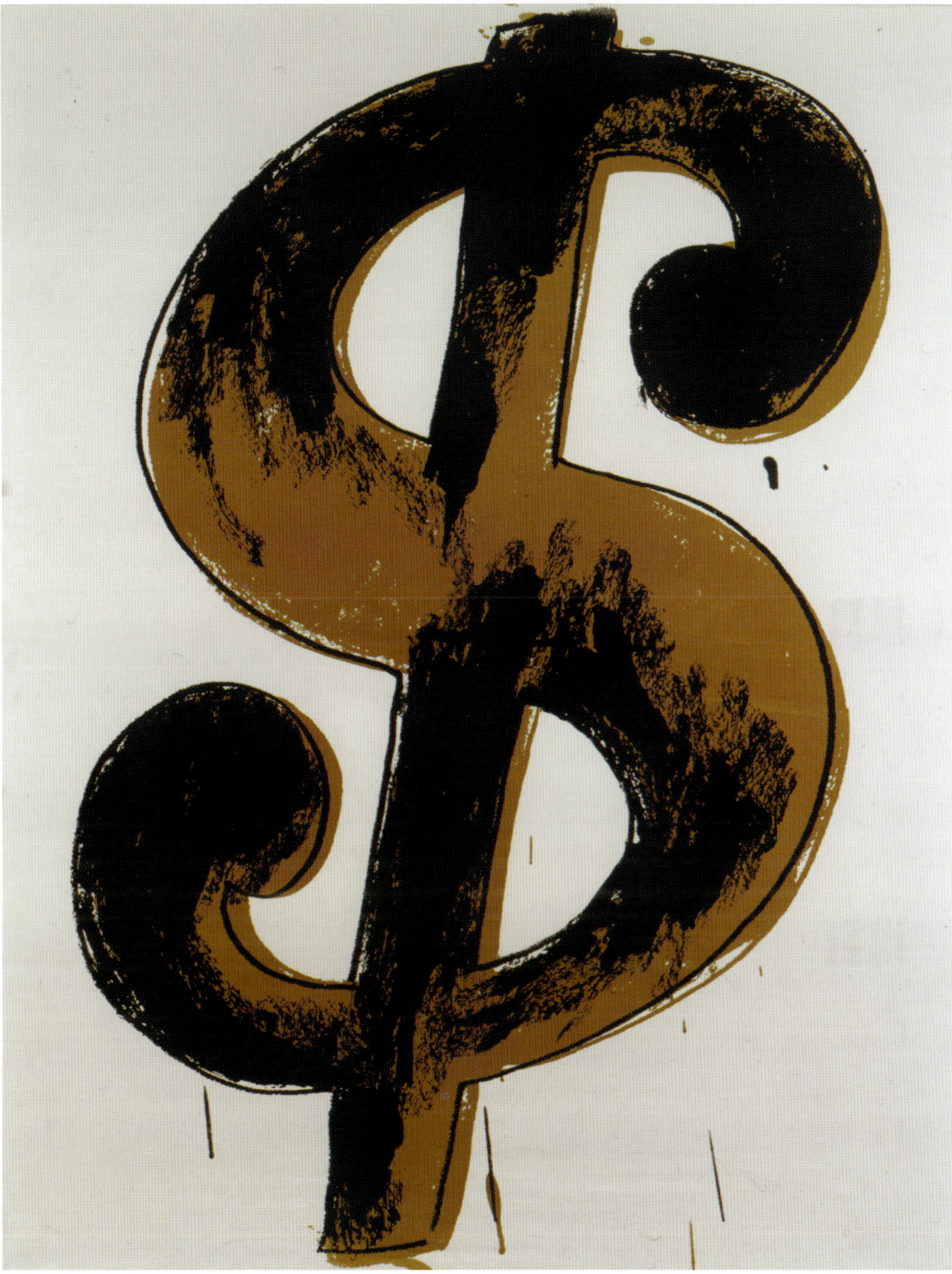

Fig. 22 Andy Warhol, *Dollar Sign*, 1981. Synthetic polymer paint and silkscreen ink on canvas, 90 × 70 in. (228.6 × 177.8 cm).

literature on the artist. With the exception of two recent exhibitions (of which only one, *Andy Warhol Enterprises* [2010], included a catalogue), there has been virtually no careful examination of Warhol's monetary paintings—particularly the 1962 *Dollar Bill* series—nor any attempt to reconstruct the historical and economic context in which they were conceived.[11] Allison Unruh, cocurator of the *Andy Warhol Enterprises* exhibit at the Indianapolis Museum of Art, suggests that this gap is due to the fact that "[t]his theme is simply all too obvious, the dollar bill too emphatically overstating Warhol's interest in postwar capitalist society."[12] Any discussion of these works cannot help but take into account the artist's well-known and self-proclaimed love of money, his fascination with consumerism, and his own success in the market. As early as March 1962, the art critic David Bourdon, in notes taken after visiting Warhol's studio, laconically reported that the artist is "now painting a series of money because 'he likes it so much.' "[13] The sheer repetition of the images themselves and their almost uninterrupted display also got in the way: between 1962 and 1975 there were no fewer than twenty-two exhibits of the *Dollar Bill* paintings and forty-five reproductions in art magazines, books, and catalogues.[14] Excessive publicity was further reinforced by the omnipresence of money itself, an object so familiar and so prosaic that it ends up being practically invisible.

In order to strip these works of their obviousness, following the example of recent research (well summarized by the 2011 *Warhol: Headlines* exhibit at the National Gallery of Art in Washington, D.C.) that has shown the dominant interpretations of Warhol's oeuvre to be inadequate, it will be helpful first to pay particularly close attention to Warhol's source images—the banknotes themselves.[15] Although these images do not belong to the history of art or even to the field of visual studies generally, their iconography, history, and contemporary relevance cannot be ignored. As for the political nature of Warhol's works, the question should no longer be posed in the terms that have focused debate for more than twenty years now, ever since the influential essays by Thomas Crow and Benjamin Buchloh, either as a biographical conjecture about the artist's point of view or as a critical disagreement over the subversive or complicit character of these works.[16] Instead, developing an argument recently advanced by John J. Curley, it will be more illuminating if we consider the ideological implications of the image of the dollar bill in a Cold War context, without ascribing to it any predetermined "intention."[17]

Let us begin by examining two overlapping activities: *making an image of money* and *making use of that image*. There is something paradoxical about their coincidence in this case. On the one hand, starting with his dollar silkscreens in the spring of 1962, Warhol sought to present an anonymous and standardized image of money. And yet, in doing this, rather than deprive banknotes of their historical and political character he managed to reveal not only the subtleties of monetary iconography, but also the power that capitalist propaganda can have by exploiting institutional language—and this at a moment when money was very much a subject on people's minds. On the other hand, and at the same time, Warhol suggested a very particular use for his images, which function as what the economic sociologist Viviana Zelizer has called "special monies," a kind of currency invested with extraeconomic values.[18] In doing this, he restored to money its anthropological quality as a *thing*, impure and profoundly human—a quality that is at the heart of exchange and the individual and collective definition of values.

From Thing to Image

In the narrative of pop art's rise to prominence, as Warhol and his biographers have recounted it, the *Dollar Bill* paintings occupy a privileged place. They came into existence at a pivotal moment in the artist's career, when he chose both a new theme, the insipidness of capitalist consumer society, and a new technique, silkscreen printing. Both the theme and the technique rapidly became identified with pop art itself. What is more, both are described in the received legend as a kind of revelation.

There are several anecdotal explanations for the adoption of money as a subject. One version has it that Warhol, dismayed by his discovery of Lichtenstein's work, which forced him to give up painting comic strips, and dispirited by the success of Claes Oldenberg's constructed environment, *The Store*, a storefront display on the Lower East Side that opened in early December 1961, turned to his friends in search of a new artistic direction. In return for a check in the amount of fifty dollars, gallery owner Muriel Latow is supposed to have suggested that he paint "what he loves most—money." According to another version, gallery owner Eleanor Ward gave him the idea, insisting that Warhol paint her a good-luck two-dollar bill and, in exchange, she would sponsor his first solo show as a pop artist, at the Stable Gallery in November 1962.[19] Although probably neither one is correct (from drawings Warhol did in the 1950s, we know that he had been interested in the subject for quite a while), the two stories display several points of resemblance. In each case the event occurs as a coup de théâtre, a dramatic turn of events at a moment of professional discouragement, when Warhol doubted his ability either to find a new style or finally to have a one-man show in New York. In each case the idea comes not from Warhol himself but from another person, confirming the artist's assumed indifference to money as a subject. And in each case the idea of money is the object of an exchange that is both symbolic and monetary: either Warhol buys the idea from Latow for real money, or else Ward gives Warhol the idea in exchange for the promise of an exhibit, which in turn will provide Warhol with a new and welcome source of income.

The *Dollar Bill* paintings are notable as well for being the first of Warhol's canvases to make use of silk-screening, a technique employed earlier by Rauschenberg, among others, that was to become emblematic of pop art. In a 1977 interview, Warhol explained that his first drawings of banknotes on paper, some of them done with watercolors, had left him unsatisfied: the subject called for a degree of detachment and neutrality that his own overly personal pencil strokes were unable to provide.[20] Tracing photographic projections turned out to be no more successful. In early 1962, Warhol began experimenting with the rubber-stamp method he used to create the famous *S&H Green Stamps* and other works with repeated images. His personal archives contain a number of engraved stamps depicting certain elements of the dollar bill, which could be arranged in various combinations within a matrix showing the frame of the banknote with blank vignettes.[21] By late winter, apparently bored by this tedious and inexact process, Warhol asked Floriano Vecchi, cofounder a decade earlier of Tiber Press (which had already been printing his Christmas cards for a number of years), to create a silkscreen with the dollar bill motif. Vecchi agreed, on the condition that Warhol draw it himself on acetate sheets; worried about running afoul of counterfeiting laws, the printer refused to work from a photograph.[22] Now that he had what he needed to print silkscreens on canvas, Warhol was elated. "[H]e got oh, so excited," Vecchi recalled. "He had great, great expectations."[23] In less than two months, beginning sometime in March up until the end of April 1962, according to the catalogue raisonné, the artist created a group of nearly forty-five silkscreens depicting dollar bills.

When one considers how short a time separated these silkscreens from the first dollar bill drawings Warhol did at the beginning of 1962—three months at most—it is striking to observe how stylistically different they are. The bills drawn with pencil (fig. 21 shows one example), in which symbols and words give way to the graphic effects of shade and volume, appear not as signs but as objects. Whether they are arranged in piles, wrinkled, folded, or rolled and torn, they are in any case far from the ideal bills imagined by classical economics, immaterial contracts ("certificates") recognized as legal tender in place of metallic money. Now they are seen for what they are—pieces of paper handled by human beings and exhibiting all the signs of such use. In moving to silkscreens (see fig. 19), Warhol substituted for bills-as-things a series of identical bills, types that no longer exist in three-dimensional space as objects, but in two dimensions as images. Their arrangement in a grid reinforces the impression of interchangeable units forming a mass, a quantity, the size of which is easily calculated: 20 bills high x 10 bills wide = 200 dollar bills—hence the title of the painting. A limited chromatic palette helps to suggest just the absence of form that Simmel spoke of, amounting to a sort of characterlessness.[24] The bills in the series are printed only in black ink, sometimes with the addition of a distinctive blue seal bearing the legend "Silver Certificate," created with a second silkscreen, as in *Printed Dollar #7* (fig. 23). Occasionally, the bills appear against a monochrome green acrylic background, as in the famous *192 One Dollar Bills*, or printed with green ink, as in *One Dollar Bill (Back)* (fig. 24). But even in these cases the color does not seem so much to give the bills some sort of character as to associate them with a predetermined identity, the "green bills" Warhol mentions in his 1975 book *The Philosophy of Andy Warhol*. They are archetypes of American money.[25]

Religion, Anti-Communism, and Inflation

In deciding to paint dollar bills, Warhol could not have picked a more symbolically American subject. Far from seeking an inoffensive, politically neutral motif, the artist saw his work as "a statement of the symbols of the harsh, impersonal products and brash materialistic objects on which America is built today."[26] Not only were dollar bills immediately identifiable throughout the world as American money (in many countries they had been used for everyday transactions after the war until the national currency was reinstated); in this case the banknote itself—the very symbol of the capitalist system—stood for the United States, its society of abundance, and its supposed fascination with money. The pictorial representation of such a currency could not help but be seen as a political and social statement. All the more, then, is the actual banknote that Warhol chose to reproduce in his *Dollar Bill* paintings worthy of closer examination.

In 1955, a Florida congressman named Charles Bennett had sponsored a bill that would require all American money to bear the inscription "In God We Trust."[27] Taken from the national anthem—"The Star Spangled Banner," written in 1814—this motto had appeared periodically on American coins since 1864, when Congress acted to approve a recommendation made during the Civil War by the secretary of the treasury, Salmon P. Chase. In the 1950s, at the height of the Cold War, the motto once more became a subject of contention. At a time when religious affiliation was at its highest level in the twentieth century—nearly 69 percent of Americans belonged to a church in 1960, as compared to 43 percent in the 1920s and 60 percent in the 1970s—the affirmation of personal faith now took on a patriotic dimension. With the fall of Senator Joseph McCarthy, a turning point in the divisive debate over anti-Communism had been reached and, with it, a new concern with restoring national unity.[28] On July 30, 1956, "In God We Trust" was proclaimed the official motto of the United States, and its inscription on American coins and paper currency became obligatory. One-dollar bills bearing the motto first appeared a little more than a year later, on October 1, 1957.

As Allison Unruh has noted, the label "Series 1957" appears very clearly on most of the drawings Warhol completed in the early part of 1962, as if to call attention to the timing of this important change in the bill's design.[29] Further evidence of symbolic renewal is found in the fact that the 1957 series was to be the first, as the press announced at the time, "to carry the signature of the new secretary of the treasury, Robert B. Anderson,"[30] an Eisenhower appointee who served from July 1957 until being replaced by President Kennedy in January 1961—a signature that Warhol includes as well (see fig. 21). Nevertheless the motto itself is not visible in these early

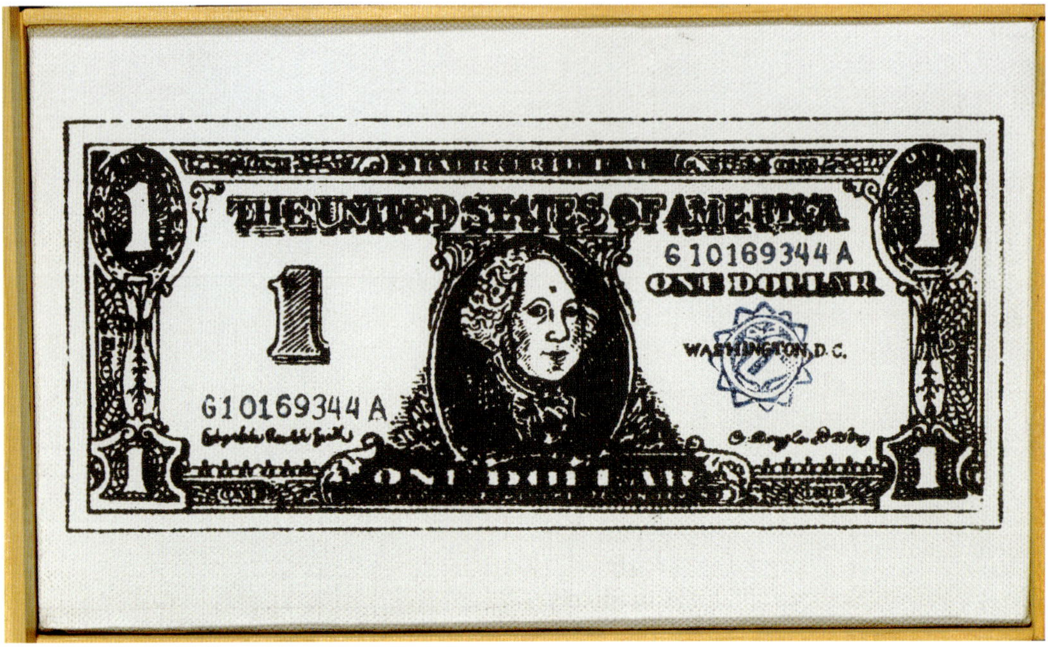

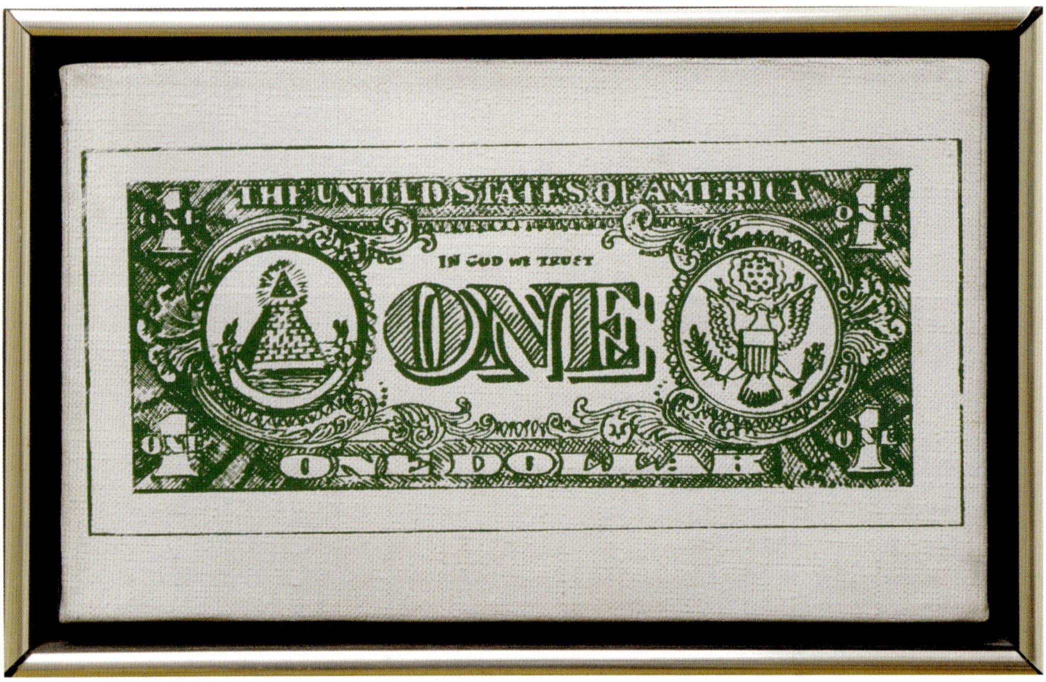

Fig. 23 Andy Warhol, *Printed Dollar #7*, 1962. Silkscreen ink on linen, 5⅝ × 10 in. (14.3 × 25.4 cm).

Fig. 24 Andy Warhol, *One Dollar Bill (Back)*, 1962. Silkscreen ink on linen, 6 × 10½ in. (15.2 × 26.7 cm).

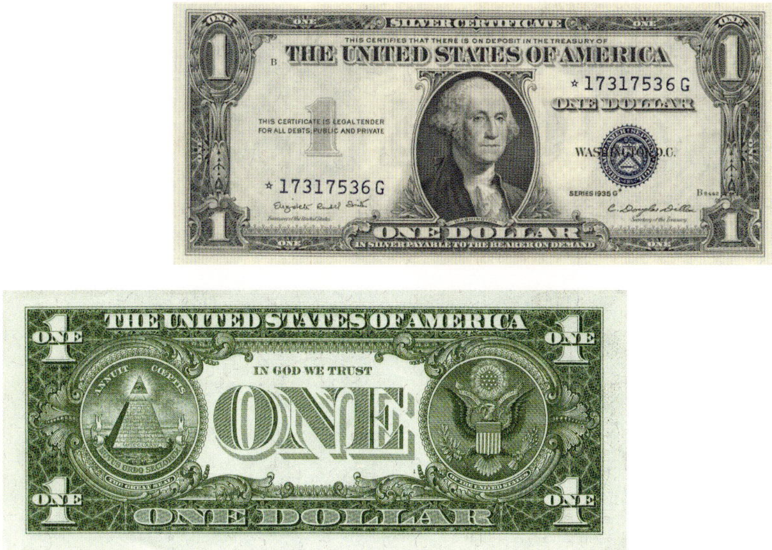

Fig. 25 Obverse and reverse of one-dollar bill, 1935-G series, signed by Elizabeth Rudel Smith and C. Douglas Dillon.

drawings, which concentrate mainly on the front of the bill. The *Dollar Bill* paintings, on the other hand, which alternate front and back views, place heavy emphasis on the words "In God We Trust," which appear above the three capital letters spelling "ONE," framed on both sides by the great seal of the United States (see fig. 24).

In dramatically increasing the size of his silk-screened banknotes by comparison with the original—in all of the paintings the bill measures about four inches (ten centimeters) high by about nine and a half inches (twenty-four centimeters) wide, about 50 percent larger than a real bill—Warhol managed to respect the law against counterfeiting while at the same time directing the viewer's attention to certain design elements that generally go unnoticed. He did not try to make an exact copy of the original, as a comparison with an actual bill readily demonstrates (fig. 25). Certain details have been deliberately omitted, such as the series date and the inscription THIS CERTIFICATE IS LEGAL TENDER FOR ALL DEBTS, PUBLIC AND PRIVATE superimposed on the number "1" on the front. Other elements are simplified or stylized, such as the blue seal on the face of the bill and the decorative motifs on the back. These alterations made it possible to highlight the elements of the design that Warhol chose to retain: the seal, the signatures, the serial number, and, on the obverse, the famous motto, "In God We Trust." The deliberately caricatural aspect of George Washington's portrait in this drawing—plump cheeks, an elaborate coiffure, pursed lips forming more of a pout than a smile—disposes of any suggestion that Warhol sought to make an identical reproduction. To the contrary, it serves to emphasize the artificiality and conventionality of the design, equally distributed among the bill's chief emblems: seal, signature, portrait, and motto.

These various elements also make it possible to identify precisely which type of bill is being represented. The one-dollar bill used as a model for the *Dollar Bill* silkscreens is not the same as the one in the drawings: it belongs to the 1935-G series, issued in 1961, as the signatures of Elizabeth Rudel Smith as treasurer of the United States and C. Douglas Dillon as secretary of the treasury attest. This same bill was a subject of controversy during the fall of that year through the early months of 1962. In spite of the widely reported announcement that one-dollar bills displaying the mandatory legend "In God We Trust" were immediately forthcoming, many bills continued to be printed without the motto after 1957, even ones belonging to the latest installment of the 1935 series and bearing the signatures of the newly appointed treasurer and secretary of the treasury. This apparent breach of promise aroused the anger of both religious and anti-Communist groups, eventually causing a scandal. A report circulated privately in 1964 by the Bureau of Engraving and Printing, which bore responsibility for the design and manufacture of banknotes, summed up the situation: "Prompted by newspaper, radio, and television accounts that were misunderstood, or by statements that the missing inscription from some new notes was tied in with atheistic intent, these people wrote to the White House, the Treasury Department, and the Bureau about the matter. More than a thousand complaints have been received, many of them multiple signed petitions and resolutions of protest by religious, civic, and veterans' organizations."[31]

There was a great stir in the press. Suspicion grew that high officials in the Treasury and the Bureau of Engraving and Printing were involved in sabotage and complicit in Communist subversion. A resolution was even passed in the Arizona House of Representatives in April 1963 demanding that "$1 silver certificates that do not carry the motto 'In God We Trust' be withdrawn from circulation" on the ground that they would "give aid and comfort to atheist Communist countries."[32] Earlier, in October 1961, the *Los Angeles Times* had quoted the director of the Bureau, Harry Holtzclaw, noting that "his moral and political integrity has been assaulted by irate citizens who find a new bill, complete with signature by California's Elizabeth Rudel Smith, but lacking 'In God We Trust' on the reverse. Mrs. Smith, who ran into some criticism for proposing different colored bills soon after her appointment as U.S. Treasurer, has also caught some of the fire on motto-less currency."[33] At this point, in the autumn of 1961, the controversy reached its height. The Bureau promised that all dollar bills produced from December onward would bear the inscription, which prompted the same newspaper to note that this was six years after Congress had required it to be included on all coins and currency.[34] In 1962, the motto was also inscribed on the dais of the Speaker of the House of Representatives, as if to reassert the importance of what was now plainly understood to be a national article of faith.[35] These events had the effect, as the *New York Times* observed, of "attracting greater attention to paper money in general."[36]

In the midst of this controversy, Warhol made up his mind to depict the dollar bill of the 1935-G series, featuring, in addition to "In God We Trust," the now well-known signatures of Smith and Dillon. In the spring of 1962, one-dollar bills bearing the motto were still relatively rare: only 13 percent of the 226 million bills of the 1935-G series displayed it.[37] It was, therefore, quite deliberately that the artist chose to illustrate the new inscription. In this way he underlined not only the connection between religious values and capitalist instruments, but also the subliminal impact that such a message is apt to have when it appears on an object as frequently handled as a one-dollar bill. More than this, in uncovering visual evidence of a sort of "banal nationalism"[38] he implicitly criticized a larger official and bureaucratic aesthetic that formed one of the chief pillars of capitalist propaganda at a moment when the Cuban missile crisis was soon to open a new chapter in the Cold War.

The reason why the Bureau of Engraving and Printing was not able to produce one-dollar bills bearing the "In God We Trust" motto before the end of 1961 was a purely technical one. In 1957, the Bureau took advantage of the change in the bill's design to introduce new printing presses, but not enough of them, as it turned out, to meet the demands of dollar-bill production. The existing presses therefore continued to be used to produce the old design, without the motto.

The new machines, rotary presses using a dry intaglio printing process, unlike the old flatbed presses that impressed images from steel plates onto moistened paper (fig. 26), were widely discussed at the time. They made it possible to achieve significant increases in production speed by eliminating the plate-drying time after printing and by enlarging the number of bills that could be printed from each plate—thirty-two bills to a sheet, compared to eighteen previously.[39] The 1957 series was the first to be printed with the new technique, which made it possible to print 2,400 sheets an hour, as opposed to 900 before. Indeed, contemporary press accounts emphasized that the incorporation of the nation's motto on the back of the bill was not the most important innovation. "[T]he bigger change, [though] not so apparent," the *New York Times* pointed out in October 1957, "is the new printing process."[40]

These technical details were not unconnected with Warhol's interest in the subject of money. There can be no doubt that the artist deliberately arranged the bills in some of the *Dollar Bill* paintings so as to recall the sheets that ran through the presses of the Bureau of Engraving and Printing and then were cut into individual units. Nor is it at all likely that he was unaware that dollar bills were printed, not on paper, but on cloth made of 75 percent cotton and 25 percent linen.[41] The way he described his work is revealing. Asked where he got the idea to experiment with silkscreen printing on canvas, he replied, as a counterfeiter might have done: "I started when I was printing money."[42]

The speed of the new printing process must also have excited Warhol, who in magazine profiles and interviews at the time made no secret of his fascination with the increases in productivity it made possible, seeing mass industry as a model for artistic work. "When Picasso died," he later wrote in *The Philosophy of Andy Warhol*, "I read in a magazine that he had made four

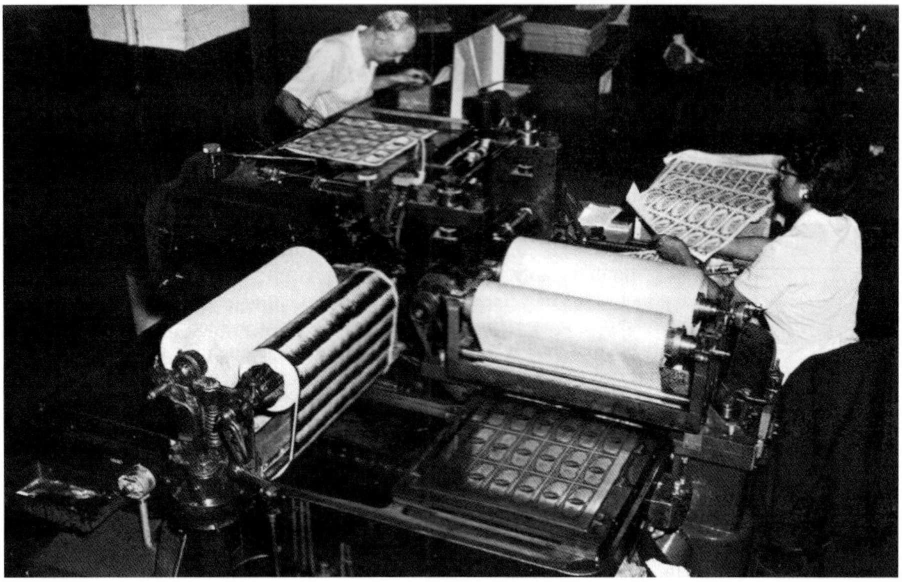

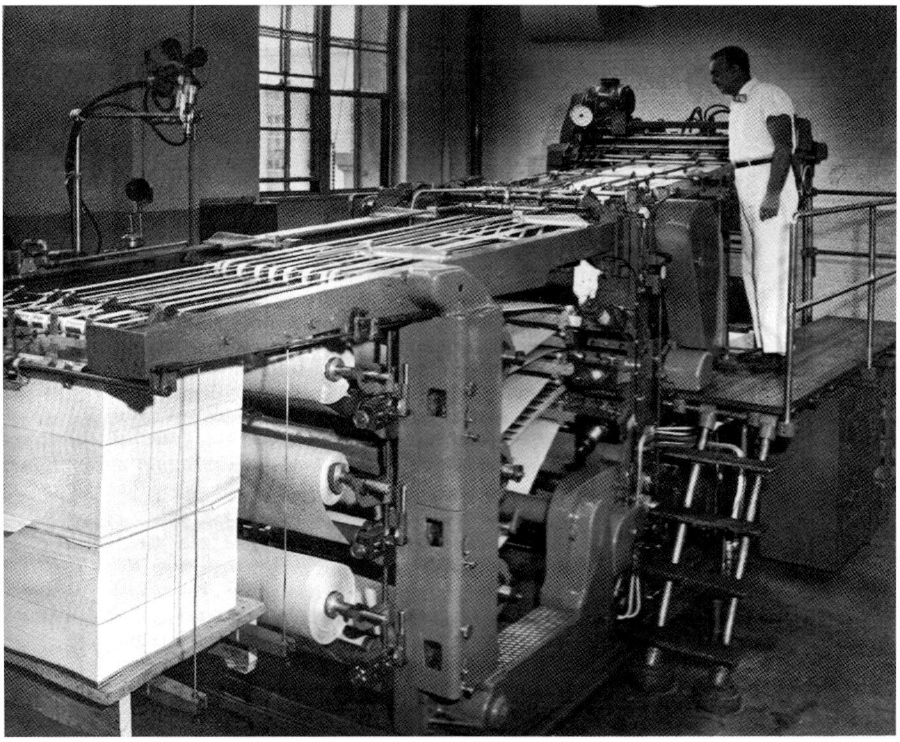

Fig. 26 Flatbed press (foreground) for printing on moistened paper, early 1950s, Bureau of Engraving and Printing, Washington, D.C.; and rotary press for dry intaglio printing, late 1950s, Bureau of Engraving and Printing, Washington, D.C. Source: *History of the Bureau of Engraving and Printing, 1862–1962* (Washington, D.C.: Treasury Department, 1964).

thousand masterpieces in his lifetime and I thought, 'Gee, I could do that in a day.' So I started. . . . You see, the way I do them, with my technique [serigraphy], I really thought I could do four thousand in a day. . . . But it took more than a day, I think it took a month. So at five hundred a month, it would have taken me about eight months to do four thousand masterpieces. . . . It was disillusioning for me, to realize it would take me that long."[43]

The advance represented by the rotary press, whose increased production capacity held such great appeal for Warhol, was not just a question of technique. It also had implications for monetary policy. Indeed, the idea that the Bureau of Engraving and Printing could now produce new bills in ever-greater quantities did not fail to elicit a skeptical reaction from observers who expressed apprehension about the prospect of repeated spikes in inflation. The *Wall Street Journal* welcomed the advent of the new dollar series with these words:

> For the first time it bears the motto long found on our coinage, "In God We Trust." Otherwise the bill is about the same as it has been since 1937, except that it doesn't buy as much. People who keep track of such things figure the 1957 dollar has only half of the purchasing power the dollar had a scant 20 years ago. . . . *Five times* as many dollar bills can be printed in the time it used to take to *print one*. We don't know what the Bureau of Engraving is preparing for, but if the Government ever gets around to a fiscal policy based on the new fiscal process, the 50-cent dollar of today will be worth a bushel basketful of tomorrow's dollars.
>
> And that gets us right back to the motto now being printed on the dollar bills. We're happy to see it circulated as widely as possible, for not only does it tell us where man's trust is best placed; it also reminds us not to place our trust, in money or other matters, too much in Government.[44]

Throughout the 1960s, inflation remained a matter of deep concern to Americans. The phenomenon of a general increase in prices, and a corresponding decrease in the dollar's value, was by no means regarded as a technical subject reserved for the financial pages. To the contrary, it was presented by the mainstream press in highly political terms as one of the major issues of the Cold War. In early 1961, Ernesto ("Che") Guevara, "the economic architect of revolutions," had notoriously declared that inflation was a "capitalist concept."[45] The historian T. J. Clark has noted that Soviet theoreticians long considered inflation to be an ally of Communism, confident that it would bring about the collapse of capitalism through the forced expropriation of shareholder wealth and, in the long run, a loss of confidence in the very foundation of the capitalist system: money. Thus, for example, E. A. Preobrazhensky dedicated his *Paper Money in the Epoch of the Proletarian Dictatorship* (1921) to the "printing press of the People's

Commissariat of Finance . . . , that machine which attacked the bourgeois regime in its rear—its monetary system—by converting the bourgeois economic law of money circulation into a means of destruction of that same regime, and into a source of financing the revolution."[46]

In the early 1960s, inflation became a spearhead of Republican attacks on the Kennedy administration, whose inability to stem the surge in prices was ascribed to its alleged lack of resolve in fighting Communism. Idaho Senator Henry Dworshak declared in October 1961 that inflation was very nearly as grave a threat as Communism itself.[47] The same argument was still being made three years later by Barry Goldwater in his presidential campaign against Lyndon Johnson. An advertisement placed by the Greene County (Pennsylvania) Republican Committee in a local paper, the staunchly conservative *Washington Observer*, denounced Democratic inaction during the Kennedy-Johnson years, charging that "[t]hey have dealt away half of the free world to Communism and more than half the value of your dollar to inflation."[48]

There is anecdotal evidence that Warhol himself was by no means indifferent to these concerns. A close friend, the curator and critic Henry Geldzahler, recounted the artist's obsession—a consequence, he claims, of Warhol's traumatizingly poor childhood—with convincing himself and others that he was on the verge of bankruptcy: "As money poured in after the middle sixties I observed him putting his money in several different banks so that . . . he could induce himself to concentrate on the account with the least funds in it and declare, justifiably, that he was almost broke. Another such spur and defense mechanism was to calculate how much money he had made in his best year and, perhaps even adjusting for inflation, point out that he was doing terribly by comparison."[49] In this way Warhol associated his personal situation with the anxiety felt by many in the 1960s, that the financial system on which American prosperity was founded was in danger of collapsing and that wealth would melt away as the dollar lost value.

The decision to depict a Silver Certificate—easily recognizable by its blue seal, which is highlighted in certain silkscreens, and because the legend SILVER CERTIFICATE is emblazoned on the front of the bill at the top (see fig. 23)—is consistent with this view. Redeemable for their value in silver coins, Silver Certificates, a legacy of nineteenth-century bimetallism, had become increasingly rare by the 1940s and 1950s (apart from the one-dollar denomination) because of the steady decline in the U.S. Treasury's holdings of silver. They were replaced by Federal Reserve Notes, bills that since the 1929 crash and the end of the dollar's convertibility into gold on the American market four years later could no longer be exchanged for precious metals. Owing to a rise in the price of silver, a one-dollar coin of this metal was worth about $1.29 in paper money in 1960. This meant that a one-dollar Silver Certificate was worth about 30 percent more than its face value. The Treasury began to limit redemptions in silver in 1964, halting them altogether in 1968, with the result that this type of bill disappeared completely.[50]

In depicting a Silver Certificate, then, Warhol had elected to portray what was soon to be the obsolete symbol of a monetary era that was drawing to a close, when paper money could be converted into precious metal.

One detail omitted by the artist on the silkscreens seems to have special significance. True one-dollar Silver Certificates, above the uppercased legend THE UNITED STATES OF AMERICA on the front of the bill, carried the notice "This certifies that there is on deposit in the Treasury of [the United States of America]" the amount of one silver dollar, payable to the bearer on demand (see fig. 25). By leaving out these words from his own bill (see fig. 23), Warhol seems to be silently remarking on the depletion of silver reserves and the irony of the Treasury's actual inability to reimburse its citizens for the debt represented by the bills it has put into circulation. This suggests a tacit skepticism about the nature of paper money itself. What real worth can it actually have when the Bureau of Engraving and Printing is able to produce an effectively unlimited supply of notes backed by no authority other than the notes themselves? As Warhol himself put it in a 1971 interview, "If I designed money, I'd keep it all in silver." Why? "Silver costs more."[51]

By stressing the pious sentiment of the new bills, arranged on sheets in a grid and advertising a certification of silver backing that no longer carried any genuine authority, Warhol's *Dollar Bill* paintings delivered a penetrating commentary, far subtler than is generally supposed, on a subject of public debate in which religious values, inflation, and anti-Communism were routinely invoked for the purpose of shaping American public opinion.

From Institutional to Private Uses of Money

For Warhol, however, the question of money was not only a matter of the scope of institutional power and its ability to disseminate both the instruments of capitalism and arguments for its moral and political legitimization. He was just as interested in the way the capitalist propaganda communicated by dollar bills was appropriated and subverted by ordinary citizens as he was in the message itself.

Warhol's feelings about money were deeply personal. "American money is very well-designed, really," he writes in *The Philosophy of Andy Warhol*. "I like it better than any other kind of money."[52] Many of the artist's friends have recounted his habit of tearing a bill in half, keeping one half for himself and giving them the other as a proof of loyalty. He also stockpiled cash: after his death, $14,000 in one hundred dollar bills was found in a cookie jar in his studio.[53] His hoarding shows a physical attachment to money as an object, embodied in banknotes, rather than as an abstract concept of wealth notionally residing in a bank account. "Checks," Warhol was fond of saying, "aren't money."[54] While it is true that the most famous of the *Dollar Bill* paintings depict large numbers of anonymous bills, the series mostly consists of small-scale canvases that show either the front or the back of a single bill (see figs. 23–24). These latter works were

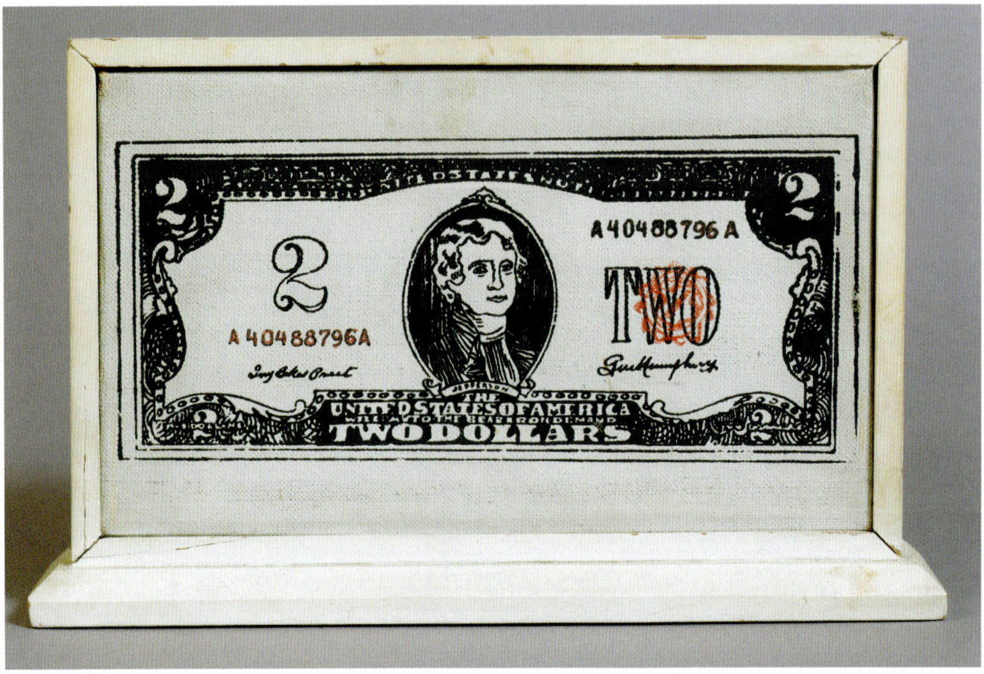

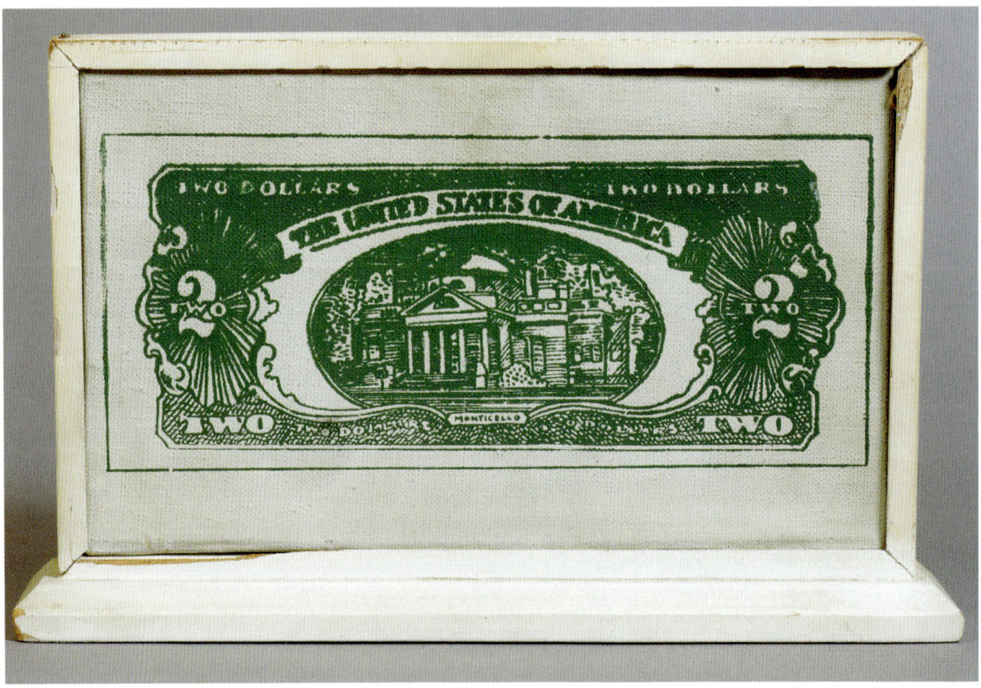

Fig. 27 Andy Warhol, *Two Dollar Bill (Front)*, 1962. Silkscreen ink and acrylic on linen, 6 × 10⅞ in. (15.24 × 27.6 cm).

Fig. 28 Andy Warhol, *Two Dollar Bill (Back)*, 1962. Silkscreen ink and acrylic on linen, 6 × 10⅞ in. (15.24 × 27.6 cm).

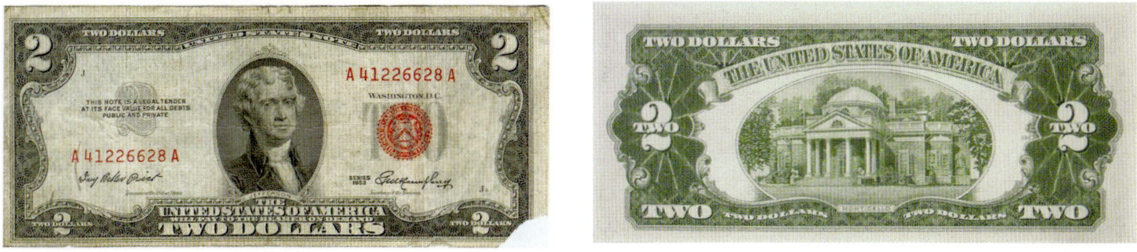

Fig. 29 Obverse and reverse of two-dollar bill, 1953 series, signed by Ivy Baker Priest and George M. Humphrey.

often signed on the back by the artist and given as presents to close friends and associates in the art world, notably the filmmaker Emile de Antonio, the art critic Gene Swenson, and the collector Emily Hall Tremaine, in addition to Geldzahler, all of whom formed a network of relationships that was both personal and professional.

By situating his work on the threshold between gift and remuneration, between symbolic exchange and monetary exchange, Warhol created an extraeconomic form of currency, the special monies so named and analyzed by Viviana Zelizer. As against the classical idea that money is simply an abstract and homogeneous instrument, Zelizer proposed a quite opposite way of thinking about it: just as the archaic currencies studied by anthropologists were associated with specific uses or particular owners, so modern money has a heterogeneous character by virtue of the many different things people do with it every day. One does not spend earned income from a monthly salary in the same way one spends money that was stolen, inherited, or won at gambling. By the same token, certain means of payment—by check, for example, or in cash—are given precedence over others for certain kinds of expenditures. These uses remove money from the purely rational sphere of *Homo economicus* and assign it a particular kind of value: "Money is neither culturally neutral nor morally invulnerable. It may well 'corrupt' values into numbers, but values and sentiments reciprocally corrupt money by investing it with moral, social, and religious meaning. . . . What is the relationship of money as a medium of exchange and measure of utility to money as a symbol of social value?"[55] If money as an image, as a representation, is bound up with institutional and political interests, Warhol also saw individual practices as a means of socially reclaiming money as a vehicle of extramonetary value. The best example of the power of money to subvert the institutional role it is supposed to promote is provided by the *Two Dollar Bill* paintings (figs. 27–28). Like the old Silver Certificates, two-dollar bills were far from common in the 1960s; indeed, they were already quite rare the decade before, and their production was officially halted in 1966. The reason for this, however, had to do not with monetary policy but with cultural preferences and their actual use.

The two-dollar bill that Warhol chose to represent belongs to the 1953 series, recognizable by its red seal (included on certain silkscreens), by the signatures of Ivy Baker Priest and George M. Humphrey, and, of course, by its iconography, a portrait of Thomas Jefferson on the front and, on the back, a view of Jefferson's Monticello residence (fig. 29). First issued in 1862 as legal tender in the United States, the two-dollar bill never managed to establish itself among the other denominations of American money. Only two series—1928 and 1953—were produced between the initial release of small-size banknotes in 1929 and the appearance of the *Dollar Bill* corpus in 1962. They were always printed in limited quantities, especially in the 1950s. The Treasury was adapting to a social fact of life, namely, that Americans were reluctant to adopt this denomination; indeed, many were suspicious of it. Many stores refused to accept two-dollar bills, and consumers tended to hoard rather than circulate them.[56] According to the *Baltimore Sun*, "It was only in New England that the $2 bill was accepted. In other parts of the country this unpopular bill, with its many associated superstitions, was spurned and ignored by Mr. Average Citizen."[57]

Linked in the popular mind with the lowest numerical rank of playing cards, the two-dollar bill was suspected of bringing bad luck in card games. Its reputation also suffered from association with sports betting, political corruption, and prostitution—two dollars being, at the end of the nineteenth century, the minimum wager on a horse, the smallest bribe in an election, and the cost of a cheap prostitute.[58] The Treasury Department, for budgetary reasons, nonetheless tried to encourage its use in the 1950s and 1960s, as an article in the *Washington Post* explained: "The way the Treasury sees it, if two-dollar bills became more popular, more could be printed. Then more one-dollar bills could be retired and it would take fewer two-dollar bills to maintain the same amount of money in circulation, thus cutting printing costs." The writer goes on to mention, with a hint of irony, the department's fruitless efforts to make the two-dollar bill more popular: "Kathryn O'Hay Granahan, the Treasurer of the United States, has waged a low-key effort to increase the use of the neglected twos and created such enthusiasm within her staff about it that they carry a few around at all times to pay bills."[59] By depicting a bill that had, for the most part, gone out of circulation and now become little more than a curiosity and a collector's item (thus, for example, Eleanor Ward's good luck bill), Warhol showed that, much to the displeasure of financial authorities, the daily use—or non-use—of money is capable of undercutting its role as a mere medium of exchange. However much it may appear to be the rational tool of capitalist bureaucratic society, modern currency remains part of a cultural context made up in no small measure of superstitions and shared beliefs, on which its very existence depends.

On April 6, 1962, *Life* magazine published a special issue, called "Your Money." The cover shows a drawing of a dollar bill reminiscent of the one on which Warhol was then working as part of his *Dollar Bill* series. The editors wished to draw their readers' attention not only to certain areas of concern for the American economy (balance of payments, precious metal bullion reserves, inflation), but also to the various ways in which private citizens coped with these challenges in their daily lives. No doubt Warhol would have concurred with the editors' own conclusion that "money values are finally set by people, not by governments."[60]

Warhol's *Dollar Bill* paintings are often associated with another series of canvases completed twenty years later, the *Dollar Sign* paintings (see fig. 22).[61] From what we have just seen, however, the two need to be clearly distinguished. The dollar sign ($) does not figure on any coin or bill. Its principal function is syntactical. It simply allows a quantity of money to be identified with a particular national currency, the U.S. dollar. By itself, it has no semantic content. In Warhol's paintings, it has the grammatically illogical and empty form of an auxiliary verb lacking a main verb, as it were, a connective lacking any terms to connect; with repetition, it takes on a sort of tragic and obsessive absurdity that imbues these vividly colored images with an air of profound uneasiness. A superficial reading of these works—conflating the *Dollar Sign* and the *Dollar Bill* paintings, looking at them both through the misleadingly simplistic prism of "money"—misses what should be obvious, namely, how very different they are. In the 1980s, a decade that in so many ways was very different from the 1960s, Warhol was exploring the pointlessness of a concept that had been reduced to a mere sign itself, divested of all significance. Twenty years before, by contrast, he had demonstrated the banknote's layers of unsuspected meaning as both object and image, at once an institutional instrument of Cold War capitalist propaganda, a reflection of the indecisiveness and missteps of the monetary policy of the period, and, finally, a familiar object appropriated for private use as a store of noneconomic values.

LARRY RIVERS, DE LA BANQUE FRANÇAISE

Though less famous than Warhol's *Dollar Bill* paintings, Larry Rivers's *French Money* series was created the same year and the works composing it were no less numerous and no less important for his career. In the spring of 1971, the Swiss collector Éric Meyer, unsure of the authenticity of a canvas he had acquired depicting a bill of one hundred new francs, wrote to Rivers asking him if it was, in fact, by his own hand. "I did it in Paris in early 1962," the artist replied. "I think it was purchased at the time by my gallery dealer Jean Larcade who ran the gallery Rive Droit [*sic*]. . . . The solution would lie in your keeping this letter as an identifying factor & we can put down for history right here and now its name [so] it stands distinguished from the others in the series. It is [henceforth] called 'French Money—Right Bank.'"[62]

The choice of a new title for this work was not only the occasion of a play on words ("Right Bank" referring both to the English name of his gallery in Paris and to the idea of a sound banking institution). A title uniquely identifying the work was also a necessity in view of the large number of paintings Rivers had done on this subject, probably fifteen or so in the first half of the 1960s, the majority of them dated 1962.[63] This degree of repetition, unusual even for Rivers, who often produced variants of a particular work, points both to his predilection for money as a theme and to the commercial success of his *French Money* paintings, which made them very good banks indeed.

All the works of the series take as their motif the new one hundred franc banknote featuring Napoleon Bonaparte (figs. 30–31). Drawn in pencil on paper or painted in oil on canvas, in different formats, the front and back sides of the note are shown, either singly or in pairs, and repeated up to six times on the same support. In each case, the design is perfectly recognizable and at the same time freely executed: certain details—decorative ornaments, numbers, written legends—are rendered with the greatest accuracy; others are merely sketched, or omitted, or transformed into abstract patches of color. Reproduced many times in various journals, these paintings became the trademark of an artist who came to be known as "Larry Rivers, de la Banque française."[64]

And yet they have seldom been closely examined, either by art critics at the time or by the few historians who have taken an interest in them since. The received view of Rivers's work during this period, from the late 1950s to the early 1960s, is that it was related to pop art through its subjects and to abstract expressionism through its handling of form.[65] In the case of the *French Money* paintings, this simplistic interpretation insists, on the one hand, on the ordinariness of a theme taken from contemporary life—money being neither more nor less interesting than the packs of cigarettes in *Amel-Camel* (1962) or the restaurant menu in *Cedar Bar Menu* (1959); and, on the other, emphasizes formal elegance, abstraction, and treatment of surfaces.[66] On this view, the choice of money as a subject has no special importance of its own; instead it is seen as something trivial, at most a topic of casual conversation. Nor is the work done in Paris seen as having any social content or contextual significance. The critic Pierre Schneider, writing in 1962, went so far as to say that the "only local influence discernible is that . . . a 100 new francs note rather than a ten dollar bill will serve as the theme for the artist's variations, that a pack of Gitanes is likely to sit for its portrait rather than a pack of Camels."[67]

Rivers himself spoke of his work during the 1960s in much the same formalistic manner. He maintained that his interest in borrowing images from mass culture was a matter of aesthetic and moral indifference, and that his paintings were not to be understood as making "[s]ome socially significant statement." Among the factors influencing his choice of subjects he cited "[a]vailability . . . a cheap easily gotten model, any store almost any time" and "[f]latness . . . [t]he reduced conflict between what you are looking at and what you end up with on your canvas."[68] If these criteria are indisputably satisfied in the case of the *French Money* paintings, they seem nonetheless to account only to a very small degree for what made Rivers regard the note worth one hundred new francs as an object of exceptional interest. A statement he read at an October 1963 symposium at the Museum of Modern Art in New York testified to the lasting influence on his generation of the formalism

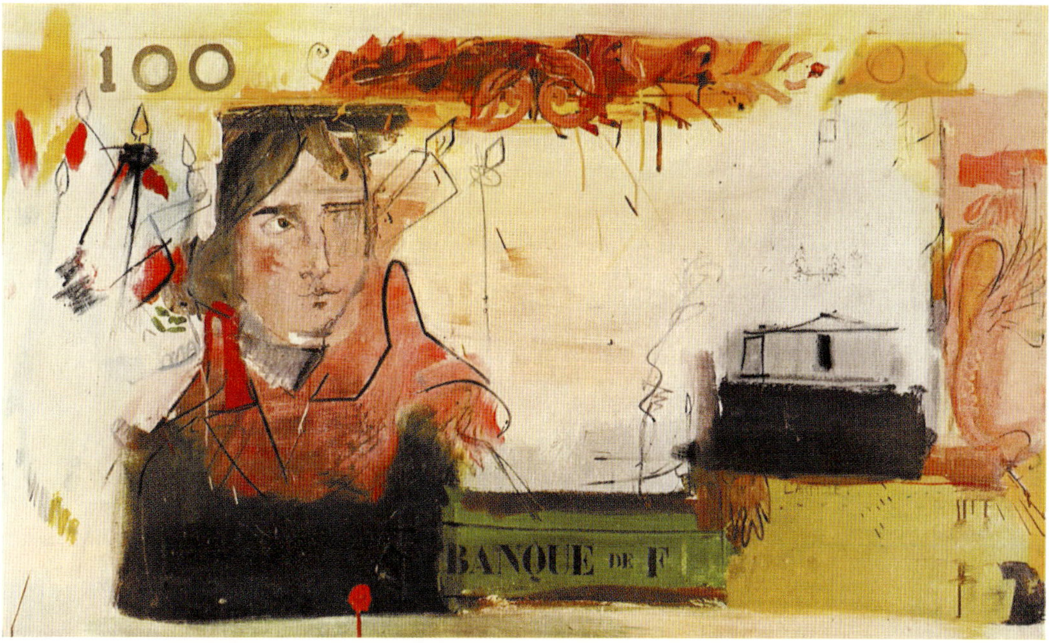

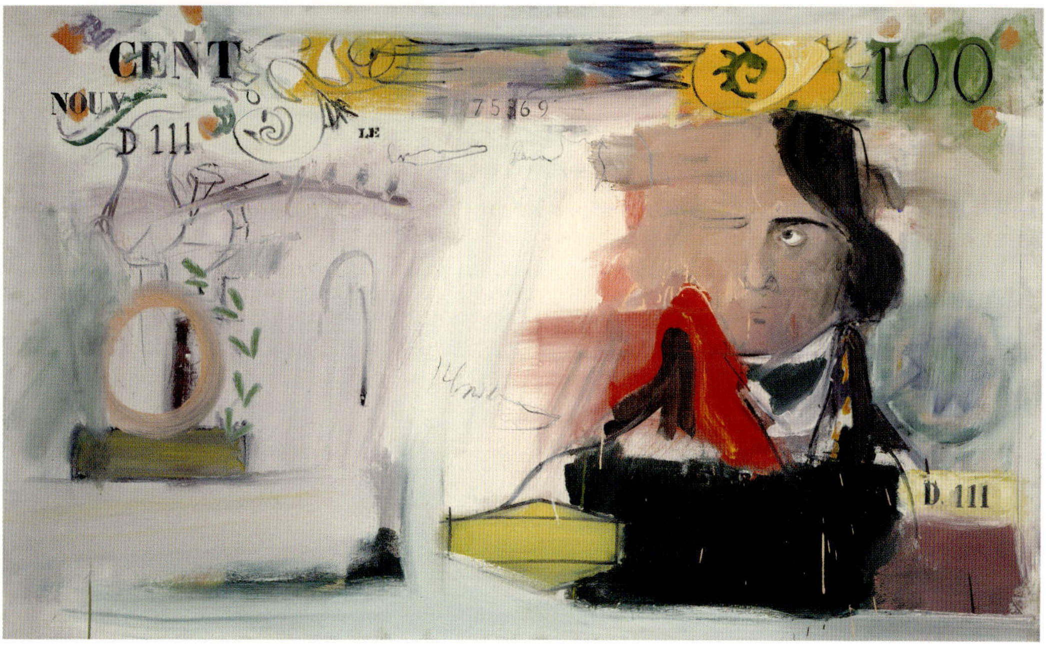

Fig. 30 Larry Rivers, *French Money I*, 1962. Oil and charcoal on canvas, 35⅜ × 59 in. (90 × 150 cm). Private collection.

Fig. 31 Larry Rivers, *French Money II*, 1962. Oil and charcoal on canvas, 35⅜ × 59 in. (90 × 150 cm). Hirshhorn Museum and Sculpture Garden, Smithsonian Institution, Washington, D.C.

championed by the critic Clement Greenberg. Under the sway of abstract expressionism, he later admitted, "it took me a long time to accept my concern with subject matter."[69] A careful examination of the artist's archives, only recently made accessible to scholars through the Fales Library and Special Collections at New York University, now makes it possible to show how the new French banknote provided Rivers with an opportunity to challenge conventional notions of economics, politics, and morality at a time when France was deeply divided over the wars of decolonization in which it was engaged.

The Search for Commercial Success

In early 1962, when Rivers began work on the *French Money* series, the theme of money was bound to have held a very personal meaning for him. He had just then entered a crucial stage of his career. Born in 1923, five years before Warhol, Rivers was already well known in the New York scene: first noticed by Clement Greenberg, his figurative paintings enjoyed great critical success in the 1950s; the Museum of Modern Art had purchased his famous *Washington Crossing the Delaware* shortly after its completion in 1953.[70] Now, at the beginning of the 1960s, he was poised to take a decisive step forward by embracing a new iconography that would have important consequences for both his artistic reputation and his commercial prospects, in America and abroad.

In the autumn of 1961, having been approached by European galleries interested in sponsoring exhibitions of his work the following spring, Rivers took up residence in Paris with his young Welsh-born wife, Clarice, in the Impasse Ronsin, an alley in Montparnasse where many artists had studios. He lived there for almost a year, and after a visit to Italy returned to New York.[71] This long stay in France, Rivers's second (he had spent six months in Paris some ten years earlier), was a formative experience. Yves Klein, whom he had met the previous year in New York, introduced him to the circle of artists, critics, and dealers associated with the Nouveau Réalisme;[72] he also struck up a friendship with his neighbors in the Impasse Ronsin, the sculptor Jean Tinguely and his companion, the artist Niki de Saint Phalle, who, as Rivers later recalled, "spent their time bombarding the wall of their studio next door, shooting a .22 rifle."[73]

On the advice of his dealer and friend John Myers, cofounder of the Tibor de Nagy Gallery in New York, Rivers gave up the idea of using his upcoming exhibits in Paris (at the Galerie Rive Droite) and London (at Gimpel Fils), in April and May 1962, to mount a retrospective of his earlier work, which could not help but have a certain wistfulness about it. "The image you have created for yourself [in England]," Myers wrote him in December 1961, "is one of radicalism, of satire, humor, etc. etc. (as reported in the press and from your lecture). Your older pictures are quite different from this. . . . The advanced artists and critics may well attack the show as old hat or god knows what. . . . Try to remember that you have now a *new* public quite separate and different from your old following. I'm not sure you need or want that old public—either in America or Europe."[74] In response to Myers's urging, Rivers undertook to create wholly new canvases for the two exhibits. *French Money I* and *French Money II* (see figs. 30–31), the two pictures of the money series exhibited in Europe, were therefore conceived at the beginning of 1962 as part of an attempt to consolidate this new audience by highlighting the radicalism, satire, and humor it was thought to appreciate. Contrary to what several authors have maintained, they were not a response to Warhol's *Dollar Bill* paintings, created during the same period and at once caught up in the media's infatuation with pop art and the commercial success that accompanied it.[75] Rivers's *French Money* pictures were shown for the first time in April 1962, in Paris, and reproduced almost simultaneously in the April issue of *Art International,* whereas Warhol's series, produced between March and the end of April, was seen in a New York gallery show and in a magazine article only the following month, in May.[76] In all probability, then, it is a matter of the same subject spontaneously emerging on both sides of the Atlantic, not of some sort of imitation or one-way influence.

Rivers's financial situation up to this time had been precarious. The struggle to make ends meet would have naturally recommended money as a subject to an artist casting about for a satirical, if not also a scandalous, theme that might enlarge his audience and attract more buyers. Rivers's correspondence with his dealers in New York and London during the winter of 1961–62 foreshadows the sudden change in fortune that would soon turn a critically admired but commercially unsuccessful artist into a successful and internationally recognized artist. In December 1961, a discouraged Myers had written to Rivers in Paris, describing the relative failure of his most recent New York exhibit: "I don't know *why* so little has sold. . . . I am sure we will eventually sell all our Riverses but it is a headache when we're so strapped for cash to see it all on the walls."[77] Adding to these preoccupations, New York and Paris galleries alike were shaken by a crisis in the art market in the spring of 1962. The topic is frequently mentioned in his correspondence of the period. "The stock market has crashed in May," Myers glumly reported, referring to the so-called Kennedy Slide, "which, of course, is terrible news for galleries and painters."[78] The success of his European exhibits—particularly the London show that same May—therefore came as a most welcome surprise for Rivers. "We're really going aren't we," he wrote enthusiastically to Peter Gimpel.[79]

This happy turn of events, crowning months of particularly productive and satisfying work for Rivers, gave him new confidence and ambition. "With those pictures of the French 100-franc notes," he confided a few months later, "I thought I might have a formula, a formula for the perfect painting."[80] On his return to the United States he left the Tibor de Nagy Gallery, which had supported him from the beginning, and signed on with Marlborough Gallery, which was more prestigious and, he felt, better equipped to help him in the next phase of his career. In the words of a June 1973 *Time* magazine article, Marlborough under its current director, Frank

Lloyd, was "[l]ess a gallery than a multinational corporation," whose policy was to "promote established artists" by poaching them from rival galleries. Rivers chose Lloyd—a highly controversial dealer, famous for saying "I only collect money, I don't collect pictures!"—to sell the *French Money* paintings for him.[81] Myers, for his part, made no attempt to conceal his bitter disappointment, telling Rivers, "I deeply regret that 'international fame' moved you so very far away from us."[82]

Between Inflation and Decolonization

It is tempting, then, to conclude that the preoccupation with money, never far from Rivers's mind during the period from late 1961 until early 1963, was merely a reflection of the sudden reversal in his professional circumstances, which in the space of little more than a year—and, in part, thanks to these very paintings—had brought him a measure of material comfort he had not known up to this point, and, at the same time, had intensified his artistic ambitions. This can only be a partial explanation, however. It reduces money simply to the financial challenges Rivers faced in spite of his early critical success, while ignoring the manner in which he treated so distinctive a theme in his work. The aesthetic exuberantly embraced in the *French Money* paintings makes it clear, however, that they are not primarily concerned with money in a general sense, but with a particular currency, the new French franc, physically embodied by a banknote having an iconography all its own.

The two most accomplished works in the series, *French Money I* (see fig. 30), today in a private collection, and *French Money II* (see fig. 31), held by the Hirshhorn Museum and Sculpture Garden in Washington, D.C., were shown together in Paris and London and frequently reproduced in magazines and journals.[83] Conceived as companion pieces, each one represents a face of the 100 new francs Bonaparte banknote, 1959 series (fig. 32): the back in *French Money I*, the front in *French Money II*, with the shape of the canvas following the form of the note, though with noticeably enlarged dimensions (35⅜ × 59 in. [90 × 150 cm]).[84] The treatment of the note's content is a free, but nonetheless meticulous, interpretation of a quite singular visual landscape. In keeping with the symmetry of the two faces of the note, the portrait of Bonaparte appears on the right in *French Money II* and on the left in *French Money I*, his gaze directed to the opposite side in each case. In both portraits, one half of the face is precisely drawn—an alert eye, a well-shaped nose, pursed lips underscored by a shadow—whereas the other half is erased or fades into the background. An exaggeratedly high red collar serves metonymically to suggest Bonaparte's uniform. In *French Money II*, a scarcely recognizable architectural element drawn on a patch of purple gray stands for the Arc de Triomphe. In *French Money I*, the flags behind Napoleon are evoked only by their arrowhead finials, and on the right it is possible to make out the church of Les Invalides, its dome almost wholly effaced.

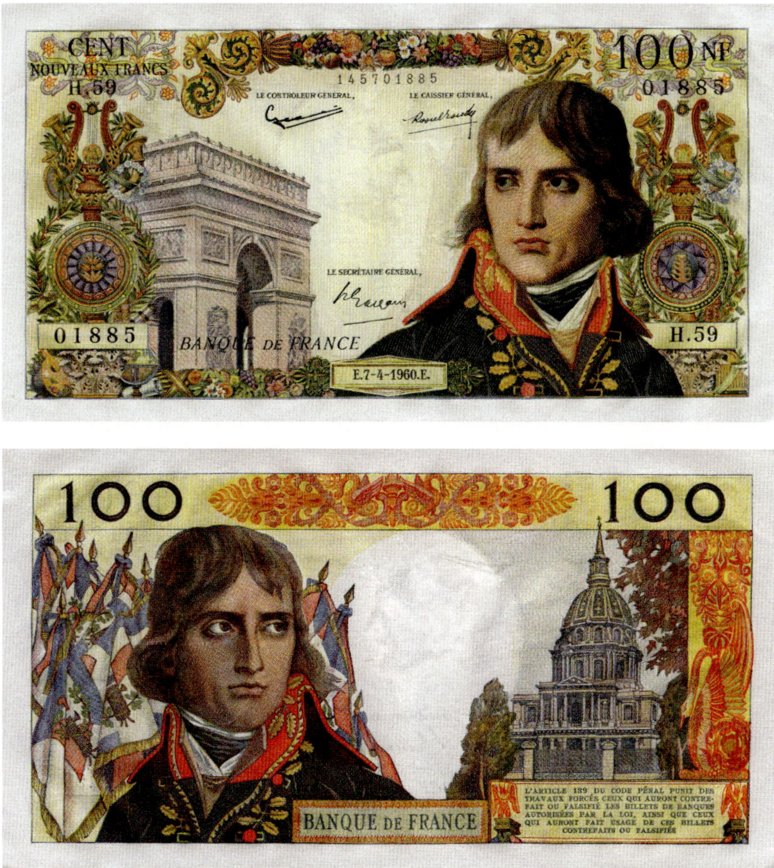

Fig. 32 Obverse and reverse of 100 new francs (Bonaparte) banknote, 1959 series.

Adopting the vivid polychrome palette of the banknote—olive green and flesh color dominant on the front, red and orange on the back—the two pictures offer a contrast of colors, applied sometimes in pure, sometimes in diluted form. The brushwork is masterful, and in places very precise; the treatment of the number "100," for example, at the top right of the front face and the top left of the back, seems almost calligraphic. Elsewhere, however, the brushwork is broad and rapid; uneven surfaces are set off by heavy strokes and smudged by visible fingerprints. The decorative elements along the edges of the note are sometimes faithfully reproduced, as in the case of the swan that appears on the right of *French Money I*; sometimes they are altered, as with the flower that embellishes the front of the note, comically transformed into a snail in *French Money II*; elsewhere they fade away into a vivid abstraction, as with the overhanging garland of flowers and fruits in *French Money II*. A charcoal pencil is used to emphasize certain details, such as the signatures of three high-ranking treasury officials (the contrôleur général, the caissier général, and the secrétaire général), all faithfully reproduced in *French Money II*; sometimes, however, it tarnishes the colored surfaces, leaving indistinct streaks. The artist's careful handling of his materials is apparent also in the thickness of the paint: some layers are so thin that the canvas beneath can still be seen, as in the central area of the

Fig. 33 Preparatory drawing by Clément Serveau for the 10,000 francs banknote, c. 1955. Banque de France, Paris.

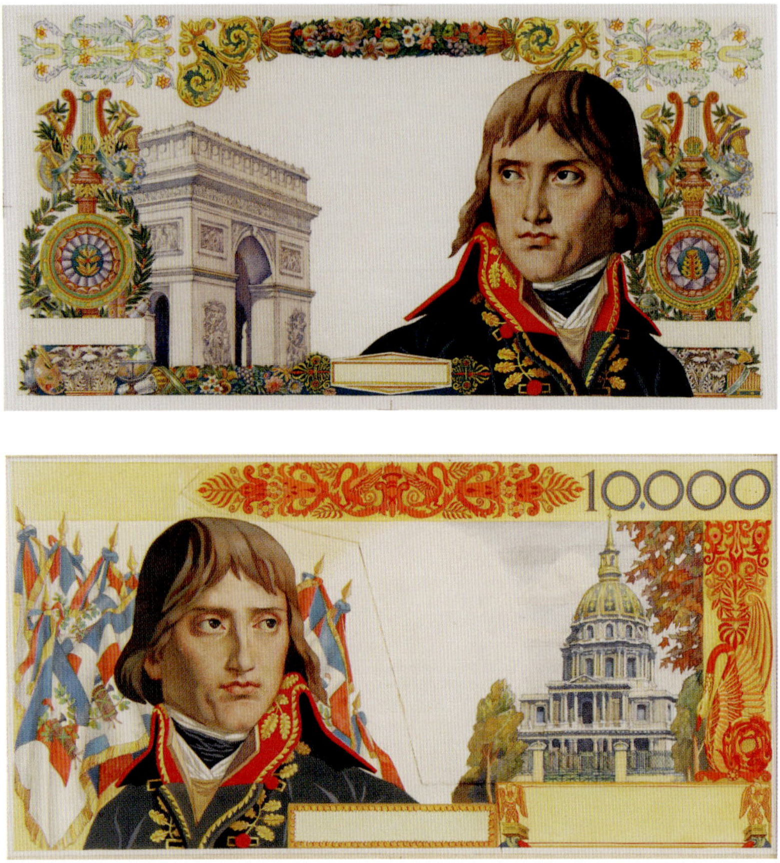

two compositions; other surfaces are built up and then, using the pencil again, hollowed out.

Since the early nineteenth century, central banks had sought to outdo one another in an attempt to create a kind of paper money whose authenticity and trustworthiness would be guaranteed by an ingenious use of polychromy, complex decorative ornamentation, lettering, numerical values, serial numbers, signatures, and raised or impressed markings (including transparent watermarks), while at the same time discouraging counterfeiters. Rivers, while he treated colors, textures, and motifs with great care, seemed at the same time to be intent on offsetting their very effect: the words and numbering are half finished, the faces half erased, the cartouches and ornamental borders left empty. This emptiness recalls the unfinished preparatory drawings by Clément Serveau, the artist commissioned to design the Bonaparte banknote in the mid-1950s (fig. 33). In *French Money I*, article 139 of the penal code, printed on the reverse of all notes as a warning of the penalty incurred by counterfeiting (forced labor), is only faintly suggested by the first word alone ("L'article"). Both paintings give the impression of being the work of an expert forger, wearied by too great a task, who then abruptly abandoned it.

At the beginning of the 1960s in France, as we have seen, the franc was a subject of intense public debate. The new (so-called heavy) franc, worth one

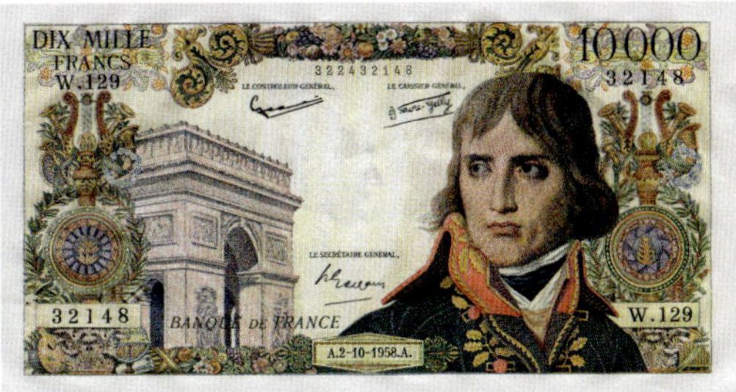

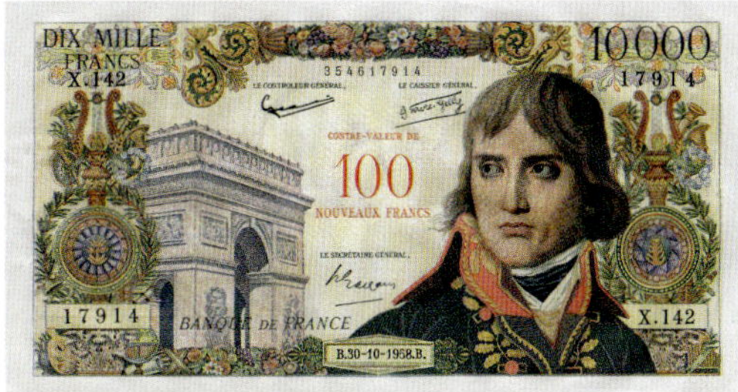

Fig. 34 Obverse of 10,000 francs (Bonaparte) banknote, 1955 series; and obverse of 10,000 francs (Bonaparte) banknote, 1955 series overprinted in red with equivalent value in new francs.

hundred times the old franc, was introduced on January 1, 1960, in order to reestablish trust in a currency chronically strained by inflation and trade imbalances. This symbolic and economically neutral adjustment attracted comment at once in the international press—thus the title of a report in the *New York Times*, "A Franc Method to Change Money: Value of Currency Is Same, but Dropping of Zeros Brings a New Look."[85] The notes themselves reflected the artifice employed: the 100 new francs note (1959 series) that Rivers chose to illustrate, which came into circulation on January 4, 1960, exactly reproduced the design of the 10,000 old francs note, 1955 series, except for one detail—the denomination; during a transitional phase, specimens of the old note continued to circulate, now overprinted in red ink with the number *100* in order to indicate its equivalent value in new francs (fig. 34).[86] The critic Michel Ragon, apparently getting the arithmetic wrong in his review of Rivers's exhibit at the Galerie Rive Droite, spoke of the "Bonaparte of the 1,000 francs bill."[87]

What value, then, was to be attached to a paper banknote from which the government could suddenly remove two zeros, leaving the economy unaffected while nonetheless claiming to have restored public confidence? These zeros haunt the *French Money* paintings. Plainly present in the upper right-hand corner of *French Money I*, and, more subtly, in the form of pink and green circles that appear at the middle left and middle right respectively of *French Money II*, the pair of zeros that separate *10,000* from *100*, the old franc from the new franc, underscore the purely conventional character of a currency's face value—and all the more powerfully in view of the fact that, in the space of a few years, inflation can dramatically erode, even destroy, its real value. What was fundamentally new, then, about a new franc dressed up in an old note? This is the question that the impertinent legend "NOUV," in the upper left-hand corner of *French Money II*, seems to ask. Cognate with the English word *new*, here the root *nouv-* (from which the corresponding French word *nouveau* is formed) concentrates in four letters the whole of the word's meaning for an artist who was then trying with some difficulty to learn French, taking evening classes at the Alliance française.[88] Considered in light of the vain pretensions of the new paper money, Bonaparte—creator of the Banque de France and the so-called germinal franc of 1803, symbol of the stability and durability of French currency—cannot help but seem a rather pathetic figure.

At the very moment when Rivers chose it as a subject, the 100 new francs Bonaparte banknote was about to disappear: on January 1, 1963, the new franc lost its qualifying adjective and French money once more became simply the franc, with fresh notes of its own.[89] Rivers's canvases were doomed almost at once to live on as magnified representations of a demonetized currency, a piece of paper now having no worth other than what collectors were willing to pay for it. It seems scarcely possible that an artist who frankly admitted "[t]he business section of the N.Y. Times is much more exciting to me than all the opinions on this & that show or dance or whatever" could have been unaware of this.[90]

The reasons for introducing the new franc, as commentators at the time well understood, were more political than economic. "For a regime bent on restoring what is considered France's natural place in the world, the monetary changeover is a logical one," the *New York Times* observed in January 1960. "A great nation should not have a cheap currency."[91] The determination to affirm France's independence, notably in response to the global reach of American power, was symbolized by the new regime's approach to monetary reform: unlike previous devaluations, the introduction of the new franc—intended by de Gaulle to be the last such devaluation, inaugurating a new and lasting era of stability—was not calculated on the basis of parity with the dollar, but directly as a function of gold content, 1.8 milligrams of pure gold for one franc, the rate of conversion into dollars (one dollar = 493.7 francs) being only a secondary equivalence derived from gold parity. As the *New York Times* put it in December 1958, the "new franc rate mirrors gold and French pride."[92]

Moreover, at a time when decolonization threatened to reduce the French Empire to a small fraction of its former extent, the will to reassert France's place in the world took on a special urgency. It was not uncommon during this period to see a direct connection between de Gaulle's monetary reforms and the prosecution of the war in Algeria. As Pierre Mendès-France wrote in 1959, "M. Jacques Rueff declares that the devaluation of the franc has been calculated so that we might continue the Algerian war for years; thus our whole economic, monetary, social policy . . . continue[s] to be dominat[ed] by military considerations."[93] Rivers's stay in Paris, from autumn 1961 to spring 1962, coincided with the final phase of the war of Algerian independence. The artist mentioned the subject in his correspondence, though in a rather detached tone, giving his view of the conflict and noting the daily threat of attacks in Paris. In early March 1962, for example, after months of uninterrupted violence in both Algiers and Paris—including an attempt on André Malraux's apartment in Boulogne-sur-Seine—Rivers wrote: "As for bombs plastiques [*sic*] O.A.S. & such, it goes on but it is such a big city & busy [every]one is so caught up in their own small 'gorgeous' lives it is only newspaper headlines like Muggings Rapes etc. at any rate it'll be over soon & like all selfish sweet human beings I hope it quiets down at least a few days before my show."[94] Rivers may have been thinking

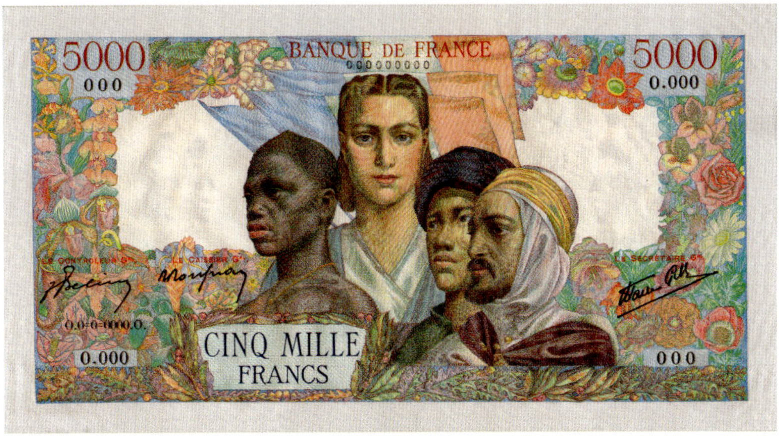

Fig. 35 Obverse of 5,000 francs (French Empire) banknote, 1945 series.

of Robert Rauschenberg's mishap at the Galerie Daniel Cordier the previous spring, in April 1961: the opening of his exhibit coincided with the failed coup d'état against General de Gaulle, the so-called Generals' Plot, and the gallery had to close its doors temporarily.[95] Nevertheless, the sight of France torn by internal conflict was bound to be of great concern to an artist of liberal views, keenly interested in politics, someone who could not begin the day without reading the newspaper from front to back and who, a few years later, described himself as an inveterate signer of petitions, someone who was even contemplating a career in politics.[96] Rivers's show at the Galerie Rive Droite opened on April 10, 1962, two days after the referendum approving the Évian Accords, which provided for a cease-fire and a second referendum concerning self-determination to be held in Algeria. There can be no doubt that Rivers followed events all the more closely as he was in daily contact with artists such as Niki de Saint Phalle, herself very much affected by the course of the war and its consequences.[97]

The iconography of the new banknote was strongly influenced by a desire to insist upon France's international stature as a great power, present appearances to the contrary notwithstanding. The painter commissioned to design the Bonaparte banknote, Clément Serveau, had distinguished himself some years earlier with the 5,000 francs (French Empire) note, issued in 1945 (fig. 35).[98] On the front of this note, at the center, appears a young blond woman, representing metropolitan France, with three "indigenous" men—a black African, an Asian, and a Berber—placed slightly beneath her in the foreground. Set against a backdrop of French tricolor flags, the ensemble was plainly meant to symbolize the greatness of the French nation, and the mother country's domination of its colonies no less than the protection it afforded them.

For his Bonaparte bill, Serveau chose instead to highlight the theme of conquest. Here the emperor is shown surveying his realm before an array of flags, the standards of the armies he commanded in Egypt and Italy. The force of this martial iconography was immediately appreciated by the dissident paramilitary group that carried out terrorist attacks in opposition to de

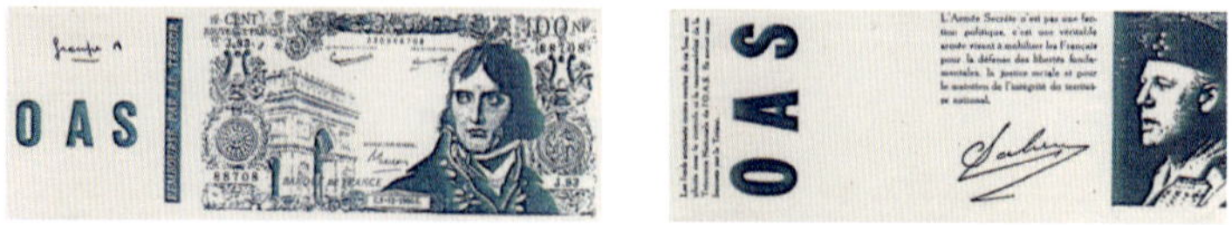

Fig. 36 Obverse and reverse of bill issued by the Secret Army Organization (OAS in its French initials) in return for financial support, January 1960. Dimensions unknown. Collection of Sergeant Major (ret.) Herbert A. Friedman.

Gaulle's policy in Algeria, the Secret Army Organization (OAS in its French initials), which in 1960 appropriated the design of the 100 new francs note for the purpose of advertising bonds that were issued in exchange for financial contributions (fig. 36).[99] Signed by the group's leader, General Raoul Salan, the bonds featured a copy in blue ink of the 100 new francs bill together with the legend "Reimbursed by the Treasury," explained on the back as meaning that all financial support for the activities of the OAS would be reimbursed by the state once victory had finally been achieved. The figure of Bonaparte was regularly invoked by the defenders of French Algeria; indeed, one combat unit was named the "maquis Bonaparte."[100]

What was at stake, then, with regard both to monetary iconography and the debate over the Algerian war, was nothing less than a rereading of French history itself, at least in relation to the prospect, which many found alarming, that the nation's imperial geography might soon be diminished still further. Among opponents of the war, a connection between the obsolescence of economic values and French colonial values had been made as early as January 1960 by a trenchant critic of the new note, who detected in its iconography the fantasy of finally winning battles that had long been lost:

> New franc does not mean new franchise. . . . Who therefore pretends that this regime has no sense of history? It is pleased to go against the tide and swim upstream when everyone else is floating down. . . . Already the Sower [a familiar allegorical figure pictured on new franc coins] speaks to us of annuities and savings. Already [on the Bonaparte notes], flags flying in the breeze, we make our way back along the route of our African conquests. . . . Tomorrow, no doubt, the Sun Kings of Versailles and the Sun Emperors of Austerlitz will be reborn between old moons and by their dusty light illuminate our triumphant march backward toward original novelties.[101]

What remained of these vague longings for domination and conquest in the work of Larry Rivers in 1962? Flags reduced to a ridiculous scattering of arrowheads in *French Money I*; a national hero with an outsized collar but a receding visage in *French Money II*.

The Banknote as History Painting

By its nature, the banknote is an exercise in selective history, and so perhaps it is not surprising that Rivers himself should have been regarded as a "reinventor of history painting."[102] Certainly he succeeded in making a profound impression on the Paris art scene. The critic Gérald Gassiot-Talabot, looking back on the 1962 Galerie Rive Droite exhibit a decade later, saw it as "one of the most memorable [shows] of the early 1960s" on account of the "confusion" it caused and its "influence" on the younger generation.[103] The writer André Warnod, he recalled, had mocked an overly polished painting for being "as lovely as a banknote." In the case of Rivers, by contrast, "the banknotes of the *French Money* series were the excuse for a dazzling feat whose virtuosity fortunately did not conceal a rather bitter and detached philosophy of the present moment. For this very reason, Rivers has been one of the most effective corrosive agents in the resurgence and the crisis of the image." In startling counterpoint to the luminous finish of Jacques-Louis David's reverential portraits of Napoleon celebrating a glorious historical past, Rivers's deliberately defaced canvases perpetrated "the most arrogant heresy" on a scale amounting to "visual and mental sedition."[104]

This was not the first time that Rivers had treated national heroes and patriotic emblems in a humorously unorthodox manner. He had already attracted notice for his pictures of the American flag (1953) and the last veteran of the American Civil War (1959). But it was another painting from 1953, his reworking of Emanuel Leutze's academic pomposity *Washington Crossing the Delaware* (1851), that announced his unexpected entry into the field of history painting.[105] Just when McCarthyism and the Red Scare of the early Cold War were at their height, he dared to poke fun at the grandiose patriotism of Leutze's famous picture in a spirit somewhere between homage and satire.[106]

Yet, in fact, Rivers had Napoleon in mind when he began work on his portrait of the American general and future first president. "In 1953," he later recalled, "I read *War and Peace*. . . . By meshing Napoleon's invasion of Russia with contemporary life, Tolstoy set me on a course that produced *Washington Crossing the Delaware*."[107] In 1961, Rivers added to Washington and Napoleon another pair of leaders in *The Friendship of America and France (Kennedy and de Gaulle)*, produced with the help of Tinguely, who mounted the canvas on a revolving base.[108] In one version of the painting, the juxtaposed portraits of the two presidents surmount a grid of alternating packs of French cigarettes (Gauloises, Gitanes) and American cigarettes (Lucky Strike, Camel, Marlboro). The pseudo-patriotic confrontation was no less impertinent than in the case of Washington, since, if Rivers's correspondence with his friend Bill Brooker in December 1961 can be credited, the picture was privately envisaged as a homoerotic nude study. "The painting sounds marvelous," Brooker wrote him. "But following your point about de Gaulle and Kennedy in the nude, what about the tangle (sex not stated) of that USA and that Gallic cock? It could be nasty!"[109]

It seems likely that Rivers had in mind a similar private joke when he began sketching the irreverent *French Money* paintings. As many commentators at the time were quick to point out, there is scarcely any hint of military authority in his Bonaparte. Critics agreed that Rivers's bills were notable for their "romanticism,"[110] the refinement of their leafy borders, and a setting nearer in mood to sentimental fable than satire. A December 1962 *Newsweek* article even spoke of a "sensual Napoleon."[111] James Schuyler, who was personally acquainted with the artist, wrote in *Art News*: "Rivers' own disheveled elegance is most overt in the *French Money* [paintings], with their dewy-lipped, languid-eyed Napoleon dreaming on the petal-colored cash."[112] Schuyler's choice of words seems to cast some doubt on Bonaparte's virility. The mention of the artist's "own disheveled elegance" lends support to this interpretation: Rivers was one of the rare artists of the period who made no secret of his homosexual experience, and for those who were aware of what went on behind the scenes in the art world, the allusion was plain.[113] Schuyler went on to notice the mannered but "touching" poses depicted in Rivers's portraits, as well as the "seductive and strangely intimate figments of desire" betrayed by his otherwise apparently ordinary, pedestrian subjects.

Two years later Rivers exhibited a work that further confirmed this heretical view of Napoleon: a portrait, loosely based on a famous painting by David now at the National Gallery in Washington, D.C., *The Emperor Napoleon in His Study at the Tuileries* (1812), of a hero whom now he called *The Greatest Homosexual* (fig. 37). The historian Gavin Butt has shown how Rivers delighted in exaggerating certain features of the David portrait that were supposed, in keeping with the stereotypes of the period, to betray exactly the kind of sexually deviant behavior that was hunted down in America during the Cold War: the inviting look, the weight on the back leg, the unnatural placement of the hands.[114] Rivers later explained that he had been struck by David's work, not in 1964, but in the spring of 1961, passing through Washington on his way back to New York from Los Angeles.[115] Three years later he referred to the "large, clear reproduction" he had purchased at the National Gallery in making his picture. He therefore already had a certain idea of Napoleon in mind in the fall of 1961 when he next encountered the emperor's visage, in France, on the 100 new francs notes. This time it seems to have been the boyish appearance and sullen pout that captured his imagination. Serveau's preliminary sketches for the note indicate that he had initially leaned toward a Napoleon with more mature and more pronounced features, and a moustache. In the end he decided on an unfinished drawing by David, now at the Louvre, dating from 1797–98 (fig. 38). Made during the Italian campaign, it is in many respects a preromantic portrait, showing a very young general Bonaparte, beardless, long hair tousled by the wind, staring into the distance. As he was later to do in *The Greatest Homosexual*, Rivers accentuated these details in his *French Money* paintings, making the fleshy lips, the dreamy gaze, and the disheveled locks the signs of a suspect sexuality. In so doing, he turned a way of looking at the male physique that was typical of the homophobia of the period against itself. He was not the first to have seen Napoleon in this light, however. A few years

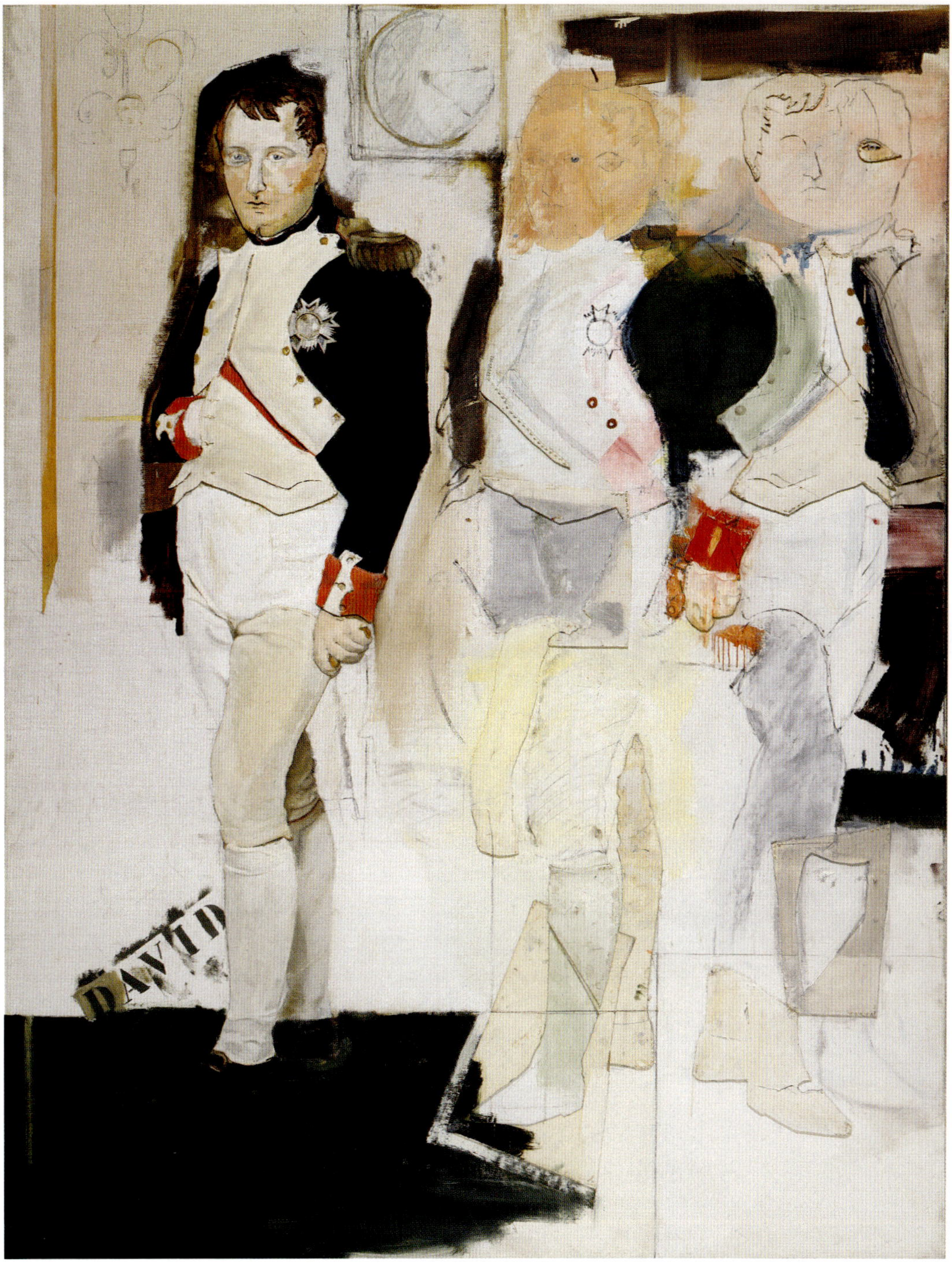

Fig. 37 Larry Rivers, *The Greatest Homosexual*, 1964. Oil, collage, pencil, and colored pencil on canvas, 80 × 61 in. (203.2 × 154.9 cm). Hirshhorn Museum and Sculpture Garden, Smithsonian Institution, Washington, D.C.

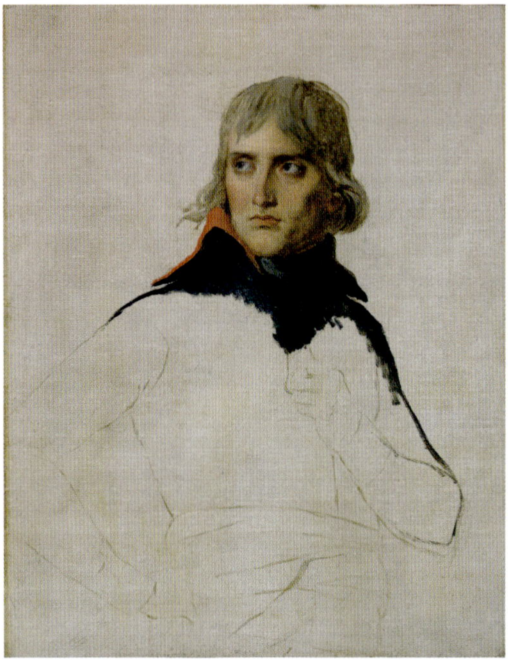

Fig. 38 Jacques-Louis David, *Le général Bonaparte*, c. 1797–98. Oil on canvas, 31⅞ × 25⅝ in. (81 × 65 cm). Musée du Louvre, Paris.

earlier Louis-Ferdinand Céline had remarked that "Bonaparte rather resembles a young lady, fine features, delicate hands à la Fragonard. . . ."[116]

It is quite true, of course, as Butt points out, that in *The Greatest Homosexual*—and, I would argue, in the *French Money* paintings as well—"Rivers's painterly manipulation . . . is not meant as a serious or 'scurrilous' accusation."[117] Even so, the subversive impact of Rivers's allusiveness, implicitly in the one case, more overtly in the other, if only because of the title, was felt no less in France—where the 1960 Mirguet amendment had added homosexuality to the list of "national scourges"—than in the United States, where a period of heavy persecution of homosexuality, regarded during the McCarthy years as a sign of culpable weakness likely to encourage Communist conspiracy, had only recently come to an end.[118] Unsurprisingly, then, the gallery owner Charles Gimpel, in a letter dated July 1964, wrote Rivers to tell him that Joseph Hirshhorn had purchased *The Greatest Homosexual*: "[It] is going into the Greatest Collection of all i.e. Joe H. He is going to ask you to change the title!?!!!"[119] The wealthy American collector was not the only one to be offended by the title. Rivers later recalled receiving a furious letter from a French historian who had seen the picture in Washington. "Never, in all my years of study," he wrote the artist, "have I read that Napoleon was a homosexual." Demanding that the painting be withdrawn from the Hirshhorn Museum's collection, the historian asked how, as Rivers put it, "we Americans would feel coming across a painting of George Washington, the father of *our* country, called, in effect, *The Greatest Cocksucker*."[120]

Rivers was not looking to provoke a scandal on this scale, certainly not with the *French Money* paintings. There, Bonaparte's homosexuality is no more than a suggestion, a witty aside meant for the amusement of a small circle of intimates. Whatever evidence there may be of "inversion" is perceptible more in the composition of the paintings and the treatment of the subject than in any explicit detail. The important point is the desacralization of the hero, the challenge to his authority as the guarantor of national values. For it is by virtue of defending exactly these values that a currency is able to claim legitimacy—as the embodiment, in the economist André Orléan's phrase, of a "primordial debt" that binds the members of society to one another. "If they accept currency in exchange for the goods they sell," Orléan observes, "it is because they have confidence in the sovereign's ability to ensure that the values it upholds are respected."[121] The economy, in other words, is not a separate domain: the value of money rests on other values, be they political, moral, or historical, that are generally shared and that are incarnate in the national hero. In implicitly attacking French history painting, Rivers heaped scorn on the entire system it supports. The doubt he cast on Bonaparte as a figure of authority was liable to spread, undermining the political foundations of the great nation for which he stood, and the stability of the currency that he was understood to guarantee.

Furthermore, in exposing monetary conventions for what they are, mere agreements entered into by members of society that form a basis for common beliefs, Rivers demonstrated how fragile the prevailing assumptions about money, patriotism, sexual behavior, and morality really were. The moment doubt creeps in, even if ever so slightly, it is bound to grow, eventually causing agreements to break down and make what once enjoyed the full authority of a social norm suddenly to seem altogether arbitrary and pointless. In Rivers's *French Money* paintings we find a subtle and illuminating picture of a society to which he nonetheless remained an outsider, as an American artist living for a short time in a country whose language he had not mastered, whose national heroes he did not admire, and whose patriotic values he did not share.

CHAPTER 3

Speculation as Spectacle

In France, the art market entered into a prolonged slump toward the end of 1962. In the United States, by contrast, the 1960s were a time of almost uninterrupted prosperity and accelerating economic growth in the arts. Soon after its emergence in New York galleries in 1962, the pop art craze was swept along by an exceptional wave of rising prices.[1] Quickly it became the symbol of the commodification of art, as much because it trafficked in images of commercial culture and advertising as because it was embraced by collectors. A 1965 *Esquire* article (illustrated by photographs of Andy Warhol, James Rosenquist, Larry Rivers, and Jasper Johns) spoke for many in admitting that "the idea that there are no longer any painters both reputable and short of funds comes as a shock. It is hard to adjust to the rapidity of change in the United States."[2]

The advent of conceptual art at about the same time, in a highly politicized atmosphere colored by strong anti-imperialist and anticapitalist feeling, appeared to many observers as a radical rejection of the extreme commercialism of the art market. The critic Lucy Lippard was a leading exponent of this view. "The artists who are trying to do non-object art are introducing a drastic solution to the problem of artists being bought and sold so easily, along with their art," she argued, noting that this kind of art lent itself less readily to "capitalist marketing devices."[3] In support of this very widely shared opinion, beginning around 1968, critics pointed to a set of physical characteristics common to a large number of works grouped under various rubrics in addition to conceptual art, from performance art to land art and even arte povera. Perishable, invisible, reproducible (or, in the case of earthworks, actually inseparable from a fixed and permanent installation), this art appeared to be "[i]mpossible for collectors to collect, for museums to show, for dealers to handle, for critics to appraise." This led the critic Thomas Messer to conclude in 1969, "it will most likely not be bought or sold."[4] In the case of conceptual art, for example, who would pay for a few words scribbled on a sheet of paper? Who would purchase an idea that one could make one's own simply by reading the artist's statement of it?

Only a couple of years later, however, these same critics were forced to admit that they were wrong: conceptual art was being exhibited, sold, and collected, particularly on the European market. "All we can do today," Catherine Millet conceded in 1971, "is acknowledge the success of conceptual art, its happy career on the gallery circuit, the number of international exhibits that have been devoted to it."[5] In their astonishment, observers were inclined even to exaggerate the commercial success of the movement. "Instead of being quite unusable within the sinister structure of the art market," one writer claimed the following year, "an enormous amount of money has been made out of conceptual art."[6] For the most politically committed of the movement's supporters, the disappointment that followed its unexpected profitability was commensurate with the hopes it had initially aroused.[7]

Three decades later, the historian Frances Colpitt described the supposed failure of "dematerialization" to subvert the traditional artistic economy as a "myth," arguing that anticommercial bias played little or no role in the thinking of the first generation of conceptual artists, and that it was mainly owing to the efforts of leftist critics such as Lippard, Gregory Battcock, Ursula Meyer, and Barbara Rose that the idea gained currency, subsequently being adopted with reservations by a few artists from 1969 onward.[8] Colpitt's findings were corroborated by the research of another historian, Alexander Alberro, on the career of Seth Siegelaub, a prominent dealer in conceptual art. Alberro uncovered evidence of an elaborate publicity strategy that had been put into effect from the movement's beginnings.[9] What is more, Siegelaub made no secret of his motives: "My interest as a businessman," he said more than once, "isn't in circumventing the commercial system. . . . Artists having their work go out as printed matter can be just as viable as selling [Kenneth] Nolands."[10]

My purpose here is not to take sides in the debate over the commercial or anticommercial nature of conceptual art. I wish instead to examine conceptual art in relation to the economic life of the period. Hopes that the dematerialization of art would make it possible to break free of market constraints seem to have been based on a view of the economy that was very largely outmoded by the late 1960s. When Barbara Rose, in an article in *New York Magazine* in March 1969, claimed that "[a]rtists today are virtually fleeing the art world and the political economy on which it rests,"[11] she was referring to a commodity-based economy, fed by the accumulation of consumer goods required by the system of production and distribution that produced the spectacular growth of the decades immediately following the war. She ignored a sector of the economy already assured of a bright future: the financial economy—the immaterial economy par excellence. What could be more conceptual than an economy founded on contract alone, on a form of credit ("representative" or "bank" money) that circulates through a manipulation of accounting entries without ever having to assume material form? What could please a conceptual artist more than stock shares and financial derivatives—purely speculative instruments of increasing sophistication, each one more removed from an underlying reality than the last—if not the phenomenon of inflation itself, through which money begets money without any productive human intervention? In the spring of 1969, the very moment when Rose wrote that "[a] great deal of the new art cannot be bought, sold, owned or traded like a blue-chip investment,"[12] some American artists were making investment, sales, and money the very basis of their work.

Indeed, 1969 was the year when the vogue for so-called monetary art reached its height, with the success of the exhibit *The Art of Money* at the Chelsea Gallery in New York that spring.[13] There, in addition to one of Warhol's *Dollar Bill* drawings and one of Rivers's *French Money* paintings, a number of variations on the banknote theme were displayed, including the latest *Accumulation* by Arman. The main attraction, highlighted in the advertisement for the show, was Abraham Lubelski's *Sculptural Daydream*, a minimalist cube composed entirely of piles of dollar bills amounting to a quarter of a million dollars.

In the work of conceptual artists the theme of money took a less literal form that sprang from the dematerialization of transactions. The likening of art to a financial security, long a commonplace among journalists and economists, had now become a source of inspiration for artists themselves. In what follows I look at six of them. Whereas Bernar Venet and Dennis Oppenheim took finance as their subject, converting its mathematical abstractions into a visual and plastic material, Les Levine, Robert Morris, Dan Graham, and Lee Lozano entered into the life of the stock market as agents in their own right.

ART AS AN INVESTMENT

The British art historian Gerald Reitlinger, introducing the third and final volume of his influential *The Economics of Taste*, devoted to the art market during the 1960s, expressed alarm at what he considered to be one of the most pernicious developments of that decade: the increasingly widespread idea that art can legitimately be regarded as a financial investment. Taking aim at the many authors of books and articles who "teach the tyro not how to acquire a discriminating taste, but how to get a return on his money," he held these "propagandists" responsible for "the deliberate and indoctrinated confusion of artistic appreciation with self-interest." "The lesser slump of 1968–69," Reitlinger argued, "produced a paradox which threatened to become an orthodoxy. It is that works of art go up in proportion as capital values, profits and dividends decline, that as substitutes for money, works of art are not liable to the same erosions as money itself."[14] By the end of the 1960s, to consider art not merely as an investment, but as a particularly profitable investment, had in fact become, if not quite an orthodoxy, as Reitlinger claimed, at the very least a staple of popular writing about economics. "Art has long been recognized as a sound area of investment," a columnist for the *Montreal Gazette* observed, "and the sums of money made in the art markets of the world have at times been staggering."[15] As early as

1961, a *Washington Post* critic had remarked that "'art as an investment' has become a household phrase."[16]

And no wonder, for the phenomenon of investing in art had taken root still earlier, in the mid-1950s. In the United States, a December 1955 article in *Fortune* magazine entitled "The Great International Art Market" can be seen in retrospect to have been a harbinger. Taking the already hackneyed example of Impressionist paintings sold for a pittance at the end of the nineteenth century that now fetched hundreds of thousands of dollars, the authors maintained it was possible to "draw useful parallels between investment in the art market and investment in the stock market."[17] Speaking of works of art as "commodities," they suggested that the art market combined risk with opportunities for profit in exactly the same way as financial markets. Thus Old Masters were the equivalent of gilt-edged securities, virtually risk-free investments—in the language of financiers, "as good as gold, or better." The Impressionists were blue-chip investments, the most profitable homes for money at any given moment. Contemporary artists were speculative investments ("growth issues"), riskier but over time possibly more profitable still; Jackson Pollock, Ad Reinhardt, and Bernard Buffet were cited as examples.[18]

The chief argument advanced to explain the superiority of art over any other form of investment was that art, like a precious metal, is a hedge against inflation—a central preoccupation in the climate of rising prices that emerged a few years later. But specific tax advantages made art a potentially lucrative investment as well. In the United States, a work of art donated to a nonprofit institution was tax-deductible at its fair market value. A work purchased by a collector and then given a few years later to a museum might therefore qualify for a tax credit greater than the purchase price if in the interval its trading price had gone up. This increase was all but assured, according to the authors of the *Fortune* article, because the art market was booming. "From the broadest point of view," they concluded, "art *is* an investment: the prime investment that men of great wealth can make."[19]

In the late 1950s, two highly publicized public auctions in New York—the first in November 1957, involving the trove of Impressionist works amassed by the Franco-American banker Georges Lurcy, succeeded a year later by the American hotelier and real estate investor Arnold Kirkeby's collection of French modern art—gave weight to this claim by realizing record prices. "Investment has been called an art; it's less usual to think of art as an investment," the *New York Times* noted. "But in 1957 the works of postimpressionists [*sic*] such as Gauguin, Renoir, Matisse, Monet, Dufy, Seurat, and van Gogh turned out to be among the world's best investments."[20] During the following decade this new state of affairs was more and more frequently acknowledged in the press. The comparison, disparaging more often than not, between a work of art and a tradable financial asset was hardly new: one finds it in Émile Zola, for example, in the late nineteenth century.[21] The true novelty had to do with the fact that this idea was now not only taken seriously by economists, but regarded by financial experts as a rigorously established proposition having immediate practical consequences for investors.

Perhaps the most prominent of these experts was the economist and journalist Sylvia Porter, a respected investment advisor whose columns were syndicated in newspapers throughout the United States. As late as 1966, she still looked askance at the notion of art as an investment, considering it a "fad" that survived mainly because it was "aggressively publicized and promoted," and urged her readers to exercise caution.[22] Several more years of rising prices for art convinced her otherwise. By the end of the decade her growing interest in what she called "far-out investments" had prompted her to write a regular column about how to profit from nonconventional assets, foremost among them works of art. "Today's 'smart money,'" she noted in 1969, "is recoiling with horror from such fixed-income investments as bonds and savings accounts, and is also fleeing world-famous corporation stocks which appear to have only modest growth potential. Instead, the smart money is searching for both tangible hedges against inflation and escape hatches from federal taxes."[23]

Making money in the domain of art was within the reach of all her readers, Porter insisted, not only connoisseurs: "What's behind the art boom? How can *you* buy into it—with the expectation of making significant profits when *you* resell?"[24] The ordinary investor had only to follow the advice that she liberally dispensed in her many columns. The Barbizon School, she explained, was now "out of vogue" (among its members she doubtfully included the academic painter William Bouguereau, misspelled "Bougereau"). Instead, she strongly recommended buying "any good American painting of a subject of unusual historical, social, or geographical interest," as well as primitive Oceanian engravings and small Mediterranean bronzes—all these were "bound to rise."[25] The same enterprising tone characterized advertisements for publications such as the *Art Market Guide and Forecaster*, which promised to teach subscribers "How to Invest for *Super*-Profits in Art."[26] The booklet *Taxes and Art*, published by the New York art dealer French and Company in 1961, was aimed at ordinary investors looking to take advantage of tax legislation with a view to making patronage of the arts both a charitable and a financially attractive activity.[27]

The appeal of art as an investment vehicle, although it was particularly pronounced in the United States, was felt wherever prices for art were sharply increasing. In Europe, yearbooks and specialist periodicals began to appear in the 1960s.[28] The uniformity in outlook across national markets is remarkable. Everywhere emphasis was placed chiefly on art's value as a rampart against inflation. But it was also seen as an expanding market owing to the rise in living standards and to the "elevation of standards of culture" that followed from it, inevitably encouraging the "development of a taste for painting."[29] Most authors were nonetheless careful to forestall charges of cynicism by arguing, as Gilbert de Knyff did, that "the contradiction between the essential freedoms of the fine arts and the constraints imposed by government management of the economy is only apparent,"[30] and that buying art as an investment in no way prevents the buyer from taking aesthetic pleasure in it. To the contrary, as André Parinaud put it in his preface to Mayer's international yearbook of art sales for 1964, the "quoted value . . . is akin to a proof of genius." So far from being the result of a "lottery," current market price reflects better than any other indicator the real artistic value of a work over time. What is recognized to have true artistic quality will necessarily prove to be an attractive financial investment. Conversely, price is bound to be the most reliable signal of artistic value: "In the extreme case one might say that a work for which a price is not, and cannot be, quoted does not matter. It points to something beyond the world we live in. No better way of maintaining the world of values has been found than by nourishing it with the prices of things."[31]

The most striking thing about these publications, however, is the presumptively scientific method of analysis they brought to bear on the art market. The promotion of expertise and the claim to quantitative objectivity made it possible to devise a "ranking system" whose various grades and classifications were first publicized in the 1950s.[32] If the *Art Market Guide and Forecaster* actually was able to spot the "new unknowns" and "rediscovered masters" before anyone else, then there was no longer any place left for intuition. By employing "the same disciplined analytical methods and careful research technology used by successful *stock market* investors," the purchase of art could be established on a "factual, no-nonsense basis."[33] Recent studies have shown that the popularity of the first speculative art investment funds in the 1960s and 1970s depended on creating elaborate databases and increasingly sophisticated analytical tools that gradually convinced investors of the transparency of information and the trustworthiness of predictions.[34]

The scientific pretensions of those who urged the value of art as an investment were bolstered by the numerical tables, charts, and graphs that routinely accompanied their writings and presentations (figs. 39–40).[35] These visual displays are remarkable not only because they illustrate the first incursions of statistical and economic analysis into the domain of art, but also because they were a result, in Reitlinger's justly skeptical phrase, of "fooling around with computers to produce an allegedly scientific averaging of a given painter's prices."[36] As key instruments of persuasion, graphic representations were deliberately manipulated to support the claim that, on the one hand, works of art can be considered the equivalent of shares and that, on the other hand, they are in both the short and the long term more profitable than any rival investment portfolio. The almost invariable use of continuous lines to represent what was in fact only a small number of separate public sales was a deeply misleading way of producing a plausible analogue of the historical course of a stock price. Moreover, these graphics typically covered long periods without taking inflation into account. The curves they

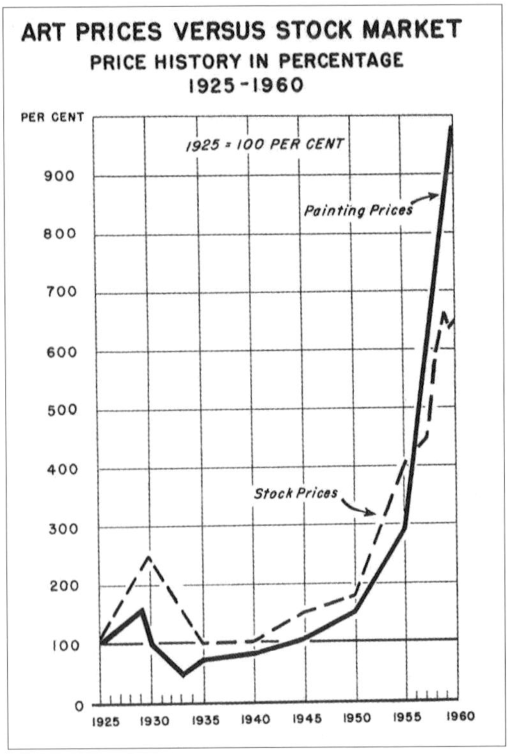

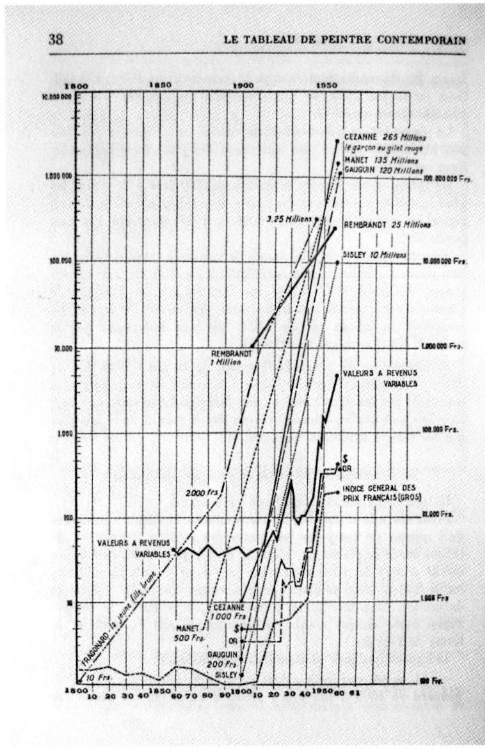

Fig. 39 Chart published in Richard H. Rush, *Art as an Investment* (Englewood Cliffs, N.J.: Prentice-Hall, 1961), 385.

Fig. 40 Chart published in Maurice Pariat, *Le tableau de peintre contemporain comme valeur de placement* (Paris: R. Pichon/R. Durand-Auzias, 1961), 38.

traced therefore rose more steeply than actual stock price curves, which reflected the corresponding rise in the consumer price index. Making matters still worse, the underlying analysis was contaminated by a patent retrospective selection bias: the graphics did not display information concerning all works sold at a given moment, only a "representative" sampling that, in reality, was made from a small pool of the most famous artists. As a coauthor of the pioneering Times-Sotheby's Index unwittingly revealed, "[t]he Impressionist index, for instance, is based on the work of six artists: Monet, Renoir, Sisley, Pissarro, Fantin-Latour, and Boudin."[37]

Visual displays of this kind nonetheless had a considerable impact in the 1960s, fooling even informed readers. The *Wall Street Journal*, reviewing Richard H. Rush's 1961 book *Art as an Investment* (see fig. 39), was impressed that it "almost succeeded in applying Dow-Jones averaging techniques to the suddenly expanding world of art brokerage."[38] Eight years later, in 1969, the editors of *Art News* were still marveling at the "impressive graphs in the shape of an ascending slalom run" published in the Times-Sotheby's Index.[39] Already at the turn of the decade, in 1960, even the staid journal *Art in America* had launched its own "Market Letter," reporting sales figures and making purchase recommendations in the manner of a Wall Street broker. The time was not yet ripe, however. The letter was almost at once discontinued in the face of readers' indignation.[40]

More rigorous analysis subsequently showed that, in exchange for a very high level of risk, works of art actually promised only a rather modest return on investment.[41] In the meantime, however, certainly until the mid-1970s, the inadequate sampling methods endorsed by apparently scientific studies managed to convince the whole of the artistic community that the opposite was true, and little by little economistic terminology and reasoning came to be adopted by critics, collectors, and artists alike. When Robert Scull and Leon Kraushar compared the pop art works they were purchasing in the mid-1960s to shares of AT&T and IBM stock, they seemed to be echoing the authors of the 1955 *Fortune* article ("General Motors has done a little better than Cézanne, but not so well as Renoir").[42] Many years later, the artist Allan Kaprow distinctly recalled where he first came across this idea: "I remember one particular article in *Fortune* magazine that advised collectors how to make more money buying modern art than they could in the stock market. And they actually gave tables of appreciation over a five-year period. Like, buy Larry Rivers because it was no longer affordable to buy Pollock or Newman or de Kooning. And the art market began to pick up everywhere, including a market for work by younger artists."[43]

Kaprow's famous 1964 essay "The Artist as a Man of the World" painted a new portrait of the artist in the age of pop: far from having to endure the poverty and isolation romanticized by the abstract expressionists, the artist was now perfectly integrated into the economic and social milieu of the upper-middle class. From the collector's point of view, thanks to tax advantages, a "good investment" in art might prove to be a "pleasant sort of philanthropy."[44] The old and new clichés associated with the art world of the period are brilliantly encapsulated in a cartoon by Whitney Darrow Jr. that appeared in the February 1963 issue of *Art in America* (fig. 41). A bourgeois collector is shown paying a visit to an unkempt artist (probably an abstract painter) in his attic studio. Instead of looking at the canvases, however, he addresses the artist in the manner of a businessman discussing investments with his banker: "Show me something about 36" × 48" in blues

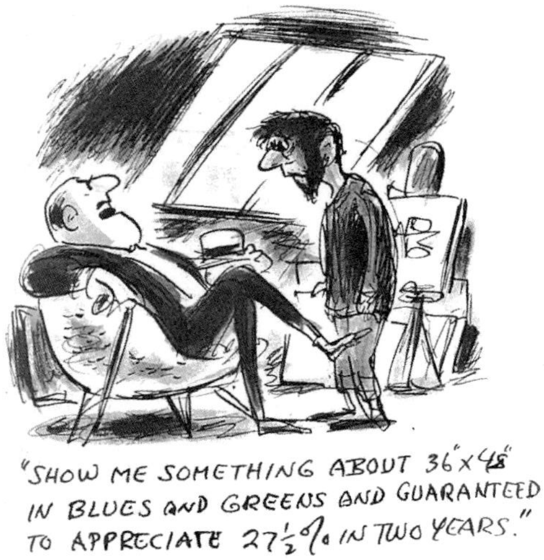

Fig. 41 Cartoon by Whitney Darrow Jr., in *Art in America* 51, no. 2 (1963): 25.

and greens and guaranteed to appreciate 27½% in two years." Here, the speculative potential of a painting is mentioned in the same breath as the format and palette, as though it, too, were a physical characteristic of a work of art. Rightly or wrongly, artists themselves were convinced that the price of art was bound to rise. In John Baldessari's *Information Paintings Never Completed* (1969)—unrealized works that were destined to remain nothing more than ideas—the first such work asserts: "This painting will last and increase in value."[45] Whether art was celebrated or condemned, everyone was persuaded that no investment was more profitable.

PERFORMANCES AT THE NEW YORK STOCK EXCHANGE

The vogue for art as an investment did more than transform the popular image of the artist and lend credence in the minds of a great many people to the analogy between art and rising asset values. It also suggested a new visual dimension to artists themselves. The world of the stock exchange—its graphs, its tables of figures, and its trading floors—now came to be associated with the world of art. Often regarded as the supreme manifestation of technological rationality and the compression of space-time, the financial sphere presented conceptual artists with a vast unexplored terrain while at the same time providing them with the sources of a novel plastic art, cold, dry, mathematized. Bernar Venet and Dennis Oppenheim stand out among a group of artists on the New York scene in the late 1960s who had the idea of making this visual universe its own stage. Their work, at the boundary between conceptual art and performance art, was a peculiar kind of theater, a balancing act made all the more difficult by the risk inherent in treating speculation as a spectacle: in adopting its professional codes and working on-site, artists were in danger of falling under the spell cast by the stock exchange itself, of becoming fascinated by the object of their own gaze. For this reason, their works tended sometimes to reinforce the process of ideological legitimation associated with a system of licensed wagering guided by mathematical models amid the controlled frenzy of the trading session.

Bernar Venet and the Financial Economy as a Scientific Enterprise

Beginning in 1968, by which point works of art were firmly identified in the popular mind with financial investment, Bernar Venet made the stock exchange the focus of a series of works that assumed a great variety of forms over the next two years. One of the first consisted of a panel-mounted photographic enlargement of the "American Stock Exchange Transactions" listing in the *Wall Street Journal* (*WSJ*). There followed more than thirty such "blow-ups," to use the artist's favored term, of extracts from the financial columns of the *WSJ*, *New York Times*, and *Newsweek* (figs. 42–43), some of them in numbered editions.[46] These static images were often displayed, especially in 1969–70, alongside works having a serial element. For a group

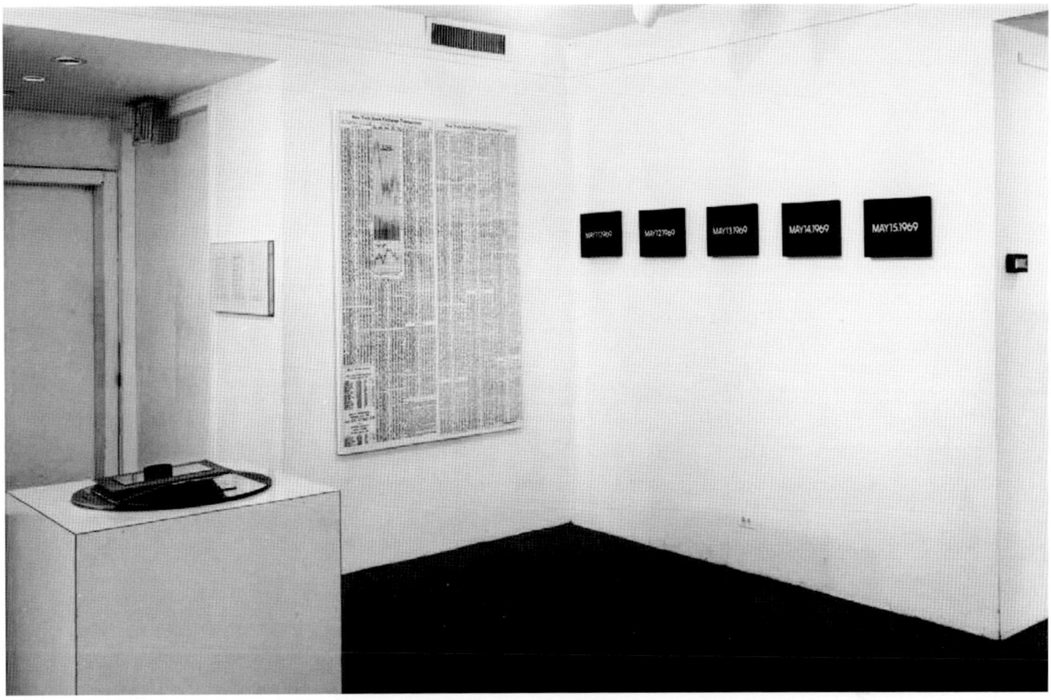

Fig. 42 Partial view of the installation of *Language III*, an exhibition at the Dwan Gallery, New York, May 24–June 18, 1969. Photo by Walter J. Russell. Dwan Gallery records, Archives of American Art, Smithsonian Institution, series 2, box 4, folder 1.

show put together by Lucy Lippard at the Paula Cooper Gallery in the spring of 1969, for example, Venet stapled together a week's worth of issues of the *WSJ* between two plywood panels painted black to suggest a bound volume of copies (fig. 44).[47] In conjunction with this event, he sent an issue of the same paper to twenty-five personal acquaintances and to twenty-five people selected at random from the New York City phone book.[48] He also took out subscriptions for a small number of figures in the art world (thus, in January 1970 he wrote to Lippard asking if she had been "receiving all the issues of the Wall Street Journal during one entire month").[49] Later that year, as part of his solo exhibition at the Museum Haus Lange in Krefeld, West Germany, Venet unveiled a telephone that, by dialing a certain number, made it possible to obtain stock quotes in real time.[50] For the large group exhibition *Information*, held at the Museum of Modern Art in New York in the summer of 1970, the artist installed a television on the floor of the gallery. The catalogue informed viewers that it "will be turned on whenever Stock Market and classroom programs are presented. The rest of the time the TV will be turned off."[51] Not long afterward, Venet cast himself in a cameo role: a photograph in the February 1972 issue of the French magazine *Chroniques de l'art vivant* showed him reading the *WSJ*.[52]

Bernar Venet—he dropped the final *d* from his first name in the 1950s in order to distinguish himself from Bernard Buffet, whom he much admired—was born in Château-Arnoux in 1941 and began his career in Nice, where the art scene was dominated by the Nouveaux Réalistes and Fluxus.[53] His early works reflected an interest in abstraction and the use of raw materials.

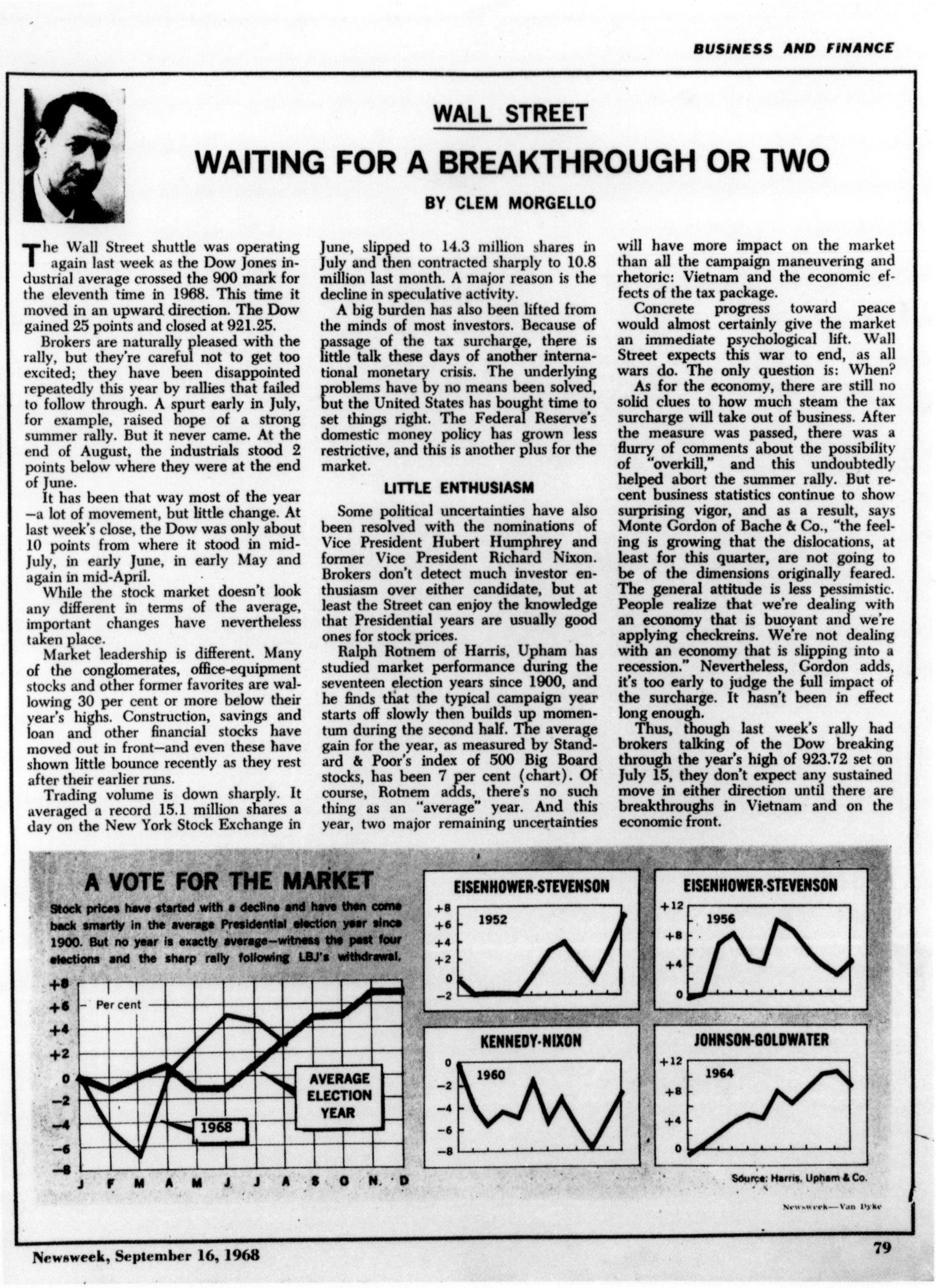

BUSINESS AND FINANCE

WALL STREET

WAITING FOR A BREAKTHROUGH OR TWO

BY CLEM MORGELLO

The Wall Street shuttle was operating again last week as the Dow Jones industrial average crossed the 900 mark for the eleventh time in 1968. This time it moved in an upward direction. The Dow gained 25 points and closed at 921.25.

Brokers are naturally pleased with the rally, but they're careful not to get too excited; they have been disappointed repeatedly this year by rallies that failed to follow through. A spurt early in July, for example, raised hope of a strong summer rally. But it never came. At the end of August, the industrials stood 2 points below where they were at the end of June.

It has been that way most of the year—a lot of movement, but little change. At last week's close, the Dow was only about 10 points from where it stood in mid-July, in early June, in early May and again in mid-April.

While the stock market doesn't look any different in terms of the average, important changes have nevertheless taken place.

Market leadership is different. Many of the conglomerates, office-equipment stocks and other former favorites are wallowing 30 per cent or more below their year's highs. Construction, savings and loan and other financial stocks have moved out in front—and even these have shown little bounce recently as they rest after their earlier runs.

Trading volume is down sharply. It averaged a record 15.1 million shares a day on the New York Stock Exchange in June, slipped to 14.3 million shares in July and then contracted sharply to 10.8 million last month. A major reason is the decline in speculative activity.

A big burden has also been lifted from the minds of most investors. Because of passage of the tax surcharge, there is little talk these days of another international monetary crisis. The underlying problems have by no means been solved, but the United States has bought time to set things right. The Federal Reserve's domestic money policy has grown less restrictive, and this is another plus for the market.

LITTLE ENTHUSIASM

Some political uncertainties have also been resolved with the nominations of Vice President Hubert Humphrey and former Vice President Richard Nixon. Brokers don't detect much investor enthusiasm over either candidate, but at least the Street can enjoy the knowledge that Presidential years are usually good ones for stock prices.

Ralph Rotnem of Harris, Upham has studied market performance during the seventeen election years since 1900, and he finds that the typical campaign year starts off slowly then builds up momentum during the second half. The average gain for the year, as measured by Standard & Poor's index of 500 Big Board stocks, has been 7 per cent (chart). Of course, Rotnem adds, there's no such thing as an "average" year. And this year, two major remaining uncertainties will have more impact on the market than all the campaign maneuvering and rhetoric: Vietnam and the economic effects of the tax package.

Concrete progress toward peace would almost certainly give the market an immediate psychological lift. Wall Street expects this war to end, as all wars do. The only question is: When?

As for the economy, there are still no solid clues to how much steam the tax surcharge will take out of business. After the measure was passed, there was a flurry of comments about the possibility of "overkill," and this undoubtedly helped abort the summer rally. But recent business statistics continue to show surprising vigor, and as a result, says Monte Gordon of Bache & Co., "the feeling is growing that the dislocations, at least for this quarter, are not going to be of the dimensions originally feared. The general attitude is less pessimistic. People realize that we're dealing with an economy that is buoyant and we're applying checkreins. We're not dealing with an economy that is slipping into a recession." Nevertheless, Gordon adds, it's too early to judge the full impact of the surcharge. It hasn't been in effect long enough.

Thus, though last week's rally had brokers talking of the Dow breaking through the year's high of 923.72 set on July 15, they don't expect any sustained move in either direction until there are breakthroughs in Vietnam and on the economic front.

Newsweek, September 16, 1968 79

Fig. 43 Bernar Venet, *Waiting for a Breakthrough or Two*, 1969. Photographic enlargement of a page of *Newsweek* (September 16, 1968), 39¼ × 29 in. (99.8 × 73.7 cm). Edition of 55 copies, plus 25 signed and numbered, published by Bruno Bischofberger Gallery, Zurich.

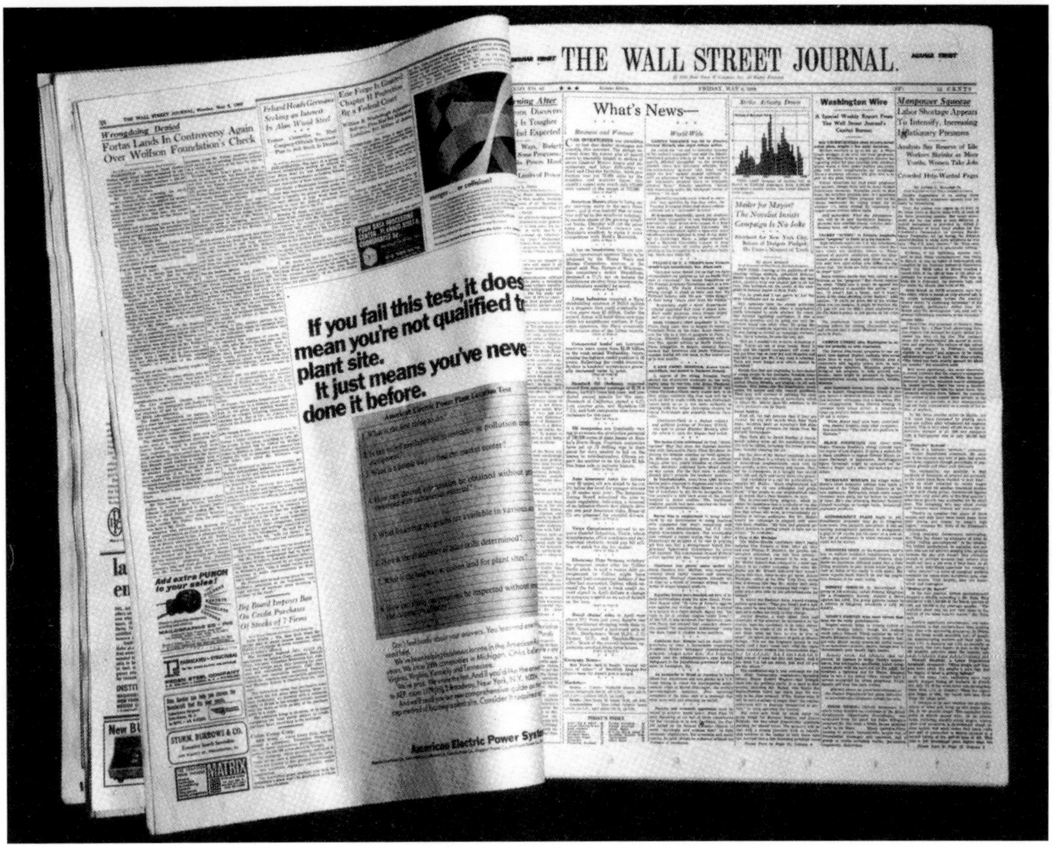

Fig. 44 Bernar Venet, *One Week of the "Wall Street Journal,"* 1969. Newspapers stapled inside a painted plywood cover.

In 1966, he moved to New York with help from his friend Arman, who put him up in his studio apartment for a time and introduced him to a circle of friends that included artists, critics, and collectors.[54] Here, his work took a more conceptual turn. One of his first projects involved annotating technical illustrations of various objects by means of hand-drawn diagrams cataloguing their mathematical, physical, and chemical properties.

Venet described this pivotal period as a gradual but thoroughgoing rejection of all forms of subjectivity in art. "My work," he declared in July 1967, "is a manifesto against aesthetics, against the expression of the individual's personality."[55] Increasingly preoccupied with the "hard" sciences, whose cold objectivity provided him with material that was devoid of expressiveness and personal character, he ended up perfecting a spare style that relied on photographic enlargements of pages from published mathematical and scientific works, chosen precisely, or so it appeared, for the complexity of their notation, comprehensible only to experts. The value of the fragments he reproduced—from the papers of the information theorist Robert Ash, the set theory of the Bourbaki group, and the theoretical physics of Martin Krieger—was not aesthetic; it depended exclusively on the fact that they transmitted objective and scientifically useful information.[56] As Venet put it in a 1971 interview, "I do not present my work as art, but I present mathematics and other scientific disciplines for what they are, *i.e.*, pure knowledge as such."[57] From a formal point of view, the artist disclaimed any aesthetic purpose, contenting himself instead with a mode of display that would most effectively "facilitate apprehension of the message" without modifying its meaning.[58]

Venet sought the advice of specialists in selecting results that were representative of the most recent advances in various fields. Jack Ullman, a physicist at Columbia University whom he met in January 1967, advised him in consultation with colleagues in mathematics and the physical sciences.[59] With regard to finance, and the workings of the New York Stock Exchange (NYSE) in particular, Venet looked to his friend Paul Schups, a francophone art collector working on Wall Street, who recommended the commentary of the financial analyst Clem Morgello in *Newsweek*.[60] Venet subsequently did blow-ups of all the articles Morgello published in 1969. The artist maintained that he was seeking not only to convey a sense of the objectivity of scientific research, but also to exploit its imagery, which (drawing on the semiotic theory developed by the cartographer Jacques Bertin) he described as "monosemic" in the sense that it exhibits "only one level of signification." Graphs, tables, diagrams, and mathematical symbols appeared to him to be the best examples of such "rational" imagery because they provide "a simplified and abstract representation of an object from the outside world as a message in which *semantics take over from aesthetics*."[61] In this way two things were unambiguously asserted: on the one hand, a principle of aesthetic neutrality and inexpressiveness, and, on the other, a view of science as the privileged domain of objective knowledge. On both these points, however, Venet's works concerning the New York Stock Exchange raise important problems that reveal the ambivalence of conceptual artists' attitudes toward the financial world in the late 1960s.

With regard to the first point, the technique of photographic enlargement—no less than the other techniques that Venet experimented with—is not so easily disentangled from formal and expressive considerations as he seems to have imagined. "Blown-up photographs have a built-in aesthetic property," the critic and curator Lawrence Alloway pointed out in a March 1970 article. "As print expands in size, for example, little imperfections show up in the characters and oddities in the spacing between letters open before our eyes, factors of which we are unaware when reading. . . . Although [Venet] is indifferent to the aesthetic status of his work, to which [he] assigns a didactic function, the spectator has ways of subverting (or enlarging) the artist's intention."[62] Evidently photographic enlargement does not solely have the effect, as Venet supposed, of improving the legibility of printed characters; it creates a new form of plastic art. Venet himself later admitted that he had sometimes been attracted by the look of such blow-ups: "The few works that I made [about the Stock Exchange] were chosen in a very arbitrary manner and, I confess, at the risk of contradicting myself, perhaps also for their visual originality. To enrich, as it were, the detail of my propositions overall, to enrich them at the level of content, of course, but I also found the technicity of this imagery and the various configurations of these lists of figures interesting in themselves."[63]

The dryly technical visual appearance of these works was meant to have as little in common with traditional artistic forms as possible.[64] In this respect, Venet resembled many other conceptual artists of the period who were interested in a kind of creativity that had nothing to do with pleasing the eye; renouncing sensual pleasure, they looked for inspiration to definitions, numbers, and symbols, and the ways in which they could be combined to transmit information in a formalized and impersonal manner.[65] Nevertheless the graphs, the statistical tables, the charts of stock performance these artists consulted were not as far removed from the artistic idiom of the late 1960s as they seemed to imagine. As we saw earlier, the penetration of the artistic sphere by the visual appendices of economic theory was just then at its height. When Venet exhibited his blow-ups of the financial columns of the *New York Times* in the late spring of 1969 at the Dwan Gallery in New York (see fig. 42), the shift of perspective he brought about mirrored the one that the *Times* had already introduced by discussing art in its financial pages. At a time when economists were using works of art to chart price movements, Venet made works of art out of price-movement charts. In doing this, he sought to show that such works could compete with, and indeed replace, "black-and-white reproductions of good paintings."[66]

On closer inspection, however, it becomes clear that the tools of financial analysis are hardly neutral or inexpressive. Photographic reproduction captures the distinctive style and the characteristic subject of a painting. Quantitative graphics (see figs. 39–40) tell another and no less fascinating story, not of the evolution of styles, but of the amassing of fortunes and the vagaries of careers and reputations. Notwithstanding Venet's strenuous efforts to eliminate all traces of ambiguity and emotion from his works, the columns of stock prices he replicates, and the graphs plotting their rise and fall, betray a feverish excitement every bit as intense as the feeling that inspires the general public's fascination for art, considering not only the aesthetic pleasure that art gives but also, in Barbara Rose's phrase, "the sensation created by the huge sums of money attached to art now."[67]

The artistic forms Venet employed were calculated to reinforce the dramatic aspect of financial markets. The formats selected for the blow-ups, roughly 180 centimeters (or about 70 inches) high, greatly magnified the graphs and columns of figures displayed (see fig. 42). The succession of copies of the *Wall Street Journal*, whether bound in the form of a book for purposes of exhibition, as in his work *One Week of the "Wall Street Journal"* (see fig. 44), or sent to a select list of recipients every day through the mail, imposed a narrative dimension on the constant stream of ephemeral financial information by creating a mood of anticipation, suspense, and, finally, resolution. The communication of financial information in real time by television or telephone within the gallery itself created an atmosphere

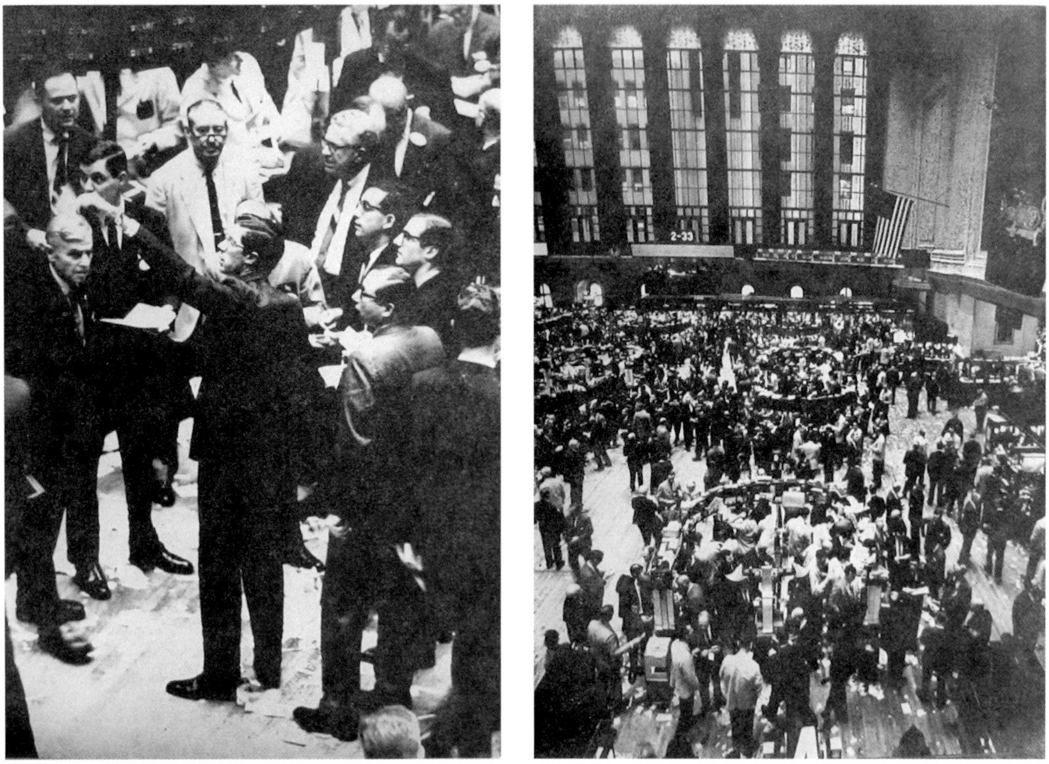

Fig. 45 Bernar Venet, *Inside New York Stock Exchange Building*, May 1969. Two black-and-white photographs, dimensions variable.

suggesting the chronic state of excitement in which stock exchanges operate throughout the world, twenty-four hours a day.

The explicitly dramatic and theatrical dimension of financial markets particularly interested Venet. In 1968, he sent invitations to his circle of acquaintances in the New York art world, asking them to come to Wall Street at a given date and hour to attend a session of the NYSE.[68] As it turned out, the "performance" he promised could not take place since nonprofessional groups were denied entry to the Stock Exchange during trading hours. Venet had to settle for photographing activity on the floor of the Exchange the following year, in May 1969 (fig. 45). Looking back on this project many years later, Venet still vividly recalled the high hopes he had for it:

> I wanted [my guests] to experience a reality very different from the one we're always presented with by the world of art. I intended for them to be plunged into a strange and unfamiliar atmosphere in which they would discover the world of financial transactions and experience the frenzy, the agitation, the exaltation, and the periodic exasperation, an experience that would lack none of the drama of theatrical constructions built on artifice, the drama of caricature and simulated spectacle. By proposing this other type of event, I hoped to move performance into a new kind of space without the principal "actors" being aware of it. I was proposing that the public enter the zone of real action.[69]

The world of finance, far from being "dry and rigid, cold, and objective,"[70] as Venet described it in one interview, appears here as a theater of anxiety and unpredictable mood swings. One sees this clearly in the May 1969 photographs (see fig. 45), which capture the tense faces of men in dark business suits and the immensity of the hall in which crowds of nervous speculators bustle about. The art historian Alberto Toscano has recently called attention to the challenge posed by modern financial markets to older theatrical conventions, drawing in large part on an unfinished play by Bertolt Brecht about the Chicago Mercantile Exchange—a choice of subject that required what Brecht called "a new dramatic and theatrical form" capable of accommodating the "cyclical crises," "abortive actions," and "fields of force" generated by the collective decisions of groups of anonymous traders.[71]

For Venet, staging the activity of a stock exchange meant looking at the behavior of financiers themselves, eager to arouse the admiration of readers who followed their exploits in the financial press. The success of Clem Morgello's reporting, for example, is wholly due to his talent as a narrator, to his ability to transform financial news into tales of suspense, breathlessly told under titles such as "Why Some Stocks Go Up," "Story of a Hot Stock," and "Waiting for a Breakthrough or Two." The numbers that fill his columns are no longer the arid artifacts of corporate accountancy; here, transformed by the storyteller's art, they leap off the page. The capitalization of American Research and Development Corporation "[b]y the end of last year was worth a fantastic $266 million," Morgello marvels. "That's an increase of 441,000 percent, well beyond anyone's dreams of avarice."[72] Under the cover of a neutral and apoetic subject, Venet uses such material to imbue the New York Stock Exchange, and financial markets generally, with a mythical aura. For aesthetic pleasure, he substitutes another kind—the delight that is born of the imagination, fed by fantasies of vast fortunes won and lost on the market.

Venet's other guiding idea, that the value of science is uniquely bound up with its ability to transmit objective knowledge, poses no less of a problem. The critic Joseph Masheck, commenting on Venet's 1971 retrospective exhibition, remarked on the manifest failure of the undertaking: in every case, the information highlighted by the artist is too fragmentary, and either too technical or too trivial for the work to have any didactic value.[73] The art historian Christian Besson, for his part, observed that because most viewers are incapable of understanding the extracts they are given to look at, they content themselves with "noting that [they] belong to a certain genre, the scientific text."[74] Far from presenting specific scientific results in a transparent manner, Venet's works do no more than gesture in the direction of science in general. They rely on easily identifiable visual stereotypes that implicitly affirm the epistemic authority of the displayed text.

Although the use of rationalistic imagery, by contrast with the subjectivity of artistic expression, relies on a historical notion of scientific objectivity,[75] unwittingly it calls to mind the sense of inferiority that the social sciences have sought to overcome by imitating the technical rigor of the physical sciences.[76] Venet, without knowing it, exposes the ideological ambition to acquire scientific legitimacy through recourse to formalized codes. Why otherwise should the stock exchange, which is to say the institutional symbol of financial analysis, be a subject of special interest? Is finance really a branch of science in the strict sense, on the same level as computational mathematics and theoretical physics, that produces "objective knowledge of the world"?[77] Even in the late 1960s, a time of political confrontation and sharp ideological divisions, finance seemed to Venet to be uncontaminated by partisan feeling and opinion. Queried on this point in a recent interview, the artist made it clear that his turn toward finance was in no way influenced by current events; it derived instead from an interest in pure mathematics, of which finance seemed to him to constitute one of its most successful applications.[78]

The mathematization of economic behavior—particularly in relation to the monetary economy and finance—had, for two decades, already been at the forefront of the attempt to make economics a genuinely scientific discipline. Milton Friedman, in *Essays in Positive Economics* (1953), was one of the first to openly plead for the development of purely formal and descriptive tools of analysis, uncorrupted by politics. Economic behavior was no longer to be seen as the product of conflicting political values, but as a branch of human activity subject to a set of natural laws that in large part remained to be discovered. "Positive economics is in principle independent of any particular ethical position or normative judgments," Friedman held; it aims to be "an 'objective' science, in precisely the same sense as any of the physical sciences."[79] In every area of economic life, from the money supply to exchange rates, it is necessary as far as possible to allow the relevant laws to operate automatically, free from interference by the often misguided makers of public policy. This requires, in particular, that speculation be recognized as a stabilizing force that works to assure the smooth functioning of market mechanisms.[80] Nowhere is the essentially ideological purpose of mathematical formalization, in permitting economics to be regarded as a source of pure objective knowledge, clearer than in its fundamentally undemocratic implication that politics—and therefore elected representatives—have no role to play in managing the economy. Henceforth, only trained experts are qualified to intervene. The visual identity that a mathematized economics creates from formulas, charts, graphs, and numerical tables serves to establish the authority of the small number of people capable of understanding it.[81]

In emphasizing the scientific appearance of finance and other specialized forms of knowledge, Venet contributed to a major intellectual debate of the period whose particular interest to philosophers in his native country he seems scarcely to have suspected. The "simultaneous performances" staged in May 1969 in New York under the title *Lecture by Richard Cornfield, MD and James Rosenfeld, MBA* are particularly revelatory in this regard (fig. 46). Like other such events that Venet sponsored during this

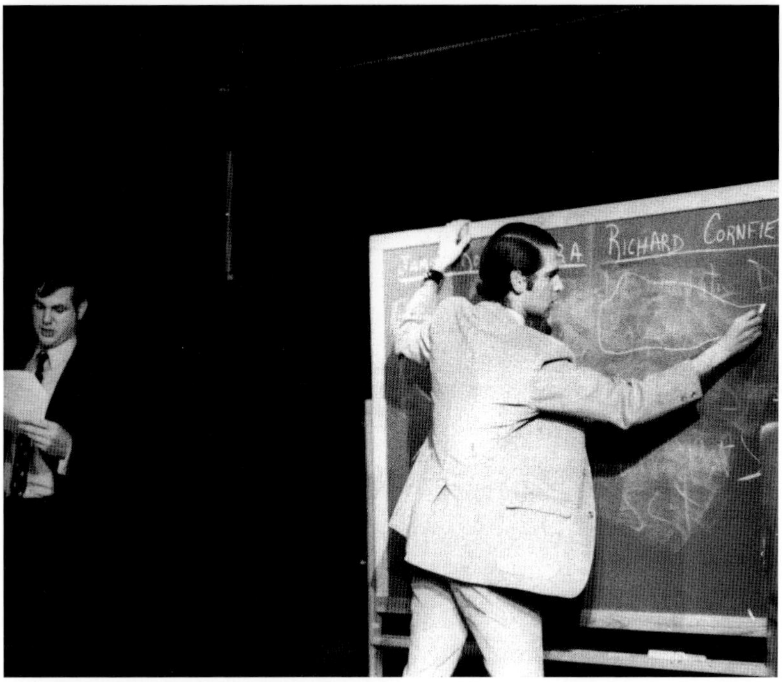

Fig. 46 Photograph of Bernar Venet's performance *Lecture by Richard Cornfield, MD and James Rosenfeld, MBA*, on May 26, 1969, at The Theater, New York.

period, consisting of two or more specialists delivering lectures at the same time on scientific matters, this one involved "different subjects, very complicated ones, very important ones."[82] Two professionals, one a physician, the other a financial specialist, were invited to deliver lectures on the effects of cystic fibrosis on pancreatic function and the performance of a company listed on the New York Stock Exchange, respectively. The academic qualifications of the two speakers, the platform from which they spoke, the blackboard on which they wrote formulas, and the abstruse subjects of their talks contributed to the aura of authority that is supposed to surround scientific discourse. The simultaneous delivery of the two speeches, which prevented the scientific information that Venet seemed to consider of such importance from being transmitted to the audience, produced an incomprehension that paradoxically reinforced the impression of scientific rigor. Precisely this effect is what attracted the interest of philosophers in France. Jean Baudrillard, considering the example of a mathematical formula, noted that "[w]hat fascinates us is always what radically excludes us in the name of its internal logic or perfection."[83] Michel Foucault went further, observing that the exclusion of laymen through the imposition of a hermetic professional code, such as mathematical formalization, is essential to the construction of a science as an autonomous discipline within a certain branch of learning.[84] In Venet's case, combining a medical lecture with analysis of the stock performance of a publicly traded company produced a sense of perplexity, not least because finance and medicine were placed on the same level, as two areas of expertise occupying an equivalent social space: financial analysis was now regarded as a natural science.

Venet's stock exchange works encouraged the view of art and finance as specialized domains, each one closed in on itself. Just as the stock exchange had come to be regarded as a separate professional space, reserved solely for experts whose feats of daring and skill fascinate a larger public, artists now had to come to terms with the fact that their trade was in the process of being professionalized in much the same way.[85] Just as the financialization of the economy had made the broker a figure of consequence, so too the artist had come to acquire a new and more dignified status. "In just twenty years the mentality of the artist, his [or her] very aspirations, have changed," the art dealer Seth Siegelaub remarked in an interview in the late 1980s. "He or she is no longer considered a worker exploited by collectors . . . but a professional in art, in the same way that a stockbroker is a professional in securities."[86] In portraying the world of finance as a highly specialized scientific endeavor, the province of savants whose prowess held great appeal for a moneyed and educated public, Venet looked upon speculation as a spectacle that enthralled spectators while holding them at a distance. This amounted to reviving the etymological sense of *speculation* (from the Latin *spectare*, "to watch"), which implies a projective gaze—only now in connection with the discovery of abstract rules, as opposed to the activity of applying them for a practical purpose. And yet, if securities speculators are ennobled by the reflected glory of mathematical abstraction, they also become true actors in their own right, taking part in the drama of the stock exchange themselves. All those who do not belong to this closed world are relegated to a lower class of mere spectators, who watch without being able to act. The spectacularization of finance, a cousin to the aestheticization of politics famously denounced by Walter Benjamin, produces a sort of reverence that thwarts all attempts at critical analysis.[87] Finance can only be contemplated, as a spectacle that excludes nonexperts and reduces them to admiring the surface appearance of an activity they are incapable of penetrating to any meaningful extent.

Dennis Oppenheim and the Stock Exchange as Gallery

Bernar Venet was not the only artist during this period who was entranced by the spectacle of the New York Stock Exchange, by the grandeur of its architecture, the swarms of traders frantically going about their priestly business beneath its high ceiling, its sacred place at the heart of a worldwide web of financial transactions. In January 1969, with the approval of the NYSE's executive officers, the American artist Dennis Oppenheim arranged with the Bay City Rubbish Collection Company for eighty sacks of debris—the residue of an entire day's trading, mostly paper and telex tapes, amounting to some four tons—to be collected and removed from the trading floor. The refuse was then "transplanted" to the spacious rooftop terrace of a tall residential building on Park Avenue South at the corner of Twenty-Seventh Street. The result of this operation was a work called *Removal Transplant—New York Stock Exchange*.

By its nature, the work was ephemeral. The sacks of debris, collected one Thursday morning at 5:30, were trucked north to the building on Park Avenue South and brought up to the roof. The following Sunday, Oppenheim and his assistants emptied the sacks onto the terrace, which had to be restored to its normal condition that same evening. Barry Bryant, the tenant who had given Oppenheim access to the building, was subsequently threatened with eviction from his apartment: despite vigorous efforts to clean up afterward, much of the paper blown about by the wind had clogged the roof gutters.[88] Only a few dozen spectators witnessed the event. For them, it survives as nothing more than a memory; for everyone else, only through its documentation, which assumed several different forms. The one preferred by Oppenheim himself consisted of two black-and-white photographs placed on either side of an explanatory text, arranged either horizontally—as in the versions presently held by the Los Angeles County Museum of Art and the Museo nacional centro de arte Reina Sofía in Madrid—or vertically. The two photographs show, respectively, the floor of the Stock Exchange, and the rooftop terrace of the building on Park Avenue South (fig. 47).[89] This arrangement made it possible to establish a strong symmetry between the two places, reinforced by a centered text that established an equivalence between the two spaces: the "spatial limits of the clearing house floor," on the one hand, and the "roof perimeter," on the other, each one acting as an "architectural mold."

This formal relationship is developed more fully in the documentary film of the event made by Douglas Collins, *Stock Exchange Transplant*.[90] It must be kept in mind that Collins's film was not subject to the artist's creative control, and that it stands as a work of art in its own right.[91] Nevertheless, the film is well worth studying, both for its insight into Oppenheim's sources of inspiration and because it was the principal medium through which his work came to be known to the public in 1969–70.

The film opens on Wall Street, with images of people hurriedly passing by on the sidewalk interspersed with low-angle shots of the colonnade and pediment of the Stock Exchange. Off-camera, Oppenheim's voice: throughout the fifteen-minute film the artist can be heard describing his motivations and responding to the questions of an interviewer (probably Willoughby Sharp). Next, the viewer is brought inside the Stock Exchange: from a balcony, the camera sweeps over the trading floor in a circular motion that gives a panoramic view of the clamor and bustle below at the height of the day's activity. With Vivaldi's *Gloria* as background music (the solemn second movement, "Et in terra pax hominibus"), overhead views of the crowd of traders in black suits alternate with close-ups of clerical employees sorting trading slips or taking orders by telephone, tight shots of electronic screens across which share quotes pass in rapid succession, and glimpses of the floor itself, littered with scraps of paper. The intercutting of disconnected camera shots and abrupt changes of perspective combine to create a powerful sense of frenzied commotion. Then a new sequence

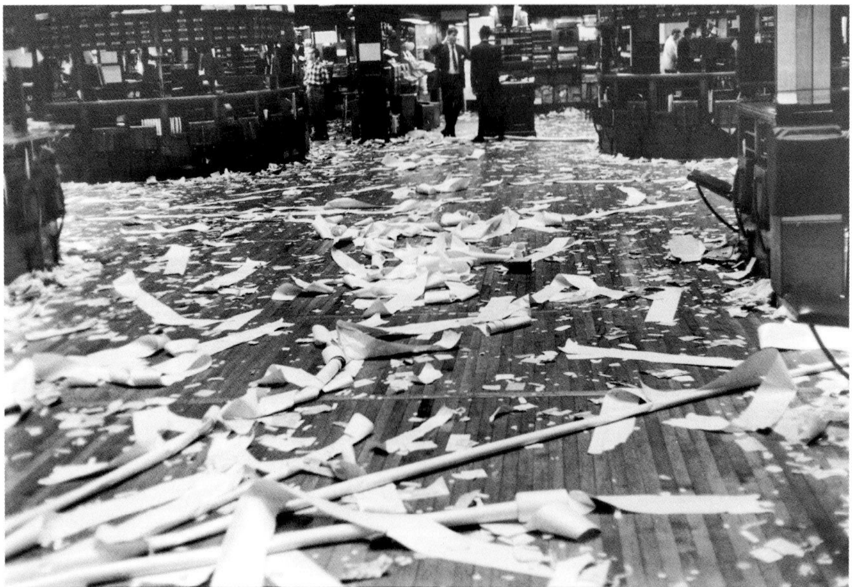

REMOVAL TRANSPLANT- NEW YORK STOCK EXCHANGE. 1968.

FOUR TONS OF PAPER DATA FROM THE FLOOR OF THE NEW YORK STOCK EXCHANGE IS REMOVED AND THIS RESIDUE IS TRANSPLANTED TO PARK AVENUE SOUTH WHERE IT WILL BE HOUSED IN AN AREA DEFINED BY THE SPECIFICATIONS OF A ROOF PERIMETER.

THE SPATIAL LIMITS OF THE CLEARING HOUSE FLOOR DICTATE THE MANNER IN WHICH THE PAPER RESIDUE ORGANIZED ITSELF. IN THE SAME WAY, A CYCLONE FENCE DIRECTS THE ACCUMULATION OF WIND-BLOWN MATTER, THUS FUNCTIONING AS AN AESTHETIC BLOCK. THE PAPER BECOMES FREE-MOVING ARCHITECTURAL FUEL, UNDIRECTED, YET RESPONDING TO THE IMPOSITION OF PRE-EXISTING BOUNDS. THE EXCHANGE FLOOR IS AN ARCHITECTURAL MOLD FOR SYMBOLS REPRESENTING DISTANT LOCATIONS.

TRANSACTIONS INVOLVING A SPAN OF THREE THOUSAND MILES TAKE PLACE ON THE STOCK EXCHANGE FLOOR. THE RESIDUE AT THE END OF THE DAY CARRIES VESTIGES OF THE DISTANCE BETWEEN TWO POINTS: THE POINT AT WHICH A BUY ORDER AND THE POINT AT WHICH A SELL ORDER HAS BEEN ISSUED. THOUGH IT LIES DORMANT ON THE FLOOR IT IS CONCEPTUALLY STILL ACTIVE. A SPATIAL TRANSACTION IS IMPLICITLY CONTAINED IN THE MATERIAL; A WEB OF COMPONENTS INTERACTING WITHIN A CONTINENTAL GRID.

AT 2 P.M. THE CLEARING HOUSE FLOOR IS FILLED WITH THE HIGHS AND LOWS OF STOCK TRANSACTIONS, THE PERMUTATIONS A STOCK HAS UNDERGONE DURING A FOUR HOUR PERIOD. BY REMOVING THIS DATA FROM A GROUND LEVEL AND CARRYING IT UP SIXTEEN STORIES, I AM RAISING THE LEVEL OF RESIDUE THAT WAS ACTIVELY HOUSED ON A LOWER PLANE. THE MATERIAL WILL BE HELD AT THE TOP OF A BUILDING: THE BUILDING FORMS A BASE FOR THE PIECE. THE ROOF IS VIEWED AS A TERMINAL STRATA FOR PASSIVE INFORMATION. THE MANHATTAN SKYLINE BECOMES A TIGHT COMPLEX OF CORE SAMPLINGS OF VARYING DEPTHS.

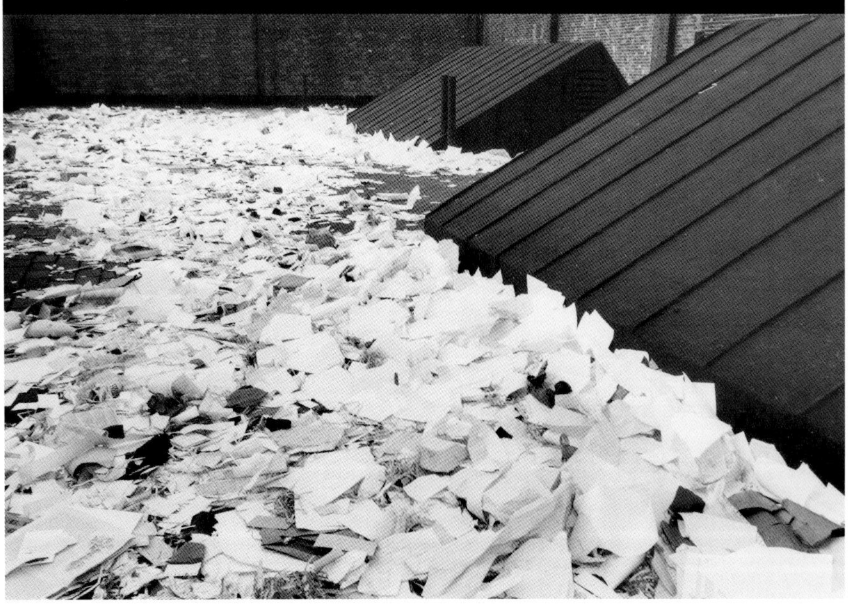

begins, introduced by an upward-looking view of the exchange's high windows, recalling those of a cathedral. The hall is now empty. The paper strewn over the floor, covering it almost like a carpet, forms what Oppenheim calls a "stratum." The camera travels down the aisles of the trading floor, examining in turn the equipment, the lines of telephones, the piles of slips. As Oppenheim photographs the scene, janitorial staff armed with brooms and trash bins go about cleaning up.

Fig. 47 Dennis Oppenheim, *Removal Transplant—New York Stock Exchange*, 1969 [text dated 1968]. Photodocumentation, three panels: black-and-white photographs, text.

At this point the music stops. The next sequence reunites the viewer with the noises of the street and traffic as the camera films from inside a vehicle. Its destination now comes into view, a tall building at the corner of Park Avenue South and Twenty-Seventh Street, shown in its full height from below. Oppenheim and his assistants get to work transporting the heavy sacks of paper up to the roof, first by elevator and then up a flight of stairs. The *Gloria* resumes, with the radiant opening chorus, "Gloria in excelsis Deo," celebrating the arrival of the sacks at the summit in the brilliant white light of a winter sky. The camera takes in the metal chimneys, silhouetted against the rooftops of neighboring buildings, as Oppenheim and his assistants empty sack after sack, blanketing the terrace with shifting piles of fluttering paper. The camera then looks down on the terrace from above, recalling the earlier shot from the balcony of the Stock Exchange. Now, the artist is seen surrounded by tangled heaps of unspooled reels of ticker tape—a scene that cannot help but evoke Hans Namuth's famous photo of Jackson Pollock painting, or the image of Allan Kaprow, surrounded by tires in *Yard*. Close-ups show pages torn from scratch pads covered with figures, discarded orders to buy or sell, long perforated ribbons of ticker tape. The *Gloria* now resumes with the joyous closing chorus, "Cum Sancto Spiritu," and the mounting sense of happiness and freedom reaches a climax. A small crowd of friends has assembled on the terrace: people of all ages, no two of them dressed the same way, laughing and frolicking amid the drifting piles of paper. They are, of course, the counterparts of the traders at the Stock Exchange—grim-faced men in identical black suits mechanically carrying out rational, dehumanized tasks. The film, like the photographic documentation of the event, shows Oppenheim throwing over the low perimeter wall of the roof long rolls of teleprinter paper and magnetic data-storage tape that waft downward among the adjacent buildings, twisted by the wind into swirling arabesques (fig. 48). Strips of magnetic tape sail through the sky, wrapping around one another and glinting in the sun's gleaming rays to the sounds of the "Amen." The whirling streams of telex paper and ticker tape are a reminder, of course, of the ticker-tape parades held in the city's financial district since the nineteenth century, celebrating momentous occasions in the life of the nation with a blizzard of shredded paper thrown out of office windows.[92] The film ends with final shots of the roof, against a background of blues chords, as Oppenheim reads aloud the statement that appears at the center of *Removal Transplant—New York Stock Exchange* (see fig. 47). This description of an inevitably evanescent work is bound to remain one of its only traces.

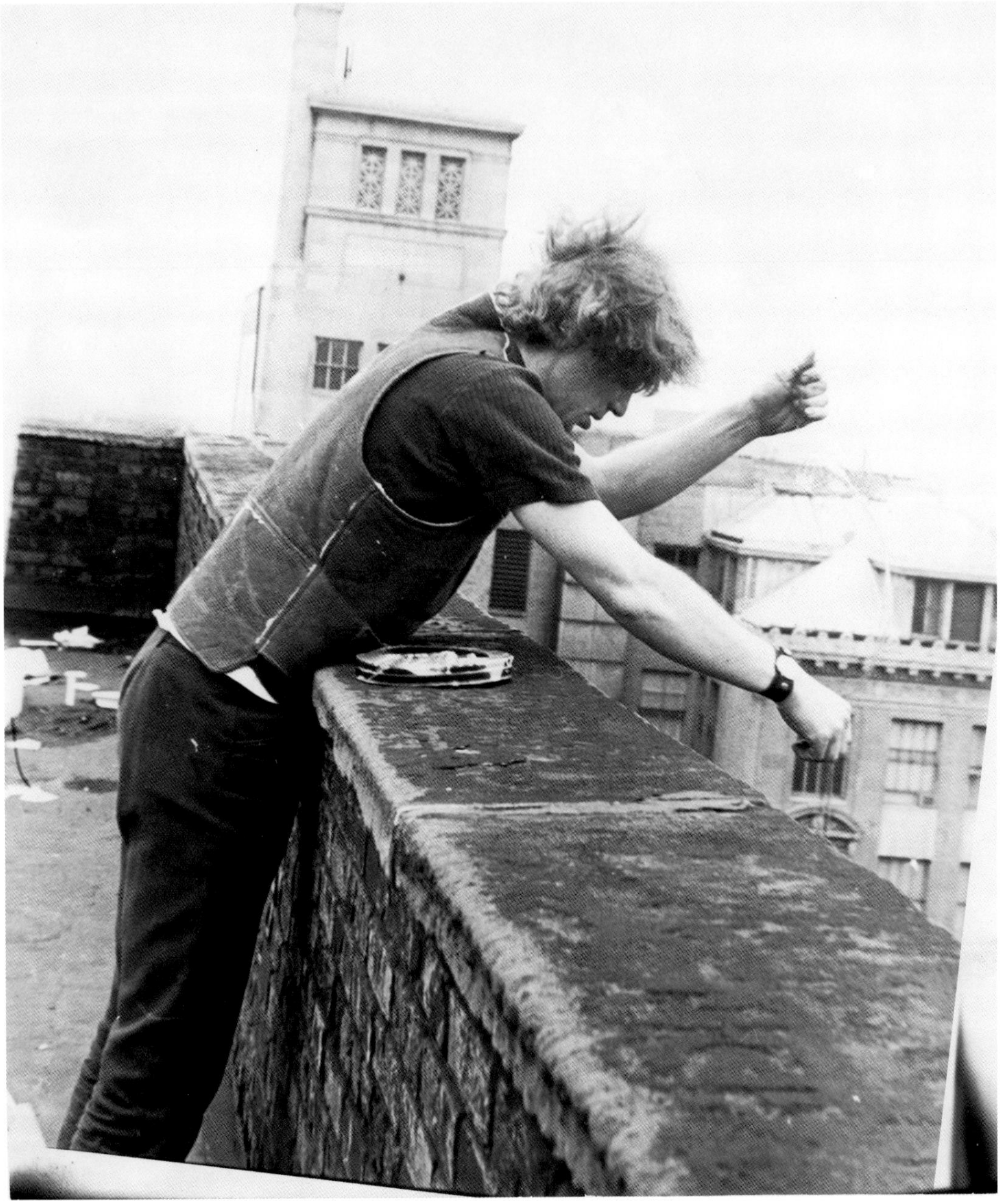

Fig. 48 Dennis Oppenheim on rooftop, 381 Park Avenue South, New York, on February 2, 1969.

Although Venet and Oppenheim were attracted by a common theme, the floor of the Stock Exchange and the frenetic atmosphere of dematerialized international transactions, they were attracted in different ways. At the beginning of Collins's film, Oppenheim says, "I knew I wouldn't be happy with merely viewing this information in the turmoil of its own location."[93] Instead he portrayed a polarity, visible in the symmetrical construction both of his photographic work and of the film, between two sites: the floor of the Exchange and the rooftop terrace, with the street (Wall Street in the one case, Park Avenue South in the other) serving as a transitional space. In each case there are two successive moments: one is a plenum, a space filled with activity where the floor is covered; the other is a vacuum, an empty space where the floor is bare and the architecture is thrown into relief—a sequence that is inverted in the case of the roof, where the plenum succeeds the vacuum. Within each space, the film has been edited in such a way as to reserve a place, a mirror image, for its double. Brief glimpses of the rooftop are inserted in the first part, set on the artificially illuminated trading floor, and momentary views of the interior of the Stock Exchange are incorporated in the second part, set on the sky-lit terrace. These two symmetrical spaces are, in many respects, opposites: on the one hand, an austere cathedral dedicated to the cult of money, where interchangeable worshippers dressed in black devote themselves to repetitive and meaningless tasks; on the other, a playground, open to the world beneath an immense sky, where men, women, and children are liberated by a colorful form of artistic and spiritual communion that is devoid of dogma. (The religious interpretation, it should be noted, is suggested mainly by musical means, and applies to the filmmaker's work rather than that of the artist; Oppenheim, for his part, is chiefly interested in contrasting two kinds of human relationship to a material environment.) Inside the Exchange, the scraps of paper and strips of magnetic tape are merely the material residue of immaterial transactions, piles of inert waste waiting to be carted away and buried in a landfill, or perhaps incinerated; on the roof, they become a luminous plastic material whose almost weightless fragments are joyfully converted into airborne sculptures. In transforming an architectural plan into a "mold" and masses of data into "strata," to recall the terms Oppenheim uses to describe his work, the artist explores the relationship between material and immaterial, container and contained, form and formlessness, immobility and mobility; and in displacing the physical traces of deadening financial activity, he manages to give the Stock Exchange, the epitome of delocalized and dematerialized labor, new roots in the fertile soil of localized and materialized recreation.

This is especially clear in the artist's own photographs, which omit the glorifying views of the high ceiling and monumental windows that were perhaps the most familiar elements of the popular conception of the Stock Exchange—and that even Collins included. Oppenheim systematically focused on the floor. He also dispensed with dramatic close-ups of the tense faces of brokers on the telephone, running back and forth, or pointing at the board. In the black-and-white pictures, the paper appears as a white fluid material sent swirling by the commotion inside the Stock Exchange or by the force of the wind on the rooftop, forming ephemeral sculptures in a landscape of dark and rigid structures, the rows of machines in the one case, the roof's architectural elements in the other. The color photographs reinforce this sense of animation. Whether in the warm orange light on the trading room or the bright bluish light on the roof, Oppenheim's sweeping views capture vibrant textures and nuances—the piles of certificates, lists of figures, selling and buying orders, financial research reports, scraps of newspaper and magazine articles, strips of ticker tape, and long ribbons of perforated paper from the teletype machines then in use at the Stock Exchange (fig. 49). The contact sheets preserved in the artist's archives include several images of legs and feet plunged in the "strata" of paper and other debris, as though they were some organic material. It was clearly the artist's intention to treat the residue of the trading floor as the equivalent of a plastic material.

In the late 1960s, even more than today, Wall Street was a focus of anticapitalist demonstrations by hippies and leftist groups. On July 14, 1968, only a few months before Oppenheim staged *Removal Transplant—New York Stock Exchange,* the artist Yayoi Kusama chose the sidewalk across from the NYSE as the stage for what a press release described as a "Naked Event outside the Stock Exchange" (fig. 50). During this event, four of the participants suddenly took off their clothes and ran naked for a few moments among passersby to the sound of a drum, while Kusama sprayed the performers with her signature polka dots in red paint.[94] The press release provocatively combines familiar countercultural themes and economic policy recommendations:

> NUDISM is the one thing that doesn't cost anything.
> CLOTHES cost money.
> PROPERTY costs money.
> TAXES cost money.
> STOCKS cost money.
> Only the dollar costs less.
> Let's protect the dollar by economizing.
> Let's tighten our belts.
> Let's throw away our belts.
> Let the pants fall where they may.
> ABOLISH:
> Clothes
> Cars
> Television
> Guns
> Atomic bombs
> Wall Street.[95]

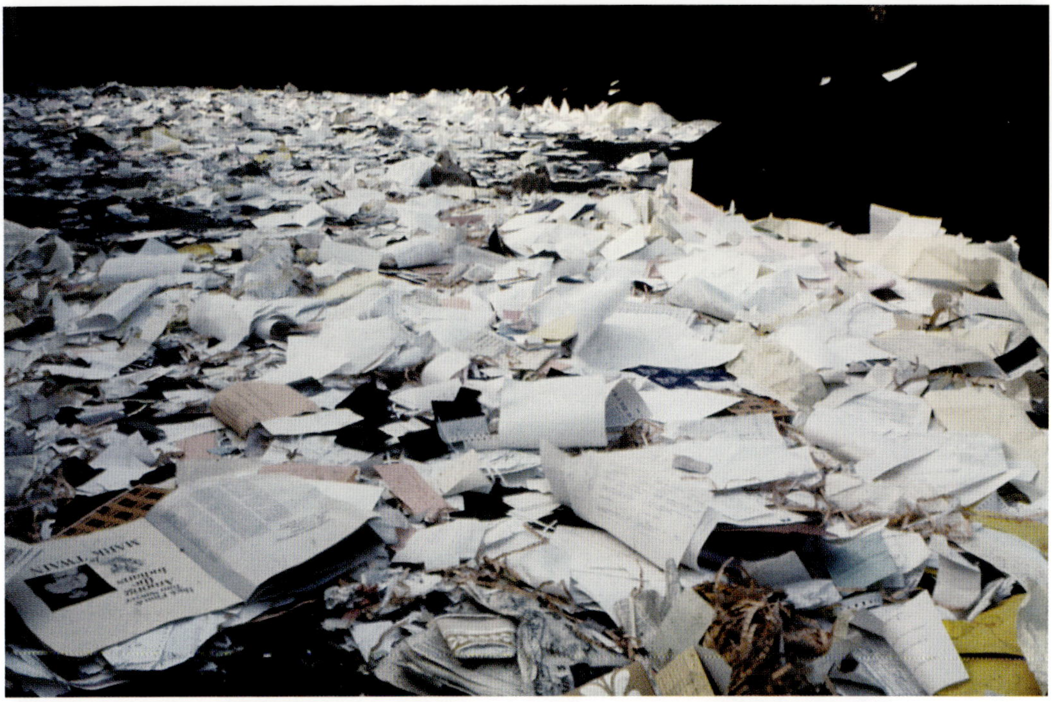

Fig. 49 Dennis Oppenheim, detail of *Removal Transplant—New York Stock Exchange*, 1969. Paper data on rooftop. Color photograph.

Kusama humorously mimics the discourse of economic austerity that was then fashionable, not neglecting to mention the covert devaluation of the dollar by price inflation and the need for thrift, while at the same time proposing an unexpected solution: doing away not only with financial speculation, but also with much of what the wealth derived from speculation is used to pay for, including clothes, weapons, and entertainment. Three months later, on October 13, 1968, she organized a second installment of the protest, again on Wall Street, this time more harshly denouncing stock shares as "a lot of capitalist bullshit" that "means nothing to the working man"; what is more, "[t]he money made with this stock is enabling the [Vietnam] war to continue. . . . Stock must be burned!" Burning stock meant burning down the Exchange itself and forcing stock traders to take up farming and fishing.[96]

Oppenheim did not see himself as making the same sort of critique. He frankly acknowledged that he had never been a politically committed artist, much less a militant one, despite the increasing pressure he felt to take a stand, especially in 1969. In retrospect, however, he perceived something like a political statement in the very nature of what he was doing at the time, well outside the traditional commercial channels of art.[97] *Removal Transplant—New York Stock Exchange* was intended primarily as a critique of artistic institutions. Oppenheim sought to liken the space occupied by the NYSE to the space occupied by an art gallery. As he explains in the opening minutes of Collins's film, "I chose the Stock Exchange because, first of all, I view the Exchange floor as a gallery continuum." Here he had in mind something more than the familiar argument made by those who recommend art as an investment, drawing an analogy between the art market and the financial market. He meant that

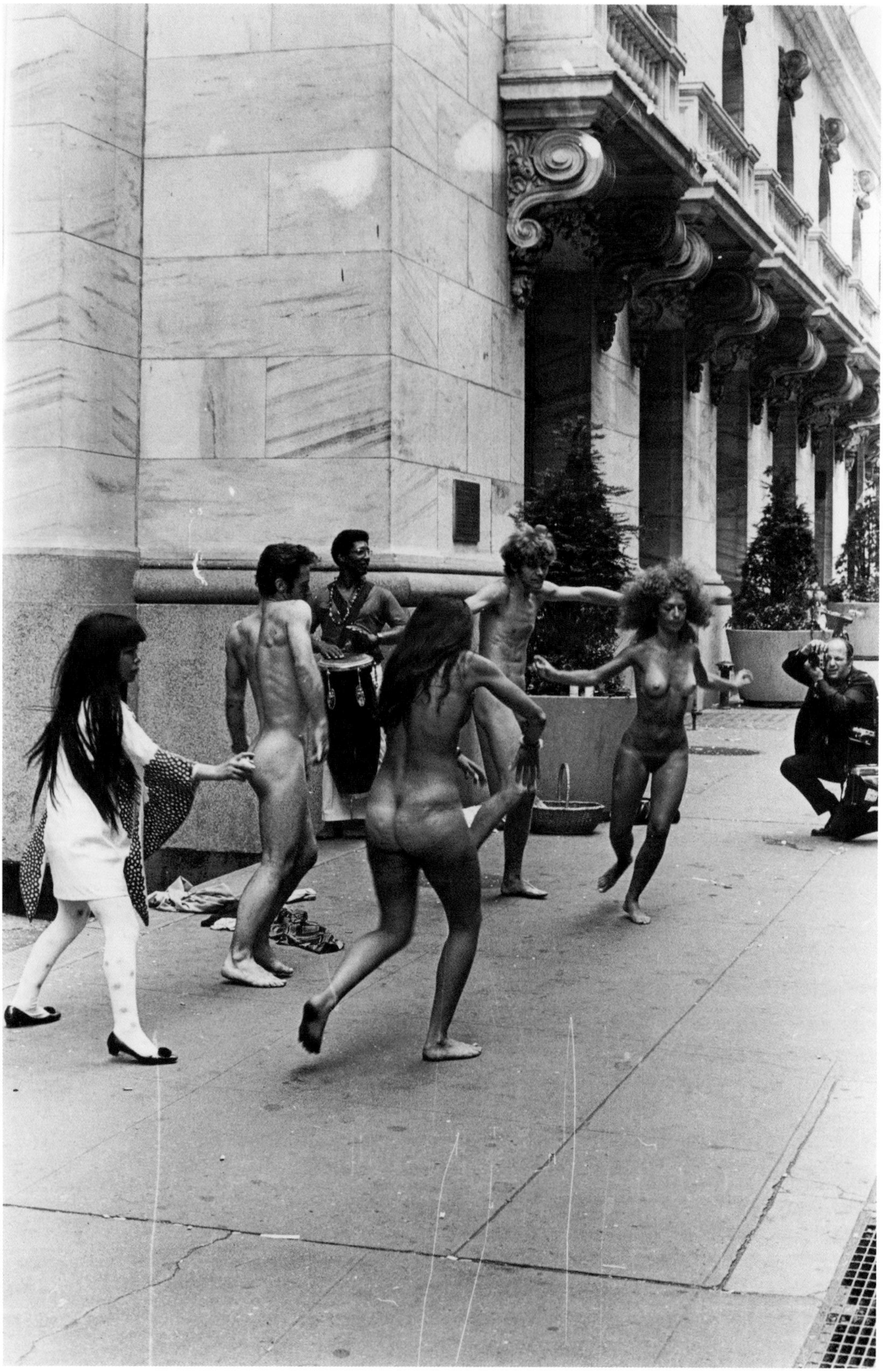

the two domains in fact exhibit comparable social behaviors: a "directed, stilted entourage" cloistered in an "enclosure" and performing outmoded "rituals"—the opening night, in the case of an art exhibition, the opening bell, in the case of the trading day. As for galleries, he continues, they "are a thing of the past . . . so far in the distance that they appear to be tombs."[98] The Stock Exchange, with its high cathedral windows, radiates the same morbid atmosphere. Financial speculation, whether in an art gallery or a stock exchange, is paradoxically on the side of the past and death, whereas artistic speculation opens onto a creative future. For Oppenheim, art, not what takes place on the trading floor, is a heroic and captivating attempt to grapple with an uncertain but exhilarating future. In doing just this, bravely going forth to meet the unknown, art is able to refresh and regenerate itself. The gallery, however, no less than the trading floor, is a thing of the past, an ancient religion stifled by obsolete rituals. Declining to reinforce the process of legitimation perpetuated by the financial world in simultaneously excluding and fascinating the general public, Oppenheim presents stock transactions as an inert material that must be brought back to life, revitalized and reappropriated not by work but by play.

The financial support Oppenheim received in making his film nonetheless exposes the precariousness of its critical position. *Removal Transplant—New York Stock Exchange* was commissioned by the contemporary art collector and patron Horace Solomon, a wealthy industrialist.[99] Solomon told a journalist that the idea of the work interested him because "the Exchange is a basic American idea, a great American institution. We thought that we could re-create the Exchange by moving all the papers to another location, and the roof did look just like the Exchange. Since I could not buy the Exchange, or the building with the papers on the roof, I had to settle for the documentation of the event."[100] Oppenheim's project could just as well be seen, then, as an enthusiastic and sincere tribute to the Stock Exchange, that "great American institution" which had helped advance Solomon's own career. The commercial success of *Removal Transplant—New York Stock Exchange* showed that art of this kind had no shortage of buyers in the contemporary market. Conceived with the intention of showing that "money is the root of all art," as the artist quipped in 1969,[101] the work itself became a source of money only a few years later. Susan Gibson (wife of the owner of the John Gibson Gallery in New York) was quoted in the *New York Times* in 1974 as saying that it was quite possible "to consider conceptual art as a good investment." Among the works whose value had "tripled in the last couple of years" she mentioned a work by Dennis Oppenheim, who "moved all the trash paper from the floor of the New York Stock Exchange to the roof of [a] building in Manhattan."[102]

Fig. 50 Yayoi Kusama, *The Anatomic Explosion Happening*, an event staged outside the New York Stock Exchange on July 14, 1968.

FOUR ARTISTIC SHAREHOLDING EXPERIMENTS

In the spring of 1969, when Venet was at work on his stock exchange pieces and shortly after the staging of Oppenheim's *Removal Transplant—New York Stock Exchange*, another type of experiment was being performed, individually but simultaneously, by four New York artists. Their aim was not to appropriate the visual appearance of the financial economy, or to repossess its discarded dross, but to participate in its actual workings. Lee Lozano's *Investment Piece*, begun in January 1969, describes her investment of $983.25 in highly speculative common stock warrants (fig. 51). The work was exhibited in May, at the same time as a work by Dan Graham entitled *Income (Outflow) Piece* (fig. 52). This project, never carried out in the event, called for advertisements to be placed in newspapers and magazines in support of an offer to purchase shares in the firm Dan Graham, Inc. By contrast with the relatively private character and limited circulation of these two works, Les Levine's *Profit Systems I* (fig. 53) was announced with press releases and related publicity. In March 1969, Levine acquired five hundred common shares of Cassette Cartridge Corporation for a sum of $2,375.00, and sold them a few months later for $7,481.25, or a net profit of 220 percent. Finally, in *Money*, a project likewise begun in March 1969, Robert Morris offered his services to the Whitney Museum of American Art in New York as an investment advisor and agent, with any profits accruing from the arrangement to be shared by the museum and himself (fig. 54).

These examples of what I call "artistic shareholding" represent some of the ways in which outsiders sought to infiltrate the financial system. At a moment when journalists, dealers, and collectors treated art as an investment, artists turned investment into art. In doing this, they scrutinized their socioeconomic position as professionals working in a specific field while at the same time examining the idea that the worlds of art and finance are self-referential, each one closed upon itself. And yet the four artists I discuss here do not share a common attitude or approach. Whereas Levine's work attempts to explore the interconnections of art and finance, Morris's work reveals an intricate system of actors whose behavior, in his view, makes the arts a financially and sociologically autonomous domain. Graham and Lozano, by contrast, sought in their own ways to shatter this system and open it up, by making money a disruptive factor.

Les Levine and the Transition from Entrepreneurial Artist to Financial Artist

In the spring of 1969, Levine sent various news organizations a bulletin marked "For Immediate Release." It announced his purchase, on March 27, 1969, of five hundred common shares of the Cassette Cartridge Corporation at $4.75 per share, and added that "[a]fter a period of one year, or at any time which it is deemed profitable prior to that, the Cassette Cartridge shares will be resold. The profit or loss of the transaction will become the work of art."[103] A few months later, in the fall, a new press release informed the public of the resale of the five hundred shares on November 26, 1969, at a price of $15.00 per share. The operation thus yielded a net gain of $5,106 in eight months, which, the announcement notes, "amounts to 220

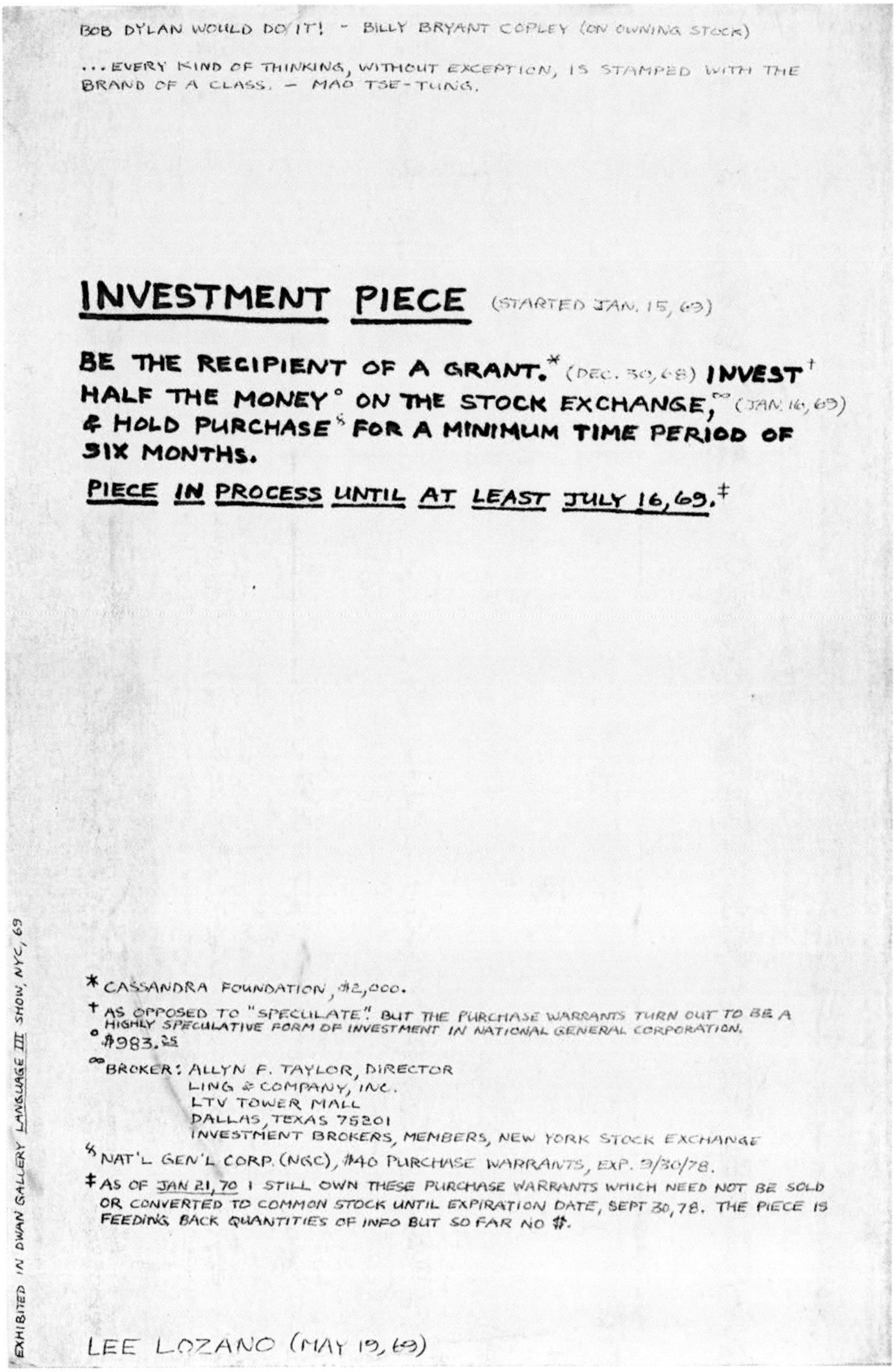
BOB DYLAN WOULD DO IT! - BILLY BRYANT COPLEY (ON OWNING STOCK)

...EVERY KIND OF THINKING, WITHOUT EXCEPTION, IS STAMPED WITH THE BRAND OF A CLASS. - MAO TSE-TUNG.

INVESTMENT PIECE (STARTED JAN. 15, 69)

BE THE RECIPIENT OF A GRANT.* (DEC. 30, 68) **INVEST**† **HALF THE MONEY**° **ON THE STOCK EXCHANGE,**∞ (JAN. 16, 69) **& HOLD PURCHASE**§ **FOR A MINIMUM TIME PERIOD OF SIX MONTHS.**

PIECE IN PROCESS UNTIL AT LEAST JULY 16, 69.‡

* CASSANDRA FOUNDATION, $2,000.

† AS OPPOSED TO "SPECULATE." BUT THE PURCHASE WARRANTS TURN OUT TO BE A HIGHLY SPECULATIVE FORM OF INVESTMENT IN NATIONAL GENERAL CORPORATION.

° $983.25

∞ BROKER: ALLYN F. TAYLOR, DIRECTOR
LING & COMPANY, INC.
LTV TOWER MALL
DALLAS, TEXAS 75201
INVESTMENT BROKERS, MEMBERS, NEW YORK STOCK EXCHANGE

§ NAT'L GEN'L CORP. (NGC), #40 PURCHASE WARRANTS, EXP. 9/30/78.

‡ AS OF JAN 21, 70 I STILL OWN THESE PURCHASE WARRANTS WHICH NEED NOT BE SOLD OR CONVERTED TO COMMON STOCK UNTIL EXPIRATION DATE, SEPT 30, 78. THE PIECE IS FEEDING BACK QUANTITIES OF INFO BUT SO FAR NO $.

LEE LOZANO (MAY 19, 69)

EXHIBITED IN DWAN GALLERY LANGUAGE III SHOW, NYC, 69

Fig. 51 Lee Lozano, *Investment Piece*, 1969. Black-and-white xerograph, 12⅝ × 8½ in. (32 × 21.5 cm).

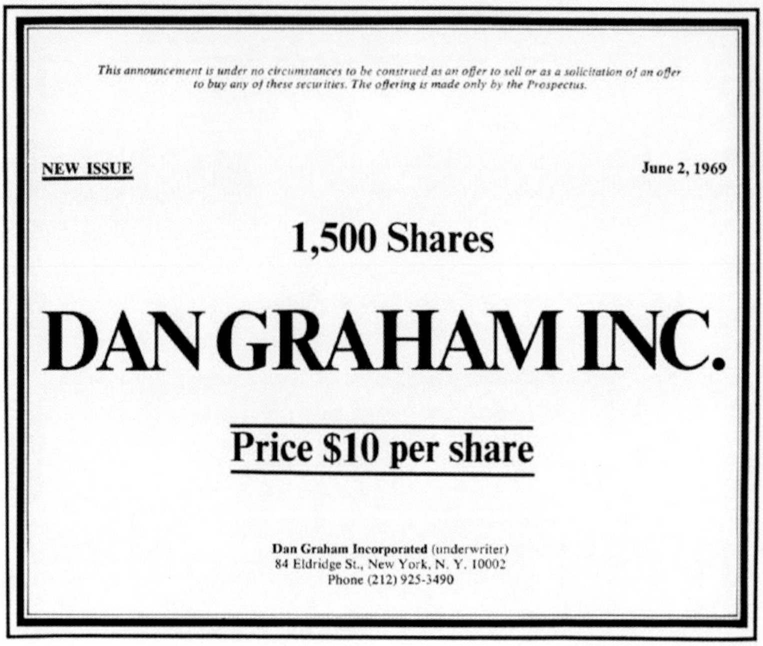

This announcement is under no circumstances to be construed as an offer to sell or as a solicitation of an offer to buy any of these securities. The offering is made only by the Prospectus.

NEW ISSUE June 2, 1969

1,500 Shares

DAN GRAHAM INC.

Price $10 per share

Dan Graham Incorporated (underwriter)
84 Eldridge St., New York, N. Y. 10002
Phone (212) 925-3490

Fig. 52 Dan Graham, *Income (Outflow) Piece*, 1969. Projected public offering, variable dimensions. Dan Graham studio, New York.

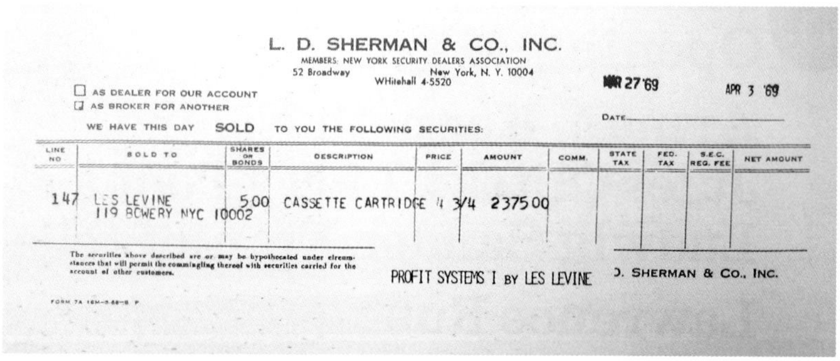

L. D. SHERMAN & CO., INC.
MEMBERS: NEW YORK SECURITY DEALERS ASSOCIATION
52 Broadway New York, N. Y. 10004
WHitehall 4-5520

☐ AS DEALER FOR OUR ACCOUNT
☑ AS BROKER FOR ANOTHER

MAR 27 '69 APR 3 '69

DATE

WE HAVE THIS DAY SOLD TO YOU THE FOLLOWING SECURITIES:

LINE NO	SOLD TO	SHARES OR BONDS	DESCRIPTION	PRICE	AMOUNT	COMM.	STATE TAX	FED. TAX	S.E.C. REG. FEE	NET AMOUNT
147	LES LEVINE 119 BOWERY NYC 10002	500	CASSETTE CARTRIDGE	4 3/4	237500					

The securities above described are or may be hypothecated under circumstances that will permit the commingling thereof with securities carried for the account of other customers.

PROFIT SYSTEMS I BY LES LEVINE

L. D. SHERMAN & CO., INC.

FORM 7A 16M-5-68-B P

Fig. 53 Les Levine, *Profit Systems I*, 1969. Advertisement in *Artforum* 7, no. 10 (1969): 16.

per cent profit on the original investment and completes *Profit Systems I*."[104] As Levine himself emphasized, the work has no "visible form," it is a "process." He nonetheless took steps to ensure that its existence was physically attested. The press releases appeared in the *Toronto Star* and a few other newspapers; a promotional insert was purchased in the journal *Artforum*, reproducing without commentary a receipt for transfer of funds (see fig. 53).[105] Levine also made a paper montage of the first press release and the receipt, which he signed and then photocopied for publication in a limited edition. He described *Profit Systems I* as "an embrace of capitalism."[106] By investing his money in a firm and advertising the result of his investment, he entered into a sphere of financial risk and public notoriety usually reserved for businessmen and entrepreneurs. Moreover, the artist claimed to be a member of their class, describing himself as a "corporate type with interests in all areas of management."[107]

By the late 1960s, Levine was a prolific and quite successful artist. His many experimental pieces, notably ones involving video technology and industrial materials, challenged the usual assumptions about making and selling works of art. He offered collectors a kind of art that could be thrown away, as in the case of plastic molds produced industrially in unlimited quantity, neither signed nor numbered, and sold on "a supply-and-demand basis."[108] In 1970, the artist signed contracts with several supermarkets for these *Disposables* at $1.25 per unit.[109] Although he was an omnipresent figure on the New York art scene, he was not well liked by other artists. "[They] resent Levine's efficiency and self-generating publicity," the art critic David Bourdon reported in 1969, citing press releases such as the ones for *Profit Systems I*.[110] If Levine's methods annoyed other artists, Bourdon maintained, it was because they exposed a marketing and financial machinery whose workings his rivals would rather be kept hidden. For the critic Jack Burnham, another influential supporter, *Profit Systems I* was the logical culmination of an attempt to lay bare the means by which the system of conventional art is perpetuated. "Levine is simply circumventing the roundabout process of producing paintings and sculptures for sale and, instead, making the message—money—become the medium," he wrote in *Artforum* in September 1969.[111] Levine's attacks on the "antibourgeois mentality" of the art world and its reluctance to admit that "[a]ll art is advertising for the individual as a profit-making entity" had earned him an undeserved reputation as a cynic.[112]

Levine himself firmly rejected charges of cynicism: "I was very serious," he insisted many years later.[113] His principal objective, plainly stated in the second press release for *Profit Systems I*, was to deal with "a 'real' societal system."[114] Like many other artists during this period who were seeking to subvert the distinction between art and life, he tried to subject art to the same economic and social constraints as other professional activities. A certain element of risk-taking was therefore unavoidable: "In order for the piece to work . . . there has to be a reasonable opportunity for loss or profit. It wouldn't work with IBM or AT&T—it just wouldn't have any point."[115] He decided to invest in Cassette Cartridge Corporation, a firm developing new sound-recording technologies, after having made a careful study of its potential profitability: "Once you choose a system, you have to succeed within that system. If I had lost money, it would have been a failure."[116] Levine linked artistic success with economic success, in other words, but rather than suppose that monetary gain follows from aesthetic value, he reversed the implication and made profit a condition of artistic validity. In this, he conformed to the prevailing opinion that art was unrivaled as a financial investment. "Obviously the idea of an unprofitable work of art is a contradiction in terms," Burnham wrote about *Profit Systems I* in April 1970.[117] Levine was not alone in using the firm as a vehicle for achieving explicit profit targets.[118] The year before, the Canadian artists Ingrid and Iain Baxter (the latter changed his name in 2005 to Baxter&, pronounced "Baxterand") had made themselves chief executives of N. E. Thing Co. Ltd., on behalf of which they issued press releases informing private investors:

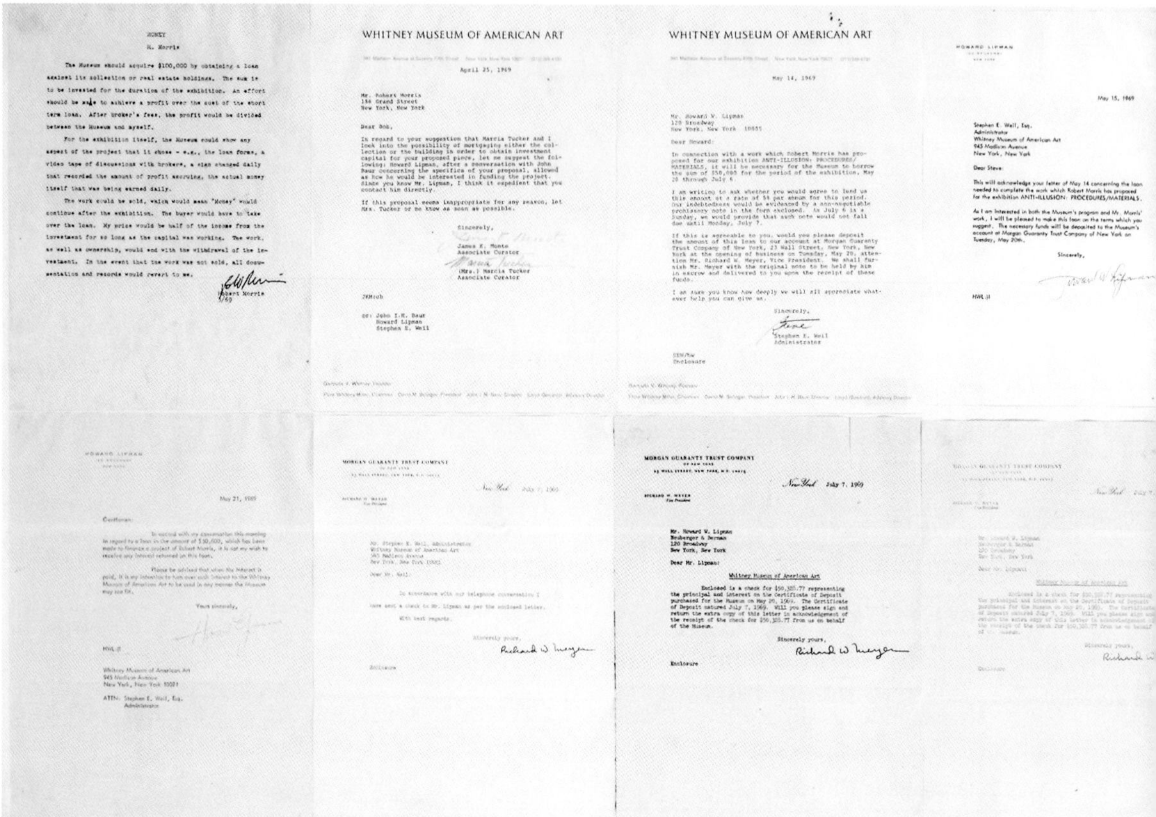

Fig. 54 Robert Morris, *Money*, 1969–73. Framed documents, 22 × 67 in. (56 × 170 cm). Whitney Museum of American Art, New York.

"Art *is* an investment. It's the greatest gamble of all."[119] Still, there was a difference. The Baxters' fascination with centralized and bureaucratic industrial conglomerates aligned them with what the sociologists Luc Boltanski and Ève Chiapello call the second "spirit of capitalism," dominant from the 1930s to the 1960s: "Its heroic figure is the director . . . , obsessed by a determination to go on increasing the size of the firm he is responsible for, in order to develop [a system of] mass production resting on economies of scale, standardization of products, the rational organization of labor, and new marketing techniques."[120] Levine's *Profit Systems I*, by contrast, anticipated a new spirit of capitalism that began to take shape in the 1970s, the motive force of a global financialized regime whose outstanding figures were the bankers and the shareholders.[121]

Having tried his hand at investment, Levine next turned his attention to the service sector. In 1970 he founded the Museum of Mott Art, Inc., which he described as both an artistic performance and a conceptual museum offering professional advice to artists and their friends.[122] A brochure issued the following year contained a listing of services and the fees associated with them, including "How to get a show at a museum" (ten dollars), "How to become an artist's spouse" (thirty dollars), and "How to avoid becoming an artist's spouse" (fifty dollars). Subscribers to the "pleasure purchase service" were promised a detailed study of the tastes of potential clients; a

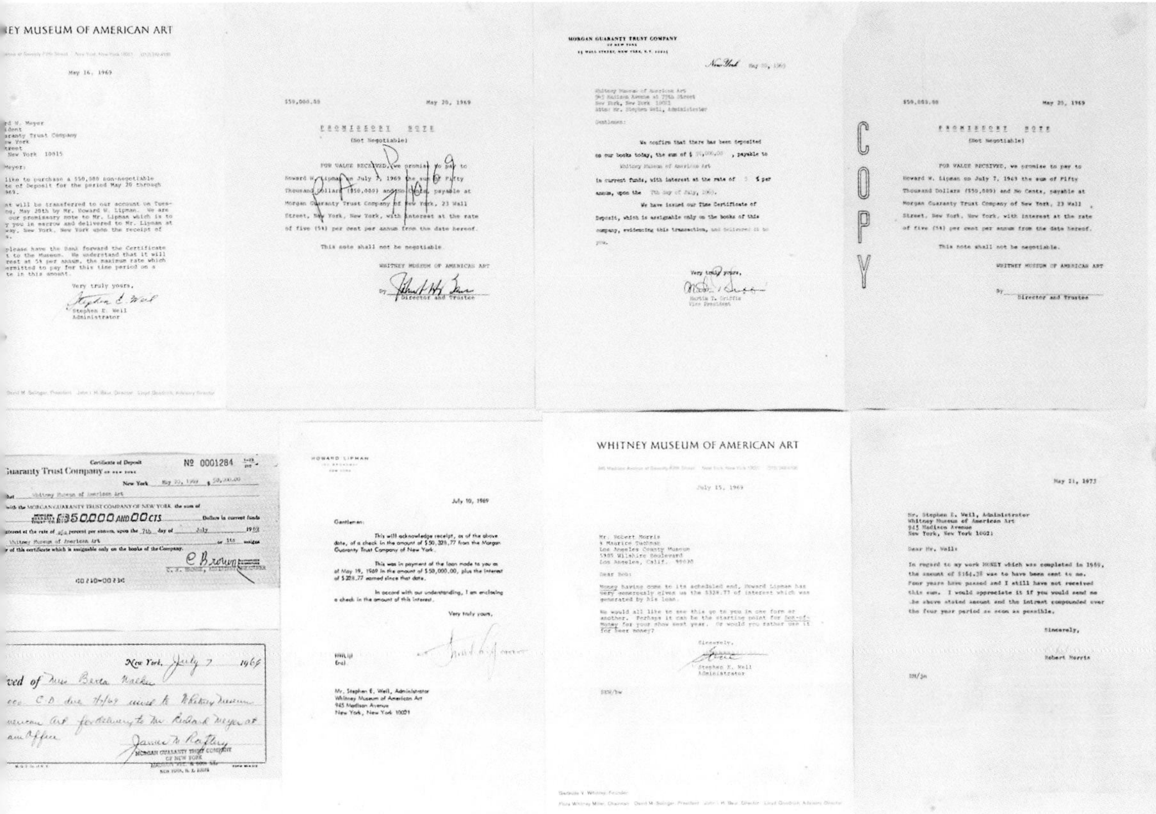

related option, "Dealing with Dealers," offered a "complete assessment of your business relationship with your dealer, including analysis of income ratio to work supplied, deductions being made . . . and contractual fulfillments."[123] The humorous tone of the brochure seemed to raise doubts about the actual availability of the itemized services,[124] but so-called public hearings were in fact held with the aid of volunteers in galleries and museums in a number of cities, including New York, Washington, D.C., and Vancouver. Recordings of these performances, as well as the equipment used for this purpose, were also the subject of exhibitions.[125]

The notional Museum of Mott Art, Inc. was inspired by the appearance, at the beginning of the 1970s, of marketing services for artists.[126] Behind this incursion by marketing specialists and financiers into the arts lay the familiar preoccupation with art as an investment, as one of the services Levine offered plainly showed: "Art for Capital Gains: An analysis of the various works over the period of the last 10 years that have increased in value and advice on what is purchasable today for capital gains tailored to the client's investment budget. When to buy, when to sell. Fee—$100."[127] At a moment when the popular press was filled with stories of bankers becoming financial consultants for the fine arts, it was perfectly natural that an artist who had proven his talent as an investor should now act as an investment advisor himself.[128] For Levine, making the transition from art to finance was a way of demonstrating the permeability of these two spheres. *Profit Systems I* was intended to demolish the idea that art stood apart from real life; that collecting art is a sort of mental vacation for bankers seeking refuge from the pressures of their professional lives.[129] But at the same time the work rejected the view of finance as a domain wholly reserved to specialists, shut off from the world. Since the financial system "influence[s] our daily lives," Levine explained in the first press release, *Profit Systems I* could not help but fit into "an open continuing system called the 'stock market,' a system directly connected to our life style."[130]

Ever alert to new market developments, Levine adapted his works to changing economic circumstances in order to make them more attractive to potential buyers. For an exhibit in February–March 1972 at the Fischbach Gallery in New York, for example, a moment when the end of dollar convertibility and the gathering economic crisis were putting sharp upward pressure on the price of gold, Levine created a set of eighteen-carat gold sculptures made from molds of pieces of Wrigley's gum that had been patiently chewed by the artist (fig. 55). Mounted on black marble bases and displayed in windows resembling those of a luxury jeweler's shop, the small sculptures whimsically contrasted the preciousness of their material with the vulgarity of their form and manner of production.[131] The aggressive tone of the show's advertising, written by the poet John Giorno, made no secret of the artist's intentions: "Buying gold gum may be a way of holding on to your money in this tiny boom year of 1972, which may become known as the last boom year that ever was. If you bought Gold Gum before Nixon devalued the dollar, you'd already have a nice profit."[132]

With his "tiny, portable, solid-gold, precious objects," the critic John Perreault remarked, "Levine is both satirizing and taking advantage of the current art market collapse"; after all, "[n]o matter what happens to the art market . . . , you can always melt down gold."[133] Levine's sarcasm and impertinence seem to have been less and less appreciated in the deteriorating economic climate of the early 1970s, however, and he rapidly lost a large part of the considerable reputation he had worked so hard to acquire. In 1974, Peter Schjeldahl observed that the role of parodist had become harder to play "in increasingly lean times, as the pleasure-loving art scene of the middle sixties has disappeared under waves of Vietnam politics, cultural breakup and now economic recession."[134]

Robert Morris, Dan Graham, Lee Lozano: Art Workers and Shareholders

Whereas Les Levine wholeheartedly embraced the artist's new status as a businessman, Robert Morris's attitude was rather ambivalent. His work *Money* (1969–73) comprises a total of sixteen documents—letters, promissory notes, a certificate of deposit, and receipts—retracing the artist's attempt to act as an investor on behalf of the Whitney Museum of

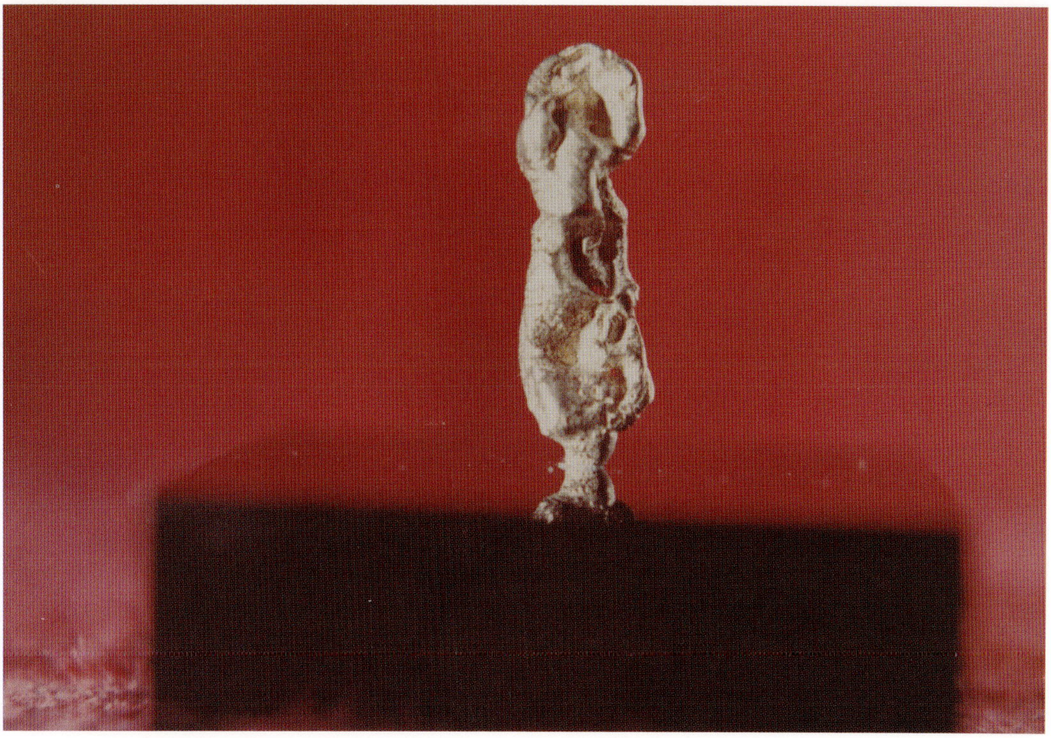

Fig. 55 Les Levine, *18-Carat Solid Gold Chewing-Gum*, 1972. Gold, height of sculpture: 1¾ in. (4.5 cm), height of cubic base: 2¼ in. (5.7 cm). Photograph conserved in Fischbach Gallery records, Archives of American Art, Smithsonian Institution, box 12, folder 29.

American Art. The project was envisioned as a contribution to the group exhibition *Anti-Illusion: Procedures/Materials* curated by the artists Marcia Tucker and James Monte and held at the Whitney May 19–July 6, 1969.[135] In his initial proposal, dated March 1969—the first document of the set, at the upper left (see fig. 54)—Morris wrote: "The Museum should acquire $100,000 by obtaining a loan against its collection or real estate holdings. The sum is to be invested for the duration of the exhibition. An effort should be made to achieve a profit over the cost of the short term loan. After broker's fees, the profit would be divided between the Museum and myself."

Unsurprisingly, the Whitney refused to expose itself to a risk of this magnitude, and the project was considerably revised, as the exchange of letters and documents that followed (and subsequently were collected in *Money*) show. At the suggestion of Tucker and Monte, the museum borrowed $50,000 at a 5 percent interest rate from Howard Lipman, a patron of the Whitney and for many years a collector of Morris's work. This sum was then invested for the duration of the exhibition in low-risk certificates of deposit paying 5 percent interest, producing the sterile result of a self-canceling transaction that generated a paper trail but no profit. Perhaps in order to alleviate a lingering sense of frustration, Lipman decided to donate the interest that was due him ($328.77) to the museum. One of the documents in *Money* is a letter that Stephen E. Weil, an administrator of the Whitney, wrote to Morris on July 15, a few days after the close of the exhibition: "Dear Bob, *Money* having come to its scheduled end, Howard Lipman has very generously given us the $328.77 of interest which was generated by his loan. We would all like to see this to go to you in one form or another. Perhaps it can be the starting point for *Son of Money* for your show next year. Or would you rather use it for beer money?" Here the collector/patron has fully entered into the process of creating a work of art. Lipman's role was decisive and productive, both from a monetary and an artistic point of view, as Morris recognized in the letter of thanks he addressed to him:

> Dear Howard,
> I wanted to thank you for your essential part in making the Whitney project possible. It is interesting how the project seems to continue to change and expand—now with your decision to turn over your interest to the Museum another step is taken. Your action inspires me to want to keep the project going . . . so if any interest is returned to me I will use it in some way to keep the project in motion. I have not yet decided what to do to implement the continuity. But this is interesting because I will now have to think of something.[136]

The reaction of the critics to this work on the "alliance of art and money" was mixed.[137] For some, Morris was a greedy "financial genius" bent on personal enrichment.[138] Others, by contrast, admired his attempt to condemn, if not also to subvert, "the commercial commodity collectors have made of his work."[139] It must be said that the carefully orchestrated arrangements made by Morris to illustrate his work in the exhibition catalogue had the effect of cultivating exactly this ambiguity. Whereas the other artists in the show were content to document the creation and display of their work within the museum space itself, Morris went a step further, producing a kind of graphic novel about money based on photographs by Robert Fiore. Here we see the artist disguised as a gangster, smoking a cigar and filling a mysterious black briefcase with wads of banknotes.[140] The visual material in the pages of the catalogue seems to have been intended as a wryly anecdotal counterpart to the dry administrative documents framed for public exhibit.[141] The complete set of Fiore's contact sheets, preserved in the archives of the Whitney Museum (fig. 56), included many photographs of Morris shaving and getting dressed, donning a long-sleeved white shirt and white suit, which indicates that initially he had thought of laying emphasis on the artist's transformation into crooked businessman before finally settling on the physical embodiment of the work's theme—banknotes—as the most effective way of getting his point across.[142]

Discussing the work in an interview on May 16, 1969, several days before the opening, Morris directly associated his purpose with the question of art as investment. If the Whitney had agreed to borrow the $100,000 originally requested, he explained, "I could have taken the money

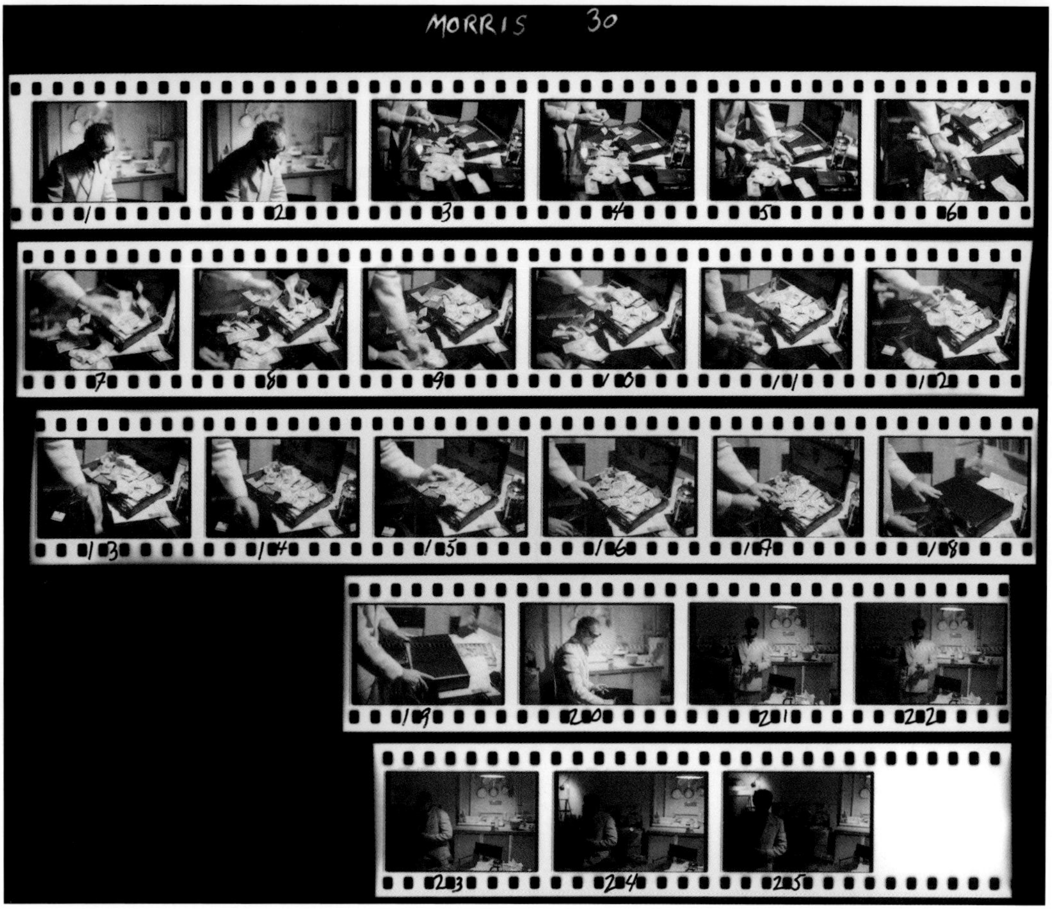

and probably doubled it by giving it to particularly shrewd art dealers to buy modern art and sell it very fast."[143] Asked to elaborate on this point many years later, Morris acknowledged that he, too, had been influenced by the first art investment funds, such as the Art Fund and the Sovereign American Arts Corporation, which were then awaiting final approval from the U.S. Securities and Exchange Commission.[144] Although they promised to encourage and financially support contemporary art by buying works by living artists, these vehicles aroused skepticism and mistrust within the artistic community. Surely it was no coincidence that Grace Glueck, in a November 1969 *New York Times* article entitled "Now There Are Mutual Funds for Art," referred in this connection to "a prominent collector of contemporary sculpture and editor of the magazine *Art in America*." This was none other than Jean H. Lipman, the wife of Howard Lipman. "To me," she quoted Jean Lipman as saying, "the concept of art investment is as bad as air pollution. It's dealing with art as a commodity, a total confusion of values."[145] Implicitly, then, Lipman was suggesting that Morris's work, supported by her husband, was to be interpreted as attacking this very concept.

Fig. 56 Robert Fiore, photographic contact sheet prepared in connection with the *Anti-Illusion: Procedures/Materials* exhibit held at the Whitney Museum of American Art, New York, May 19–July 6, 1969.

The first months of 1969, during which Levine produced *Profit Systems I* and Morris produced *Money*, also saw the founding of the Art Workers' Coalition. The AWC brought together artists, critics, and museum employees with the purpose mainly of defending the rights of artists, but it also took political positions, against the war in Vietnam, sexual and racial discrimination, and the economy of the art world.[146] One of the group's central concerns was to combat the notion of art as an investment. Some historians have been puzzled by what they take to be a paradox—that artists should have protested their treatment as underpaid economic producers most vehemently just when the art market was expanding at an unprecedented rate.[147] When one recalls, however, that over the course of the 1960s art had come to be considered the most profitable investment of all, it is hardly surprising that artists felt they were prevented from sharing in the very considerable gains that others had realized from their own works. On April 10, 1969, an "open hearing" attended by several hundred people was held by the AWC at the School of Visual Arts in New York. One of the liveliest topics of discussion was speculation on art.[148] The image of the artist proposed by one of the participants, as someone "living in penury while his pictures fetch outrageous prices,"[149] seemed to be a plausible and direct consequence of the idea promoted by Richard Rush and others, that art is an excellent way to get rich—for the collector. Further proof of the impact of studies on art as an investment may be found on the next-to-last page of the collection of documents published by the AWC that same year, where a familiar series of charts comparing the performance of Impressionist paintings and the stock market is immediately recognizable at the bottom (fig. 57).

If the artists in attendance were unanimous in reviling investors who profited financially from their work, they were not always in agreement about the measures needing to be taken in response. Minutes of the April 1969 public hearing describe two divergent positions. On the one hand, many felt that a system linking art to the economy was not necessarily bad in itself, but that "society in general must guarantee that artists get their share of the money." On the other hand, some were convinced that "the monetary construction of society" simply had to be "abolished," and that "artists should dissociate themselves from all commercial politics."[150] These positions found clear expression in the two "propositions" adopted by the AWC at the end of the hearing. Alternative A endorsed the principle that "[t]o be free, the artist must have control over and receive reasonable value for his work." On this view, artists deserve to be fairly compensated for the display and reproduction of their works, are entitled to a percentage of the profits earned from the sale of their work and to a certain degree of control over its future disposition, and have the right to health insurance and other benefits. Alternative B, by contrast, maintained that "[t]o be free, the artist must not [reckon] the value of his work." As a consequence, "[t]he Coalition should not be concerned with attempting to enforce proprietary rights or with helping artists to become rich."[151]

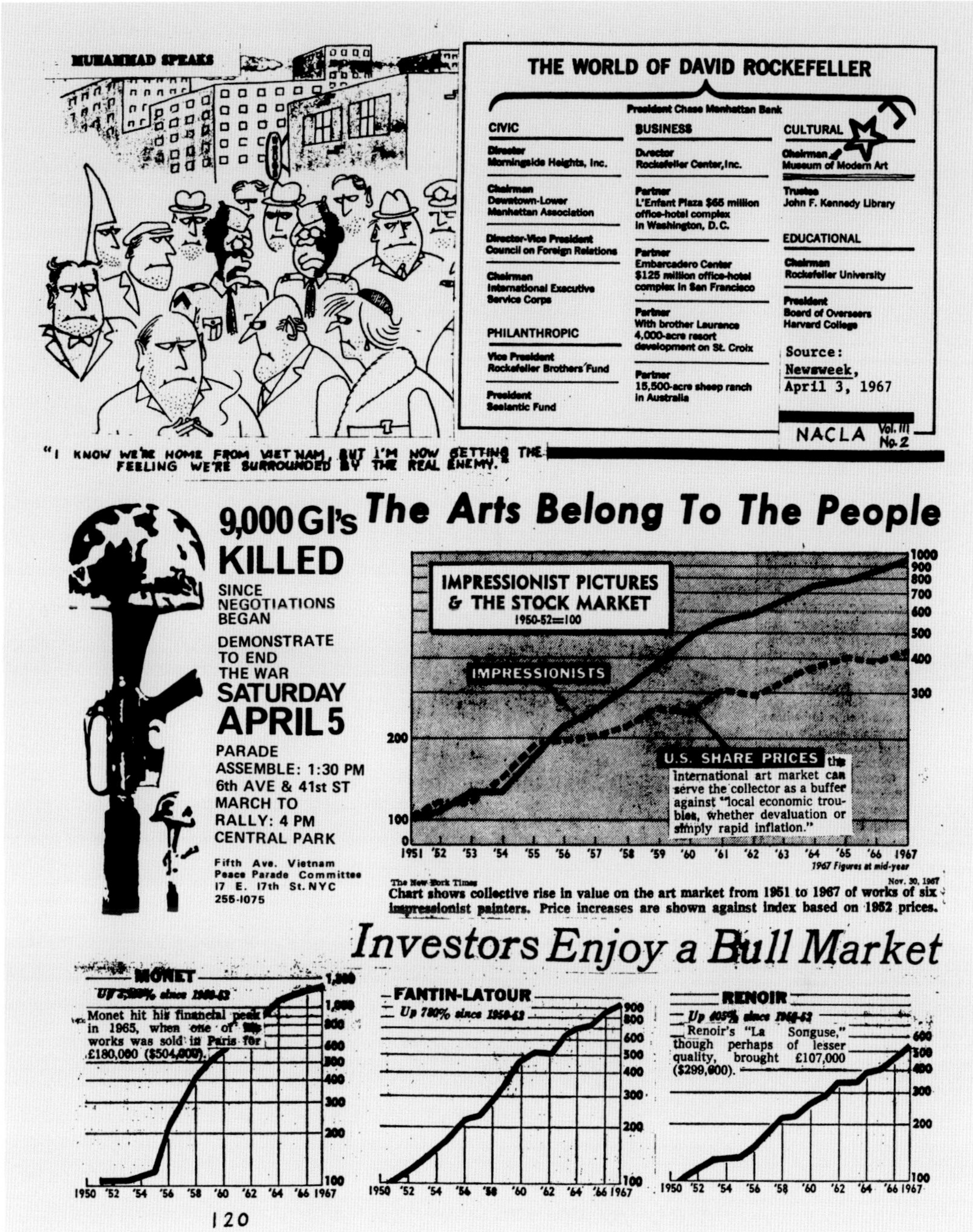

Fig. 57 Documents collected in Art Workers' Coalition 1969 publication *Documents I*; reprinted as *Open Hearing: Art Workers' Coalition* (New York: Primary Information, 2008), 120.

Like most of the New York artists of their generation, Levine, Morris, Graham, and Lozano were all personally involved to one degree or another in the AWC protests.[152] Although Morris denied having had the group's concerns in mind when he created *Money*, Graham looked back on Morris's work in precisely this light.[153] In a December 1973 lecture, Graham conceded the merits of *Money* on its own terms, while arguing that it amounted to a perversion of the concerns raised by the AWC that threatened to transform artists' newly awakened political consciousness into a self-reflexive and, ultimately, inoffensive way of thinking about art, in the manner of Duchamp.[154] Rather than force artists to confront larger social issues, *Money* had the effect of narrowing their outlook, confining their attention to matters that were of interest to the art world and no one else. More than this, *Money* seemed to collapse the AWC's two options into one: Alternative A. Morris had manifestly asked to be paid for the exhibited work, since he demanded half of the profits earned by the Whitney's investment during the course of the exhibition and sought to participate in any financial gains subsequently realized on the art market. Graham and Lozano, by contrast, had taken a radical stance during the public hearing that put them squarely on the side of Alternative B. As Graham put it, "the subject is the artist, the object is to make art free."[155] Lozano, for her part, had declared herself to be an "art dreamer" who was prepared to "participate only in a total revolution simultaneously personal and public."[156] For both of them, Morris's work for the Whitney was a shabby piece of self-serving politics.

At the moment he was creating *Money*, Morris appeared to be sympathetic to the view that conceptual art was a means of breaking free from the constraints of the traditional art market and its obsession with objects: "You could overemphasize that, but I think it's undeniably there [in my work]—that resistance to art as a commodity," he told Patricia Norvell in May 1969. "I mean, art that remains an object and is put in the marketplace is the most amiable kind of capitulation to capitalism." When Norvell asked how art should be financed in the future, Morris recommended a greater reliance on the generosity of wealthy patrons: they are ready to forego "an investment kind of value [in] supporting art that doesn't produce objects, but they certainly get the prestige kind of return."[157] And indeed there is some evidence that the prospect of escaping the usual market mechanisms may have held a certain appeal for prominent collectors. Robert Scull, for example, confided in a November 1970 interview that "[m]y present involvement with non-saleable or non-ownable art may be a manifestation of my need to get into art with profit-less possibilities. I think I need it to restore my essential gratitude for an artist allowing me to become part of his creative process. Now it is pure and has the least to do with the money value of a work of art. It is an affirmative involvement in what I hope will be the development of a man and his work."[158]

The idea that conceptual art was able to attract financing because it did more to satisfy an appetite for social prestige than a desire for monetary gain is strikingly confirmed in the case of *Money* itself, which, as we have seen, was charitably supported by Howard Lipman. Lipman started out as a sculptor, then switched careers and joined the investment firm Neuberger and Berman. Together with his wife, Jean H. Lipman, he had begun to collect popular American art in 1937 and subsequently developed a deep interest in contemporary art. In 1940, with the death of Frederic Fairchild Sherman, the founder and editor of *Art in America,* the couple purchased the magazine, and for three decades, from 1941 to 1970, Jean Lipman served as its editor-in-chief. As it happens, an article she wrote for the magazine in January 1970, "Money for Money's Sake," prominently featured Morris's *Money.*[159] Howard Lipman, for his part, was elected a trustee of the Whitney Museum in 1969, then served as its president (1974–77) and as chairman of the board of trustees (1977–85). It was therefore the monopolistic functioning of the economy of contemporary art as a whole, encompassing private collections, art journals, and museums, that Morris's work both described and profited from.

Graham and Lozano, who were lovers at the time, heard about Morris's project for the Whitney before he had actually begun work on it and decided that each of them would create a work in response. Although they came up with the idea together, the two artists worked separately without consulting each other.[160] Graham's production was titled *Income (Outflow) Piece,* Lozano's *Investment Piece*; the two works were shown together at the Dwan Gallery in New York as part of the *Language III* exhibit held there in May–June 1969. Both works addressed the same theme as *Money,* of art as an investment, but with the quite different aim not only of stimulating debate within the art world, but also of encouraging reflection about the place of money in society in general, in the case of Graham, and about the relations between individual members of society, in the case of Lozano.

Income (Outflow) Piece was to consist of a public offering of shares (see fig. 52) outlined in a letter of intent, dated June 1969 and printed in the form of black-and-white photography, that was acquired by the Belgian collectors Herman and Nicole Daled two years later.[161] In this letter, Graham asserts his intention to offer the public an opportunity to invest in himself as a commercial enterprise, Dan Graham, Inc.: "The 'object' (my motive) of this company will be to pay Dan Graham, myself, the salary of the average American citizen out of the pool of collected income from the stock's sale. All other income realized from the activities of Dan Graham beyond [this] amount *will be returned to the investors* in the form of dividends."[162] The scheme involved drafting an official prospectus announcing the purchase offer and placing legal notices ("tombstones") in various newspapers and magazines as part of a general solicitation for the purpose of raising capital. Owing to the complexity of the undertaking from the administrative point of view, Graham finally abandoned the project, and the promised prospectus was never issued.[163] For Graham, the point of

Income (Outflow) Piece was to rethink the relationship between the public "self" and the private "self" by regarding money as a vehicle connecting the individual with society as a whole.[164] In making information about his commercial prospects generally available and offering anyone the opportunity to participate in the proceeds from his work, Graham sought to redefine the artistic economy. In place of an economy resting on a small number of predetermined actors—artists, museums, collectors, as in Morris's work—the idea was to make the general public an investor in art, both intellectually and financially, and in this way create the sort of economic interdependence that obtains between the directors of a firm or a mutual fund and its shareholders. In his letter of intent, Graham expressed a particular interest in the various "feedbacks" that the proposed arrangement would generate.[165]

The unusual problems posed by the sale of a "proposition" such as *Income (Outflow) Piece* suggested a novel contractual relationship between artist and collector that would curb speculation and act as a brake on the increase of resale prices. The price list for the May–June 1969 show at the Dwan Gallery specified the following terms:

> This proposition is for rent from the artist to the collector who has taken an interest at 5% per annum of its gallery price. The gallery takes its established percentage from the artist's realized principal as it comes in. Thus, all interest is directed to the artist with dividends for the gallery: the artist's rights are protected as he has legal possession of the object. When (if) a collector's interest has been played out, he has the option to return the work for further rental. If the collector dies still retaining the piece, it is to be destroyed.[166]

By offering his work for rent, rather than for purchase, Graham could assure himself of continuing legal control. Under this conception, the status of the collector is ambiguous: on the one hand, he never acquires full possession of the work, which he can be obliged to return to its author; on the other, because the work is not meant to survive him, a strong mutual bond is created among the collector, the work, and the artist, who in the event of the collector's death no longer receives any remuneration.

According to Graham, whereas his work was concerned with "collectiveness," Lozano's was "more subjective, she wanted to bring the subject into it."[167] It may seem surprising at first sight to characterize her *Investment Piece* (see fig. 51) in this fashion, for it gives the appearance of being a neutral and impersonal document in which the artist orders herself, in the imperative mood, to invest in financial markets half of a grant she had just received, amounting to $983.25. Two enigmatic quotations preface the text, the first due an artist friend named Billy Bryant Copley: "Bob Dylan would do it!"; the other to Mao Tse-tung (as his name used to be spelled in Roman characters): "Every kind of thinking, without exception, is stamped with the brand of a class."[168] Notes at the bottom of the page specify the type of common stock warrants purchased and the broker with whom Lozano dealt. A final annotation, dated January 21, 1970, added that the artist still held the warrants, a particularly risky financial product, since the work was "feeding back quantities of info but so far no $." The same might be said of Morris's *Money*.

Investment Piece figures among the so-called language pieces that Lozano created in 1968–69. Working professionally in New York from 1960 onward, she had experimented for a few years with a variety of techniques, from expressionist figurative painting to Surrealist-inspired drawings infused with sexuality and violence, before turning to an almost monochrome style of abstract painting, meticulously executed, which led her to adopt an increasingly conceptual approach.[169] The language pieces were an outgrowth of her notebooks, simple ideas to begin with that she developed as she went along. The majority of them formulated a series of self-addressed instructions that made it possible to conduct experiments on her own life over longer or shorter periods of time. Despite the great variety of projects undertaken, the language pieces had a uniform format: Lozano made a clear distinction between, on the one hand, the work itself, "an act or series (set) of acts in time," which were explained in her notebooks; and, on the other hand, "write-ups," which she expressly identified as drawings—fair copies, made by hand and on blank paper, of the titles of the works on the occasion of their being exhibited.[170] The write-ups could be photocopied and offered for purchase. One of the first mentions of the investment project occurs in a notebook entry from January 1969, under the title "Lace Piece."[171] A write-up for the finished *Investment Piece* was done some four months later, on May 19, 1969, a few days before the show's opening at the Dwan Gallery.

The "subjective" perspective of *Investment Piece* can be understood only in relation to another work that Lozano had begun the month before, in April. Originally titled "Real Money Piece" in her notebook (fig. 58), it was included as a write-up in the Dwan Gallery show under the title *Cash Piece*. Not only did *Investment Piece* and *Cash Piece* share a common theme, money, Lozano herself always made sure that they were exhibited side by side.[172] *Cash Piece* described an experiment the artist conducted in her apartment. She took $585 from the sale of a painting and put it in a jar, in five, ten, and twenty dollar bills. She then invited visitors to take a little money for themselves from the jar, as if it were a box of chocolates, carefully observing and recording their reactions. While many were embarrassed, even offended by the offer (one friend, she noted with amusement, closed the jar and "screw[ed] the lid very tightly back on"), some accepted the offer, pleading financial need. Lightheartedly, without judging the behavior of her visitors, Lozano observed the way in which money affected individual psychology and attitudes toward others. By bringing out the difference between a gift of money and a traditional gift, her work

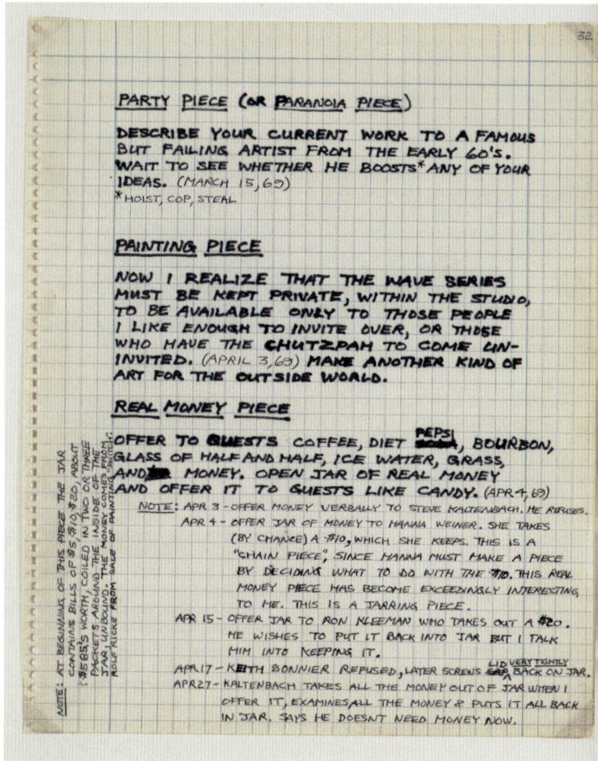

32

PARTY PIECE (OR PARANOIA PIECE)

DESCRIBE YOUR CURRENT WORK TO A FAMOUS BUT FAILING ARTIST FROM THE EARLY 60'S. WAIT TO SEE WHETHER HE BOOSTS* ANY OF YOUR IDEAS. (MARCH 15, 69)

*HOIST, COP, STEAL

PAINTING PIECE

NOW I REALIZE THAT THE WAVE SERIES MUST BE KEPT PRIVATE, WITHIN THE STUDIO, TO BE AVAILABLE ONLY TO THOSE PEOPLE I LIKE ENOUGH TO INVITE OVER, OR THOSE WHO HAVE THE CHUTZPAH TO COME UN-INVITED. (APRIL 3, 69) MAKE ANOTHER KIND OF ART FOR THE OUTSIDE WORLD.

REAL MONEY PIECE

OFFER TO GUESTS COFFEE, DIET PEPSI, BOURBON, GLASS OF HALF AND HALF, ICE WATER, GRASS, AND MONEY. OPEN JAR OF REAL MONEY AND OFFER IT TO GUESTS LIKE CANDY. (APR 4, 69)

NOTE: APR 3 - OFFER MONEY VERBALLY TO STEVE KALTENBACH. HE REFUSES.
APR 4 - OFFER JAR OF MONEY TO HANNA WEINER. SHE TAKES (BY CHANCE) A $10, WHICH SHE KEEPS. THIS IS A "CHAIN PIECE", SINCE HANNA MUST MAKE A PIECE BY DECIDING WHAT TO DO WITH THE $10. THIS REAL MONEY PIECE HAS BECOME EXCEEDINGLY INTERESTING TO ME. THIS IS A JARRING PIECE.
APR 15 - OFFER JAR TO RON KLEEMAN WHO TAKES OUT A $20. HE WISHES TO PUT IT BACK INTO JAR BUT I TALK HIM INTO KEEPING IT.
APR 17 - KEITH SONNIER REFUSED, LATER SCREWS LID VERY TIGHTLY BACK ON JAR.
APR 27 - KALTENBACH TAKES ALL THE MONEY OUT OF JAR WHEN I OFFER IT, EXAMINES ALL THE MONEY & PUTS IT ALL BACK IN JAR. SAYS HE DOESN'T NEED MONEY NOW.

NOTE: AT BEGINNING OF THIS PIECE THE JAR CONTAINS BILLS OF $5, $10, $20, ABOUT $585's WORTH, COILED IN TWO OR THREE PACKETS AROUND THE INSIDE OF THE JAR, UNBOUND. THE MONEY COMES FROM ROLF RICKE FROM SALE OF PAINTING "SWITCH".

Fig. 58 Lee Lozano, notebook write-ups ("Party Piece" [or "Paranoia Piece"]; "Painting Piece"; "Real Money Piece"), vol. 2, pages 32, 33, 33A, nos. 394, 395, 396, March 15, 1969–July 9, 1969. Graphite and ink on paper, three sheets, 11 × 9 in. (28 × 22.9 cm) each. Wadsworth Atheneum Museum of Art, Hartford, Connecticut. Alexander A. Goldfarb Contemporary Art Acquisition Fund, 1998.6.10a–c.

examined the relationship between objective economic constraints and her visitors' own highly personal feelings about money.

Investment Piece and *Cash Piece* were matching works, then, that together constituted an inquiry into the impact of money on individuals, the latter being informed by the reactions of others, the former having no experimental frame of reference beyond the artist's own reactions. In 1968, in her notebooks, Lozano had begun to question the commercial arrangements that governed the world of art and the way in which artists renounced their creative liberty and made themselves economically dependent on their dealers. In May 1969, she wrote: "Paul Bianchini lays a check for $500 on me for drawings he hasn't picked [out] yet. After he leaves . . . I have utterly empty feeling. Empty feeling is not because of visit, which was a lot of fun, but somehow is related to getting money."[173]

Whereas Levine tried to make his investment in *Profit Systems I* as public as possible, Lozano conceived of *Investment Piece* as an intimate exploration of her own feelings about monetary transaction in its most abstract form. If, as Mao claimed, all thinking bears the mark of class, how would the artist's way of thinking be affected by her new status as a holder of securities—as a capitalist? In one of the notes at the bottom of *Investment Piece*, Lozano makes it clear that she wishes to "'invest,' as opposed to 'speculate.'" While she did, in fact, acquire high-risk warrants, she was content merely to possess them and to hold on to them; selling them,

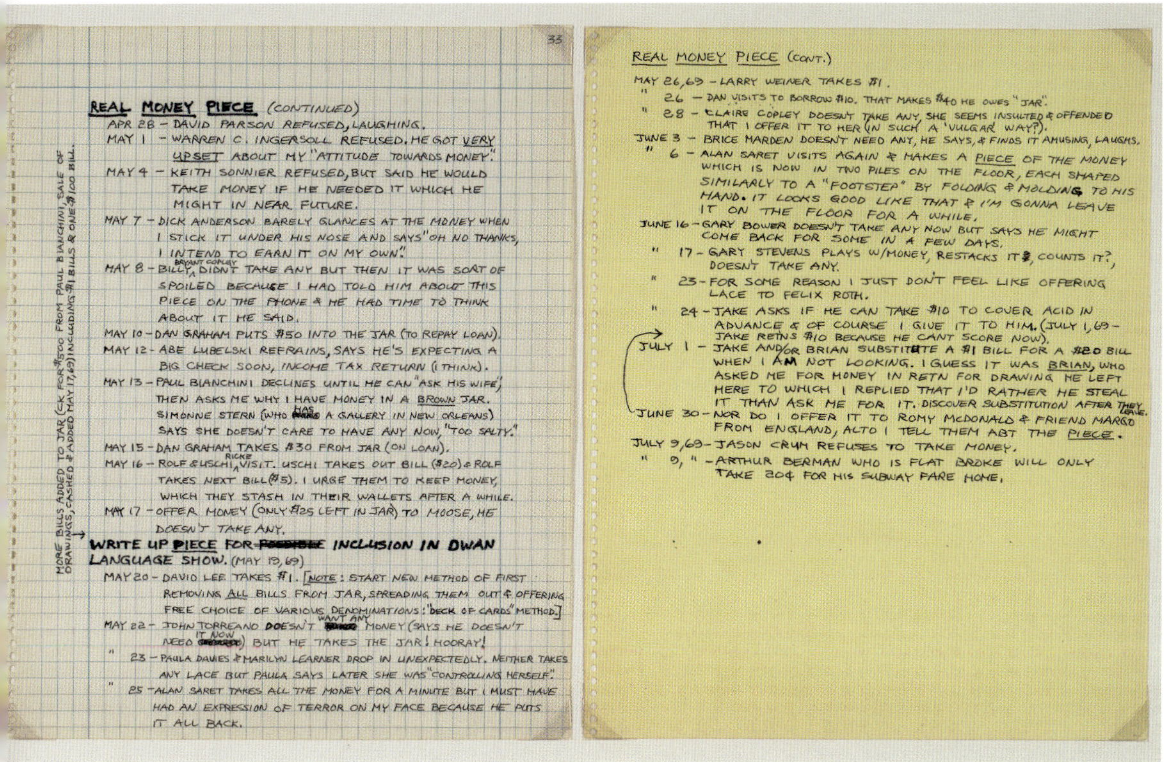

33

REAL MONEY PIECE (CONTINUED)

APR 28 – DAVID PARSON REFUSED, LAUGHING.
MAY 1 – WARREN C. INGERSOLL REFUSED. HE GOT VERY UPSET ABOUT MY "ATTITUDE TOWARDS MONEY."
MAY 4 – KEITH SONNIER REFUSED, BUT SAID HE WOULD TAKE MONEY IF HE NEEDED IT WHICH HE MIGHT IN NEAR FUTURE.
MAY 7 – DICK ANDERSON BARELY GLANCES AT THE MONEY WHEN I STICK IT UNDER HIS NOSE AND SAYS "OH NO THANKS, I INTEND TO EARN IT ON MY OWN."
MAY 8 – BILLY BRYANT COPLEY DIDN'T TAKE ANY BUT THEN IT WAS SORT OF SPOILED BECAUSE I HAD TOLD HIM ABOUT THIS PIECE ON THE PHONE & HE HAD TIME TO THINK ABOUT IT HE SAID.
MAY 10 – DAN GRAHAM PUTS $50 INTO THE JAR (TO REPAY LOAN).
MAY 12 – ABE LUBELSKI REFRAINS, SAYS HE'S EXPECTING A BIG CHECK SOON, INCOME TAX RETURN (I THINK).
MAY 13 – PAUL BIANCHINI DECLINES UNTIL HE CAN "ASK HIS WIFE," THEN ASKS ME WHY I HAVE MONEY IN A BROWN JAR. SIMONNE STERN (WHO HAS A GALLERY IN NEW ORLEANS) SAYS SHE DOESN'T CARE TO HAVE ANY NOW, "TOO SALTY."
MAY 15 – DAN GRAHAM TAKES $30 FROM JAR (ON LOAN).
MAY 16 – ROLF & USCHI RICKE VISIT. USCHI TAKES OUT BILL ($20) & ROLF TAKES NEXT BILL ($5). I URGE THEM TO KEEP MONEY, WHICH THEY STASH IN THEIR WALLETS AFTER A WHILE.
MAY 17 – OFFER MONEY (ONLY $25 LEFT IN JAR) TO MOOSE, HE DOESN'T TAKE ANY.

MORE BILLS ADDED TO JAR (CK FOR $500 FROM PAUL BIANCHINI, SALE OF DRAWINGS, CASHED & ADDED MAY 17, 69) INCLUDING $1 BILLS & ONE $100 BILL. →

WRITE UP PIECE FOR INCLUSION IN DWAN LANGUAGE SHOW. (MAY 19, 69)

MAY 20 – DAVID LEE TAKES $1. [NOTE: START NEW METHOD OF FIRST REMOVING ALL BILLS FROM JAR, SPREADING THEM OUT & OFFERING FREE CHOICE OF VARIOUS DENOMINATIONS: "DECK OF CARDS" METHOD.]
MAY 22 – JOHN TORREANO DOESN'T WANT ANY MONEY (SAYS HE DOESN'T NEED IT NOW) BUT HE TAKES THE JAR! HOORAY!
" 23 – PAULA DAVIES & MARILYN LEARNER DROP IN UNEXPECTEDLY. NEITHER TAKES ANY LACE BUT PAULA SAYS LATER SHE WAS "CONTROLLING HERSELF."
" 25 – ALAN SARET TAKES ALL THE MONEY FOR A MINUTE BUT I MUST HAVE HAD AN EXPRESSION OF TERROR ON MY FACE BECAUSE HE PUTS IT ALL BACK.

REAL MONEY PIECE (CONT.)

MAY 26, 69 – LARRY WEINER TAKES $1.
" 26 – DAN VISITS TO BORROW $10. THAT MAKES $40 HE OWES "JAR."
" 28 – CLAIRE COPLEY DOESN'T TAKE ANY, SHE SEEMS INSULTED & OFFENDED THAT I OFFER IT TO HER (IN SUCH A 'VULGAR' WAY?).
JUNE 3 – BRICE MARDEN DOESN'T NEED ANY, HE SAYS, & FINDS IT AMUSING, LAUGHS.
" 6 – ALAN SARET VISITS AGAIN & MAKES A PIECE OF THE MONEY WHICH IS NOW IN TWO PILES ON THE FLOOR, EACH SHAPED SIMILARLY TO A "FOOTSTEP" BY FOLDING & MOLDING TO HIS HAND. IT LOOKS GOOD LIKE THAT & I'M GONNA LEAVE IT ON THE FLOOR FOR A WHILE.
JUNE 16 – GARY BOWER DOESN'T TAKE ANY NOW BUT SAYS HE MIGHT COME BACK FOR SOME IN A FEW DAYS.
" 17 – GARY STEVENS PLAYS W/MONEY, RESTACKS IT, COUNTS IT?, DOESN'T TAKE ANY.
" 23 – FOR SOME REASON I JUST DON'T FEEL LIKE OFFERING LACE TO FELIX ROTH.
" 24 – JAKE ASKS IF HE CAN TAKE $10 TO COVER ACID IN ADVANCE & OF COURSE I GIVE IT TO HIM. (JULY 1, 69 – JAKE RETNS $10 BECAUSE HE CANT SCORE NOW).
JULY 1 – JAKE AND/OR BRIAN SUBSTITUTE A $1 BILL FOR A $20 BILL WHEN I AM NOT LOOKING. I GUESS IT WAS BRIAN, WHO ASKED ME FOR MONEY IN RETN FOR DRAWING HE LEFT HERE TO WHICH I REPLIED THAT I'D RATHER HE STEAL IT THAN ASK ME FOR IT. DISCOVER SUBSTITUTION AFTER THEY LEAVE.
JUNE 30 – NOR DO I OFFER IT TO ROMY McDONALD & FRIEND MARGO FROM ENGLAND, ALTO I TELL THEM ABT THE PIECE.
JULY 9, 69 – JASON CRUM REFUSES TO TAKE MONEY.
" 9, " – ARTHUR BERMAN WHO IS FLAT BROKE WILL ONLY TAKE 20¢ FOR HIS SUBWAY FARE HOME.

actively seeking to realize a profit, was not part of the instructions she had given herself at the outset of the experiment. Rather than play the role of the artist turned businessman or speculator, in the manner of Levine and Morris, Lozano assumed her new status as part of a plan for living that had less to do with what she did than who she was. Jo Applin has convincingly argued that the pose of "not working," while at the same time deploying the tools and procedures of work, is a constant theme throughout the artist's career that should be understood as inherently political.[174] Here, in thinking about her (non)involvement in a process through which capital begets capital, she interrupted a sterile, self-perpetuating cycle by introducing her own perception of herself as both a deeply personal being and a social creature. Art and finance were therefore conceived as two wholly interrelated spheres of existence, ways of simultaneously expressing individual and collective experience.

The language pieces do not seem to have produced the opportunity Lozano expected for subverting existing economic structures, however. From 1969 onward she gradually and, in the end, completely removed herself from the art world—this at the very moment when her success seemed most assured in view of the continuing support she enjoyed from gallery owners on both sides of the Atlantic (Bianchini in New York and Rolf Ricke in Cologne), and in advance of solo exhibits at the Whitney Museum (1970) and at the Nova Scotia College of Art and Design (1971). In February 1969, with *Withdrawal Piece*, she pulled out of a group exhibition organized by Richard Bellamy; five months later, in July, with *General Strike Piece*, she set for herself the objective of "gradually but determinedly avoid[ing] being present at official or public 'Uptown' functions or gatherings related to the 'art world.'"[175] Finally, with *Dropout Piece*, begun in 1971 as a month-long trial that became permanent, Lozano pushed the experiment to the point of no return: after editing her notebooks, she disappeared from the New York conceptual art scene and went underground, embarking on the ultimate stage in her "Life-Art" project.[176]

All four of the artistic shareholding experiments we have considered in this section, conducted simultaneously during the first half of 1969, were undertaken in reaction to the vogue of art as an investment that reached its height at the end of the decade. Nevertheless they have one crucial feature in common, namely, that they make the artist an actor in the spectacle of speculation, not merely a spectator. In so doing, they provided fresh insight into the interaction between the worlds of art and finance, and the grounds for comparing them. At the same time, a single principle—making investment in securities a work of art—was acted on to express four quite distinct positions. Levine considered *Profit Systems I* as a means of rethinking the role of the artist in society, of calling into question the mutual exclusion of art and daily life. He deprived art of its hermeticism by integrating it with what he took to be its opposite: the pedestrian world of business and finance, formerly seen not only as a closed and specialized domain, but also as the site par excellence of the exercise of practical reason. In so doing, Levine illuminated a paradoxical aspect of modern financial capitalism, where artists turn themselves into businessmen and Schumpeterian entrepreneurs take artistic activity as their model.

The experiments in artistic shareholding made by Morris, Graham, and Lozano, by contrast, did not inquire so much into the distance—and the convergence—between art and finance as the supposed isolation of each of these domains from social life in general. Morris used *Money* to explore from the inside the way in which a small number of actors (artists, museums, collectors, journals, and patrons) interact to produce artistic and financial value without reference to the rest of society. He thus likened art and finance in a manner that recalled John Maynard Keynes's famous comparison in the *General Theory* of the functioning of financial markets with that of a beauty contest.[177] Those among the contest's judges who will have foreseen the result in voting for the winning contestant are the real winners, more than the winning contestant herself. For the judges do not choose the "prettiest" contestant on the basis of their personal tastes, which is to say their subjective judgment; to the contrary, the ones who are able to guess which contestant will be preferred by a majority of their colleagues will prevail. Each judge must attempt to anticipate the reaction of his fellow judges, in other words, rather than consult his own personal opinion in arriving at a judgment. What Keynes did was model a completely self-referential financial system, in which no external—in this case, no aesthetic—factor needed to be taken into account, where no validation by the so-called real economy was necessary. Graham and Lozano took issue with this closed system. They tried to reintroduce an external factor, the general public in Graham's case, the social and psychological individual in Lozano's case. If finance and art are supposed to be self-referential spaces, reserved solely to a small number of interested parties, then both must be put to the test, assaulted, and forced to open up—or, failing that, abandoned altogether.

CHAPTER 4

Circuits of Commerce

By the early 1970s, artistic innovations were not solely responsible for changing the way artists thought about politics and the economy. The growth of international commerce, with the completion of the European Customs Union and the progressive enlargement of the European Community, went hand in hand with a geographical reconfiguration of the market for art in Europe, which now occupied an area whose centers were in the Netherlands, West Germany, and Switzerland. In the meantime the world economic situation continued to deteriorate, until finally a grave economic crisis put an end to the sustained cycle of growth that had characterized the postwar years. It was against this background that both the European and American art scenes became highly politicized after 1968, in large part because of the controversies surrounding wars of decolonization in the Third World. At a moment when the continuing prosperity of the major capitalist economies seemed suddenly to have been cast in doubt, and when the countries of the developing world were protesting their exploitation by developed countries, artists were naturally led to ask whether international commerce was a source, not of wealth and peace, but of domination, oppression, and impoverishment.

The idea that "the natural effect of commerce is to lead to peace" by establishing a relation of mutual dependence among nations, as Montesquieu famously argued in *The Spirit of the Laws*,[1] has been one of the chief justifications of free trade ever since. Keynes, following classical economists of the nineteenth century such as John Stuart Mill and Alfred Marshall, made the same argument in objecting to the Treaty of Versailles in *The Economic Consequences of the Peace*.[2] The close connection between the growth of commerce and the progress of peace was further insisted on by liberal thinkers between the wars, and it lay at the heart of the plan to unite Europe after World War II.[3] Jean Monnet expressed a widely shared view in holding that the creation of a common market was not only an economic matter; by bringing one into existence, "we shall have made an essential contribution to the cause of progress and peace."[4]

By the early 1970s, however, this assumption had lost much of its obviousness. Commercial liberalism was now widely seen, at least on the left, as a form of imperialism—war conducted by other means, to recast Carl von Clausewitz's celebrated formula. Once again the art market functioned as a laboratory for larger economic questions. Over the course of the 1960s, having been internationalized and financialized, it had demonstrated its capacity to absorb the most varied forms of contemporary art. Artists themselves were struck by the new geography of power that had taken shape, and by the intense, sometimes ruthless, competition that played out between the major centers of influence on both sides of the Atlantic. Until 1973, the persistence of high prices and speculation in spite of the looming crisis confirmed the impression of an artificially boosted demand for art and of a market that was headed for a fall that would be all the more dramatic the longer it was delayed.

Up to this point artists had explored the mechanisms of price and value, including a period of brief but concentrated interest in the role played by banknotes, and examined the functioning of stock markets. Now they ventured to take up the more general question of commerce. Whether it involved currencies or commodities, commerce was understood above all as a process of circulation, of encounter and exchange. Artists studied this process not only in its trade and monetary aspects, but also, and at the same time, as a social relationship founded on dialogue and communication—in the sense that one has commerce *with* someone, deals *with* someone. It will be useful, then, to adopt the notion of circuits of commerce elaborated by Viviana Zelizer in order to reject the separation of the "impersonal rationality" of market transactions from the "intimacy" of the world of human intercourse, in which money has no place.[5] Among artists, no one inquired more deeply into the permeability of these two domains than Ray Johnson and Marcel Broodthaers. In their own quite different ways, they brought out the human and social consequences of an expanding commercial sphere and reimagined the ways in which commerce, peace, and war are connected with one another.

RAY JOHNSON AND THE CRITIQUE OF COMMODIFICATION AND HUMAN COMMERCE

In a letter dated September 18, 1968, to his dealer and friend Richard Feigen, Ray Johnson wrote in characteristically cryptic fashion: "I have a planned TWIGGY face that has those Virginia Woolf kind of black boots walking across her face mascara running eyes but how to say TWIG PIG hasn't been worked out."[6] A few months later, the problem had been solved, and *Twiggy with Dollar Bill* (fig. 59) was shown at the Chelsea Gallery as part of an exhibition titled *The Art of Money* in April 1969. The collage was a great success, reproduced in a number of leading publications.[7] Johnson had long been in the habit of recycling familiar images disseminated by the mass media. In this case, he had borrowed from the cover of the April 10, 1967, issue of *Newsweek* featuring the smooth-skinned visage of Lesley

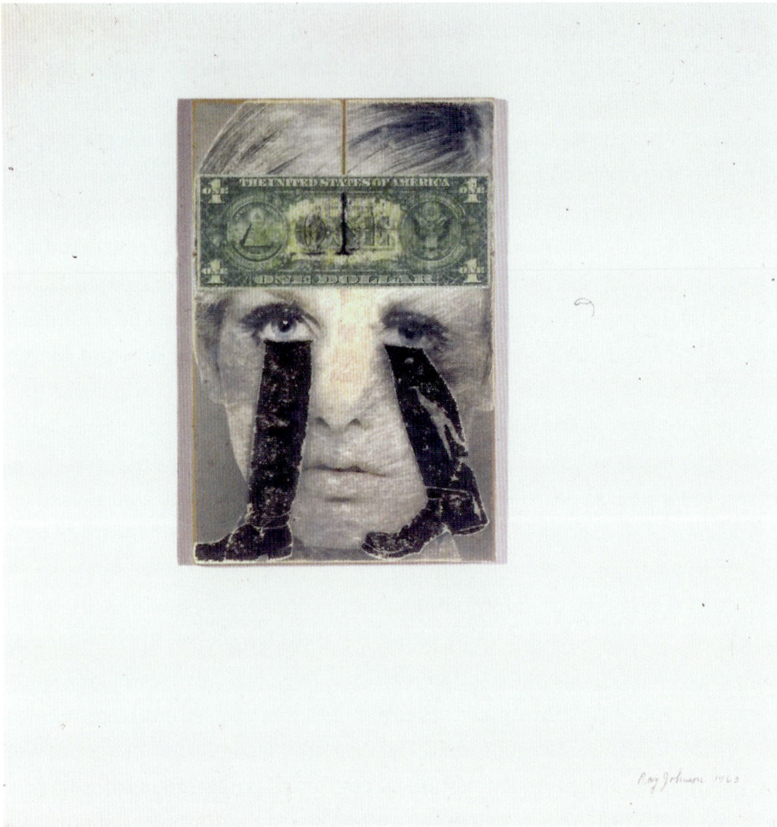

Fig. 59 Ray Johnson, *Twiggy with Dollar Bill*, c. 1969. Collage, 17 × 17 in. (43.2 × 43.2 cm). Collection of Lois and George de Menil.

Hornby, a slender English model known as Twiggy who had become an icon of pop culture in the 1960s, famous the world over for her androgynously youthful looks. Bert Stern's photograph of her for *Newsweek* emphasized the flawless contour of her unblemished face, the pouting lips and the big blue eyes. In Johnson's version, her girlish looks (she was only seventeen years old at the time) had faded: cut out and stuck to a cardboard backing, rubbed with an eraser and drawn over with pencil, the face is devoid of color except for the iris of each eye. Two misproportioned boots upset the equilibrium of Stern's picture still more strikingly. Glued to the bottom rims of the eyes and following their curves, the boots extend Twiggy's long eyelashes in two vertical strips that obscure her cheeks and appear to walk along the bottom edge of the work in such a way as to accentuate its rectangular frame. A dollar bill, damaged and stained, is pasted horizontally over her forehead, covering up the sweep of her blond hair. A faded red line running from the top edge straight down the middle, almost as far as the eyes, completes the composition, pointing to the almost imperceptibly oblique angle of the nose, which softens the cold symmetry of the original portrait.

Johnson's enigmatic letter to Feigen nonetheless provides a key for decoding the collage. Through a phonetic elision typical of his work, "Twiggy" has become "Twig Pig," an American slang term for a forest ranger (*pig* referring to a cop and *twig* standing metonymically for a wooded wilderness). The association of Virginia Woolf with high stiff black boots, symbolizing order and security in an almost Fascist manner, is to be interpreted as referring to a homophone of the author's last name, the wolf (an animal that logically enough calls to mind the forest) and dangers that lurk there. This consonance had been made famous scarcely two years earlier with the film adaptation by Mike Nichols of Edward Albee's play *Who's Afraid of Virginia Woolf?*, in which the phrase is sung to the tune of "Who's Afraid of the Big Bad Wolf?" from the 1933 Disney cartoon.[8] The film aroused attention and scandal at the time, as much for its glittering stars (Elizabeth Taylor and Richard Burton) and formal innovations as for its uncensored use of foul language. The movie tells the story of two couples who tear themselves apart. Repeating a classic rhyme of English literature, Nick (played by George Segal) confides that he was attracted to his wife, Honey (Sandy Dennis), mostly for her money.[9]

Is the dollar that blots out Twiggy's forehead therefore a talisman or an anathema? For Johnson, who throughout his career desperately courted and fled from success, money, and celebrity, the question remained unresolved. By following the visual and textual clues planted by the artist, looking carefully at the works themselves, and searching for their sources of inspiration in the arts, popular culture, and cinema, it will nonetheless be possible to decipher the series of dollar bill collages that Johnson produced between 1969 and 1971. We will see, too, that he managed to reconcile the tensions between his collages and his mail art by means of an elaborate system in which commerce was treated as both a monetized trading relationship and a relationship of friendly and cost-free exchange. Far from enforcing a strict separation between the personal and the monetary, he explored their interactions in an attempt to exploit the fundamental ambiguity of using commercial exchange for humane purposes, restoring the social dimension of trade while at the same time warning against the threat commerce poses of converting human beings into commodities.

The Economics of Collage and Mail Art

Born in 1927 in Detroit, Johnson belonged to the same generation as Robert Rauschenberg. Like Rauschenberg, he studied in the late 1940s at Black Mountain College in North Carolina, where he took courses with Josef Albers and developed an interest in the art of Marcel Duchamp and the tradition of collage.[10] With the help of friends from Black Mountain he was able to settle in New York in 1949. There he was introduced to the abstract painter Ad Reinhardt, soon becoming his assistant. At this time Johnson was experimenting with small collages mounted on reclaimed sheets of cardboard, sanded, and painted, which he called "moticos"—an anagram of *osmotic*—signifying something permeable and perpetually changing. Reinhardt photographed them in 1955 and two years later put together a group exhibition, the first show in which Johnson took part.[11] His early compositions, such as

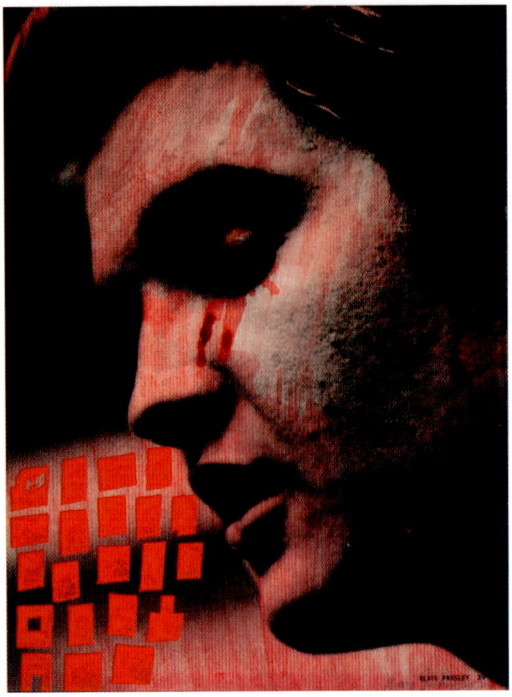

Fig. 60 Ray Johnson, *Oedipus (Elvis Presley #1)*, 1956–57. Collage, 10 × 7 in. (25.4 × 17.8 cm). Private collection.

Oedipus (Elvis Presley #1) from 1956–57 (fig. 60), drew inspiration from magazine images of entertainers and public figures, and rapidly brought him to the attention of critics. (One reads in the January 1958 issue of *Art News*, for example, that Jasper Johns's "first one-man show places him with such better-known colleagues as Rauschenberg, Twombly, Kaprow, and Ray Johnson.")[12] This initial notoriety eventually led to his being classified as "pre-pop," a term that haunted him in later years. In the mind of an artist who never enjoyed the same popular acclaim as Warhol or many of the others who came to prominence before and after, the term was synonymous with missed opportunity or failure.

And yet this lack of success—particularly commercial success—seems almost to have been orchestrated throughout his career, in large part by Johnson himself. As the historian Donna De Salvo, organizer of one of the very few large-scale exhibitions of the artist's work, observed several years after his death, "Johnson's ambivalence for the institutions of the art world and marketplace led him to develop other ways of circulating and exhibiting his work."[13] More than three decades earlier, in April 1965, Grace Glueck had written in the *New York Times* about his solo exhibition at the Willard Gallery:

> Though Johnson's collages have for years been creeping into first-rate collections, he's never before had a gallery show. His previous exhibitions have been fairly impromptu—on side-walks, in Grand Central Station and down on Peck Slip. "I've never really believed in the gallery thing," said Johnson, a baby-bald young man in a leather

> motorcycle jacket. "But at the same time I've been dying for a show. Ambivalence, you see. Occasionally I visit collectors with a box of collages wrapped in newspaper under my arm, like a Fuller Brush man. That pleases me."

Johnson, Glueck concluded, lived in "voluntary poverty" on the Lower East Side and was certainly "New York's most famous unknown artist."[14] Five years later, in March 1970, Rosalind Constable made the same observation in a long article in *New York Magazine*: "If Johnson didn't make the same splash [as Rauschenberg or John Cage] it was partly due to his own reticence." Shocked by the nearly fatal attack on his old friend Andy Warhol in June 1968, and "[r]efusing all gallery offers," he left Manhattan for the town of Glen Cove, on the north shore of Long Island, settling shortly afterward in nearby Locust Valley, "[w]here he continues to live in almost total seclusion."[15] The main vehicle of Johnson's underground celebrity, outside the commercial system, was a postal network that he called the New York Correspondance School (NYCS), slightly altering the name given it by the painter Edward M. Plunkett sometime in 1962.[16] Through this network Johnson sent out letters combining text and images with collage fragments and miscellaneous scraps of material. As early as 1955, a columnist for the *Village Voice* had reported that scores of people were receiving mysterious mailings on an occasional or regular basis: "I'd heard about them from a friend who inexplicably found himself on a moticos mailing list one day. 'I send lists to people I think would be interested or to people I think won't be interested,' explained Ray. There are 200 people on his mailing list so far, including [gossip columnist] Elsa Maxwell and the Museum of Modern Art's James [*sic*] Barr."[17]

Johnson's postal communications shared the themes, style, and materials of his collages as well as what the critic John Gruen described as their "enigmatic playfulness."[18] Sometimes these two branches of his art were fused: fragments of written correspondence were apt to find a new place within a collage; conversely, a work considered unsatisfactory for one reason or another might be torn in pieces and mailed in an envelope to someone. The fundamental distinction that Johnson made between the two had less to do with a difference in kind—though it is true the collages were generally more elaborate, whereas the postal pieces were rapidly executed and often had a more spontaneous quality—than with a difference in economic status, as the artist made clear in a document from the early 1970s titled "My Career" (fig. 61):

> I developed two activities:
> (1) Free distribution of mailed envelope-enclosure art. . . .
> (2) Creation of collage compositions containing sandpapered painted cardboard chunks casting shadows with hand-lettered poems, ink drawings of combs, condoms, massage balls and snakes, lists of Famous

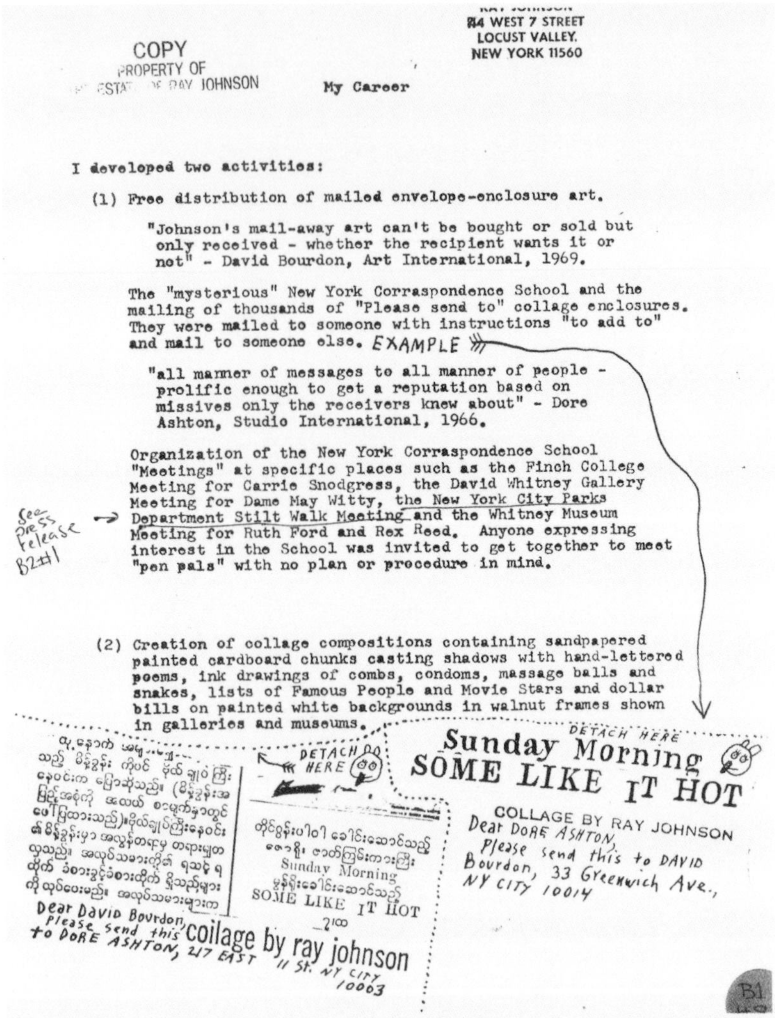

COPY
PROPERTY OF
ESTATE OF RAY JOHNSON

RAY JOHNSON
44 WEST 7 STREET
LOCUST VALLEY,
NEW YORK 11560

My Career

I developed two activities:

(1) Free distribution of mailed envelope-enclosure art.

"Johnson's mail-away art can't be bought or sold but only received - whether the recipient wants it or not" - David Bourdon, Art International, 1969.

The "mysterious" New York Corraspondence School and the mailing of thousands of "Please send to" collage enclosures. They were mailed to someone with instructions "to add to" and mail to someone else. EXAMPLE

"all manner of messages to all manner of people - prolific enough to get a reputation based on missives only the receivers knew about" - Dore Ashton, Studio International, 1966.

See Press Release B2#1 → Organization of the New York Corraspondence School "Meetings" at specific places such as the Finch College Meeting for Carrie Snodgress, the David Whitney Gallery Meeting for Dame May Witty, the New York City Parks Department Stilt Walk Meeting and the Whitney Museum Meeting for Ruth Ford and Rex Reed. Anyone expressing interest in the School was invited to get together to meet "pen pals" with no plan or procedure in mind.

(2) Creation of collage compositions containing sandpapered painted cardboard chunks casting shadows with hand-lettered poems, ink drawings of combs, condoms, massage balls and snakes, lists of Famous People and Movie Stars and dollar bills on painted white backgrounds in walnut frames shown in galleries and museums.

Fig. 61 Ray Johnson, artist's statement titled "My Career," c. 1972. Ray Johnson Archives.

People and Movie Stars and dollar bills on painted white backgrounds in walnut frames shown in galleries and museums.[19]

The strictly "free" status of the mail art, by contrast with the collages "shown in galleries and museums," was emphasized in this same document by a quote from a 1969 article by David Bourdon: "Johnson's mail-away art can't be bought or sold but only received—whether the recipient wants it or not."[20] Anyone who exhibited the often-collective products of the NYCS's activity or, worse, put them up for sale, was liable to incur Johnson's wrath and find his or her name removed from the mailing list.[21] By the late 1960s, Johnson had acquired a reputation as a profoundly unselfish artist, devoting eight to ten hours a day to his "non-profit" and "all free" enterprise, with the result that, for want of "a patron willing to furnish an endowment fund," he was "driven by economic necessity to exhibit marketable collages" in order to finance his other activities.[22] This view of Johnson's motivations caused a sort of legend to grow up around him, propagated in France by the art historian Jean-Marc Poinsot, who asserted that "sending collages, theoretical writings, [and] objects to various recipients without financial compensation is tantamount to challenging the laws of the marketplace."[23] Johnson was considered a pioneer for developing a new conception of the economy of art, founded not on money but on free exchange. As the authors of a tribute to the artist published in 1999, four years after his death, put it: "We celebrate his attempt to forge a new art, based on the correspondence between artists, rather than the competition and commerce making mainstream art. . . . Johnson's mailings provoked a new art with no center, no financial reward and little chance for widespread recognition. Art was a gift for Johnson, who challenged fellow artists to emulate him through his own natural generosity."[24]

And yet this view is too simple. As the historian Ina Blom has shown, Johnson himself did not subscribe to the basic principles of mail art that came to be formulated in the 1970s: communication, creation of a nonhierarchical and democratic social network, ritual generosity, and interactivity.[25] To the contrary, under Johnson's direction the New York Correspondance School was characterized by a centralized and unapologetically hierarchical mode of operation, exclusive, elitist, and, above all, nonreciprocal. The practice of "Add and Send To," which assumed the form of triangular communications among NYCS members supervised by the artist himself, subverted the very logic of exchange—constituting, in effect, a critique of the concept of gift giving as something personal and mutual. Moreover, Johnson's relationship to money and the system of market recognition was much more complex than a mere attitude of rejection would suggest. Far from dissociating himself from these things, he constantly positioned himself in relation to them. "Something went foul with my career," he told a journalist in early 1969. "I was not the success I wanted to be."[26] For Johnson, mercantile commerce became instead a pretext for social commerce, so that the act of negotiating the price for a work of art was transformed into a collaborative form of artistic innovation. As the artists Christo and Jeanne-Claude later recalled, "discussing the price [was] a continuation of the creative process." Once the terms of sale had been agreed upon, an endless sequence of letters and telephone calls was set in motion, often in their turn announcing future mailings that would entail reusing or adding to or cutting up existing works.[27] The very personal system of commerce constructed by Johnson's dual practice of collage and mail art will be easier to understand if we look at the *Dollar Bill* collages he created in 1970.

The Dollar Bill Collages and Artistic Commerce

It may have been Johnson's success with *Twiggy with Dollar Bill* that led him to undertake a series of works inspired by this same banknote. The *Dollar Bill* collages formed the basis of two exhibitions, first at the Richard

Feigen Gallery in Chicago, in September 1970, where nineteen works were shown, and then at Feigen's New York gallery in April 1971.[28] At the beginning of 1970, preparing for these shows, Johnson found himself swamped with work. "Have been up to my neck in polka dots and dollar bills," he wrote to his friend the painter Richard Lippold, "trying to finish another $ ten paintings the Gypsy Rose Lee tombstone was a flop the Frank O'Hara tombstone was a flop but Marilyn Monroe dollar bill and Cornell dollar bill a success so that's only eight more to go. Am very behind in my schedule & full of anxiety but it will all get done."[29] A few months later, in June, he was pleased to be able to inform the artist Dana Atchley (in a letter signed "Peggy Guggenheim") of his progress: "I am doing the Ted Kennedy dollar bill today, finished Midnight Cowboy and will do an Ed Ruscha dollar bill. His nose!"[30]

The *Dollar Bill* collages are, in many respects, the most ambitious series Johnson had attempted up until then, considering not only their format but also their extreme sophistication, meticulously conceived compositions that exploit startling contrasts between geometric shapes and curvilinear silhouettes. Each collage comprises a great many related elements: moticos, fragments of letters and press clippings, postcards, and photographs, some mounted on cardboard, which create layers of uneven thickness giving rise to an interplay of relief and shadow. Black and white are dominant, but colored elements—particularly the green of the banknotes neatly glued to the surface of each work, perfectly level with it—heighten the overall effect. Flowers and birds form ornamental friezes; innumerable polka dots are elegantly scattered over black surfaces; certain raised elements are further emphasized by being framed with chevrons. The finishing decorative touches that impart an air of fastidious refinement to these works give some idea of how much time the artist spent laboring over them. Just so, the *Dollar Bill* collages were offered for sale in Chicago at a higher price than his earlier works, between $1,200 and $1,800 each.[31]

By incorporating actual dollar bills in his work, Johnson reaffirmed a system of artistic value founded on the dichotomy between free mail art and expensive collages—this at a time when the market seemed capable of accommodating any form of art through vast inflows of money in search of investment opportunities. Since the late 1960s, in fact, Johnson had seen his letters sold at auction.[32] "He had always been very clear about never letting NYCS material be sold," Michael Findlay, manager of the Feigen Gallery in Chicago at the time and the organizer of the 1970 exhibition there, recalled many years later, "but he reinforced his position at that time."[33] The invasion of the domain of art by money is plainly an important theme of the *Dollar Bill* collages; in the case of *Marilyn Monroe Dollar Bill* (fig. 62), it is the central concern. Here the viewer is presented with the silhouette of a person seen from behind, arms raised. The line of the neck and the shoulders is sinuous, the ears and hair are sharply delineated; moticos mark the armpits. Ink drawings of flowers, animals, fairies, and sirens cover the upper

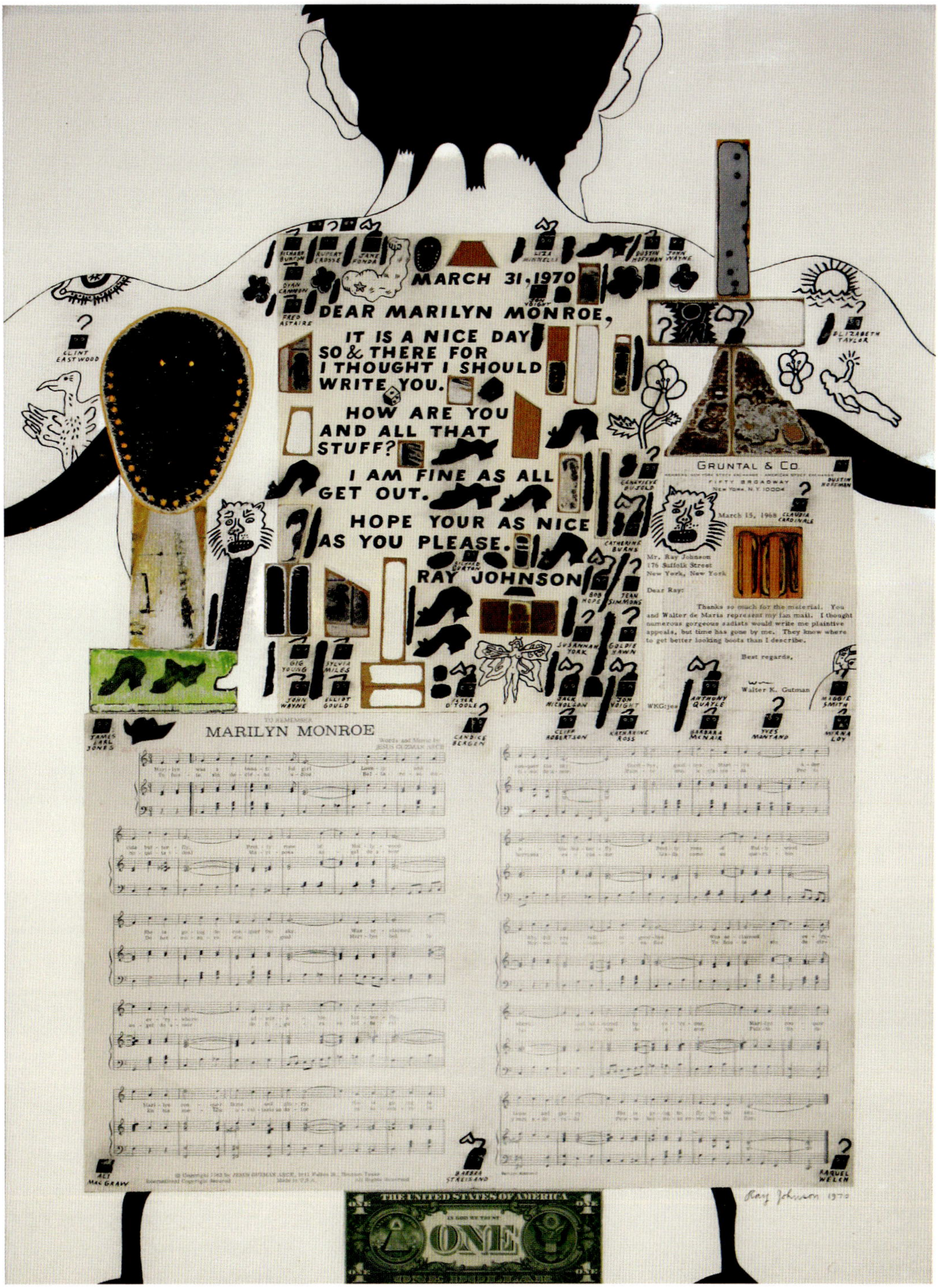

Fig. 62 Ray Johnson, *Marilyn Monroe Dollar Bill*, 1970. Collage, 30 × 20 in. (76.2 × 50.8 cm). Private collection.

back like tattoos. Glued to the surface at the center, just below the nape of the neck, is a letter dated March 31, 1970, and addressed to Marilyn Monroe, who had died almost eight years earlier. The lower back is marked off by the horizontal line of a piece of sheet music for a hymn titled "To Remember Marilyn Monroe" by Jesús Guzmán Arce, which constitutes the rest of the body, apart from two short legs and feet at the bottom, drawn in ink, between which appears the back of a dollar bill. Strewn throughout the composition are small black square legends bearing the names of film actors who were popular in the late 1960s, notably (and more than once) Elizabeth Taylor and Richard Burton, the stars of *Who's Afraid of Virginia Woolf?*, and Jon Voight and Dustin Hoffman, who had recently won praise for their performances in *Midnight Cowboy*.[34]

Success and celebrity are linked in this work with anxieties of death and oblivion. The letter to Marilyn Monroe, which starts off in a bantering tone ("How are you and all that stuff?"), reads like a tragicomic provocation. The stationery—actually a form letter Johnson frequently used in 1970 and afterward, as though to deprive his correspondence of any personal quality—is covered with women's shoes drawn in ink. They cannot fail to recall the shoe drawings that first brought Andy Warhol attention in the field of advertising and graphic design (he was still working as a commercial illustrator when Johnson met him in the mid-1950s).[35] By 1970, when Johnson created this collage, Monroe and Warhol were bound together by success and its potentially morbid consequences: Warhol's images of the movie star had made him a celebrity in his own right, though he did survive the attack on his life two years earlier. Attached to this letter to Marilyn Monroe is another letter, addressed to Johnson and dated March 15, 1968. It is signed by Walter K. Gutman, a man who worked both as an artist and as a broker on Wall Street. Gutman was also a stock market analyst and advisor to several investment funds, known in particular for his witty and inventive weekly letters on the market, collected in 1969 under the title *The Gutman Letter*.[36] For Johnson, it would appear, it was but a short step from a noncommercial NYCS letter, addressed to a deceased actress, to correspondence with the author of a market letter circulating among financiers and investors.

The connection between art and the acquisitive desire it arouses among wealthy collectors, repeatedly stressed by the carefully wrought detail of the collage, is made explicit in a long funny letter Johnson sent to Feigen and Findlay in late December 1968.[37] The artist adopts the persona of "BB"—not Brigitte Bardot, the French sex symbol of the 1960s, but Miss Bill Blass (a reference not only to the well-known American fashion designer but also to a banknote ["bill"])—a wealthy lady inquiring about the works of art offered for sale in their gallery. "I just love modern art," the letter begins, "and I happen to have a big house with a lot of waltz [*sic*] space." The collector goes on to say exactly what it is she has in mind. Frustrated in her attempt to buy the collages of Kurt Schwitters ("snatched up years ago by discerning collectors"), she is now looking for "a really gorgeous batch of lovely sort of collage things in well-made frames that have a refined look so people seeing what I have bought for my waltz can see what good taste I have and I like things to have a sort of relief-shadow effect with maybe a humorous looney black and white ink drawing thrown in on the side for comic relief like I just love shoes. . . ."

Wryly hinting at the great value such "refined" collages cannot help but have, Johnson makes fun of collectors for treating them as precious objects. He goes on in the rest of the letter to examine the collector's motivations. They are of three kinds: narcissistic and sociological—displaying Johnson's work, so that Miss Blass (sounding like Robert Scull in *Life* magazine) can go on "explaining to the art tours how much I love it"; speculative—"invest[ing] in the right artist"; and philanthropic—aiding the starving artist.[38] Artist, art dealer, and collector all have their place in this perfectly functioning system: after all, as Miss Blass observes of the artist, "his job [is] to do and make just as it is your job to sell his things and my role to buy these things." There is just one point on which she is unsure, which interferes with this coherent vision of the art world:

> And now in closing I must ask you if you happen to know where I can get some of that correspondance art I have been hearing about? I think I read in Vogue about this free art you can get by writing for it and all these gorgeous free things get mailed to you and you just have to ask for them and you get put on a list and someone somewhere has all this art that is made just for you alone to look at in a quiet place. . . . We got to watch this love stuff we really can't have people sending out free art work because people like me so concerned with helping the artist by buying their work don't like to think someone else has a great collection of things they got free from some mysterious place like the North Pole. . . . But if these things are being given away through your gallery perhaps I'd rather get these than buying the work. But I hear it isn't quite the same thing. Isn't what you pay for much better than what you get free? I have to have all this explained to me I don't know much about politics or economy.

With the *Dollar Bill* collages, Johnson managed to come to grips more directly than he had before with the problem of money and its influence in the art world. In a December 1970 letter to Findlay about preparations for the New York exhibit, composed in a style that could only recall Miss Blass, Johnson described it as "[a] satiric document of an artist living on the planet Earth creating enduring and everlasting important art products attempting to organize a presentation of *Dollar Bill* works in elegant wooden frames for the waltz with sensitive lighting and white walls whisked ever so clean with Fantastic spray. I think it humorously expresses the feeling so many other sensitive artists must feel at this time of national economic confusion and a necessity to think of costs, sizes and survival."[39] The "national economic confusion" Johnson mentions went beyond the depressed state of the art market, jocularly described in the letter from Miss Blass and later with a certain morbid sense of unease in *Marilyn Monroe Dollar Bill.* In a subsequent letter, written in early January 1971, Johnson associated the lukewarm reception given to the *Dollar Bills* exhibit in Chicago the previous fall with the deteriorating economic and political situation: "Mr. Nixon is in the White House and things are so bad all over the country and prices are soaring and the blacks have it so bad."[40] Artistic commerce, monetary crisis, and racial struggle all come together in Johnson's economic system.

Demonetized Collages vs. Mail Art as Circulating Currency

Between the two wars, the German artist Kurt Schwitters—to whom Johnson was often compared in the early stages of his career, and whose work he mentions in the Miss Blass letter—had likewise incorporated banknotes in his collages, which became particularly coveted items during the 1950s (fig. 63). But there it was a case, as historians noted, of "devalued post-World War I marks . . . before the extreme inflation that a little later made German currency so valueless that Schwitters might almost have picked up thousand-mark notes with the other scrap paper he found on the sidewalk."[41] In Johnson's *Dollar Bill* collages the opposite process was at work—not elevating refuse to the rank of precious works of art, but degrading monetary assets by treating them as the dregs of a consumer society. The artist accomplished singlehandedly what intensifying inflation was then threatening to do on a far larger scale, namely, undermine the worth of financial assets by reducing currency itself to a paper image, all the less valuable the more massively it was printed. Johnson was quite conscious that including money in his collages had the effect of demonetizing it, and confided in his dealer about his concerns regarding the legality of this practice: "[I] spoke to Michael [Findlay] quite some time ago about the legal problem which doesn't seem to exist at this time but to exhibit twenty paintings featuring dollar bills, I do not want to have any trouble in Chicago with the Mayor or the American Legion Daughters etc so *please* assure me . . . if you can consult one of your lawyers that what I—we are doing is [in the] legal realm of art."[42]

Johnson was doing two things in these *Dollar Bill* collages, then, both guaranteeing the value of the collage by incorporating real money in it and depriving money of value by making it merely one of the component materials. On this view, whereas commerce serves to establish a scale of equivalence among assets, art operates as a differentiating process that disrupts the economic order. Paradoxically, the works that Johnson considered to have monetary value, his collages, had the effect of demonetizing money by withdrawing it from circulation—for the very fact that a currency is current, as the seventeenth-century English economist Nicholas Barbon observed, the fact that it is used and accepted as legal tender, is what gives

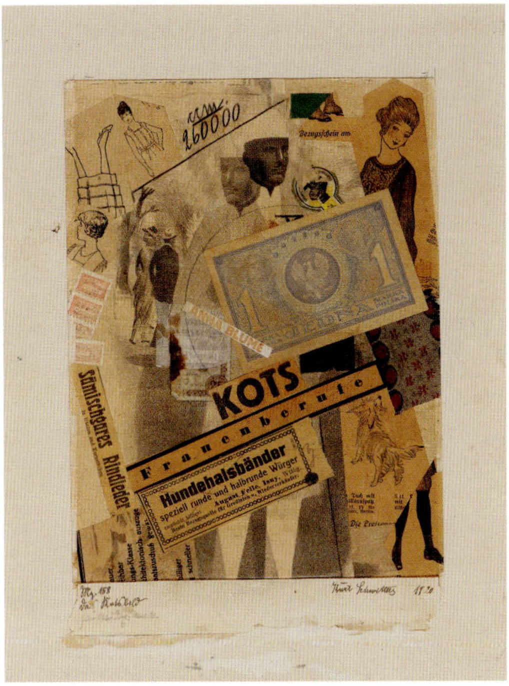

Fig. 63 Kurt Schwitters, *Mz. 158 Das Kotsbild*, 1920. Collage, 10⅞ × 8⅛ in. (27.5 × 20.7 cm). Sprengel Museum, Hannover, Germany.

it value.[43] Mail art, by contrast, conceived of as something free and standing apart from the commercial system, is "constantly in motion."[44] In this sense it is more like a currency, if we are to believe those philosophers, economists, anthropologists, and historians who regard currencies primarily as the expression of a social relation, specifically one of indebtedness. According to these authors—in France, members of what Michel Aglietta calls the "regulation school" or analysts of what Jean-Pierre Dupuy and André Orléan call the "economy of conventions"—social ties, and the sanctions and honors associated with them, brought about the birth of money, whose value derives from the perceived legitimacy of these bonds.[45]

The question arises, then, whether the New York Correspondance School, hierarchically structured around Johnson, can be thought of as a system of indebtedness in which mail art became a form of money, a circulating currency. It seems that Johnson himself had considered the idea. In 1968, for example, he sent obviously counterfeit banknotes (apparently taken from a children's board game) to the art critic Lucy Lippard, a member of the NYCS (fig. 64).[46] Emblazoned on the front with the image of an eagle (the symbol that figured so prominently in Broodthaers's work of this same period), the bills—representing a total of 167,132 units in various denominations—are clearly identified as "PLAY MONEY" and bear the legend "NO VALUE." Johnson also sent her a Western Union message concerning a money order from "Mrs. Sarah Harris" to "Sam Wong," with the instruction: "Please send to Sam Wagstaff, Detroit Art Institute" (fig. 65). Lippard was, therefore, only a transitory link in the service of a notional currency advertised as "Money Sent by Telegraph and Cable to All the World."

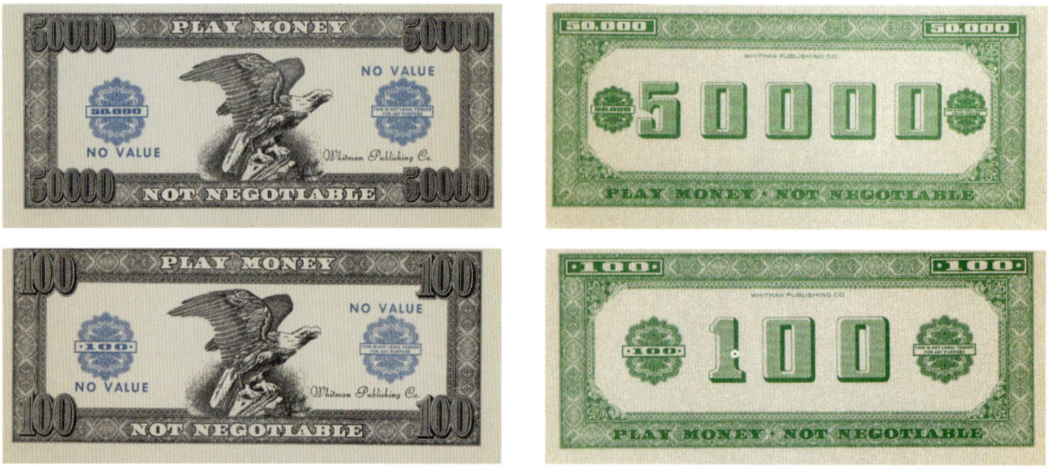

Fig. 64 Ray Johnson, untitled mailing (play money), 1968. Lucy R. Lippard Papers, Archives of American Art, Smithsonian Institution, series 2.1, box 10, folders 33–37.

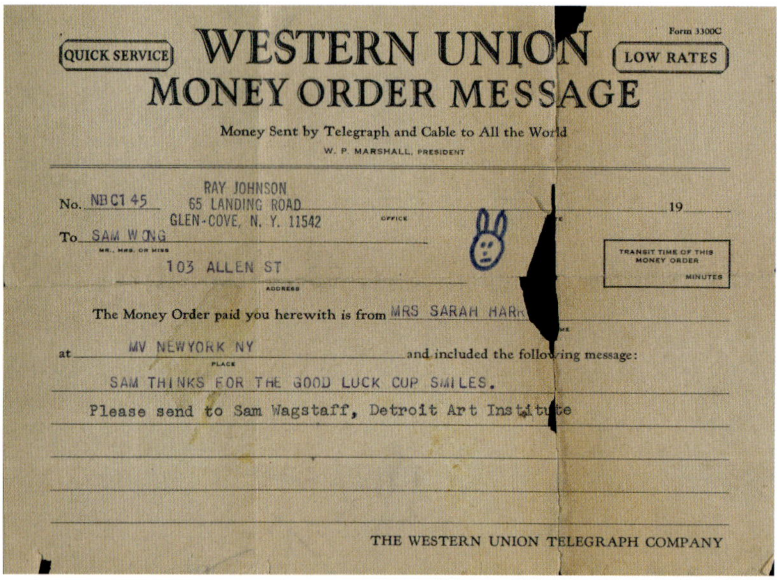

Form 3300C

QUICK SERVICE — WESTERN UNION — LOW RATES

MONEY ORDER MESSAGE

Money Sent by Telegraph and Cable to All the World

W. P. MARSHALL, PRESIDENT

No. NBC1 45 — RAY JOHNSON, 65 LANDING ROAD, GLEN-COVE, N. Y. 11542 — OFFICE — 19

To SAM WONG

MR., MRS. OR MISS

103 ALLEN ST

ADDRESS

TRANSIT TIME OF THIS MONEY ORDER — MINUTES

The Money Order paid you herewith is from MRS SARAH HAR

at MV NEWYORK NY (PLACE) and included the following message:

SAM THINKS FOR THE GOOD LUCK CUP SMILES.

Please send to Sam Wagstaff, Detroit Art Institute

THE WESTERN UNION TELEGRAPH COMPANY

Fig. 65 Ray Johnson, untitled mailing (telegram), 1968. Lucy R. Lippard Papers, Archives of American Art, Smithsonian Institution, series 2.1, box 10, folders 33–37.

Some of Johnson's recipients seem to have liked the idea, and toyed with it themselves on several occasions. In 1970, in response to Johnson's "play money" mailing, Dana Atchley—a Boston-born artist who traveled throughout the United States on his Ace Space bus showing the work of more than three hundred artists—sent NYCS members sheets of "real money" for them to cut out and personalize.[47] "Take this sheet of real money," Atchley instructed his correspondents, "cut out the bills and fill them in with your own images. See what you can get with them."[48] Another artist, Eleanor Antin, sent a check dated October 31, 1969, payable to the order of "Ray Johnsong," on which she said she was "thinking of you sinking of you thinking of dollars."[49] The Image Bank, an artists' collaborative founded by Michael Morris and Vincent Trasov in 1969, went further than anyone else in using mail art as an alternative and free currency. The group's name played on the ambiguity of a phrase that could refer to both a database created by Morris and Trasov in organizing their postcard shows and a financial institution that puts images into circulation as money.[50] Thus, for example, the group's contribution to a 1972 volume titled *Art Work, No Commercial Value*, consisted of a photocopied postcard stamped with the notice: "Post Card/Legal Tender."[51] The members of Image Bank referred to themselves as "[i]mage bankers" and distributed an annual report, as ordinary businesses do, in which they claimed to have created "a valid information economy" based on "process rather than product economics." The reason for doing this, they explained, is "simply that money earned in the conventional way costs more than it is worth."[52]

It would therefore be mistaken to set the ordinary commerce of art, founded on impersonal monetary relationships, against mail art, seen as instituting an alternative circuit of commerce in which money played no part. In many respects, Johnson himself made this interpretation untenable by demonetizing money in his *Dollar Bill* collages and by actively working to make postal correspondence a form of currency among the agents of an artistic economy based on trade.

From the Commodification of Art to the Commodification of Human Beings

Once a monetary system can no longer be clearly distinguished from social and personal relations, the problem of treating human beings as commodities naturally presents itself, particularly in connection with slavery and prostitution. At the beginning of the 1970s, a time when, as we have seen, financial crisis in the United States aggravated not only a volatile art market and an inflationary economy but also divisive debates about racial and sexual inequality, this question came to occupy a central place in Johnson's work.

An April 1968 interview, in which Johnson wondered about the feasibility of one day "sell[ing] my meetings,"[53] represented a decisive step in the direction of transgressing the ultimate economic taboo: the sale of human beings. These events, held by Johnson at irregular intervals beginning that same year, were a kind of "happening," intended to attract members of the NYCS and anyone else interested in its activities.[54] Usually they amounted to nothing more than simply getting people to talk about various subjects in person. Like everything connected with the NYCS, the meetings were free of charge, but in this interview Johnson imagined how they might be made to generate a stream of revenue. In buying a meeting, "you would get for about one month, if one is interested, the whole creative process." The sort of commercialization he had in mind was so radical, however, as to be tantamount to prostitution. "[W]ith some sum of money like $1,000," he suggested to the interviewer, "a person can buy a meeting, can buy Ray Johnson, can buy you."[55] The sale of art, under these circumstances, would be indistinguishable from the sale of a person—the artist himself.

One of the *Dollar Bill* collages, *Joe Buck Dollar Bill* (fig. 66), a work from the 1970 series, takes up the question directly. From a formal point of view, the work plays fast and loose with the modernist conventions of collage, particularly the enclosure of a work by a rectangular frame and the flatness of the plane surface. The white background of the support, set off by an elegant wooden frame (not visible in the figure), frames in its turn a black background that covers a nonrectangular surface whose boundaries are everywhere overstepped by a set of outsized elements. Some elements, such as the dollar bill, are glued flat onto the surface; others—the legend "Joe Buck," a photograph of Josephine Baker, fragments of the comic strip "Nancy," painstakingly copied by Johnson in blue ink—are mounted on thick cardboard, contradicting the supposed flatness of the image. The relief is completed by moticos, ranged on two levels in the upper part of the work. The collage functions visually as a puzzle in three dimensions, in which various pieces overlap, not only superficially but also in a layered fashion.

The puzzle is further complicated by a sophisticated scheme of correspondences among the various elements of the collage, in particular the photographic portrait surmounted by a dollar bill, at the center of the work, which itself is surmounted by the name of the work's title character, spelled out in black letters on a white ground. A phonetic similarity accounts for the transition from "Joe Buck" to "Josephine Baker." The related passage from masculine to feminine, and vice versa, is explained by the dancer's masculine style of dress in the photograph: top hat, black tuxedo, white shirt, and white bowtie—visually echoed by the white bow in Nancy's hair. Joe Buck is the name of the hero of *Midnight Cowboy*, the ground-breaking film directed by John Schlesinger that came out in May 1969. Johnson's fascination with the movie is evident: it figures in another collage in the 1970 series called *Midnight Cowboy Dollar Bill*, the object of several mailings as well.[56] It tells the tragic tale of Joe Buck, "a funny, dim-witted variation on the lonely, homosexual dream-hero," in the words of one prominent critic of the period,[57] who has come to New York from Texas to make his fortune as a male prostitute catering to rich women of a certain age, dressed in his immutable cowboy outfit. His hopes are quickly dashed. Reduced to poverty, he is forced to sell his services to an increasingly abject clientele, male and female.

Midnight Cowboy was an early milestone in the emergence of a "New Hollywood" in the late 1960s and 1970s, winning several Oscars. One of the first films aimed at a general audience to deal frankly with the themes of homosexuality and male prostitution, it also testified to the frictions between Hollywood and the avant-garde cinema of the period, as well as the influence that each exerted on the other. The themes of Schlesinger's movie, and its treatment of scenes and characters, freely borrowed from Warhol's films, especially *My Hustler* (1965) and *Lonesome Cowboys* (1968); indeed, the director hired Viva and other members of Warhol's entourage

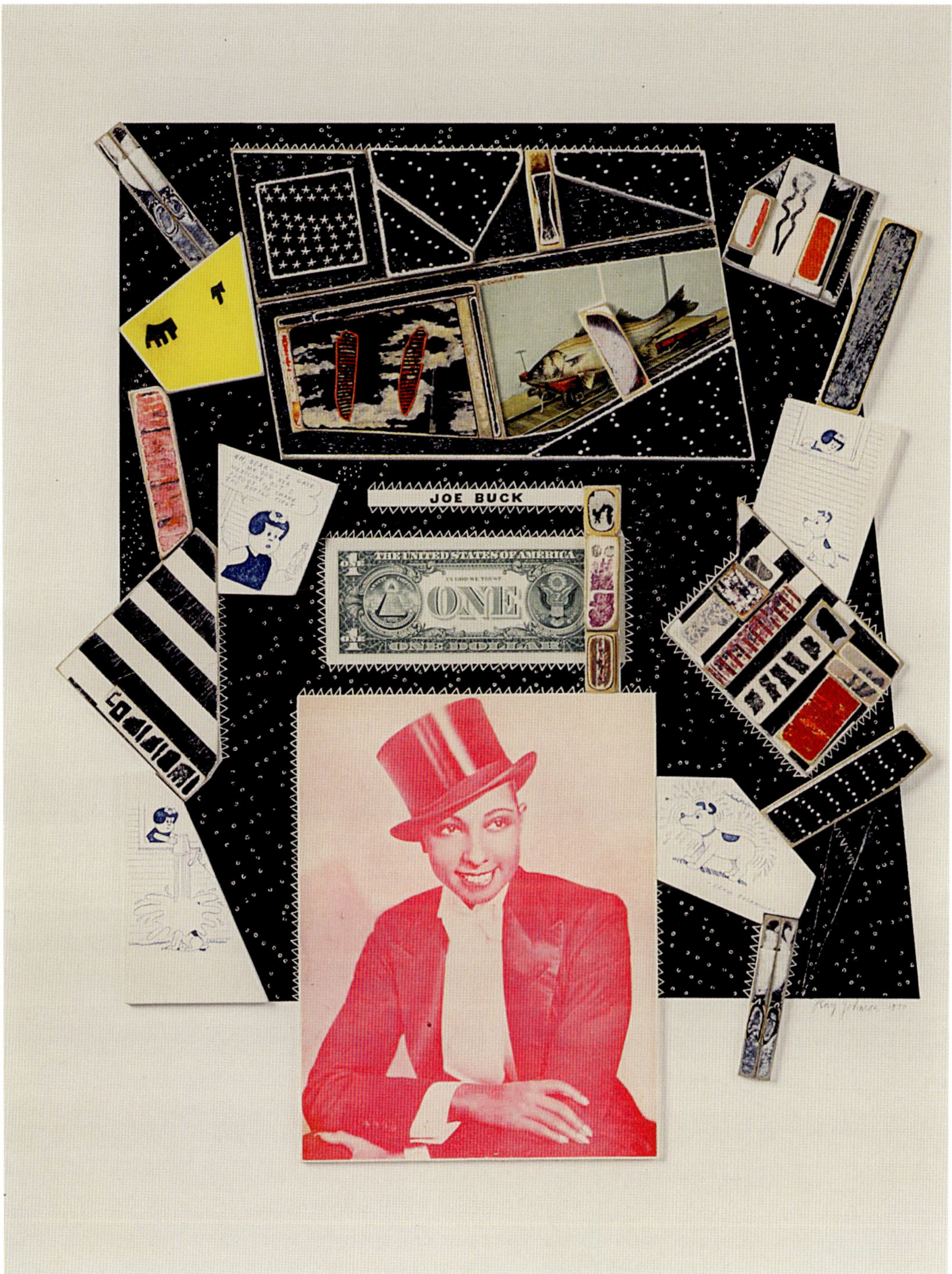

Fig. 66 Ray Johnson, *Joe Buck Dollar Bill*, 1970. Collage, 30 × 20 in. (76.2 × 50.8 cm). Collection of Frances Beatty and Allen Adler.

from the Factory to re-create the ambience of an underground party.[58] Warhol himself, then recuperating in the hospital after his shooting, could only look upon what he saw as a piece of Hollywood hijacking with a mixture of jealousy and bitterness.[59] It is hardly surprising that Johnson, a regular visitor to the Factory who was well aware of what smuggling the avant-garde into mainstream cinema implied for the already uneasy coexistence of art and commerce, should have seen *Midnight Cowboy* as a natural subject for his *Dollar Bill* collages.[60]

Schlesinger's film is fundamentally a meditation on money and the way in which it affects social and sexual relationships. The very name "Joe Buck" refers to money: in American slang, a buck is a dollar. At one point the illiterate hero misspells the word *money*, fooled by a neon sign he sees from his window into thinking he should write "mony." But a buck is also a male animal, especially a bull or a horse—a term that during antebellum slavery came to be used as a polite substitute for the crudely demeaning insult "nigger" (with the implied suggestion of animal strength and sexuality) and then, more generally, to refer to a criminal.[61] Joe Buck himself was lowered to the status of a sexual slave, exploited for his body like an animal; through the polysemy of his name he is associated with the condition of American blacks, then in the midst of a fierce struggle to obtain their civil rights, more than a century after the abolition of slavery. In this light, the photograph of Josephine Baker takes on a new aspect: American expatriate entertainer and international star, she is seen here as an ambiguous symbol of the emancipation of blacks in the United States. Active in the struggle against racism and discrimination, she nonetheless owed her celebrity to the fact that she embodied a certain number of racial stereotypes and male-chauvinist fantasies. Was she really a buck as well, then, a piece of animal property, a commodified body, enslaved by another form of prostitution? The dollar hanging over her head supports such an interpretation: it seems to say that a price has been put on her head. More than this, it evokes an iconography peculiar to the world of antebellum American slavery—printed announcements offering a reward for recapturing slaves who have fled their masters, so-called runaway advertisements (fig. 67).[62]

In a piece of mail art dating from 1973 (fig. 68), Johnson annotated the "rectified readymade" that Duchamp had created fifty years earlier and that the French artist had himself chosen to illustrate the poster for his celebrated retrospective at the Pasadena Art Museum in the fall of 1963.[63] In this work, Duchamp reprinted a faux wanted persons notice for a criminal at large, in which he had inserted photographs of his own face, front view and profile. Johnson, in his collage, has simply pasted between the images of Duchamp—who had become extremely famous in the 1960s—a supermarket label reading: "Prime Rib 69¢/lb." This label is evidently meant to call to mind an avatar of the search for wanted persons: the bull, or buck (the poster itself asks for "information leading to the arrest of George W. Welch, alias Bull," who is said to have "operated a bucket shop in New York"). The point of

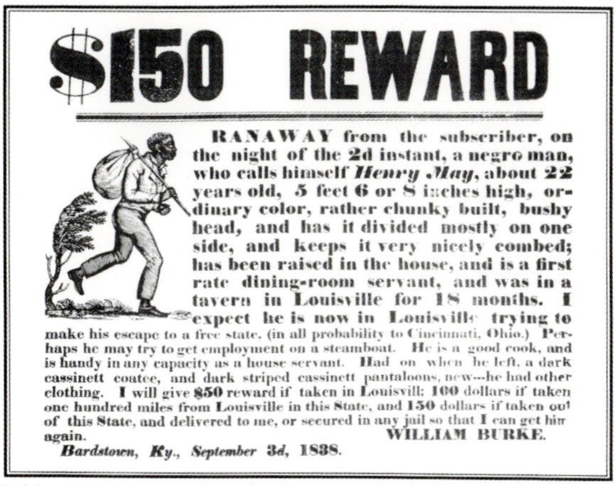

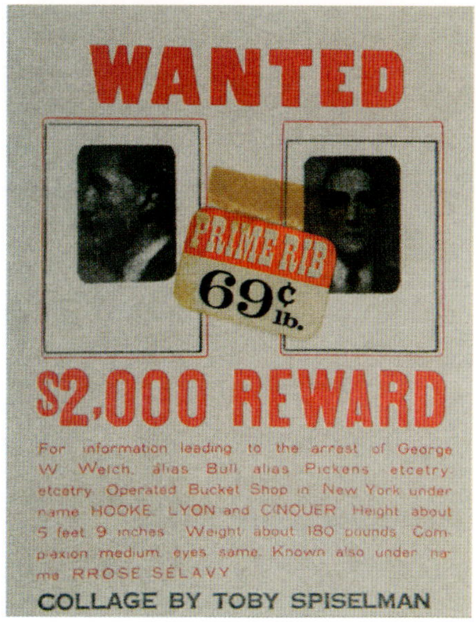

Johnson's sudden detour through the grocery store meat department is to emphasize the kinship between an escaped criminal and a head of cattle, and the commodification of the body implicit in the commodification of art. Whereas currency, as a circulating standardized mass image, must be immobilized in a collage to lose its value and its power to harm, the body/slave, a fixed asset of the capitalist economy, must be put into circulation, like mail art itself, which is always in motion. Whereas traditional commerce reifies individuals and fetishizes works of art, the circuit of artistic commerce must allow criminals to circulate, must allow postal works to continue on their wayward course.

But how far did Johnson himself believe that he could really break free, having made his own escape from the traditional circuits of commerce? In a series of mail-art pieces sent in April 1973, Johnson unilaterally declared the death of the New York Correspondance School. The postal dispatches did not cease, of course, but the demise of the NYCS, like a "very tired and ill" animal, marked a new stage in Johnson's gradual withdrawal from the art world; beginning in the mid-1970s, he took the further step of absenting himself from galleries and exhibitions altogether.[64] A few years later he started to send out a new round of mailings accompanied by notices such as "Letters $10,000 each" and "Ray Johnson free artworks three million dollars each."[65] Had Johnson abandoned all hope of circulating his mail art outside the commercial system? Or did he once more affirm, albeit rather bitterly, the gratuitousness of this art by giving it an absurdly high price? However this may be, he cannot have helped but see that by the mid-1970s the economic system that had permitted him to sell his work without selling himself, making it possible to preserve the positive dimension of artistic commerce as a vehicle of productive, amicable, and free exchange, was increasingly being undermined.

Fig. 67 Anonymous, runaway advertisement, 1838. Wood engraving, reproduced in Marcus Wood, *Blind Memory: Visual Representations of Slavery in England and America, 1780–1865* (Manchester: Manchester University Press, 2000), 88.

Fig. 68 Ray Johnson, untitled mailing (Duchamp wanted/prime rib), 1973. Location unknown.

MARCEL BROODTHAERS AND THE CRITIQUE OF INCONVERTIBILITY AND ECONOMIC WARFARE

In the autumn of 1975, Marcel Broodthaers was invited to present a retrospective of his work at the Kunstmuseum in Basel. As if to acknowledge this city's newly preeminent position in the circuits of modern artistic commerce (it had by then been host for five years to the world's largest international contemporary art fair), he gave careful thought to the scene awaiting visitors to the exhibition.[66] At the focal point of the first room, two strikingly similar works were hung side by side: *Museum-Museum* (1972; fig. 69) and *Gedicht-Poem-Poème/Change-Exchange-Wechsel* (1973; fig. 70). Silkscreens on cardstock of equivalent dimensions, each one forms a diptych, with a very ordered composition in rows and columns. The dialogue they instituted is not only formal. The unity of the subject matter is manifest as well: a succession of gold ingots bearing the names of artists and commodities, on the one hand, and, on the other, columns of initials followed by numbered results, some labeled in francs, some in pounds, some in dollars, some in marks. But if the common theme of these works—art and commerce—was clear at once, the way in which it was to be interpreted was rather less obvious.

In the foreword to the catalogue of another retrospective exhibition, this one posthumous, held almost twenty years later at the Galerie nationale du Jeu de paume in Paris, in 1991, Alfred Pacquement wrote that Broodthaers was one of a small number who had "most acutely posed the question of the social role of the artist and the commercial function of the work of art."[67] Indeed, the idea of an artistic economy—involving both the artist as producer/merchant and the work of art as a commercial commodity—is at the heart of the legacy of an artist who in 1975, a few months before his death, expressed grave doubt "that it is possible to give a serious definition of art, unless we examine the question in terms of a constant, I mean the transformation of art into merchandise."[68] This idea has long been a touchstone for scholarly research, which over the past few years has produced a sizeable literature.[69] Few works have attracted greater attention than the *Museum of Modern Art, Department of Eagles*, a multiform project carried out between 1968 and 1972 through exhibits, events, open letters, objects, and films.[70] Broodthaers placed it under his own supervision as "curator," in keeping with the idea that a museum is to be understood more as something that contains than is contained. For want of a permanent collection to oversee, he adopted the codes and conventions of the traditional museum as an institutional and bureaucratic framework through which his Museum, as an actor standing outside the artistic economy, might likewise perform a legitimizing function for the artistic sphere as a whole. Among the "sections" into which it was divided during the brief period of its existence—Nineteenth-Century Section, Cinema Section, Figures Section, Advertising Section, and so on—Broodthaers eventually incorporated a Financial Section, whose exact contours and content have yet to be agreed upon by historians.

I am chiefly concerned here with Broodthaers's economic thought, relying once more on the notion of commerce in order to understand the artist's position in an economy of social and monetary exchange, as well as the ambiguous status of art and language, which fall somewhere between meaningful instruments of communication and mere consumable commodities. Nevertheless my aim is not to look at Broodthaers's view of art in relation to commodification in theoretical terms, as several authors have already tried to do.[71] Instead, I want to consider a selection of his works, drawn from within the Financial Section and from outside it, in the light of a specific historical context: the state of the art market and of the international economy during the period between the rise of the German art fairs, the expansion of European commerce under the aegis of the Common Market, and the crisis of the international monetary system.

The Financial Section at the Cologne Art Fair

In 1970, Broodthaers began work on a film that was finished the following year in Cologne, with the enigmatic title *Projet pour un poisson (Projet pour un film)* [*Plan for a Fish (Plan for a Film)*].[72] Faithful to his poetical bestiary, Broodthaers chose the motif of a fish to represent art that had become a commodity.[73] He had employed it before, though never in so finished a form; henceforth it became a recurrent theme in his work. The film was made using engravings that alternated images of headless fish and fish scales with printed names of fish, signs, and sentence fragments, sometimes displayed within the frames of a roll of film, itself a drawing. The film was shown for the first time at the Galerie Michael Werner in Cologne in November 1971. The invitation card for the opening contained an explanatory note in French, English, and German:

> 1. Is it a gothic fish? Style is the eagle of the sea.
> 2. The fish as an idea of non-communication. The fish itself as a motionless film.
> 3. The fish as childish art market. (dumping fish on the market)[74]

Art, in other words, having become a commodity, is reduced to a marketable "style" (1). In so doing, it loses all possibility of true communication, for it becomes a merely formal and fixed set of variants, as mute and devoid of influence as a "motionless film" (2). As a further consequence, the commerce of art, insofar as it paradoxically ensures the circulation of an inert, "motionless" commodity ("dumping fish on the market"), is harmful to the circulation of meaning (3). Commercial exchange and social exchange therefore stand opposed to one another as incompatible phenomena: the fish-commodity is an "idea of non-communication."

The many drawings Broodthaers made in preparation of *Projet pour un poisson* were subsequently used in a second film, *Le poisson est tenace* [*The*

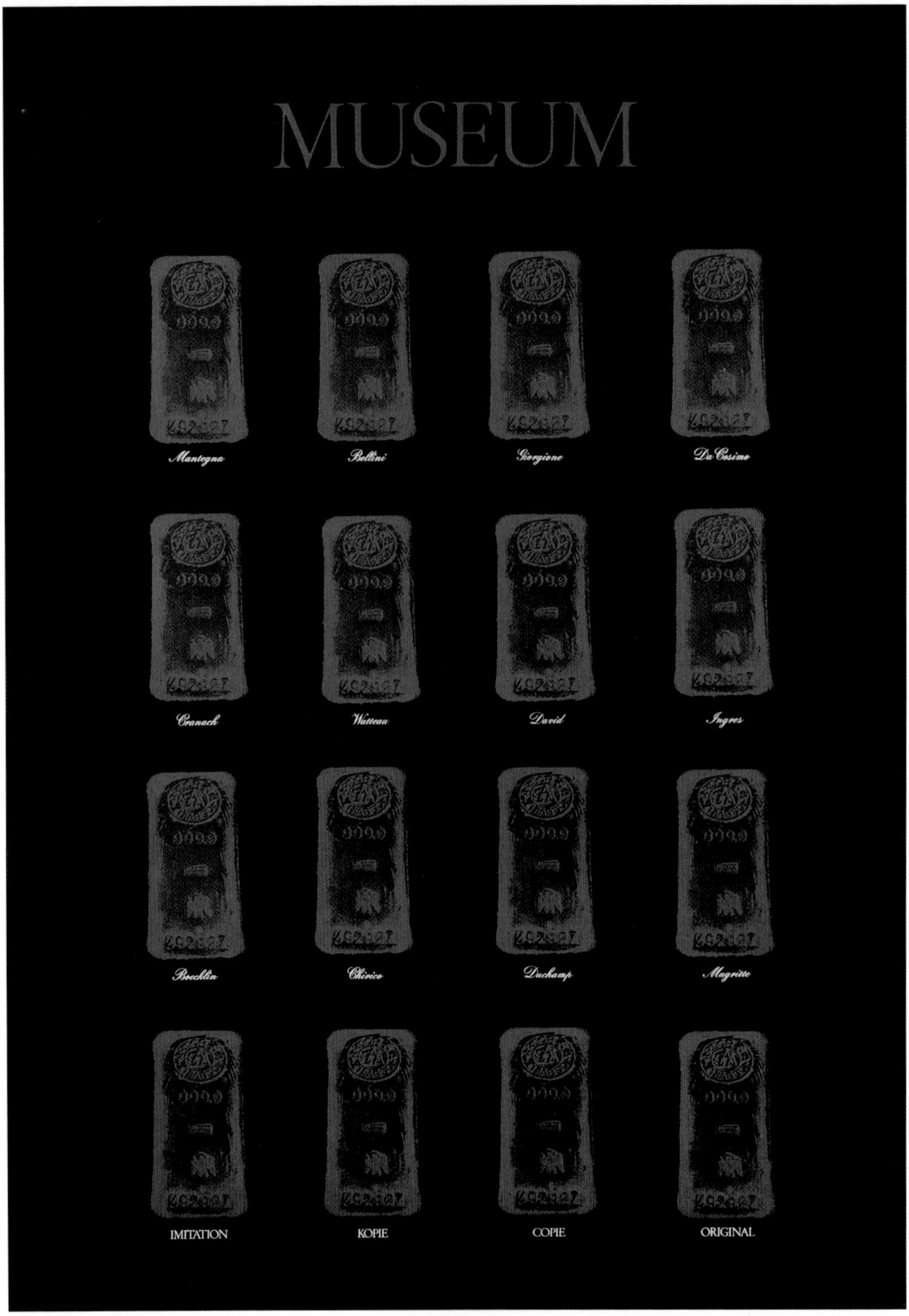

Fig. 69 Marcel Broodthaers, *Museum-Museum*, 1972. Gold, white, and black silkscreen on cardstock, two sheets, 33 × 23½ in. (84 × 59.5 cm) each. Edition of 100 copies, numbered and signed, published by Edition Staeck, Heidelberg.

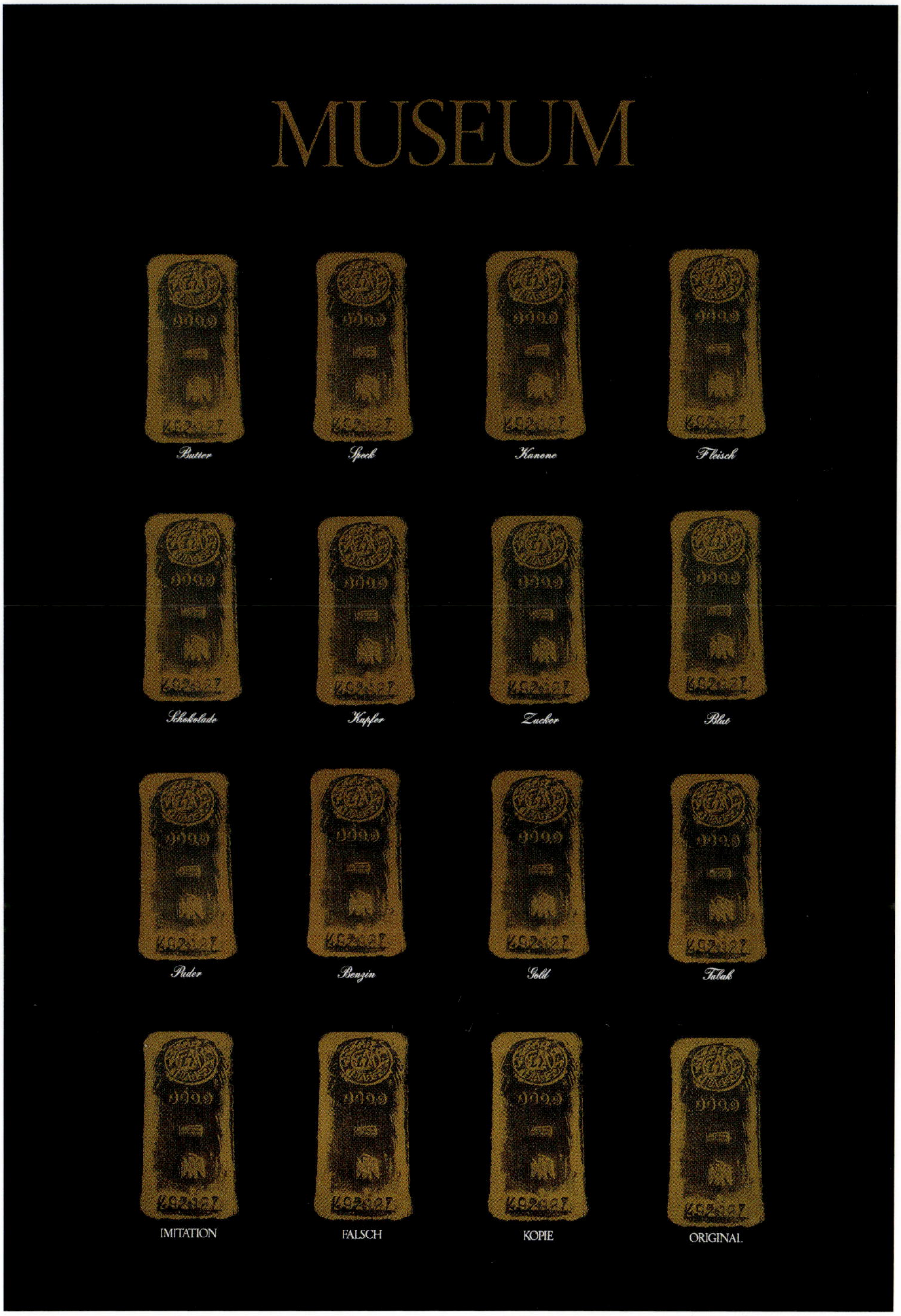
MUSEUM
Butter
Speck
Kanone
Fleisch
Schokolade
Kupfer
Zucker
Blut
Puder
Benzin
Gold
Tabak
IMITATION
FALSCH
KOPIE
ORIGINAL

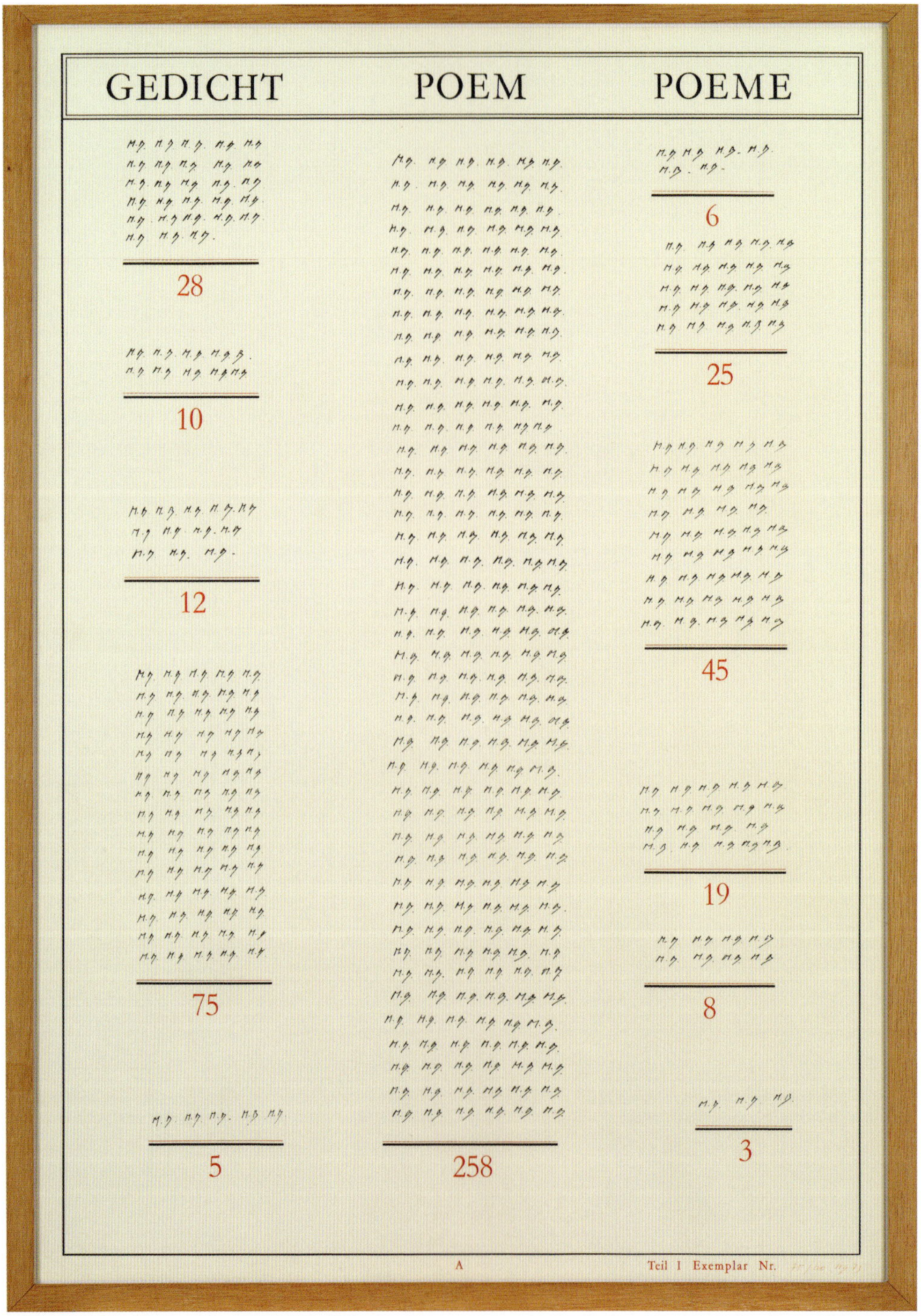

Fig. 70 Marcel Broodthaers, *Gedicht-Poem-Poème/Change-Exchange-Wechsel*, 1973. Red and black silkscreen on cream cardstock, two sheets, 38½ × 27 in. (98 × 68.5 cm) each. Edition of 100 copies, numbered and signed, published by Edition Staeck, Heidelberg.

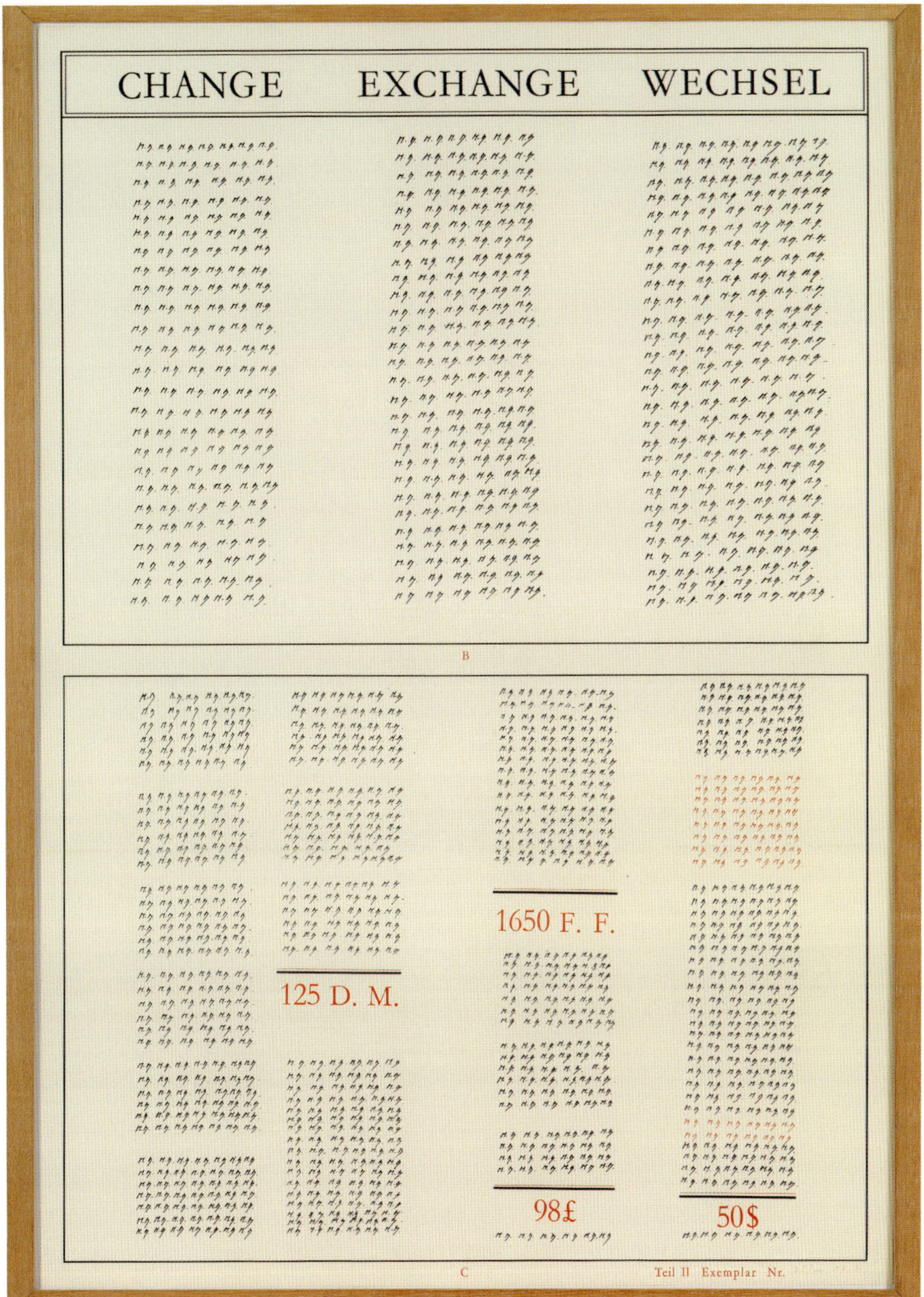
CHANGE EXCHANGE WECHSEL
B
1650 F. F.
125 D. M.
98£
50$
C
Teil II Exemplar Nr.

Fish Is Tenacious], as well as in a book published by Galerie Michael Werner in 1973, *Jeter du poisson sur le marché de Cologne* [*Dumping Fish on the Cologne Market*].[75] The book's title refers to the great annual art fair in that city, the Kölner Kunstmarkt. On each page of the book, illustrated by fish tails and scales, one finds these words, dripping with menace: "The fish rots from the head." Other drawings on the same theme were published after Broodthaers's death by his widow, Maria Gilissen.[76] Still more explicitly, the French word for fish, *poisson*, becomes "poison"—the poison of business, as the artist says—and the final page of the book, dated 1975, calls upon readers to "[m]arch on Cologne" (fig. 71).

Broodthaers chose the Cologne Art Fair as the location for the opening of his Financial Section, in October 1971. A few months before, in April and May, he had begun working out a preliminary scheme that seems to have constituted the basis for it, with the working title "Contract Proposed by the Financial Service of the Department of Eagles."[77] The project, never carried out finally, was to have been sponsored by the Konrad Fischer Galerie in Düsseldorf. It contemplated the sale of an unlimited edition of gold ingots, each a kilogram in weight, stamped with the eagle emblem of the Museum of Modern Art, Department of Eagles. The first page of the contract is missing, but from the surviving clauses we know that it provided for the sale of gold ingots at double the market price, with a percentage of the profit going to the gallery and the rest to Broodthaers's museum. In making the price of his edition a function of the market price of gold, the artist was no doubt deliberately alluding to the cans of *Merda d'artista* [*Artist's Shit*]—priced by their weight in gold at the current market rate—made by the Italian artist Piero Manzoni a decade earlier, in May 1961. Broodthaers had met Manzoni nine months later, in February 1962, a decisive moment in his career.[78]

If Broodthaers's stamped ingot was worth twice the value of an ingot of equivalent weight on the precious metals market, then the strictly artistic share accounted for 50 percent of the work's total value—remunerating the artist and his dealer—and the remaining 50 percent represented the value of the raw material. This artistic value was certified by the curator's letter of authentication ("in order to prevent the production of fakes"), and by the deposit of an example of the edition in a bank. Nevertheless Broodthaers made it clear that "the purchaser is free to have his ingot or bar melted [down], so as to obliterate the mark, or to burn the letter of identification in order to enjoy fully the purity of the substance and the freshness of the original intention."[79] This clause cannot help but recall Yves Klein's "ritual rules of transfer" concerning zones of immaterial pictorial sensibility, which provided that "in order for the fundamental immaterial value of the zone to definitively belong to [the buyer] and to be made one with him, he must solemnly burn his receipt."[80] But whereas the disappearance of any authenticating trace of the work is accompanied in Klein's case by the disappearance of the gold, leaving the collector to enjoy only the immaterial

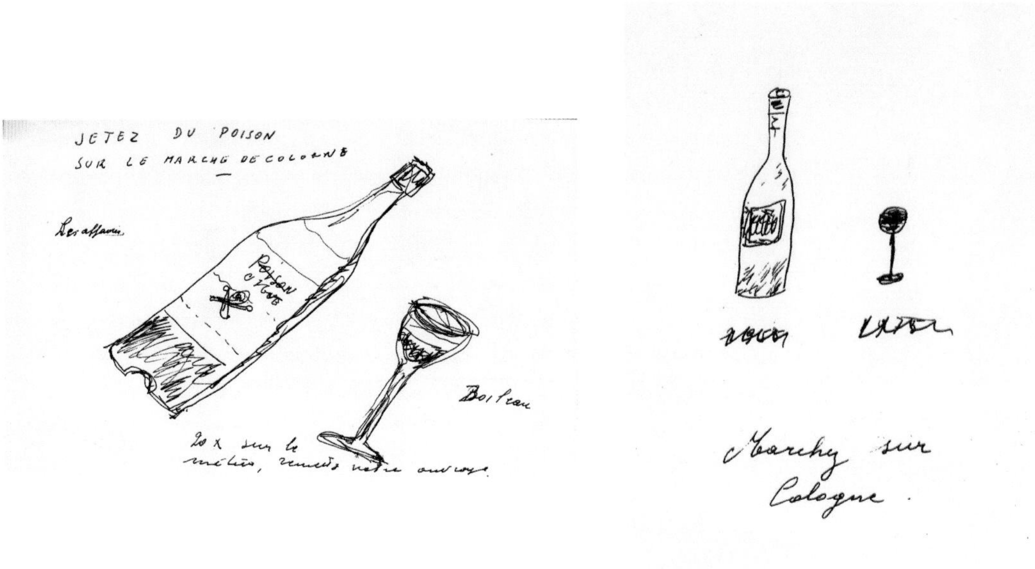

Fig. 71 Drawings by Marcel Broodthaers, published in Broodthaers, *Vingt fois sur le métier, remettez votre ouvrage*, ed. Maria Gilissen (Dijon: ADAC, 1988).

manifestation of art, in Broodthaers's case the melting down of the ingot obliterates all artistic mark and leaves the buyer with a kilo of raw gold, now once more a mere material. What with Klein implies a gain in value through the sacrifice of gold amounts with Broodthaers to a partial loss of value—assessed at 50 percent—while the gold remains. Here, the artist's irony, by comparison with the "freshness of the original intention" of the artist and the collector, is fully apparent. Although the plan formalized by the "Contract" was not put into effect, an ingot of gold had in fact been purchased, with money saved by Maria Gilissen, and stamped by a jeweler.[81] A photograph of this ingot, initially attached to the "Contract," was subsequently used in several of Broodthaers's works, notably *Museum-Museum* (see fig. 69) and *Paysage d'automne* [*Autumn Landscape*] (see fig. 76).

In the aftermath of this unfinished project, it was not until the Cologne Art Fair, October 5–10, 1971, and in the months following that Broodthaers really established the Financial Section of the *Museum of Modern Art, Department of Eagles*. During the week of the fair the artist shuttled between the Galerie Michael Werner booth at the Kunstmarkt, on the ground floor of the Kunsthalle, and the booth of the Antwerp-based Wide White Space Gallery, located in the Forum; later he appeared at the Galerie Michael Werner itself, a few blocks away in Cologne, in connection with a solo exhibit the following month, November 8–13, 1971.[82] Broodthaers's activities in these three places were evidently part of a common project, which suggests that a Financial Section, complex and multiform but nonetheless coherent (or at least thought to be so by the artist himself), actually existed by this point. Its aim was to associate the museum, a public institution having a noncommercial purpose, with the market, symbolized by the Kunstmarkt, a private institution subject to the constraints of the profit motive.

At the Galerie Michael Werner booth, Broodthaers made it known that he was putting his Museum up for sale "on account of bankruptcy." But in fact collectors attending the fair were invited to acquire the announcement of this sale, in the form of a jacket cover published in nineteen copies (fig. 72) that was to be wrapped around the official catalogue of the 1971 Cologne Art Fair, with the image of an eagle with its wings spread on the verso, above the legend "Fig. 0," and, on the back flap, a dedication to a list of figures in the art world, both real and imaginary.[83] The announcement of the Museum's sale was made not only in the form of a jacket that could be purchased; it was reproduced as part of a double-page advertisement for the Galerie Michael Werner in the catalogue itself, and also disseminated in the form of invitation cards.[84]

Why declare that the Museum was to be sold "on account of bankruptcy"? The threat of a financial failure of public cultural institutions had been raised by Broodthaers several years earlier in the context of the May 1968 protests and, in particular, of the occupation of the Palais des Beaux-Arts in Brussels, in which he took part.[85] In his "Open Letters" that same year, he called for "an increase in the budgets of the Ministry of Culture" in order to satisfy his own Museum's "need for money." "My coffers are empty," he wrote. "We are on the brink of the abyss. . . . Could the museum system be as compromised as the gallery system?"[86] When Broodthaers announced the bankruptcy of the Museum in the catalogue of the 1971 Cologne Art Fair, he therefore did not only have in mind a financial failure due to inadequate government support for the arts. He was also suggesting that his Museum had failed in its very mission. It had become an institution whose functions were modeled on those of the private market. In both the literal and figurative senses, the Museum had sold out to commercial interests. The harmful effects of this abdication of responsibility were explored in a morbid film made at the Galerie Michael Werner a month later, and summarized in its suggestive title: *Crime à Cologne* [*Crime in Cologne*].[87]

The plan to sell the Museum was never carried out; only the announcement that it was for sale was offered to prospective buyers. Broodthaers explained his reasons a few months later in an interview with the German curator Johannes Cladders: "I could have sold my museum earlier. But for the moment it's not possible. As long as I take refuge in it and identify myself with it, I can't."[88] Broodthaers continued to entertain the possibility of selling it, however, notably in an article published in April 1973, in which he insisted that "this museum can be sold only to an institution that takes all necessary measures to prevent speculation," and that in order to assure the "disinterestedness" of the artist and his "clients," "the price of the museum can be determined only by the real price of the objects (sketches, documents, books, engravings) that belong to me, and the remuneration to which I am entitled should be in line with [the salary] of the director of a modest museum."[89] To avoid speculation, in other words, Broodthaers

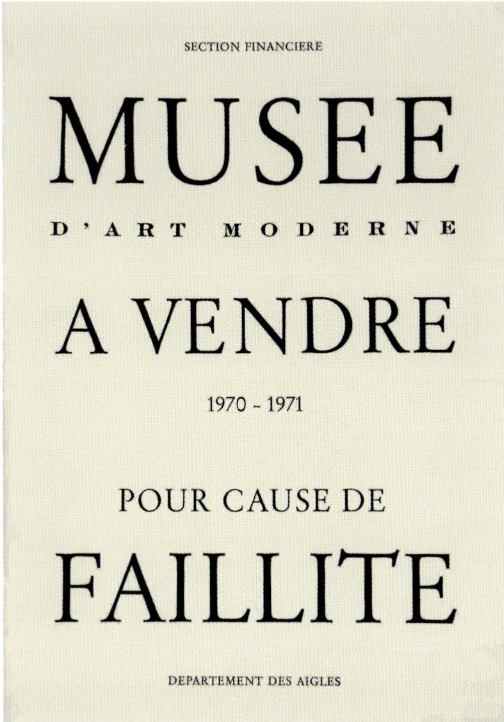

Fig. 72 Marcel Broodthaers, *Musée d'art moderne à vendre 1970–1971 pour cause de faillite* [*Museum of Modern Art for Sale 1970–1971 on Account of Bankruptcy*], 1971. Jacket for the catalogue of the Cologne Art Fair, black printing on white paper, 17¾ × 12½ in. (45 × 32 cm). Edition of 19 copies, published by Galerie Michael Werner, Cologne.

resorted to a strategy we have already noted in discussing several other artists, namely, making the price of a work equal to the combined value of the artist's materials and labor.

The pieces shown at the Wide White Space Gallery—which had devoted the whole of its exhibit at the Cologne Art Fair to Broodthaers—completed the arrangement and enriched the underlying motivation. *La Banque* (fig. 73, front view) is an old-fashioned bank counter, a row of adjacent tellers' windows about ten feet (three meters) long and carved in wood, that Broodthaers and his wife had found in the street, discarded in the course of a building renovation, in 1964.[90] It comprised three windows, each in glass and closed to view after business hours behind a pair of shutters: one window for coupons (regular income in the form of interest on bearer bonds), another for currency exchange, and the last for stock exchange orders. This object, which, as we will see, was part of the decor for a happening before becoming a work of art in its own right, underwent a series of transformations in the interval. A photograph taken in 1964 (fig. 74) shows the extreme left-hand panel decorated with two elongated curving lines, and on the panel between the windows labeled *Change* [Exchange] and *Ordres de Bourse* [Stock Exchange Orders], the frontal half-silhouette of a woman may be seen in white on black.[91] The woman is Ileana Sonnabend; Broodthaers had discovered American pop art at her gallery in Paris in 1963. In August–October 1968, when Broodthaers exhibited the counter at the Lignano Biennale in Italy, it had a still different look and a different title, being listed in the catalogue as *La Banque et le Critique* [*The Bank and the Critic*]

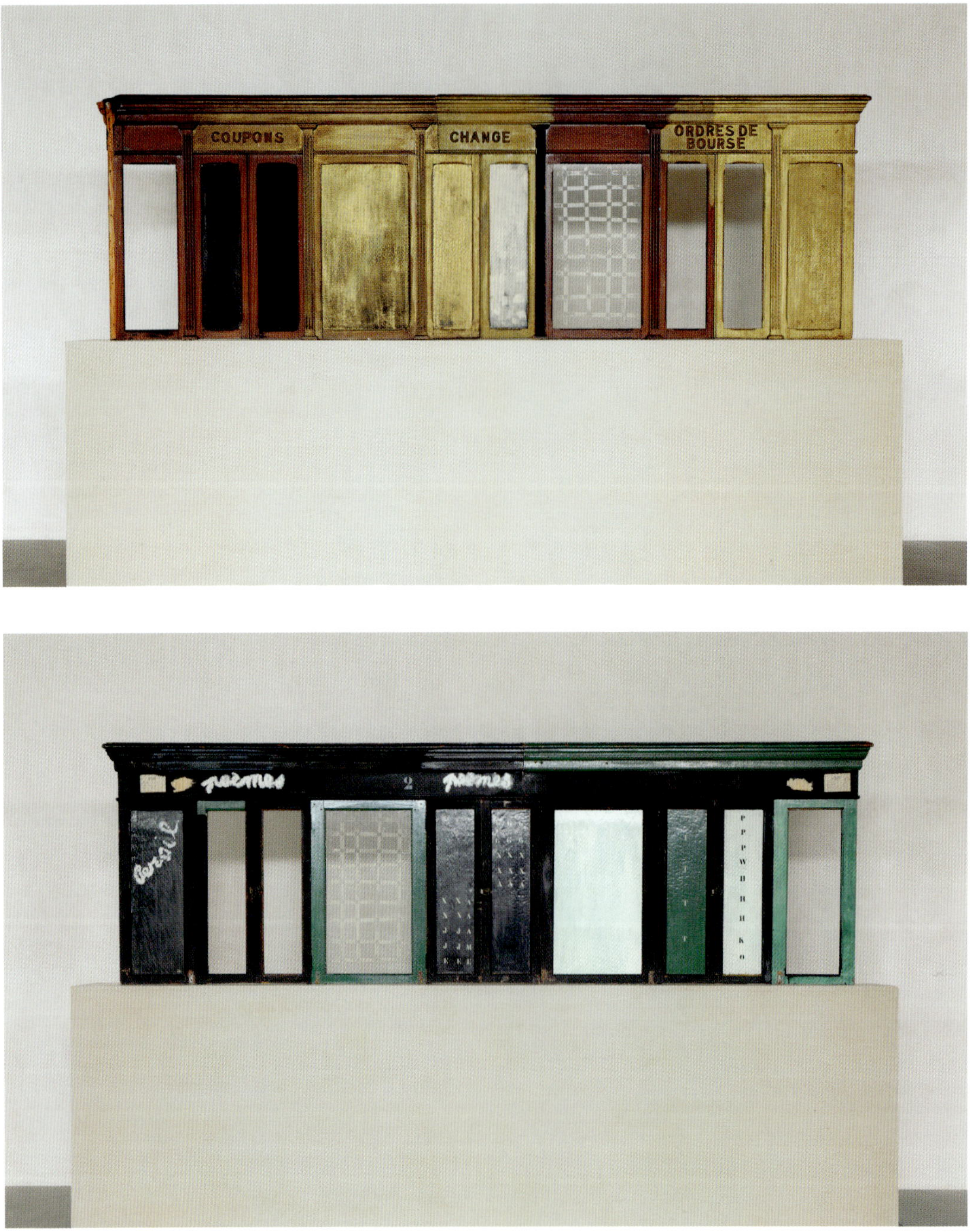

Fig. 73 Marcel Broodthaers, *La Banque*, front and rear views, 1964–68. Wood counter, glass, and oil paint, with successive modifications made during this period; the tellers' windows, 36¼ × 118⅛ × 4¾ in. (92 × 300 × 12 cm); the entire object, with base, 61⅜ × 140½ × 11¾ in. (156 × 357 × 30 cm). Raussmüller Collection, Basel.

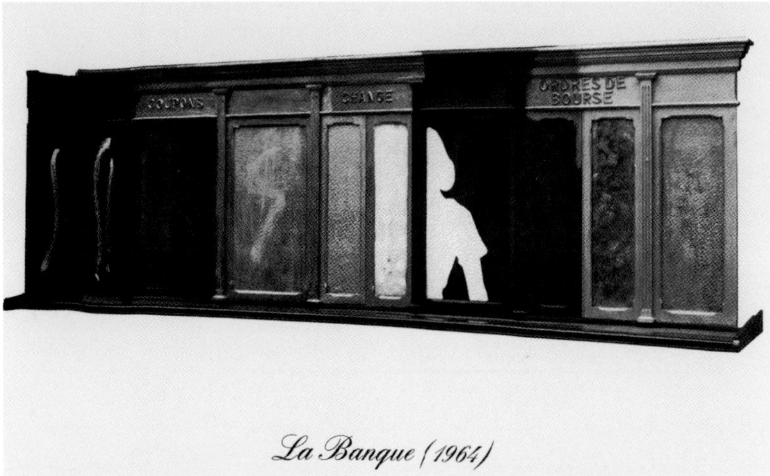

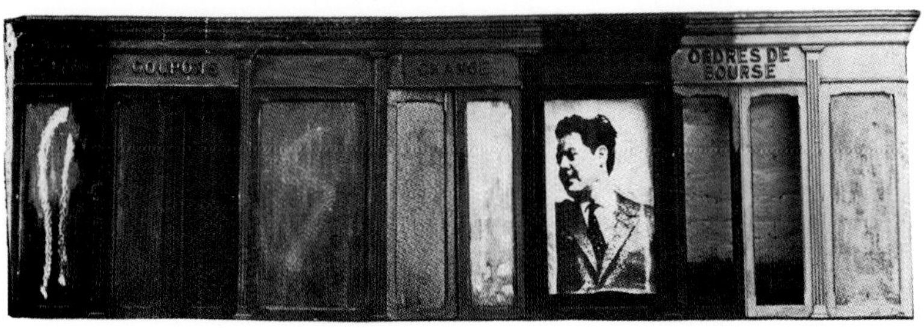

Fig. 74 Marcel Broodthaers, *La Banque (1964)*, 1964. Photograph published in the exhibition catalogue *Marcel Broodthaers*, February 25–April 6, 1975, Nationalgalerie Staatliche Museen, Berlin (Berlin: Staatliche Museen, 1975), n.p.

Fig. 75 Marcel Broodthaers, *La Banque et le Critique*, 1964–68. Photograph published in the exhibition catalogue of the Lignano Biennale, August 25–October 6, 1968 (Florence: Centro di edizioni, 1968), n.p.

(fig. 75). Here the feminine half-silhouette has given way to a photographic portrait printed on canvas of the French art critic Otto Hahn.[92] It is probable that *La Banque* was exhibited at the 1971 Cologne Art Fair in its final form, with the tellers' windows and panels uniformly obliterated by black, white, and gold paint (see fig. 73, front view).[93] The prior versions nonetheless give us some idea of how the appearance of this work as part of the Financial Section at the Cologne fair was meant to be interpreted.[94] Broodthaers was concerned not only with the relation between the world of art and the world of money, which finances the market for art, but also with the way in which the social roles of art dealer (Sonnabend, for example) and art critic (Hahn, for example) are bound up with the structures they support. For if the museum, to recall Jean Baudrillard's famous metaphor, is the "central bank" of art, the depository of its standards of value—as the gold color of the tellers' windows and the juxtaposition of gold ingots and names of famous artists in *Museum-Museum* (see fig. 69) remind us—critics and dealers are therefore its bankers, who exchange currencies and place orders, regulating and directing the market through their words and deeds.[95]

Another work, exhibited with *La Banque* and titled *Ma collection*, was created especially for the Cologne Art Fair, as we know from the handwritten inscription "Cologne 71 M.B. . . . On the occasion of an insignificant fair. . . ." The two panels constitute a summary of Broodthaers's artistic career, bringing together documents, photographs, a biographical note, and a list of his exhibitions. The economic dimension of this work is no less important than in the case of *La Banque*. In a typewritten addendum regarding contractual matters related to *Ma collection*, the artist pondered how income might be derived from what he called a "dubious readymade": "Personally, I would like to receive a tax (a royalty?) on publications, if there are any, that reproduce my statement and the images from this page of the catalogue of the Cologne 71 Fair. However, should anyone still wish to own 'Ma collection,' the physical object, then the price would be that of my conscience (Price negotiable)."[96] Broodthaers's hesitation between the two options, which naturally calls to mind the draft sale contract for gold ingots that we considered earlier, testifies to the profound unity of purpose that connects *Ma collection* and the *Musée d'art moderne à vendre 1970–1971 pour cause de faillite,* exhibited together at Michael Werner's booth at the fair. In each case, what was being offered for purchase was not so much a work of art as a meditation on the institutional structures of the art world. An act (or at least an offer) of sale was necessary in order to demonstrate that institutions and artists had both sold out ("the price would be that of my conscience"). At the same time, however, it posed a problem: the Financial Section could not be seen to be feeding the very speculation in the art market that it so forcefully objected to; in overseeing the liquidation of the museum's artistic activities, the Financial Section had to maintain its critical independence as an agent of subversion.

The 1971 Cologne Art Fair in Historical Context: Broodthaers vs. Beuys

The reasons for the advent of the Financial Section during the 1971 Cologne Art Fair will be clearer still if we consider this event in the light of contemporary events. Broodthaers was hardly alone in protesting against the fair and calling for a march on Cologne. By 1970, the increase in sale prices and the expansion of the market for art in the area stretching from the Netherlands to northern Italy, with West Germany and Switzerland at its center, had created a mood of growing discontent among European artists. The Cologne Art Fair was a primary target. Founded three years earlier by two local gallery owners, Hein Stünke and Rudolf Zwirner, in an attempt to revive the depressed European art trade, it rapidly became the focus and the symbol of the resurgent German art market,[97] criticized almost at once by critics and artists for its elitism, avowedly commercial orientation, and willingness to accommodate the methods of the capitalist world of business. "Very active from the commercial point of view," Jean-Marc Poinsot noted in 1970, "the German galleries . . . have worked hard to vulgarize the art market. What is falsely called democratization is in fact the progressive transition from art object to ordinary commercial object. . . . The artist thus tends to be a producer of goods, [ever] more dependent on the law of supply and demand, while the speculative character of art requires cultivating the public's interest without expecting any immediate return."[98]

At the 1969 Cologne Art Fair, Joseph Beuys became the first German artist to see one of his works fetch a record price, 110,000 deutsche marks, the result of a sale conducted by the West Berlin–based Galerie René Block.[99] An event of this sort was bound to make a profound impression, and all the more as memories of May 1968 were still fresh in many people's minds. In February 1971, with the support of a small number of artists and dealers, Beuys publicly attacked the organizers and forced the gates of the fair to be opened ahead of schedule. The campaign was continued by "A Call to Action" issued by Beuys and two other German artists, Erwin Heerich and Klaus Staeck, calling for an end to "the monopoly of the Cologne Art Market" and "the subjection of the artists to gallery owners who belong to the Association of Progressive German Art Dealers." The statement concluded with the following appeal: "We demand a free art market, able to meet the public demand for full information. We demand that the Cologne Kunsthalle and the Berlin Kunstakademie be made available for a free producers exhibition."[100]

Some four hundred people, mainly artists, signed their petition in the next few months.[101] René Block, organizer of the art fair held in Berlin that summer, responded in the catalogue with concrete proposals: equal booths for all, and even "a limit on the price of works to 10,000 deutsche marks (16,000 francs) in order to avoid speculation."[102] But these initiatives were perceived by the most radical artists as marginal reforms that did not permit the system of commerce in art to be thoroughly reconceived. On September 6–7, 1971, Beuys, Heerich, and Staeck held an "International Meeting for a Free Kunstmarkt" in Heidelberg, attended by artists, gallery owners, and art critics, to prepare a boycott of the upcoming Cologne Art Fair and to propose alternative solutions.[103] The twenty-four participants came from West Germany, Belgium, France, the Netherlands, and Italy, but none from the United States, much to the regret of the leaders of the boycott, who felt that the success of their undertaking "depend[ed] on the cooperation of the American side."[104] Indeed, the many exchanges between Staeck, Beuys, and the New York conceptual art dealer Seth Siegelaub, who had asked them to circulate his "artist's agreement," show that the European opponents of the existing art market system were seeking to coordinate their protests with those of the Art Workers' Coalition in the United States.[105]

Yet Broodthaers declined to sign the "Call to Action." An interview he gave to the Belgian poet and critic Freddy de Vree during the 1971 Cologne fair, in the wake of Beuys's highly publicized attempt to boycott it, suggests how great their differences were. De Vree asked Broodthaers about his "attitude toward a fair where art is sold," leading to this exchange:

> MB: Ah, but I feel much more at ease at the Cologne Fair than in my own Museum, for in the Kunstmarkt we find ourselves right inside the reality of contemporary society, right in the middle of its system, which reveals itself to be crassly commercial.

> FDV: And why do you feel at ease there?
>
> MB: Because it's everyone's life, the existence of practically all artists, museum directors, and gallery owners. Crassly commercial—I don't mean that all these people are odious, or vile, but that art is sold there as a contemptible commodity.[106]

Resisting Beuys's call for exhibiters to withdraw from the fair in order to preserve their artistic integrity, Broodthaers professed to be more comfortable living with the commercial consequences of his work as an artist than acting as the curator of his own Museum, which is to say on behalf of a noncommercial effort to reach the general public. Works of art, Broodthaers seemed to suggest, are unavoidably caught up in an elitist and profit-seeking system of publicity; everyone is better off in the end if the system does not pretend to be something it is not. The interview goes on to reveal Broodthaers's preferred way for dealing with this state of the affairs:

> FDV: Do you feel that you are haggled over in such a Kunstmarkt or do you think that, by its very nature, your work escapes this sort of commerce?
>
> MB: I try, particularly in the works that are shown here at the Cologne Fair, to introduce something that comprehends the negation of this situation, a situation that I expected. There are two or three objects here that might pass for a contemptible commodity, but I hope that, through their structure or through the words that surround them, they contain a warning that says: "I am here, it's not my fault" . . . I hope I'm not the one who says this, I hope the object itself indicates it.[107]

Broodthaers's position could not have been more different than that of Beuys, who was quoted at the same time, in October 1971, as saying: "A potato that is cultivated and cared for by a farmer doesn't suffer any damage even if the merchant who sells it is dishonest. The area of creativity, art, and human freedom rests upon a different principle—the social and democratic principle of a just administration of justice. Therefore, the art is not degraded by the abuses of the market; it remains thoroughly and absolutely intact."[108]

For Beuys, in other words, human creativity and art are protected against commercial corruption by virtue of the fact that they operate on a different level. The gallery system must be combated and transformed because it alienates artists as workers, but in no case does it imperil works of art themselves, which remain foreign to it. For Broodthaers, by contrast, the work of art is not independent of the economic circumstances of its production, still less of its conversion into a commodity. But it is precisely this intrinsic compromise, this indissociability of art and commerce, that opens up the possibility of inserting a warning, as he put it—of formulating a critique from within. Whereas Beuys insisted on staying away from the Cologne Art Fair, Broodthaers tried to make himself even more a part of it than before.[109] Thus the *Musée d'art moderne à vendre* not only wrapped itself around the fair's catalogue on the outside, in the form of a limited edition jacket (see fig. 72); inside, it insinuated itself in the form of a double-page advertisement for the Galerie Michael Werner. This amounted to an assertion of principle, that any external critique of a system of art has a duty to ensure that it is formulated within the same system. Thus the Financial Section, in taking up advertising space inside the fair catalogue, not only called attention to itself as a saleable object but left open the possibility that favorable critical notice might actually add to its market value. A letter written by Michael Werner to the collector Herman Daled shortly afterward, emphasizing the topicality of *Musée d'art moderne à vendre* in the light of intervening events, this in the hope of improving his chances of selling it to Daled, suggests as much. In a postscript, Werner specified his price: 300 deutsche marks.[110]

Beuys was not the only author of the "Call to Action" with whom Broodthaers took issue. Klaus Staeck published several of his graphic works in Heidelberg, including *Museum-Museum* in 1972 (see fig. 69) and *Gedicht-Poem-Poème/Change-Exchange-Wechsel* in 1973 (see fig. 70). Staeck had joined the German Social Democratic Party (SPD in its German initials) in 1960, and by the end of the decade came to specialize in works of propaganda denouncing capitalism, the exploitation of workers, the influence of religion, and environmental pollution. His favored vehicles for reaching the largest audience at the lowest cost were posters and postcards, published in almost unlimited numbers and distributed, displayed, or sold at a modest price.[111] This method of desacralizing the art object, in order to stimulate a more democratic interest in art and its political message, is precisely what Broodthaers stood on its head in marketing his own productions, notably in the case of *Paysage d'automne* [*Autumn Landscape*] (fig. 76), published by the Galerie Yvon Lambert in 1973. As the handwritten certificate accompanying the work stipulates: "The complete edition—140 copies—is offered for sale, en bloc, and thereby constitutes a single item."[112] In this way, Broodthaers turned a limited edition into a unique art object, which later he archly described as "a copy numbered from 1 to 1."[113] Contrary to Staeck's ambition of promoting multiple ownership, then, Broodthaers deliberately revived the old fetishistic desire of exclusive possession.

Appropriately enough, *Paysage d'automne* took the economy as its theme. Part A consists of an orthonormal graph inscribed with an irregularly ascending curve bearing the legend "Rise in Art Prices—1972–1973." Broodthaers's sense of humor is readily apparent in this representation: while mimicking the practice (still very much in vogue) of using the visual tools of economics and statistics to describe the course of the art market, the freehand drawing evidently owes more to an artistic sensibility than to mathematical exactitude; the curve turns back on itself in a comical loop that leads on after a moment's hesitation to a dizzyingly steep climb portending, or so it would seem, an imminent plunge into the abyss. Part B, described as a "Reproduction on the Scale of a Kilo of Gold (No. F36040)," presents an image of the gold ingot that the artist contemplated selling as part of the unexecuted "Contract" we considered earlier, similar to the ones in *Museum-Museum* (see fig. 69). Finally, Part C, soberly titled "Landscape," displays four two-dimensional geometrical figures: a rectangle, an isosceles triangle, a right triangle, and a circle. Geometrical forms such as these in Broodthaers's work often refer to the "primary structures" of American minimalist artists, who enjoyed a considerable institutional and commercial success in Europe at the time while nonetheless maintaining a studied silence on political matters. Broodthaers had said of them earlier that, like "fish-commodities," they "obey the laws of the sea."[114]

Inconvertibility and Economic War

While Broodthaers was working on *Paysage d'automne* there was a lull in the art market, as the curve showing the rise in prices during 1972–73 seemed to suggest was inevitable: once a peak had been reached, collapse would follow sooner or later. In the fall of 1973, the Cologne Art Fair experienced the first recession in its history.[115] The last months of the market's rise came to a close just as the rest of the economy felt the first shocks of the OPEC embargo—with art, like gold, still serving as a safe haven for investors. But the economic crisis was not only an oil crisis, it was a monetary crisis as well. The year 1971, when Broodthaers stamped his gold ingot, had marked the end of the dollar's convertibility into gold and, as a consequence, the disappearance of the system of fixed exchange rates established by the Bretton Woods agreement and of the role of gold as the standard used to back national currencies. Broodthaers was fully aware of this. On December 7, 1972, at the Palais des Beaux-Arts in Brussels, he showed a compilation of films under the title *Rendez-vous mit Jacques Offenbach* [*Appointment with Jacques Offenbach*], prefaced by the following notice that appeared on the screen: "Made between 1968 and 1972. / This program covers the period / that saw the birth and development / of inflation and its consequences. / Marcel Broodthaers / (Cfr. Nixon Speech, summer 1971)."[116] The speech referred to here was Nixon's solemn address to the nation on August 15, 1971, broadcast on radio and television, describing the "cruel" consequences of inflation—unemployment and international exchange rate imbalances—and pledging to make its elimination the priority of his administration. Then, to the surprise of most of those listening and watching, the American president announced the suspension of the dollar's convertibility into gold.[117]

This decision, as Broodthaers noted, was in reality the culmination of a crisis that had been gathering since 1968. Already by that point the price of

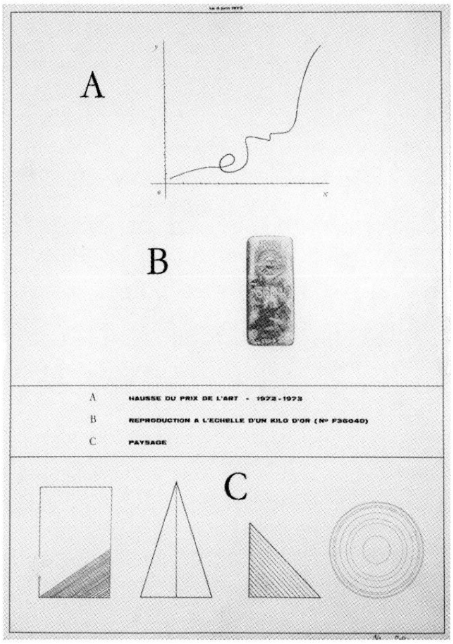

Fig. 76 Marcel Broodthaers, *Paysage d'automne* [*Autumn Landscape*], 1973. Color lithograph on white glossy cardstock, 27½ × 19¾ in. (70 × 50 cm). Initialed "M. B." on lower right of some copies; numbering "1/1" on lower right of one copy. Edition of 140 copies, published by Galerie Yvon Lambert, Paris.

gold had reached unprecedented levels, while the dollar was in steep decline, leading to the emergence of a dual market for gold: an open market on which the metal's price continued to rise, and a market for central banks where the official rate of thirty-five dollars an ounce was artificially preserved. Hopes for stabilization were short-lived: as the dollar continued to fall, the deutsche mark found itself subject to correspondingly strong upward pressures. Fueled by speculation, this disequilibrium widened further until finally West Germany decided to let its currency "float" on May 9, 1971, against the wishes of some of its partners among the six founding members of the European Economic Community (France, in particular). With the drastic reduction in American precious metal reserves and no end in sight to the dollar's loss of value, the end of convertibility was unavoidable. A monetary crisis had precipitated both a financial and an economic crisis.

Broodthaers's gold ingot, purchased in 1971 and reproduced twice—first in *Museum-Museum* in 1972, and then in *Paysage d'automne* in 1973—therefore had a quite particular significance, symbolizing at once the instrument of the fall of the international monetary system and the ultimate rampart against its collapse. The urge to hoard treasure was shared by many Europeans at the time. Broodthaers himself acquired pieces of gold bearing the emblem of the eagle from various countries.[118] According to Maria Gilissen, Broodthaers encouraged his friends at this time to buy gold and expressed pessimism regarding the international situation. He assiduously followed the economic news—particularly in *Le Monde*, which he sent his daughter to buy at Victoria Station when he and his family were living in London. Occasionally, he asked her to read him the exchange rates for currencies and gold.[119] Broodthaers meant to evoke this arid litany of alarming figures when he inserted six financial pages from *Le Monde* and other international newspapers in his 1975 book *En lisant "La Lorelei"* [*While Reading "Lorelei"*] (fig. 77). Among the cities whose names punctuate the columns of stock market news, the major centers of the art market of the period ring out: Düsseldorf, Berlin, Amsterdam, Brussels, Milan, Paris, and New York.

This is hardly surprising. The health of the art market, as we have seen, is closely tied to the performance of the general economy, particularly in relation to the stock exchange and monetary policy. As the Belgian artist Pol Bury put it in November 1972: "When the stock exchange catches cold, the fine arts sneeze."[120] What is more, then, as now, the geography of the art market was largely a function of monetary considerations. Otto Hahn, in a January 1972 article titled "The Avant-Garde Chooses the Mark," argued that the success of German fairs such as the one in Cologne was to be attributed to the difficulties of Wall Street and the dollar.[121] Another French critic, Michel Ragon, concurred in an article published a few weeks later: "Money is undoubtedly the real magnet that 'polarizes' artistic schools. Avant-garde art, more than that of the center and the rear, doggedly follows the geographical movements of the Stock Exchange. Wherever the most money is, modern art flourishes most brilliantly. This was the case in France before 1914, in the United States before the devaluation of the dollar. And now that the mark keeps on rising. . . ."[122]

The purpose of *Museum-Museum* (see fig. 69) and *Gedicht-Poem-Poème/Change-Exchange-Wechsel* (see fig. 70) therefore appears all the more plain in retrospect: they constituted exactly the sort of "warnings" Broodthaers was resolved to issue, in this case, about a crisis of currencies and international commerce that threatened to provoke a crisis of artistic values. Like *Paysage d'automne*, his 1973 work *Gedicht-Poem-Poème/Change-Exchange-Wechsel* consists of three parts, labeled A, B, and C (in small red type at the bottom of each section). Part A, "Gedicht-Poem-Poème," is laid out in three columns corresponding to the German, English, and French terms. The visual display calls to mind a calculation as much as it does a poem: the end of each "stanza" is indicated by a double line (consisting of a fine red line set above a thick black line), with the numerical "result" of adding up the figures above the line marked in red beneath. But the figures of this poem/calculation are neither words nor numbers, only a succession of initials, "M. B.," which the artist used to sign his work. The first panel reduces the literary to the numeric, and the second panel, part B, "Change-Exchange-Wechsel," converts the numeric into the monetary. Below that, in the untitled part C, the results of this second set of calculations are now labeled in monetary units, the final stage in the commercialization of a work of art.

Interpreting this work turned out to be more challenging than many commentators were inclined to suppose. Michael Compton, along with other authors, claimed that in part A, the number of sets of initials—of the artist's signatures—in each "stanza" corresponds to the number indicated under the double line beneath, whereas in part C they manifestly do not.

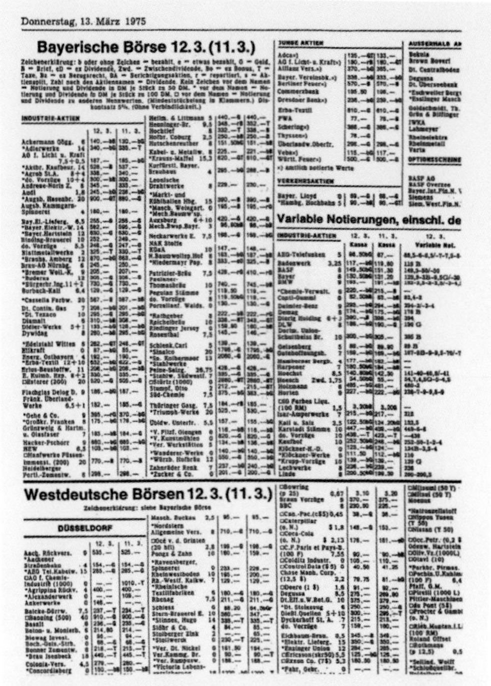
Donnerstag, 13. März 1975

Bayerische Börse 12.3. (11.3.)

Variable Notierungen, einschl. de

Westdeutsche Börsen 12.3. (11.3.)

DÜSSELDORF

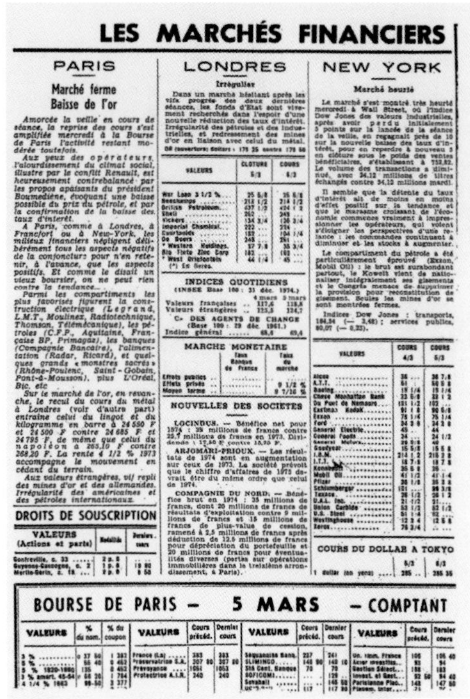
LES MARCHÉS FINANCIERS

PARIS

Marché ferme

Baisse de l'or

LONDRES

NEW YORK

INDICES QUOTIDIENS

MARCHÉ MONÉTAIRE

NOUVELLES DES SOCIÉTÉS

DROITS DE SOUSCRIPTION

COURS DU DOLLAR A TOKYO

BOURSE DE PARIS — 5 MARS — COMPTANT

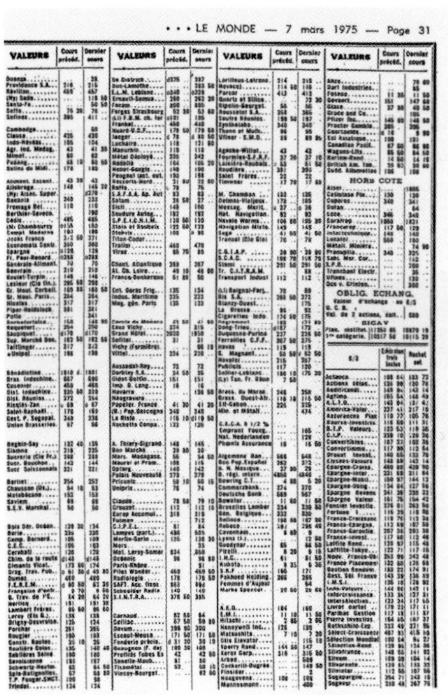
• • • LE MONDE — 7 mars 1975 — Page 31

Fig. 77 Three pages from Marcel Broodthaers, *En lisant "La Lorelei"* [*While Reading "Lorelei"*] (Munich: Galerie Heiner Friedrich; Paris: Galerie Yvon Lambert, 1975), n.p.

From this Compton concluded that "the calculations of [*Gedicht-Poem-*] *Poème* prove to be clear and exact, whereas those of *Change-Exchange-Wechsel* are false and dishonest," and that "Broodthaers thus gives us to understand that art pertains to truth," whereas commerce is the province of the lie.[123] This interpretation is untenable, however, for two reasons. First, an error has deliberately been allowed to slip into the calculations of part A.[124] Second, the "truth" of an addition means something different if its result is simply numerical, rather than labeled in monetary units. The result "125 D.M.," for example, is equivalent to the addition of 125 signatures only if one signature is "worth" one deutsche mark. The same is true for all the other results: "1,650 F.F." is equivalent to 1,650 signatures only if a signature is worth one French franc, and so on. This amounts to assuming that 1 DM = 1 FF = 1 £ = 1 $, which, of course, makes no sense in economic terms. Everything depends on the actual rate of exchange between currencies. But how was the rate to be determined at a moment when these currencies were undergoing wildly irregular swings? Part B, which serves as a conversion table, is indecipherable. Small wonder—the franc and the deutsche mark, whose rate of conversion had proved so difficult to negotiate, the pound sterling of the United Kingdom, which had just joined the Common Market in 1973, and the dollar, still under siege, were all part of an unfolding drama whose uncertain outcome forms the theme of this work.[125]

The whole problem raised by *Gedicht-Poem-Poème/Change-Exchange-Wechsel* therefore has to do with the search for equivalence, without which international commerce would be impossible. Here again, commerce is at once a social encounter, a linguistic encounter (between English, French, and German), and a monetary encounter (between the pound, the dollar, the franc, and the mark). The artist seems to suggest that there is a close parallel between the translation of a poem from one language to another (part A) and the conversion of one currency to another (part C). And yet the intervening section (part B), which purports to provide the key for linking the two others, but which in fact refuses to unlock the secret of their association, seems to undermine the possibility of both translation and conversion—a sign not only of monetary crisis but also of misunderstanding among nations. In part C, the column of signatures labeled in dollars is printed partly in red ink, as though to signal that the American currency, which in 1973 was continuing to lose value against the others, was now "in the red." The worth of the initials "M.B." likewise varies as a function of the contingencies of artistic geography: overvalued in francs (1 M.B. = 8.33 FF), it is undervalued in dollars (1 M.B. = $0.20).[126]

The effect of all this is to portray the market—whether for art, commodities, or currencies—as a place of conflict rather than of peace. For Broodthaers, the incompatibility between the two senses of the word *commerce* is manifest: commercial and monetary exchange preclude social harmony. As we saw earlier in connection with his film *Projet pour un poisson*, a commodity seemed to him to be identical with the "idea of non-communication."

Broodthaers had explored this same idea some years before in a happening called *Au pied de la lettre*—the name translates literally as "At the Foot of the Letter," or, less literally, as "Literally"—held at the artist's home in Brussels, 30 rue de la Pépinière, on December 8, 1966, a fairly detailed account of which may be found in a review by the journalist Pierre Bourgeois. "[T]hrough simultaneities of actions and through encounters of different ways of talking," Bourgeois wrote, "Broodthaers sought to confront, by means of language, the difficulties and impossibilities of poetic communication." The event involved a great many participants, writing, playing music, manipulating letters of the alphabet, and, above all, reciting verse and whispering enigmatic phrases in very different languages. A poet seated on the mantelpiece, with a dove perched on his shoulder, sporadically wrote down a few words while others recited in loud voices. After the declamation of a poem in English, "Icelandic and Hebrew were laid on top of an African dialect, when French texts were not being superimposed on one another." Not the least of the "annoyances," as Bourgeois called them, was that throughout the performance "a young woman sold a stenciled sheet of paper for ten francs, self-service literature."[127]

In the midst of this anarchic confrontation of incomprehensible speeches and incommensurable languages—a situation, in other words, in which there was no chance of mutual understanding—there stood the archetypal instrument of exchange: the tellers' windows of *La Banque*. According to Maria Gilissen, this object was placed in such a way that the inside was visible, rather than the outside, with the window shutters open (see fig. 73, rear view).[128] The inside is painted in black, green, and white; the panes of the tellers' windows are painted over or else are missing. Under the molding, at the level of the exterior horizontal panels marked *Ordres de Bourse* [Stock Exchange Orders] and *Change* [Exchange], the word *poems* is written twice, by hand and in white paint; traces of a third instance, partially erased, are still visible in the *Coupons* window. On the vertical wooden panels, covered in black, green, or white paint, the letters X, A, J, M, E, G, T, P, W, H, K, and O are stenciled several times in various more or less complete combinations. At the extreme left, the word *Persil* (referring to a popular brand of laundry detergent made and distributed by Henkel) has been painted by hand in white over black.

These inscriptions illuminate the role played by *La Banque* in the 1966 happening. Through the cacophony of words and letters, and in keeping with the detergent metaphor that recurred throughout the event, Broodthaers and the other participants undertook a thorough cleansing of language, by going back to its source.[129] This process ruled out any possibility of clear communication, implying an irremediable clash among untranslatable languages. It could only end, as Bourgeois saw for himself, in an "imbalance of accounts": "Poets, artists, and performers began to cry out figures in dollars, rubles, liras, francs. This accountants' auction led them into the streets—and no doubt into the bistro next door. The audience found itself left all alone. Incommunicability had triumphed."[130]

Broodthaers's happening supplies the missing elements needed to complete the interpretation of *Gedicht-Poem-Poème/Change-Exchange-Wechsel.* Here again, one encounters the same themes: the sale of a work of art (in each case, a poem), the substitution of figures for poetry, the conflict between languages and currencies. Only seven years separate the two works, but they are nonetheless very different in spirit. In *Au pied de la lettre*, the confrontation between languages and currencies is anarchic, delirious, and resolves itself through a riotous celebration in which incommunicability triumphs in the name of artistic creativity. In *Gedicht-Poem-Poème/Change-Exchange-Wechsel,* economic order gains the upper hand at the expense of plastic form: the columns, carefully arranged to facilitate calculation, immobilize language in the straitjacket of an economic system in crisis: the violence of economic and monetary rivalry is mirrored by the brutality of international artistic competition. At the 1966 happening, turning the bank counter around to expose its interior was meant to suggest the possibility not only of arresting the process of commodification, of coming to terms with the irreducibility of poetical languages, but also of bringing forth from the collision of languages and currencies—from their communion—a truly human, amicable, and joyous form of commerce, a festival of goodwill that ends up in the bistro next door. After this event, however, the counter was exhibited and photographed only from the front, as in the case of the Financial Section at Cologne, once more soberly assuming its role as guarantor of institutional and financial authority.

The pessimism of *Gedicht-Poem-Poème/Change-Exchange-Wechsel* regarding the possibility of creating a peaceable commercial regime that would respect the diversity of economic and social values seems to have grown as the crisis of the 1970s deepened. In 1975, Broodthaers published a miniature book (1½ × 1 in. [38 × 25 mm]) titled *La conquête de l'espace: Atlas à l'usage des artistes et des militaires* [*The Conquest of Space: An Atlas for the Use of Artists and Soldiers*]. Each of the thirty-two pages features the outline of a country, in black ink on a white ground.[131] If artists now needed a military atlas in order to set out to conquer space, it is because the art market, at once a source and specimen of the disorder of international commerce, had made them soldiers in a global conflict. "It rains money," Broodthaers wrote that same year. "Is it economic war that prevents me from sleeping?"[132] At this moment of crisis, inconvertible currencies and untranslatable languages were caught up in a general confrontation in which commerce contributed neither to social peace nor to material well-being, but instead stirred up hatred and strife among peoples and nations.

For both Johnson and Broodthaers, a tension exists between commerce in the sense of social interaction and commerce in the sense of economic exchange. And yet, as each one recognized, art cannot reject the latter in favor of the former: an economic system is needed to join these two aspects together. In Johnson's work, the articulation is made possible by doing two things: on the one hand, producing marketable *Dollar Bill* collages for sale in galleries, which entailed immobilizing—and therefore demonetizing—the currency itself; on the other, disseminating mail art free of charge, which put an alternative form of currency in circulation as a means of communication within a community of artistic fellowship. In Broodthaers's conception, a work of art cannot avoid being a part of commerce, which, in turn, can only lead to economic warfare. But by incorporating a particular kind of warning in its own internal economy, it can interfere with the normal functioning of the market and, out of the inconvertibility of currencies and languages, bring into being authentic poetic exchange. The public and private faces of the bank counter in *La Banque* illustrate the two aspects of commerce: on the outside, the Coupons, Exchange, and Stock Exchange Orders windows assure convertibility and the market's normal trading function—accounting efficiency having become an "engine of terrible precision" (to recall Mallarmé's phrase)[133] in the service of the economic warfare Broodthaers sought to combat; on the inside, poems and dispersed letters proclaim the reign of incommunicability, in which the irreducibility of poetic language to economic language allows inconvertibility to be seen as a value-generating and life-giving force.

For many artists in the 1970s, the idea that the development of international commerce went hand in hand with the spread of peace no longer appeared plausible. Ruinous competition among developed economies and commercial exploitation of the Third World had largely discredited it. Robert Filliou, who during this period knew both Johnson and Broodthaers well, ridiculed the European Community's decision to place all of its hopes for peaceful development in commerce.[134] "In Europe now," he was quoted as saying in 1978, "we are talking about [the] Common Market, [the] unity of Europe—in the sixties . . . I [argued] that [the] countries of Europe, in order to seal their new-found friendship and point out the obscenity of war, should exchange their War Memorials."[135] This project, titled *Commemor*, urged that peace be founded not on free-market exchange, but on the commemoration, protection, and advancement of human values.

The situation outside Europe was still more discouraging for artists worried about the outlook for countries injured by the terms of commerce imposed by the great powers. The Uruguayan artist Luis Camnitzer, in a 1969 lecture entitled "Contemporary Colonial Art," denounced the hypocrisy of the idea of commerce based on cooperation and joint development, in art no less than other consumer goods:

> There is a rhetoric and a mental process of the Empire which are very particular and which are not new. . . . As with Commerce, Art is above stingy political games: "it helps the communication and understanding of the people," "it is a common denominator for understanding." "The world is smaller every day," and under the rug

> of this phrase one sweeps the moment-by-moment growing difference between the cultural needs of economically developed countries and those [that are] underdeveloped or developing. . . . The United States of America, with 6% of the world['s] population, consumes 50% of the world['s] consumer goods. In addition to the necessary military consequences to maintain this situation, this rather monstrous proportion allows the United States of America to also fix the conditions of the market for those goods. The art-consumer goods do not escape this rule.[136]

In condemning the United States for exporting a liberal rhetoric that masked the reality of commercial, military, and cultural imperialism,[137] Camnitzer exhorted artists to create new networks of circulation, new areas of free trade that are no longer predicated on capitalist competition, but on genuine friendship and respect for cultural differences.

Conclusion

Robert Filliou, who crossed paths directly or indirectly with most of the artists we have encountered in the previous pages, from Paris in the late 1950s to New York in the mid-1960s and then shortly afterward in Cologne and Berlin, shared many of their concerns. Like Klein and Gallizio, he sought to make art a laboratory for investigating economic life in all its aspects, on the basis of a new "theory of values."[1] Like them, too, he felt a need to reconceive the place of creativity in an increasingly automated world, and tried to imagine a system in which "technology would serve to create freedom and art to indicate different ways of making use (consuming) this freedom."[2] Like Jorn, he rejected the division of labor in a capitalist economy, arguing on behalf of a conception of "work as play" that would permit the natural "genius" of humanity to flourish, rather than encourage the search for new and ever more specialized forms of practical knowledge.[3] Filliou aimed to create a "brilliant Republic," kindred in spirit to Gallizio's Alba laboratory, dedicated to experiment and free inquiry—precious things that are "not the privilege of those who know, but rather the domain of those who do not know."[4]

PRINCIPLES OF POETICAL ECONOMY

In 1966, Filliou called attention to "[a] problem, the one and only, but massive: money, which [artistic] creation does not necessarily create."[5] Yet he did not himself venture to create money through his art, as Warhol and Rivers had done. Their cleverly contrived currencies provided a skeptical (and often quite funny) perspective on the most noticeable conventions of the changing capitalism of the 1960s while shrewdly carving out a lucrative place for themselves in the art market. Filliou, like the conceptual artists we looked at in chapter 3, preferred to address another, less obvious aspect of this transformation: mathematical formalization and technical expertise. Unlike Venet, however, who was fascinated by the hermeticism of mathematized finance, or Levine, who mimicked the rationalistic efficiency of investment analysis, Filliou was drawn instead to approximation and amateurism. Disencumbering himself of his own professional knowledge of economics, Filliou delighted in toying with absurd calculations. The blackboard that figures in his 1971 installation at the Stedelijk Museum in Amsterdam, for example, is covered with erroneous mathematical equations (see fig. 1). In this work the artist set himself the task of measuring the "speed of art," which is to say how long it takes for a work to be assimilated into public consciousness, from the time of its conception to its fabrication, display, and reception—the rate, in other words, at which art and life are joined together.[6] But the derivative of the function he gives here is wrong. As for the supplementary unit *h*, normally a pure mathematical convention, it becomes "drinking, for inst[ance]"—wryly suggesting that alcohol can accelerate the artistic process.

Filliou's view of the pretensions of professional economists in claiming to enjoy a monopoly on economic decision making is fraught with irony. "If I dwell on scientists," he explained, "it is because I also tease them on their own terrain"—the better to remind them that imaginative genius always trumps intellectual talent and technical expertise. "A mathematician who talked to [me] about modern mathematics the other day, a simply incredible conversation, concluded by saying that in order to solve the world's problems it is necessary to learn modern mathematics—that way we will understand a bit of what the computers that govern us decide. This is naïve."[7] In mocking the gullibility of those who seek to make the study of capitalist economies a "hard" science, and their workings something that powerful electronic computational devices can optimize, he reaffirmed the human responsibilities of economic and social policy.

Like Johnson and Broodthaers, Filliou adopted the pose of a merchant in order to promote a closer alliance between social intercourse and commercial exchange. He kept what he called a "legitimate gallery" in his hatband, so that he could show his work wherever and whenever he happened to run into a potential buyer.[8] A tip of the hat—what Erwin Panofsky famously pointed to as the paradigmatic example of visual symbolism—now became a way of greeting an acquaintance while at the same time conveying an invitation to purchase an artist's work. In 1965, Filliou opened a "nonshop" shop called La cédille qui sourrit [The Smiling Cedilla] in the Mediterranean seaside resort of Villefranche-sur-Mer that served as a meeting place for artists for several years.[9] Like Johnson, Filliou was alarmed by a capitalist system of commerce that forced the artist to participate in an "economy of prostitution." Nevertheless, he suspended moral judgment in the face of the practical obligation to earn a livelihood, holding that anything an artist "could do well (or badly) to make money was *legitimate*."[10] And like Broodthaers, he inveighed against terms of trade that made commerce a source of injustice and exploitation. He was more optimistic than Broodthaers, however, and set himself the task of devising a "true rate of exchange" (VTE in its French abbreviation). According to this calculation, exchange would no longer be based, as in classical economics, on a relation of equivalence, an equilibrium state requiring an estimation to be made of the quantity of some principle common to each of the commodities exchanged, whether it be the amount of labor involved in their manufacture or the amount of utility created. Instead, exchange would be "fair" only insofar as it preserved a dissymmetry that reflected ineliminable differences between the commodities exchanged (this is what he called the "principle of noncomparison"). Because the singular qualities and imperfections of these items would be deemed enriching in themselves, the untranslatability of languages and the inconvertibility of currencies would no longer lead to economic warfare, but to a mutually fulfilling appreciation of the diversity of human values.[11]

Yet Filliou's career also illustrates the frustration that the artistic practices we have examined are apt to arouse. In 1966, Filliou attached the highest importance to writing his *Principles of Poetical Economy*; five years later, he considered it to hold "the keys to my work."[12] It will nonetheless be clear to anyone who looks at the question closely that the principles themselves were never worked out in any formal way, as Jorn's critique of economic policy had been, for example. Was anything else to be expected from a "café genius" who celebrated the "not done" as an "ideal stage" and who proclaimed the necessity of staying "calmly seated, doing nothing"?[13] The notional manuscript remained in fragmentary form, consisting only of incantatory keywords and paradoxical statements that were subsequently developed in writings, films, and artworks, sometimes ironically called "chapters"—chapters of a treatise that did not in fact exist.[14] Their very nonexistence has fed a certain, rather fantastical, confidence in their revolutionary promise. "Once written down and applied," the historian Sharla Sava dared to suggest, "these principles could resolve major world problems."[15] In the absence of practical solutions, however, and faced with the capitalist art market's ever-increasing powers of absorption, one may be forgiven for wondering whether works of art can have any real impact on economic life. The most ambitious attempts, such as those of Gallizio, often left artists themselves with a sense of failure. As Allan Kaprow noted in 1964, "[a] picture never changed the price of eggs."[16]

WHAT ART CAN DO FOR ECONOMICS

What contribution can artists make to economic thought? There was a time when economists looked to the arts for inspiration. We know that the famous *Tableau économique* [*Economic Table*] published by François Quesnay in 1759, the first schematic representation in the history of economics, was inspired by a cabinet of curiosities of the period and valued both as a tool of scientific analysis and as a means of visual re-creation.[17] More generally, economists such as David Hume, A. R. J. Turgot, and Adam Smith gave careful thought to the place of luxury and the arts in the economic development of nations and in the moral growth of individuals. The influence of artistic appreciation on economic analysis was felt even at the level of terminology: as the late American economist Craufurd Goodwin noted, for example, "[w]hat economists nowadays think of as 'demand' was often called 'taste' in the eighteenth century."[18] But then, in the nineteenth century, classical (and later neoclassical) economics excluded art from its field of study. It was only with the work of John Maynard Keynes, a member of the Bloomsbury Group and close friend of the painter and critic Roger Fry, that economics was able once more to profit from fresh thinking on aesthetic subjects.[19]

In the 1960s, capitalist economies were chiefly concerned with managing monetary stability and fighting inflation; capitalist economics laid a corresponding emphasis on technical expertise, as we have seen, and claimed to constitute a branch of science unaffected by subjective perceptions or political considerations. This reorientation was accompanied by the emergence of a visual culture peculiar to economic analysis, cloaked in the presumptive authority of graphs, formulas, charts, and tables of figures. At a time when economics was triumphantly applying quantitative methods to the study of every sphere of human activity—notably in connection with the art market—it presented itself as a specialized domain of expert knowledge, inaccessible to the uninitiated.

When artists began to scrutinize the assumptions of economic theory in their works, they did not pretend to be acting as enlightened economists. The ones I have discussed in this book were interested in economics—most of them read the financial pages, some had a passing knowledge of Marx's writings, perhaps even a bit more—but none of them laid claim to expertise in the subject. Only Filliou had been trained as an economist; all the more readily, then, did he indulge a taste for error in his work, for the deliberately improper use or confusion of technical terms—as though to stress the importance of nonexpertise, of not knowing. In proportion as economics jealously insisted on its exalted status as a science, a discipline reserved for experts, artists forced economics to disclose its secrets, by submitting it to the test of arts that were foreign to it. In doing this, they implicitly endorsed the attitude described by Georges Bataille in his preface to *La part maudite* [*The Accursed Share*]:

> For some years, being obliged on occasion to answer the question "What are you working on?," I was embarrassed to have to say: "A work of political economy." . . . Indeed, I had to add that the book I was writing (which I am now publishing) did not consider the facts the way qualified economists do, that I had a point of view from which a human sacrifice, the construction of a church or the gift of a jewel were no less interesting than the sale of wheat. . . . Moreover, neither psychology nor, in general, philosophy can be considered free of this primary question of economy. Even what can be said of art, of literature, of poetry has an essential connection with the movement I study. . . .[20]

It remains for us to determine whether these unorthodox ways of looking at capitalism called it into question in any serious way. Current events in both the arts and politics have given rise to a great many exhibitions and much critical commentary reinterpreting historical and contemporary developments from an anticapitalist perspective, often with frankly militant intent.[21] Because the avowed aim of these artists and critics is to propose an alternative to the present system, their outlook is fundamentally ideological. In the present book, by contrast, I have not assumed that criticism of a dominant economic regime by works of art is the prerogative of committed or even politically progressive artists. Some of the artists I discuss did, indeed, take anticapitalist and revolutionary stands; Gallizio, as a member of the Situationist International, is perhaps the foremost example. But most were less dogmatic in their views. In many cases, the very ambivalence of their attitude—poised somewhere between outright condemnation and unconditional celebration, between pure intentions and a cynical awareness of self-interested motivations—enriched the practice of their art. In their resolute opposition to the grim disciplinary specialization of economics (what Walter Benjamin called its "papal solemnity"),[22] these artists brought to bear the formidable resources of humor, utopianism, and a proud amateurism. This was their most lasting contribution.

Not only were Filliou's principles of poetical economy never actually written down, the artist himself missed no opportunity to mock those who expected him to solve the problems of the capitalist world. In 1977, for example, he identified his limited-edition work *Je meurs trop* [*I Die Too Much*] (fig. 78) as the "fourth chapter of the 'Principles of Poetic[al] Economy.'"[23] The object resembles a book, with a handwritten label bearing the title and the name of the author, and a printed publicity wrapper in the French style. And yet the reader eager to discover what his fourth chapter contains will have a very hard time opening this weighty tome: it is a fireproof brick. Brick was a material prized by Filliou, who contrasted its impenetrable density with the airy presumption of fluid and unimpeded access to the profundity of a thinker's ideas.

The fact that the principles of poetical economy were never cast in the form of a systematic critique is revelatory. It tells us that it is futile to look to artists for alternative economic solutions that are both socially meaningful and readily translated into a political program. No contribution that art might be able to make to economic thought could possibly have a form comparable to that of an economic treatise. But because art stimulates reflection, imagination, laughter, and aesthetic pleasure, it has the power to change the way we look at economic behavior, by demonstrating that, however determined economic theory may be to hide behind the veil of science, it remains a human activity that must always be open to critical examination by people from all walks of life. Ultimately, like all the other artists we have met in this book, Filliou invites us to think about what artistic representations of the economy can, and cannot, be expected to achieve.

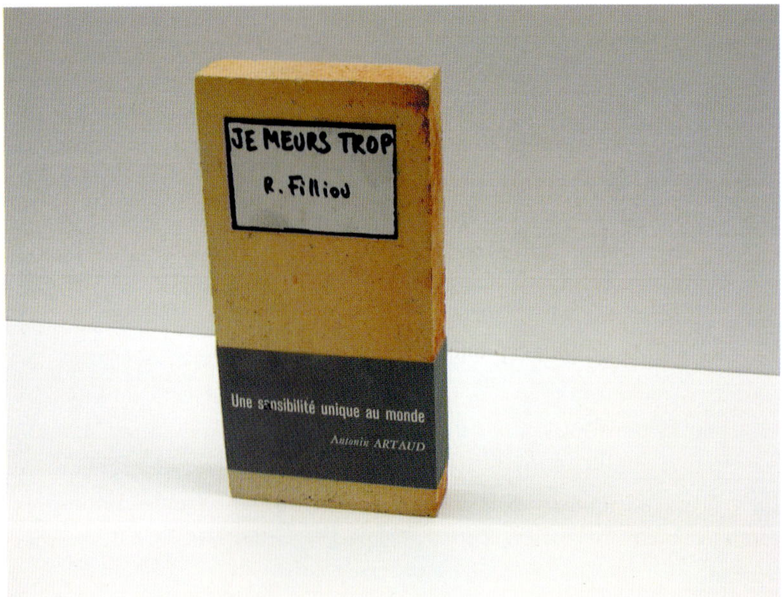

Fig. 78 Robert Filliou, *Je meurs trop* [*I Die Too Much*], 1977. Brick, label, and printed publicity wrapper, 9⅛ × 4⅜ × 1⅛ in. (23.3 × 11 × 3 cm). Edition of 50 copies, published by Éditions Lebeer-Hossmann, Brussels.

To be sure, none of them seriously challenged the economic orthodoxy of the period. Indeed, considering the resurgence of neoliberal capitalism in the decades since, it is tempting to say that artists during the 1960s not only failed to deflect its trajectory, but actually helped to hasten its ascendency.[24] To this one may nonetheless respond, with Filliou, that the impact of a work of art cannot be measured on such a limited scale. "My artistic propositions are advanced within the framework of a period of five billion years," he explained. "Over the long term, there can be no doubt that these prospects will be realized."[25] It is up to all of us who look at art and the world today, and to all of those who will come after us, to imagine what poetical economy may one day be able to do for political economy.

Notes

INTRODUCTION

1. Robert Filliou, "A Proposition, a Problem, a Danger, and a Hunch," in *Manifestos* (New York: Something Else Press, 1966), 14.

2. Robert R. Nathan Associates, *An Economic Programme for Korean Reconstruction* (New York: United Nations, 1954).

3. On his departure from the United Nations Korean Reconstruction Agency, Filliou noted that he "would have been fired as a 'security risk' anyway": he had joined the Communist Party after taking part in the Resistance during the war, and "gave up [C]ommunism after [President Josip Broz] Tito was excommunicated from the Cominform." Robert Filliou, *Teaching and Learning as Performing Arts* (Cologne: König, 1970), 8. See also Pierre Tilman's biography, *Robert Filliou, nationalité poète* (Dijon: Les presses du réel, 2007), esp. 22–35.

4. Filliou, *Teaching and Learning as Performing Arts*, 16.

5. Ibid., 51.

6. See Max Weber, *The Protestant Ethic and the Spirit of Capitalism* [1904], ed. and trans. Stephen Kalberg (New York: Oxford University Press, 2011); also Luc Boltanski and Ève Chiapello, *The New Spirit of Capitalism* [1999], trans. Gregory Elliott (New York: Verso, 2007).

7. Paul Mattick has retraced the ideological opposition between art and commerce since the eighteenth century; see *Art in Its Time: Theories and Practices of Modern Aesthetics* (London: Routledge, 2003), 24–45.

8. Letter from Stéphane Mallarmé to Octave Mirbeau, July 8, 1889; quoted in Octave Mirbeau, *Combats esthétiques*, 2 vols. (Paris: Séguier, 1993), 1:390 n12.

9. The phrase occurs in a footnote to Mallarmé's 1894 essay "Music and Letters." See Stéphane Mallarmé, *Divagations: The Author's 1897 Arrangement*, trans. Barbara Johnson (Cambridge, Mass.: Belknap Press of Harvard University Press, 2007), 197.

10. David Ricardo, *On the Principles of Political Economy and Taxation*, in *The Works and Correspondence of David Ricardo*, ed. Piero Sraffa, 11 vols. (Cambridge: Cambridge University Press, 1951–73), 1:12. The same idea occurs in the third volume of *Capital*; see Karl Marx and Frederick Engels, *Collected Works*, 50 vols. (New York: International Publishers, 1998), 37:627. In this connection, see also Dave Beech, *Art and Value: Art's Economic Exceptionalism in Classical, Neoclassical and Marxist Economics* (Leiden: Brill, 2015).

11. See the entry "Artists" in Gustave Flaubert, *Dictionary of Received Ideas* [1913], ed. and trans. Gregory Norminton (Richmond, Surrey, England: Oneworld Classics, 2010), 8.

12. Theodor Adorno, *Aesthetic Theory* [1970], ed. Gretel Adorno and Rolf Tiedemann, trans. Robert Hullot-Kentor (London: Athlone, 1997), 225–32.

13. See, among other works, the many examples collected in Jean-Michel Ribettes and Martine Mairal, eds., *Les couleurs de l'argent*, exh. cat. Musée de la poste, Paris, 1991; also Philippe Hamon, *L'or des peintres: L'image de l'argent du XVe au XVIIe siècle* (Rennes: Presses Universitaires de Rennes, 2010). For an analysis of an individual work, see Raphaelle Occhietti, "De l'invisibilité du capital: *La junte des Philippines* de Goya (1815)," in *RACAR: Revue d'art canadienne* 38, no. 1 (2013): 65–78.

14. See, among others, Patricia Johnson and Caroline Frank, eds., *Global Trade and the Visual Arts in Federal New England* (Durham: University of New Hampshire Press, 2014), and Mark A. Meadow, "Merchants and Marvels: Hans Jacob Fugger and the Origins of the Wunderkammer," in *Merchants and Marvels: Commerce, Science, and Art in Early Modern Europe*, ed. Pamela H. Smith and Paula Findlen (New York: Routledge, 2012), 182–200; also Christy Anderson, Anne Dunlop, and Pamela H. Smith, eds., *The Matter of Art: Materials, Practices, Cultural Logics, c. 1250–1750* (Manchester: Manchester University Press, 2015). For a long-term history, see Hans-Gert Bachmann, *The Lure of Gold: An Artistic and Cultural History* [2006], trans. Steven Lindberg (New York: Abbeville Press, 2006).

15. See Svetlana Alpers, *Rembrandt's Enterprise: The Studio and the Market* (Chicago: University of Chicago Press, 1988).

16. See, for example, Richard G. Doty, *Pictures from a Distant Country: Seeing America through Old Paper Money* (Atlanta: Whitman, 2013); also Mark D. Tomasko, *The Feel of Steel: The Art and History of Bank Note Engraving in the United States* (Newtown, Pa.: Bird and Bull Press, 2009).

17. Jennifer L. Roberts, "The Currency of Ornament: Machine-Lathed Anticounterfeiting Patterns and the Portability of Value," in *Histories of Ornament: From Global to Local*, ed. Gülru Necipoğlu and Alina Payne (Princeton, N.J.: Princeton University Press, 2016), 308–19.

18. See, for example, Timothy James Clark's interpretation of *La mort de Marat* in *Farewell to an Idea: Episodes from a History of Modernism* (New Haven: Yale University Press, 1999), 15–54. On eighteenth-century currency, see Charlotte Guichard, *La griffe du peintre* (Paris: Seuil, 2018). See also Richard Taws's compelling account of visual representations of money during the Revolutionary period: Richard Taws, "Trompe-l'Oeil and Trauma: Money and Memory after the Terror," *Oxford Art Journal* 30, no. 3 (October 2007): 353–76, and *The Politics of the Provisional: Art and Ephemera in Revolutionary France* (University Park: Pennsylvania State University Press, 2013).

19. A rich literature has grown up on this subject since the pioneering works of Robert F. Chirico, "Language and Imagery in Late Nineteenth Century Trompe l'Œil," in *Arts* 59, no. 3 (1985): 110–14, Edward J. Nygren, "The Almighty Dollar: Money as a Theme in American Painting," in *Winterthur Portfolio* 23, nos. 2–3 (1988): 129–50, and Bruce W. Chamber, *Old Money: American Trompe l'Œil Images of Currency*, exh. cat. Berry-Hill Galleries, New York, 1988. See, for example,

Johanna Drucker, "Harnett, Haberle and Peto: Visuality and Artifice among the Proto-Modern Americans," in *Art Bulletin* 74, no. 1 (1992): 37–50; Paul Staiti, "Con Artists: Harnett, Haberle, and Their Accomplices," in *Deceptions and Illusions: Five Centuries of Trompe l'Œil Painting* (Washington, D.C.: National Gallery of Art, 2002); and, more recently, Dorinda Evans, "Toward Understanding Victor Dubreuil," in *American Art* 26, no. 3 (2012): 66–85.

20. For Ruskin's writings on political economy, including *Unto This Last*, *Munera Pulveris*, and *Time and Tide*, see vol. 17 of *The Works of John Ruskin*, ed. Edward Tyas Cook and Alexander Wedderburn, 39 vols. (London: G. Allen, 1903–12). On the trial, see Linda Merrill, *A Pot of Paint: Aesthetics on Trial in Whistler v. Ruskin* (Washington, D.C.: Smithsonian Institution Press/Freer Gallery of Art, 1992); also Leo G. Mazow and Kevin M. Murphy, *Taxing Visions: Financial Episodes in Late Nineteenth Century American Art* (University Park: Palmer Museum of Art/Pennsylvania State University Press, 2010).

21. See Jean-Joseph Goux, *The Coiners of Language* [1984], trans. Jennifer Curtiss Gage (Norman: University of Oklahoma Press, 1994). Goux subsequently developed the argument in several works, most notably *Frivolité de la valeur: Essai sur l'imaginaire du capitalisme* (Paris: Blusson, 2000), and *L'art et l'argent: La rupture moderniste, 1860–1920* (Paris: Blusson, 2011). Its influence has been particularly pronounced among literary theorists; see the excellent survey in Mark Osteen and Martha Woodmansee, eds., *The New Economic Criticism: Studies at the Intersection of Literature and Economics* (London: Routledge, 1999).

22. See Clark, *Farewell to an Idea*, 225–98.

23. See Rosalind E. Krauss, *The Picasso Papers* (New York: Farrar, Straus and Giroux, 1998).

24. See Marc Shell, *Art and Money* (Chicago: University of Chicago Press, 1995).

25. See Jean Fourastié, *Les Trente Glorieuses, ou La révolution invisible de 1946 à 1975* (Paris: Fayard, 1979); also Peter Temin, "The Golden Age of European Growth: A Review Essay," in *European Review of Economic History* 1, no. 1 (1997): 127–49.

26. On the art market during this period see, for France, Raymonde Moulin, *The French Art Market: A Sociological View* [1967], trans. Arthur Goldhammer (New Brunswick, N.J.: Rutgers University Press, 1987), and Julie Verlaine, *Les galeries d'art contemporain à Paris: Une histoire culturelle du marché de l'art, 1944–1970* (Paris: Publications de la Sorbonne, 2012). For New York, see Diana Crane, *The Transformation of the Avant-Garde: The New York Art World, 1940–1985* (Chicago: University of Chicago Press, 1987), and A. Deirdre Robson, *Prestige, Profit, and Pleasure: The Market for Modern Art in New York in the 1940s and 1950s* (New York: Garland, 1995). For quantitative studies, see the final volume of Gerald Reitlinger, *The Economics of Taste*, 3 vols. (London: Barrie and Rockliff, 1961–70), and Christopher Wood, *The Great Art Boom, 1970–1997*, ed. Duncan Hislop and Sharron Clarke (Weybridge, Surrey, England: Art Sales Index Ltd, 1997).

27. Katherine Kuh, "Art in America in 1962: A Balance Sheet," *Saturday Review*, September 8, 1962, p. 34.

28. Meyer Schapiro, "On the Art Market" [1960], reprinted in *Worldview in Painting: Art and Society, Selected Papers* (New York: George Braziller, 1999), 202.

29. William Seitz, "What's Happened to Art?: An Interview with Marcel Duchamp on Present Consequences of New York's 1913 Armory Show," *Vogue*, February 15, 1963, pp. 129–30.

30. On the historical origins of the sociology and economics of art, see Pierre Bourdieu and Alain Darbel, *The Love of Art: European Art Museums and Their Public* [1966], trans. Caroline Beattie and Nick Merriman (Cambridge: Polity Press, 2013); see too William J. Baumol and William G. Bowen, *Performing Arts, the Economic Dilemma: A Study of Problems Common to Theater, Opera, Music, and Dance* (New York: Twentieth Century Fund, 1966). For a historiographical survey of the economics of art, see David Throsby's introduction in Victor A. Ginsburgh and David Throsby, *Handbook of the Economics of Art and Culture* (Amsterdam: Elsevier North-Holland, 2006), 4–22.

31. See, in particular, Julie Ault, ed., *Alternative Art: New York, 1965–1985* (Minneapolis: University of Minnesota Press, 2002); Laurence Bertrand Dorléac, *L'ordre sauvage: Violence, dépense et sacré dans l'art des années 1950–1960* (Paris: Gallimard, 2004); and Francis Frascina, *Art, Politics and Dissent: Aspects of the Art Left in Sixties America* (Manchester: Manchester University Press, 1999).

32. In France, a strong tradition of research in the sociology of art grew up in the wake of seminal works by Pierre Bourdieu and Raymonde Moulin. Recent landmarks include Nathalie Heinich, *La sociologie de l'art* (Paris: La Découverte, 2004), Pierre-Michel Menger, "Artistic Labor Markets and Careers," *Annual Review of Sociology* 25 (1999): 541–74, and Alain Quemin, "The Impact of Nationality and Territory on Fame and Success in the Visual Arts Sector: Artists, Experts, and the Market," in *Cosmopolitan Canvases: The Globalization of Markets for Contemporary Art*, ed. Olav Velthuis and Stefano Baia Curioni (Oxford: Oxford University Press, 2015), 170–92. Recent landmarks in the Anglo-American tradition include Paul DiMaggio, *Nonprofit Enterprise in the Arts: Studies in Mission and Constraint* (Oxford: Oxford University Press, 1986); Olav Velthuis, *Talking Prices: Symbolic Meanings of Prices on the Market for Contemporary Art* (Princeton, N.J.: Princeton University Press, 2005). Research in the economics of art is divided between quantitative studies of the auction market, following William J. Baumol, "Unnatural Value: Or Art Investment as a Floating Crap Game," *American Economic Review* 76, no. 2 (1986): 10–14, and more qualitative analysis of the economics of culture, notably Nathalie Moureau, *Analyse économique de la valeur des biens d'art: La peinture contemporaine* (Paris: Economica, 2000), and Xavier Greffe, *L'artiste-entreprise* (Paris: Dalloz, 2012). Important biographical studies of art dealers of the period include Julie Verlaine, *Daniel Templon: Une histoire d'art contemporain* (Paris: Flammarion, 2016), Annie Cohen-Solal, *Leo and His Circle: The Life of Leo Castelli* (New York: Alfred A. Knopf, 2010), Manuela Gandini, *Ileana Sonnabend: "The Queen of Art"* (Rome: Alberto Castelvecchi, 2008), and Benoît Decron, ed., *René Drouin, galeriste et éditeur d'art visionnaire: Le spectateur des arts, 1932–1962*, exh. cat. Musée de l'abbaye Sainte-Croix, Les Sables d'Olonne (Les Sables d'Olonne: Cahiers de l'abbaye Sainte-Croix, 2001).

33. Among recent examples, see Isabelle Graw, *High Price: Art between the Market and Celebrity Culture* (New York: Sternberg Press, 2009), and Jean-Pierre Cometti, *La nouvelle aura: Économies de l'art et de la culture* (Paris: Éditions Questions théoriques, 2016). See also the issues on "Art and Its Markets," *Artforum International* 46, no. 8 (2008); on "Geld bewegt

Bild," *Zeitschrift für Bildkritik* 5, no. 4 (2013); and on "Spekulation," *Texte zur Kunst*, no. 93 (March 2014).

34. Precursors include Jürgen Harten, ed., *Museum des Geldes: Über die seltsame Natur des Geldes in Kunst, Wissenschaft und Leben: Eine Ausstellung*, exh. cat. Städtische Kunsthalle, Düsseldorf, 1978, and *Les couleurs de l'argent*, op. cit. Among more recent examples, see Jürgen Harten, *Das fünfte Element—Geld oder Kunst*, exh. cat. Städtische Kunsthalle, Düsseldorf (Cologne: DuMont, 2000), and Michael Kröger and Anne Schloen, eds., *Asche und Gold, eine Weltenreise*, exh. cat. MARTa Herford, England (Cologne: Wienand, 2012). It should be noted that two studies, dealing mainly with recent works, run counter to this tendency: Olav Velthuis, *Imaginary Economics: Contemporary Artists and the World of Big Money* (Rotterdam: NAi Publishers, 2005), and Luis Jacob, ed., *Commerce by Artists* (Toronto: Art Metropole, 2011).

35. See chapter 14 ("Money: The Poor Man's Credit Card") of Marshall McLuhan, *Understanding Media: The Extensions of Man* [1964], ed. W. Terrence Gordon (Corte Madera, Calif.: Gingko Press, 2003), 167–78.

36. In this connection my research links up with that of Pamela Lee, "How Money Looks: Man Ray's 'Perpetual Motif' and the Economy of Time," *Anthropology and Aesthetics*, no. 36 (Autumn 1999): 243–52, and Jennifer Jane Marshall, "In Form We Trust: Neoplatonism, the Gold Standard, and the 'Machine Art' Show, 1934," *Art Bulletin* 90, no. 4 (2008): 597–615.

37. See Marie-José Mondzain, *Image, Icon, Economy: The Byzantine Origins of the Contemporary Imaginary*, trans. Rico Franses (Stanford: Stanford University Press, 2005), 18–66. See also the discussion in Olivier Boulnois, *Au-delà de l'image: Une archéologie du visuel au Moyen Âge, Ve–XVIe siècle* (Paris: Seuil, 2008).

38. See Peter Read, "The *Tzanck Check* and Related Works by Marcel Duchamp," in *Marcel Duchamp: Artist of the Century*, ed. Rudolf Kuenzli and Francis M. Naumann (Cambridge, Mass.: MIT Press, 1996), 95–105. On the "fiduciary" works of Marcel Duchamp, see Francis Naumann, "Marcel Duchamp: Money Is No Object," *Art in America* 91, no. 3 (2003): 67–73; also Olav Velthuis, "Duchamp's Financial Documents: Exchange as a Source of Value," *Tout-fait: The Marcel Duchamp Studies Online Journal* 1, no. 2 (2000), accessible via www.toutfait.com/issues/issue_2/Articles/velthuis.html.

39. This subject has been extensively studied. See, in particular, Christin J. Mamiya, *Pop Art and Consumer Culture: American Super Market* (Austin: University of Texas Press, 1992); Cécile Whiting, *A Taste for Pop: Pop Art, Gender, and Consumer Culture* (New York: Cambridge University Press, 1997); Constance W. Glenn, ed., *The Great American Art Store: Multiples of the Sixties*, exh. cat. University Art Museum, California State University, Long Beach (Santa Monica: Smart Art Press, 1997); Sara Doris, *Pop Art and the Contest over American Culture* (New York: Cambridge University Press, 2007); and Jill Carrick, *Nouveau Réalisme, 1960s France, and the Neo-Avant-Garde: Topographies of Chance and Return* (Farnham, Surrey, England: Ashgate, 2010). See also Christoph Grunenberg, ed., *Shopping: A Century of Art and Consumer Culture*, exh. cat. Schirn Kunsthalle, Frankfurt, and Tate Gallery, London (Ostfildern, Germany: Hatje Cantz, 2002); and, for cultural history, Kristin Ross, *Fast Cars, Clean Bodies: Decolonization and the Reordering of French Culture* (Cambridge, Mass.: MIT Press, 1996).

40. The major references on this topic are Helen Molesworth, ed., *Work Ethic*, exh. cat. Baltimore Museum of Art (University Park: Pennsylvania State University Press, 2003), and Julia Bryan-Wilson, *Art Workers: Radical Practice in the Vietnam War Era* (Berkeley: University of California Press, 2009). See also Benjamin H. D. Buchloh, "Conceptual Art 1962–1969: From the Aesthetic of Administration to the Critique of Institutions," *October* 55 (Winter 1990): 105–43.

41. See Timothy James Clark, "On the Social History of Art," in *Image of the People: Gustave Courbet and the 1848 Revolution* (London: Thames and Hudson, 1973), 9–20.

42. See, for example, Robert L. Herbert's fine essay on Edgar Degas and the stock exchange in *Impressionism: Art, Leisure, and Parisian Society* (New Haven: Yale University Press, 1988), 50–58. For recent examples, see Matthew Beaumont, Andrew Hemingway, Esther Leslie, and John Roberts, eds., *As Radical as Reality Itself: Essays on Marxism and Art for the 21st Century* (Oxford: Peter Lang, 2007); Blake Stimson and Gregory Sholette, eds., *Collectivism after Modernism: The Art of Social Imagination after 1945* (Minneapolis: University of Minnesota Press, 2007); and Angela Dimitrakaki and Kirsten Lloyd, *Economy: Art, Production, and the Subject in the 21st Century* (Liverpool: Liverpool University Press, 2015).

43. Deirdre McCloskey, "Why Economics Is on the Wrong Track," unpublished manuscript (2006–7), available online via www.deirdremccloskey.com/articles/stats/why.php.

44. See Geoffrey M. Hodgson, *Conceptualizing Capitalism: Institutions, Evolution, Future* (Chicago: University of Chicago Press, 2015), and Joseph Vogl, *The Specter of Capital* (Stanford: Stanford University Press, 2014).

45. See Walter Benjamin, "Theses on the Philosophy of History," in *Illuminations*, ed. Hannah Arendt, trans. Harry Zohn (New York: Harcourt, Brace and World, 1973), 255–66.

46. See Andrew Shonfield, *Modern Capitalism: The Changing Balance of Public and Private Power* (Oxford: Oxford University Press, 1965).

47. These works borrow and revise Serge Guilbaut's main argument in *How New York Stole the Idea of Modern Art: Abstract Expressionism, Freedom, and the Cold War*, trans. Arthur Goldhammer (Chicago: University of Chicago Press, 1983), by restoring a central place to local scenes and actors. See, in particular, Sophie Richard, *Unconcealed, the International Network of Conceptual Artists, 1967–1977: Dealers, Exhibitions, and Public Collections* (London: Ridinghouse, 2009); Hiroko Ikegami, *The Great Migrator: Robert Rauschenberg and the Global Rise of American Art* (Cambridge, Mass.: MIT Press, 2010); and Catherine Dossin, *The Rise and Fall of American Art, 1940s–1980s: A Geopolitics of Western Art Worlds* (Burlington, Vt.: Ashgate, 2015).

48. Ikegami, *Great Migrator*, 11.

49. See the recent research by historians, geographers, and anthropologists on the long history of neoliberalism, particularly David Graeber, *Debt: The First 5,000 Years* (Brooklyn, N.Y.: Melville House, 2011); Serge Audier, *Néo-libéralisme(s): Une archéologie intellectuelle* (Paris: Grasset, 2012); Gilles Kévorkian, ed., *La pensée libérale: Histoire et controverses* (Paris: Ellipses, 2010); Philip Mirowski and Dieter Plehwe, eds., *The Road from Mont Pèlerin: The Making of the Neoliberal Thought*

Collective (Cambridge, Mass.: Harvard University Press, 2009); François Denord, *Néo-libéralisme version française: Histoire d'une idéologie politique* (Paris: Demopolis, 2007); and David Harvey, *A Brief History of Neoliberalism* (New York: Oxford University Press, 2005).

50. Thomas Piketty, *Capital in the Twenty-First Century* [2013], trans. Arthur Goldhammer (Cambridge, Mass.: Harvard University Press, 2013), 751.

CHAPTER 1
VALUING THE INVALUABLE

1. See Louis Dumont, "On Value" [1980], *HAU: Journal of Ethnographic Theory* 3, no. 1 (2013): 289.

2. D. J. Girard, "Valeur, prix," entry 818 in vol. 16 of Diderot and d'Alembert's *Encyclopédie, ou Dictionnaire raisonné des sciences, des arts et des métiers*, 17 vols. (Neuchâtel and Paris, 1751–72).

3. David Ricardo, *On the Principles of Political Economy and Taxation*, in *The Works and Correspondence of David Ricardo*, ed. Piero Sraffa, 11 vols. (Cambridge: Cambridge University Press, 1951–73), 1:12.

4. Adam Smith, *An Inquiry into the Nature and Causes of the Wealth of Nations* [1776], ed. R. H. Campbell and A. S. Skinner, 2 vols. (Oxford: Oxford University Press, 1976), 1:49.

5. Quoted by Auguste Walras, *De la nature de la richesse et de l'origine de la valeur* [1831] (Paris: Félix Alcan, 1938), 255.

6. Ibid.

7. Quoted in Firmin Oulès, ed., *L'école de Lausanne: Textes choisis de Léon Walras et Vilfredo Pareto* (Paris: Dalloz, 1950), 349. The passage occurs in chapter 3, section 226 of Pareto's *Manual of Political Economy*.

8. Charles Gide's *Principes d'économie politique* (Paris: L. Larose, 1898), which remained a standard textbook for students of economics in France until the middle of the twentieth century, was one of the last to devote the opening chapter to the question of value.

9. Raymonde Moulin succinctly described the market's development during this period: "[P]rices rose gradually from 1945 to 1950, while modern art struggled to achieve commercial recognition. By 1950 prices were moving upward at a more rapid pace, and between 1954 and 1956 the rate of increase became dizzying. Prices continued to rise until 1959–60, when the postwar boom apparently peaked; they leveled off somewhat from 1960 to 1962." Moulin, *The French Art Market: A Sociological View* [1967], trans. Arthur Goldhammer (New Brunswick, N.J.: Rutgers University Press, 1987), 166. Her conclusions have been confirmed by Julie Verlaine in her recent study, *Les galeries d'art contemporain à Paris: Une histoire culturelle du marché de l'art, 1944–1970* (Paris: Publications de la Sorbonne, 2012).

10. Geneviève Bonnefoi, "La peinture aujourd'hui," *Les Lettres nouvelles* (July 1959): 35–36.

11. The role of "values" as points of reference in evaluation, judgment, and criticism was explored by Luc Boltanski and Laurent Thévenot in *On Justification: Economies of Worth* [1991], trans. Catherine Porter (Princeton, N.J.: Princeton University Press, 2006), and then by Boltanski in *De la critique: Précis de sociologie de l'émancipation* (Paris: Gallimard, 2009). In Boltanski's new book with Arnaud Esquerre, *L'enrichissement: Une critique de la marchandise* (Paris: Gallimard, 2017), value is not defined a priori as the basis of price, but a posteriori as justifying a criticism of price. See also Nathalie Heinich's discussion of this issue in *Des valeurs: Une approche sociologique* (Paris: Gallimard, 2017).

12. Yves Klein, "Des bases (fausses), principes, etc. et condemnation de l'évolution" [1952], in *Le dépassement de la problématique de l'art et autres écrits*, ed. Marie-Anne Sichère and Didier Semin (Paris: École nationale supérieure des beaux arts, 2003), 21; emphasis in the original. [An English version of this work has since appeared as *Overcoming the Problematics of Art: The Writings of Yves Klein*, trans. Klaus Ottmann (Putnam, Conn.: Spring Publication, 2007). All translations of Klein here are my own. —Trans.]

13. Yves Klein, "L'aventure monochrome" [1959], in ibid., 235.

14. Yves Klein, "Dimanche," in ibid., 176 and 179 (among other occurrences).

15. Nan Rosenthal, "La lévitation assistée," in Dominique Bozo, Helmut Heißenbüttel, and Pontus Hulten, eds., *Yves Klein*, exh. cat. Centre Georges Pompidou, Paris (Paris: Éditions du Centre Pompidou, 1983), 221.

16. Thierry de Duve, "Yves Klein, or the Dead Dealer," trans. Rosalind Krauss, *October* 49 (Summer 1989): 79, 82. It will be clear that my own discussion in this chapter is indebted to both de Duve and Denys Riout.

17. Ibid., 78, 87.

18. There have been several illuminating recent reinterpretations of Klein's relationship with the Situationists, and particularly Guy Debord—emphasizing their friendly relations until at least 1952, and identifying certain similarities between their approaches—but they do not take into account the question of value as such. See Nicolas Bourriaud, "L'entreprise bleue, ou Yves Klein considéré comme une économie-monde," in *Yves Klein: La vie, la vie elle-même qui est l'art absolu*, exh. cat. Musée d'art moderne et d'art contemporain, Nice, 2000; and Julie Carson, "Dematerialisms: The Non-Dialectics of Yves Klein," and Sylvère Lotringer, "Traveling through the Void," both in Peter Noever and François Perrin, eds., *Yves Klein: Air Architecture*, exh. cat. MAK Center for Art and Architecture, Los Angeles (Ostfildern, Germany: Hatje Cantz, 2004). For a detailed account of Klein's dealings with Debord, see Kaira M. Cabañas, *The Myth of Nouveau Réalisme: Art and the Performative in Postwar France* (New Haven: Yale University Press, 2013), 44–56.

19. Denys Riout has reconstructed the history of these "immaterial" works, from the initial exhibit of *Surfaces et blocs de sensibilité picturale* on the second floor of the Galerie Colette Allendy in the spring of 1957 and the *du Vide* exhibition, as it was called, the following year through the conception of the "ritual rules of transfer" for the *Zones*, the introduction of receipt books, and finally the transactions completed and documented between November 1959 and February 1962; see Riout, *Yves Klein: Manifester l'immatériel* (Paris: Gallimard, 2004), 93–151, as well as the chronology on pages 173–79. Riout was also the first to dispel a persistent myth: "Klein never asked for a patent to be granted for his blue; he did nonetheless take steps to protect the priority of his invention if necessary. The method he chose—depositing an *enveloppe Soleau* [registering the date of his invention] with the National Institute of Industrial Property [INPI in its French initials]—is not to be confused with a patent application. . . . Note, too, that an *enveloppe Soleau* is valid for only five years. Finally, it must

be emphasized that the invention claimed by the artist concerned IKB as a 'binding medium,' and not the color itself—an ultramarine blue available in specialized shops." See Riout, "Imprégnations: Scénarios et scénographies," in *Yves Klein: Corps, couleur, immatériel*, ed. Camille Morineau, exh. cat. Centre Georges Pompidou, Paris (Paris: Éditions du Centre Pompidou, 2006), 34.

20. Lotringer, "Traveling through the Void," in Noever and Perrin, *Yves Klein*, 130.

21. Yves Klein, "Conférence à la Sorbonne" [1959], in Sichère and Semin, *Le dépassement de la problématique de l'art et autres écrits*, 134.

22. Dino Buzzati, "Blu, Blu, Blu!," *Corriere d'informazione*, January 9, 1957; press clipping, Archives Yves Klein, Paris (hereafter, "Klein Archives"), press book 1. Denys Riout was the first to have noticed this article, which contradicted the legend created by Klein; see Riout, *Yves Klein*, 154 n7.

23. "Nur für Kenner: Die Vollendung des Abstrakten!," *Neue Illustrierte*, January 26, 1957, and "Che coraggio blu!," *Il Corriere lombardo*; undated press clipping, Klein Archives, press book 1. See also *L'espoir de Nice et du Sud-Est*, January 26, 1957; press clipping, Klein Archives, press book H. Conversion based on United Nations data for the period.

24. M. C.-L., "Salon panoramique," *Le Monde*, February 15, 1957; press clipping, Klein Archives, press book H.

25. Emily Genauer, "Art and Artists: Have You Ever Been All Blue?," *New York Herald Tribune*, April 16, 1961; press clipping, Klein Archives, press book 8. Indeed, the five identical monochromes of 1961—roughly three times larger than the ones exhibited at the Galleria Apollinaire in January 1957, were offered at a price of $5,000 each at the Virginia Dwan Gallery in Los Angeles in May 1961, much more than in Milan four years earlier. The difference in price, which reflects the exceptional increase in the valuation of Klein's work on the international art market in the interval, is duly justified by the artist here by a difference in artistic quality. See the price list for the exhibit "Yves Klein: Le Monochrome," May 29, 1961, Virginia Dwan Gallery, in Dwan Gallery Records, 1959–ca. 1982, Archives of American Art, Smithsonian Institution, Washington, D.C. (hereafter, "Dwan Gallery Records"), box 1, folder 20.

26. Klein, "L'aventure monochrome," in Sichère and Semin, *Le dépassement de la problématique de l'art et autres écrits*, 235.

27. Riout, *Yves Klein*, 23.

28. Yves Klein, "Explosions bleues, lettre à la Conférence internationale de la détection des explosions atomiques" [1958], in Sichère and Semin, *Le dépassement de la problématique de l'art et autres écrits*, 60; see also his "Lettre adressée au secrétaire général de l'année géophysique internationale" [1958], in ibid., 59.

29. Michael Baxandall, *Painting and Experience in Fifteenth Century Italy: A Primer in the Social History of Pictorial Style* [1972], 2nd ed. (Oxford: Oxford University Press, 1988), 4.

30. Jean Ibanès, *La doctrine de l'Église et les réalités économiques au XIIIe siècle* (Paris: Presses Universitaires de France, 1967), 1. Here I sketch the economic doctrine of the canonists. The landscape of economic thought in the Middle Ages was, in fact, much more complex. Alternative views laid emphasis, for example, on the principle of free and unconstrained agreement by the two parties (according to the "romanist" interpretation), or on the principle of consensual utility (upheld by the Franciscan Petrus Joannis Olivi). See Giacomo Todeschini, *Franciscan Wealth: From Voluntary Poverty to Market Society*, trans. Donatella Melucci (St. Bonaventure, N.Y.: St. Bonaventure University Press, 2009), 105–50.

31. Georg Simmel, *The Philosophy of Money* [1900], ed. David Frisby, trans. Tom Bottomore and David Frisby, 2nd ed. (London: Routledge, 1990), 1.1.2, 95–96. See also Alfred de Tarde, *L'idée du juste prix: Essai de psychologie économique* (Paris: Félix Alcan, 1907), 31.

32. Klein, "Conférence à la Sorbonne," in Sichère and Semin, *Le dépassement de la problématique de l'art et autres écrits*, 131. Klein frequently refers to "ethics" in speaking of his work; see, for example, ibid., 149.

33. Philippe Contamine, Marc Bompaire, Stéphane Lebecq, and Jean-Luc Sarrazin, *L'économie médiévale* (Paris: Armand Colin, 1993), 217.

34. See Hannah Arendt, "The Crisis in Culture" [1954], in *Between Past and Future* (New York: Viking, 1961), 197–226.

35. Quoted by Raymond Thévenin, "La peinture est-elle devenue une valeur marchande?," *Combat*, March 14, 1962, p. 6. The debate included Alain Bosquet (writer and critic), Henri d'Amfreville (writer), Claude Rivière (art critic), Robert Lebel (art critic), Daniel Cordier (gallery director), Pro-Diaz (artist and painter), Jean-Albert Cartier (art critic), and Jean Larcade (gallery director).

36. Catherine Valogne, "Il y a tableau et tableau," *Les Lettres françaises*, no. 845 (October 13–19, 1960): 11.

37. This expression is borrowed from Nathalie Moureau, *Analyse économique de la valeur des biens d'art: La peinture contemporaine* (Paris: Economica, 2000), 7 and 93.

38. See Raymonde Moulin, "The Genesis of the Rarity of Art," trans. Jane Yeoman, *Art in Translation* 3, no. 4 (2011): 441–72.

39. Harold Rosenberg, "Defining Art," in *Minimal Art: A Critical Anthology* [1968], ed. Gregory Battcock (Berkeley: University of California Press, 1998), 300.

40. Klein's first statement on this subject dates to the *Vision in Motion/Motion in Vision* exhibit at the Hessenhuis in Antwerp. See Yves Klein, "Le dépassement de la problématique de l'art" [1959], in Sichère and Semin, *Le dépassement de la problématique de l'art et autres écrits*, 94.

41. Yves Klein, "Règles rituelles de cession des *Zones de sensibilité picturale immatérielle*" [1959], in ibid., 278–79. An eighth register, constituting series no. 0, listed unpriced zones that were reserved for friends and not sold to collectors.

42. According to the catalogue raisonné prepared by Paul Wember, there were some forty-five *Monogolds*, in different sizes, executed for the most part in 1960 and 1961; see Wember, *Yves Klein* (Cologne: DuMont Schauberg, 1969).

43. Klein, "Conférence à la Sorbonne," in Sichère and Semin, *Le dépassement de la problématique de l'art et autres écrits*, 122.

44. Pierre Restany suggested on several occasions that the gold was entirely destroyed; see Restany, "1960: L'année hors limites," in *Zero und Paris, 1960: Und heute*, ed. Renate Wiehager, exh. cat. Villa Merkel/Galerie der Stadt, Esslingen (Ostfildern, Germany: Hatje Cantz, 1997), 23. As Sylvère Lotringer put it, "No one, in other words, got anything tangible from the operation"; Lotringer, "Traveling through the Void," in Noever and Perrin, *Yves Klein*, 129. Thomas McEvilley, for his part, held that Klein sold "the void . . .

without however enjoying its benefits, which he cast into the river of time"; McEvilley, "Yves Klein, conquistador du vide," in Bozo, Heißenbüttel, and Hulten, *Yves Klein*, 23. This interpretation was supported by the discovery in 1979 of an ex-voto offering to Saint Rita of Cascia, consisting of three gold ingots that Klein said were "the product of the sale of the first four ZONES OF IMMATERIAL PICTORIAL SENSIBILITY." Klein, "Prière à sainte Rita," in Sichère and Semin, *Le dépassement de la problématique de l'art et autres écrits*, 276.

45. Undated letter from Iris Clert to Yves Klein, Klein Archives, correspondence. See also the letter from Iris Clert to Peppino Palazzoli, dated November 18, 1959, in which she says: "These twenty grams of gold represent I believe 20,000 lire / In principle and so that it will be perfectly valid, you should give *10,000 lire more!!!*"—further evidence that the transaction was monetary in nature; see Riout, *Yves Klein*, 168 n36. Similarly, Clert mentions having sold three "zones" (no doubt to Jacques Kugel, Paride Accetti, and Alain Lemée), in December 1959, "for ten thousand francs apiece"; see Iris Clert, *Iris-time: L'artventure* (Paris: Denoël, 1978), 92. (Riout cites this passage as well.) A letter from Accetti to Clert, dated September 17, 1959, confirms that a sale price was to be negotiated with the gallerist: "As for the price, considering the extreme difficulty of moving from the immaterial to the materiality of figures and checks, we should come to an agreement on my next visit to Paris or yours to Milan"; letter reproduced in Verlaine, *Les galeries d'art contemporain*, 314.

46. The link between current monetary developments (the government's borrowing against gold) and Klein's decision to deal in gold was first suggested by Denys Riout in a lecture for the Arts et Sociétés seminar organized by Laurence Bertrand Dorléac; see "Yves Klein: Credit via the Market," summarized in *Lettre du séminaire* 32 (April 15, 2010), available online via www.artsetsocietes.org/a/a-riout.html.

47. One may also mention the weekly column "La vie quotidienne" that Michel Bosquet wrote in *L'Express* in the late 1950s. A chart titled "Retail Prices, 1955 to 1959" showed the rise from a base index of 100 in October 1955 to 123 in October 1958; see "Économie: La vie en 59," *L'Express*, January 1, 1959, p. 8. On the warning sounded by economic experts against inflation at this time, see Éric Monnet, *Controlling Credit: Central Banking and the Planned Economy in Postwar France, 1948–1973* (Cambridge: Cambridge University Press, 2018), 69–76.

48. See Jacques Rueff, *Combats pour l'ordre financier: Mémoires et documents pour servir à l'histoire du dernier demi-siècle* (Paris: Plon, 1972), 152; also F. G., "La crise Pinay," *L'Express*, October 23, 1958, p. 6.

49. The text of this lecture ("Demain, le franc-or?") is reprinted in Jacques Rueff, *L'âge de l'inflation*, 3rd ed. (Paris: Payot, 1963), 79–101.

50. Quoted by Bruno Pays, *Libérer la monnaie: Les contributions monétaires de Mises, Rueff et Hayek* (Paris: Presses Universitaires de France, 1991), 5; see also Rueff, *L'âge de l'inflation*, 80.

51. Quoted by J. and S. S., "La nation," *L'Express*, January 1, 1959, p. 4.

52. See Rueff, *L'âge de l'inflation*, 100.

53. Claude Bourdet, "Le franc léger et le général lourd," *France Observateur*, no. 452 (December 31, 1958): 3. See also Christian Hébert, "Premier bilan de l'expérience Rueff," *France Observateur*, no. 456 (January 29, 1959): 6.

54. Tim, "La révolution (lourde)," *L'Express*, January 1, 1959, p. 10.

55. Alfred Sauvy, "Le poids du franc," *L'Express*, December 31, 1959, pp. 8–9. See also Jean Ecoche and Christian Hébert, "L'heure des économistes distingués," *France Observateur*, no. 452 (December 31, 1958): 11–13.

56. Yves Klein, "Manifeste de l'Hôtel de Chelsea" [1961], in Sichère and Semin, *Le dépassement de la problématique de l'art et autres écrits*, 309.

57. Christian Hébert, "Le scandale des 15 milliards de la dévaluation," *France Observateur*, no. 457 (February 5, 1959): 15.

58. For medieval theorists, the face (or nominal) value of money ought therefore to reflect the weight of the metal physically contained in each coin, so that exchange will have the character more of barter (one material for another) than of genuinely monetary exchange; on the development of this idea see Marc Bloch, *Esquisse d'une histoire monétaire de l'Europe* (Paris: Armand Colin, 1954). According to Michel Foucault, the shift from this conception (that it is the preciousness of a metal that justifies its use as a means of exchange) to its opposite (that it is the metal's use as a monetary instrument that gives this instrument its value) took place in the seventeenth century with the rise of mercantilism; see Foucault, *The Order of Things: An Archaeology of the Human Sciences* [1966] (New York: Random House, 1970), 189–95.

59. Klein, "Conférence à la Sorbonne," in Sichère and Semin, *Le dépassement de la problématique de l'art et autres écrits*, 131.

60. Siné, "Les vœux de Siné," *L'Express*, December 31, 1959, p. 3.

61. Jean Cau, "Le maître de finances," *L'Express*, January 8, 1959, p. 8.

62. Pierre Descargues, "Klein, l'homme qui a vendu le vide," *La Tribune de Lausanne*, October 30, 1960; press clipping, Klein Archives, press book 6.

63. The manuscript conserved in Klein's archives is not in the artist's hand, and the many references to economics that occur throughout the text seem rather foreign to his style. But even if he very probably sought assistance in composing this part of his "revolutionary" program, he nonetheless made it wholly his own in "Le dépassement de la problématique de l'art" (1959) and in his Sorbonne lecture of the same year. Following the example of Klein's editors, Marie-Anne Sichère and Didier Semin, I shall therefore consider it as fully belonging to the corpus of the artist's writings; see Sichère and Semin, *Le dépassement de la problématique de l'art et autres écrits*, 99–101, and the handwritten passages transcribed in n. 18 on pages 352–53 of this volume.

64. See Isidore Isou, *La théorie nucléaire de la monnaie et de la banque, la carte copernicienne opposée à la carte ptolémeique de la monnaie et de la banque, réforme du système monétaire, épuration ou reconversion des dirigeants et des responsables des banques* (Paris, 1966).

65. *L'Aurore*, for example, carried a front-page headline in its February 1, 1958, edition on "The Tragedy of French Finances," warning that "there remain only 186 billion [francs] to cover a trade deficit for 1958." See also, among others, Maurice Ferro, "Pour maintenir son équilibre économique, la France a lancé l'opération 'Devises,'" *L'Aurore*, January 9, 1958, p. 3.

66. For all these passages in the 1959 manuscript, see n. 18 on pages 352–55 of

Sichère and Semin, *Le dépassement de la problématique de l'art et autres écrits*.

67. Klein, "Conférence à la Sorbonne," in ibid., 149. In chapter 4 we will see that Jean Baudrillard, in 1972, also compared art to a standard guaranteeing the circulation of signs.

68. In another essay, Klein specifically condemns Soviet Communism by contrast with Christian democracy. The Soviet system, he says, "is an exasperation of form, in the sense that it is a social structure opposed to Christian societies and the civilizations illuminated by the Middle Ages. Thus Communism unifies, monochromizes, but by killing the individual, the spirit, whereas Christian democracy seeks to revitalize the individual without defining his personality, leading him [instead] to a conception of collective unity through his affective and spiritual resources and not through his material patrimony"; Klein, "L'aventure monochrome," in Sichère and Semin, *Le dépassement de la problématique de l'art et autres écrits*, 260.

69. The receipt book itself was marked "no. 0"; the individual receipts were unnumbered. See the interview with Virginia Dwan by Charles F. Stuckey, March 27, 1984, p. 1 of the transcription of the third cassette, Archives of American Art, Smithsonian Institution; also Catherine Grenier, "'Moi aussi j'ai sauté dans le vide': L'influence d'Yves Klein sur l'art de Los Angeles," in Morineau, *Yves Klein*, 208, and Riout, *Yves Klein*, 114.

70. See, in particular, Cécile Whiting, "The Los Angeles *Tableaux* of Edward Kienholz," in *Kienholz, Die Zeichen der Zeit, The Signs of the Times*, ed. Martina Weinhart and Max Hollein, exh. cat. Kunsthalle, Frankfurt (Cologne: König, 2011).

71. See Nancy Reddin Kienholz, "Chronology," in *Kienholz: A Retrospective*, ed. Walter Hopps, exh. cat. Whitney Museum of American Art, New York (New York: Whitney Museum of American Art/Distributed Art Publishers, 1996), 254. The earliest conceptual pieces of this type, such as *The Art Show*, date from 1963.

72. Edward Kienholz, "Contract for the Purchase of a Concept Tableau," reproduced in *Works from the 1960's by Edward Kienholz*, exh. cat. Washington Gallery of Modern Art, Washington, D.C. (Washington, D.C.: Washington Gallery of Modern Art, 1967), 36. The French Marxist group Supports/Surfaces had the same idea. In May 1970, in a manifesto signed by Daniel Dezeuze and Louis Cane under the title "For a Theoretical Pictorial Program," the group maintained that "the systematic exposure of the economic network underlying pictorial production must be envisaged simultaneously with the display of this pictorial production." A pricing model first tried out at Cane's exhibit at the Galerie Givaudan in 1968 broke down the sale price into the cost of materials (canvas), of equipment (ink, inking pad), of "manual labor," and of "intellectual labor," all in addition to a value-added tax and the gallery's percentage; see Lucy R. Lippard Papers (from the 1930s to 2007, the bulk of them from the 1960s to the 1990s), Archives of American Art, Smithsonian Institution, box 25, folder 1. At about the same time, the American artist Robert Morris created the Peripatetic Artists Guild, which offered various artistic services for twenty-five dollars an hour plus production and transport costs. See Maurice Berger, *Labyrinths: Robert Morris, Minimalism, and the 1960s* (New York: Harper and Row, 1989), 93–95. Adrian Piper later proposed a comparable breakdown of the costs of production in "A Proposal for Pricing Works of Art," *The Fox*, no. 2 (1975): 48–49.

73. The *Watercolors* from 1 to 10, then 25, 50, 75, and 100, then the rest of the hundreds up to 1,000, and then the rest of the thousands up to 10,000 are black. The ones from 11 to 24, from 26 to 49, from 51 to 74, and from 76 to 99 are yellow. From 101 to 499 (except for the hundreds) they are red, and from 501 to 999 (again, except for the hundreds), blue. The curator Jane Livingston suggested that these colors made it possible to establish degrees of quality: blue is "luxurious," red is "middle range," while "the cheaper ones tend to mute yellow" with monotone gray filling out the bottom end; Livingston, "Los Angeles," *Artforum* 7, no. 10 (1969): 66.

74. *Kienholz*, exh. cat. Galerie Christel, Helsinki, 1974, p. 5.

75. Livingston, "Los Angeles," 66. According to Grace Glueck, the first fifty *Watercolors* of the "monetary" series were sold almost at once; see Glueck, "Peepshows and Put-Ons," *New York Times*, April 6, 1969, p. D24.

76. *Kienholz*, Helsinki, 1974, p. 4.

77. Ibid., 3.

78. Rivers is quoted to this effect in Jean Lipman, "Money for Money's Sake," *Art in America* 58, no. 1 (1970): 82.

79. *Kienholz*, Helsinki, 1974, pp. 4–5.

80. Ibid., 5.

81. In Piedmont, as elsewhere in Italy, diminutives of *Giuseppe* are commonly used among family and friends—Giù, Beppe, Peppino, and Pippo are a few well-known examples. The artist's nickname, Pino, is a contraction of Peppino. Over time, and as a result of his association with members of the Situationist International, a terminal letter *t* came to be added (perhaps in a punning reference to the Pinot grape), together with a hyphen—converting a full name, Pino Gallizio, into an apparently aristocratic family name, Pinot-Gallizio. (Author's correspondence with the Archivio Gallizio.)

82. Guy Debord, "L'activité de la section italienne," *Internationale situationniste*, no. 2 (December 1958): 27.

83. *Pinot-Gallizio* (Paris: Internationale situationniste, 1960), n.p.

84. This strategic shift in orientation was carried on in a similar way with the resignation of the Dutch artist and architect Constant Nieuwenhuys (known simply as Constant) on June 1, 1960, the expulsion of Spur, a group of German painters, in early 1962, and the departure of Asger Jorn the previous year. The literature on the Situationist International has been greatly enriched since Debord's death in 1994 with improved access to archival resources (Debord's correspondence was published between 1999 and 2010; his personal papers were acquired by the Bibliothèque nationale de France in 2009, and those of Jacqueline de Jong by the Beinecke Library at Yale in 2012); see Emmanuel Guy and Laurence Le Bras, eds., *Guy Debord: Un art de la guerre*, exh. cat. Bibliothèque nationale de France, Paris (Paris: Gallimard, 2013). One of the most complete works, and one that gives proper attention to the Italian scene, is by the Gallizio specialist Mirella Bandini, *L'esthétique, le politique: De Cobra à l'Internationale situationniste (1948–1957)* [1977], trans. Claude Galli (Arles: Sulliver; Marseille: Via Valeriano, 1998).

85. See Selima Niggl, *Pinot Gallizio: Malerei am laufenden Meter; München 1959 und die europäische Avantgarde* (Hamburg: Nautilus, 2007); Laurent Jean-

pierre, "Pinot-Gallizio et la *Caverne de l'antimatière*, dans l'antichambre de l'anti-monde," *Palais*, no. 2 (Spring 2007): 4–13; Frances Stracey, "Pinot Gallizio's 'Industrial Painting': Towards a Surplus of Life," *Oxford Art Journal* 28, no. 3 (2005): 391–405, and "The Caves of Gallizio and Hirschhorn: Excavations of the Present," *October* 116 (Spring 2006): 87–100; and Nicola Pezolet, "The Cavern of Antimatter: Giuseppe 'Pinot' Gallizio and the Technological Imaginary of the Early Situationist International," *Grey Room*, no. 38 (Winter 2010): 62–89.

86. Note, in particular, the appearance of a catalogue raisonné, edited by Maria Teresa Roberto, *Pinot Gallizio: Catalogo generale delle opere, 1953–1964* (Milan: Mazzotta, 2001); the publication of a large part of his writings, edited by Giorgina Bertolino, Francesca Comisso, and Maria Teresa Roberto, *Pinot Gallizio: Il laboratorio della scrittura, The Laboratory of Writing*, exh. cat. Fondatione Ferrero, Alba (Milan: Charta, 2005); and, finally, the improved access in recent years to the artist's archives, now divided between the Archivio Giuseppe Pinot Gallizio, residing at the Galleria Martano in Turin (hereafter "Archivio Gallizio"), and the Galleria civica d'arte moderna e contemporanea in Turin (hereafter "Fondo Gallizio, GAM").

87. Giorgina Bertolino, "Gli anni della pittura industriale, 1957–1959," in Roberto, *Pinot Gallizio: Catalogo generale*, 100.

88. The leaflet, authored by Guy Debord, Constant Nieuwenhuys, Jacques Fillon, Giuseppe Gallizio, Franco Garelli, Asger Jorn, Walter Olmo, Piero Simondo, and Gil J. Wolman, is conserved in the *Diario-registro*, Archivio Gallizio.

89. See Pezolet, "Cavern of Antimatter."

90. Guy Debord, "Le bruit et la fureur," *Internationale situationniste*, no. 1 (June 1958): 5, and "La lutte pour le contrôle des nouvelles techniques de conditionnement," ibid., 6. The first article is available in English as "Sound and Fury," in *Situationist International Anthology*, ed. and trans. Ken Knabb, 2nd ed. (Berkeley: Bureau of Public Secrets, 2006), 47–48.

91. See Patrick Marcolini, *Le Mouvement situationniste: Une histoire intellectuelle* (Paris: L'Echappée, 2012), 36.

92. See ibid., 24, and Édouard Jaguer, "Giuseppe Pinot-Gallizio, l'albatros situationniste," *Archives et documents situationnistes*, no. 4 (Autumn 2004): 40. On the Hochschule für Gestaltung, see in particular Herbert Lindinger, *La scuola di Ulm, 1953–1968: Una nuova cultura del progretto* (Geneva: Costa e Nolan, 1988) and Valentina Anker, *Max Bill, ou La recherche d'un art logique* (Lausanne: L'Âge d'homme, 1979). On Jorn's critique of the Ulm School, see his letters to Enrico Baj, edited by Maurice Fréchuret and published as *Baj-Jorn: Lettres 1953–1961* (Saint-Étienne, France: Éditions Musée d'Art moderne, 1989).

93. See Asger Jorn, "Form and Structure" [1956] and "Against Functionalism" [1957], in *Fraternité Avant Tout: Asger Jorn's Writings on Art and Architecture, 1938–1958*, ed. Ruth Baumeister, trans. Paul Larkin (Rotterdam: 010 Publishers, 2011), 281–98 and 270–80, respectively.

94. On this subject, see Maurice Fréchuret, *La machine à peindre* (Nîmes: Éditions Jacqueline Chambon, 1994), 35.

95. The first canvas described as a product of industrial painting, *Antiluna* (late 1957), measured about 30 feet (more than 9 meters) long and almost 3 feet (86.5 centimeters) wide. It is today cut up into two distinct works: *Antiluna* (entry 57 DT 34 in the catalogue raisonné) and *Antiluna* (57 DT 35); see Roberto, *Pinot Gallizio: Catalogo generale*, 99.

96. Francesca Comisso, "Opere 1953/54–1964: Procedure tecniche, materiali," in ibid., 53–54. For a detailed description of the techniques employed, see also the report on the technical aspects of industrial painting that Debord commissioned Giorgio Gallizio to draw up in 1958, "Relazione di Giors Melanotte," Fondo Gallizio, GAM, folder V ("Movimento Internazionale situazionista [1957–1972]"), partially reproduced and translated into English as "Speech by Giors Melanotte," in *Laboratory of Writing*, 158–59.

97. Gallizio used the French expression "peinture d'ensemble." See "Le comparse éclairé: Entretien avec Giorgio Gallizio," *Archives et documents situationnistes*, no. 4 (Autumn 2004): 33–34; also the chapter "Opere collettive" in the catalogue raisonné, Roberto, *Pinot Gallizio: Catalogo generale*, 497–500.

98. "Vende quadri dipinti su chilometri di tela," *La Gazzetta del popolo*, May 31, 1958; press clipping, *Diario-registro*, Archivio Gallizio.

99. See, in particular, the letters from Debord to Gallizio dated January 30, 1958, and from Debord to Giors Melanotte, December 9, [1958], in Guy Debord, *Correspondance*, vol. 1 (June 1957–August 1960), ed. Alice Debord and Patrick Mosconi (Paris: Fayard, 1999), 57 and 164, respectively. English versions of both letters may be found in Guy Debord, *Correspondence: The Foundation of the Situationist International (June 1957–August 1960)*, trans. Stuart Kendall and John McHale (Los Angeles: Semiotext(e), 2009), 78–79, 183–85. See also the letter from Giors Melanotte to Debord, February 12, [1959], Fondo Gallizio, GAM, folder XI ("1959").

100. Thus Frances Stracey writes: "These rollers, in a parody of automation, were manually raised and lowered, each with its own sticky substance to apply: one might have resin on it, another one paint, and another a drying agent or varnish"; "Pinot Gallizio's 'Industrial Painting,'" 396.

101. Archivio Gallizio, folder "Fotografie III."

102. The French term is usually used in English writing on this topic, though sometimes translated as "diversion" (or "subversion"). See the definition given in *Internationale situationniste*, no. 1 (June 1958): 13, and the corresponding entry for "diversion" in Knabb, *Situationist International Anthology*, 45–46.

103. Debord, "L'activité de la section italienne," 28. He was no doubt influenced at this time by Constant, who opposed Jorn in rejecting "artisanal procedures, including painting," on the ground that "machine labor and serial production offer novel creative possibilities, and [that] those who know how to place these possibilities in the service of a daring imagination will be the creators of tomorrow"; indeed, he went so far as to say that "no painting is defensible from the Situationist point of view." See Constant, "Sur nos moyens et nos perspectives," *Internationale situationniste*, no. 2 (December 1958): 23. See also Philippe Dagen, "Constant: Une politique de la peinture," in *Constant: Une rétrospective*, ed. Maurice Fréchuret, exh. cat. Musée Picasso, Antibes (Antibes: Musée Picasso; Paris: Réunion des musées nationaux, 2001), esp. 27–28.

104. Asger Jorn, "Contre le fonctionnalisme" [1957], in Jorn, *Pour la forme: Ébauche d'une méthodologie des arts* [1958] (Paris: Allia, 2001), 28 and 27; a slightly different English version may be found in "Against Functionalism," in

Baumeister, *Fraternité Avant Tout*, 275 and 273.

105. Quoted by Debord in "L'activité de la section italienne," 28.

106. Giorgio Gallizio, "Relazione di Giors Melanotte," 28; in English, see "Speech by Giors Melanotte," in *Laboratory of Writing*, 159.

107. This is true even when the use of an iterative technique is apparent, as in the case of an untitled roll about 240 feet (74 meters) in length, from early 1958, that was exhibited at the Galleria Notizie in Turin. The successive mechanical impressions, modified by applying paint either with brushstrokes or by spraying, deliberately manifest marked discontinuities of style and chromatic scale while at the same time alternating impersonal gestures with quite visible traces of the artist's hand.

108. Michèle Bernstein, "Éloge de Pinot-Gallizio," in *Elogio di Pinot-Gallizio: Prima mostra di pittura industriale*, ed. Michèle Bernstein, exh. cat. Galleria Notizie/Associazione Art Figurative, Turin (May–June 1958), n.p.; in English, see "In Praise of Pinot-Gallizio," in Tom McDonough, ed., *Guy Debord and the Situationist International: Texts and Documents* (Cambridge, Mass.: MIT Press, 2002), 69.

109. Bernstein, "In Praise of Pinot-Gallizio," 70 (translation slightly modified).

110. For a summary of these arguments, see Raymond Charmet, Élise Nouel, and René Bernard, "L'art abstrait est-il condamné?," *Arts*, no. 727 (June 17–23, 1959): 7. See also the unsigned article "Présent et avenir de l'École de Paris," *France Observateur*, no. 453 (January 8, 1959): 20–21, as well as Michel Ragon, "Petit bilan pour tous," *Cimaise* 5, no. 1 (1957): 20–21, and Pierre Restany, "Le geste et le rythme," *Cimaise* 5, no. 1 (1957): 30–31. For a detailed analysis of the historical context, see Natalie Adamson, *Painting, Politics, and the Struggle for the École de Paris, 1944–1964* (Burlington, Vt.: Ashgate, 2009).

111. Mohamed Dahou, Guy-Ernest Debord, Jacques Fillon, and Véra, "Sortie des artistes," *Potlatch*, nos. 9–11 (August 17–31, 1954), reprinted in *Potlatch: 1954–1957* (Paris: Éditions Gérard Lebovici, 1985), 55; see also Dagen, "Constant," 25. In the second issue of the journal (June 20, 1954), the authors of the self-styled *Potlatch* Manifesto summarized their purpose in these words: "Political economy, love, and urbanism are means we must command in order to solve a problem that is above all ethical in nature"; see Henry de Béarn, André-Frank Conord, Mohamed Dahou, Guy-Ernest Debord, Jacques Fillon, Patrick Straram, and Gil J. Wolman, "Sans commune mesure," reprinted in *Potlatch: 1954–1957*, 16.

112. Bernstein, "In Praise of Pinot-Gallizio," 72.

113. Giuseppe Gallizio, "Discours sur la peinture industrielle et sur un art unitaire applicable," *Internationale Situationniste*, no. 3 (December 1959): 34. The French version of Gallizio's article was edited and translated by Debord. In its original Italian version, "Manifesto della pittura industriale: Per un'arte unitaria applicabile," Gallizio spoke of a "giant postage stamp, called a painting"; see the English translation, "Manifesto of Industrial Painting: For an Applicable Unitary Art," in *Laboratory of Writing*, 169 and 175. The idea that inflation was the weapon best suited to destroying the traditional arts had been introduced four years earlier: "The unbearable provocations launched or prepared by the Letterist group . . . unleashed a lethal inflation in the arts"; see Guy-Ernest Debord and Gil J. Wolman, "Pourquoi le lettrisme?," *Potlatch*, no. 22 (September 9, 1955), reprinted in *Potlatch: 1954–1957*, 154.

114. Bernstein, "In Praise of Pinot-Gallizio," 70.

115. Ibid.

116. Letter of July 27, 1957, sent to Gallizio by International Patent Research Corporation (INCO in its French initials); Archivio Gallizio, folder "Corrispondenza 1953–1960."

117. From Gallizio's welcoming address to the First World Congress of Free Artists, held in Alba in September 1956 (*Diario-registro*, Archivio Gallizio); see the translation in *Laboratory of Writing*, 130.

118. Gallizio, "Manifesto of Industrial Painting," in *Laboratory of Writing*, 171. On the importance of this subject for artists of the period, see Didier Semin, *The Painter and His Model on Deposit*, trans. Brian Holmes (Geneva: Musée d'art modern et contemporain, 2001).

119. Debord, "L'activité de la section italienne," 28.

120. Quoted by Debord in ibid.

121. One roll exhibited at the Galleria Notizie in Turin, about 46 feet (14 meters) in length, was cut up into at least four parts (almost 27 feet [8.2 meters], 2½ feet [77 centimeters], 4½ feet [1.37 meters], and about 5½ feet [1.65 meters]); see entries 58 DT 5 to 58 DT 13 in Roberto, *Pinot Gallizio: Catalogo generale*, 105–8. The Munich dealer Otto van de Loo, for his part, bought two whole rolls (*Il muro della mia casa* and *La sirena e il pirata*, both from 1958). He told the historian Selima Niggl that he considered *La sirena e il pirata* to be a work whole and entire, too coherent to be broken up into fragments; see Selima Niggl, "Intervista a Otto van de Loo," in *Pinot Gallizio: La gibigianna, magia e illusione*, ed. Maria Teresa Roberto, exh. cat. Galleria civica d'arte moderna e contemporanea, Turin (Turin: Fondazione Torino Musei, 2007), 85.

122. Debord, "L'activité de la section italienne," 28.

123. Alarmed that Gallizio might not have enough samples of industrial painting left over for his show in Paris, Debord advised the artist to raise his price per meter, if necessary; see letter to Gallizio dated July 5, 1958, in Debord, *Correspondence*, 134.

124. A resin on canvas almost 215 feet (65 meters) long was offered for 50,000 lire per meter, but 100,000 lire per 5 meters (about 16½ feet; or 20,000 lire per meter) and 400,000 lire for the complete roll (or a little more than 6,000 lire per meter). See the price list displayed by the Galleria Montenapoleone, "Prezziario," Archivio Gallizio, folder "Documenti—Mostre—Eventi (1956–1964)."

125. "Art by the Yard," *Time*, May 25, 1959, p. 50.

126. Letter from Wilfred Weiss to Giuseppe Gallizio, May 22, 1959. The letter was sent to the Galerie van de Loo in Munich, which forwarded it to Gallizio. Archivio Gallizio, folder "Corrispondenza 1953–1960."

127. Letter from Giuseppe Gallizio to Wilfred Weiss, July 7, 1959; Archivio Gallizio, ibid.

128. Letter from Weiss to Gallizio, May 22, 1959.

129. Jorn's financial support for the Situationist International (he was enjoying considerable commercial success during this period) is attested in many letters from Debord. See, for example, his letter to Gallizio of September 27, 1958; to Jorn,

December 31, 1959; to Maurice Wyckaert, February 14, [1960]; and especially the one to Jorn dated July 16, 1960 (reproduced in Debord, *Correspondence*, 161, 304, 332, and 371–72, respectively). That Jorn continued to make significant financial contributions even after his withdrawal from the group in 1961 is confirmed by Guy Atkins, quoted in Stewart Home, *The Assault on Culture: Utopian Currents from Lettrism to Class War* (London: Aporia Press and Unpopular Books, 1988), 34. According to Home, Gallizio played the same role during the time he was a member of the SI; see ibid., 34. Mirella Bandini concurs: see *L'esthétique, le politique*, 96, and her essay, "Pinot Gallizio, de l'expérimentation à la situation," in *Figures de la négation: Avant-gardes du dépassement de l'art*, ed. Martine Dancer and Jacques Beauffet (Paris: Paris-Musées; Saint-Étienne: Musée d'art moderne de Saint-Étienne Métropole, 2004), 97.

130. Jorn's text was initially published in French as *Critique de la politique économique, suivi de La lutte finale* (Paris: Internationale situationniste, 1960). The Danish manuscript, later extensively revised, has been translated into English as "Critique of political economy," in *The Natural Order and Other Texts*, ed. Peter Shield (Burlington, Vt.: Ashgate, 2002), 121–46. The French version published by the SI, with its implicit emphasis on the analysis of "reification" developed by Goldmann and Lukács, is the one that Gallizio read and worked from. Its genesis may be traced back to a letter Debord wrote to Jorn in July 1959: "If your booklet were to present a critique of Goldmann, who touches on the same theme you do—and if possible a critique of Lukács's book [*History and Class Consciousness*, 1923] which you can read in German (Lukács is now very much in fashion here)—this would in any case be a very useful element of your exposition. But above all it would be very positive if you could find yourself in agreement with Goldmann's ideas, at least for our effectiveness in [attracting the notice of] the Parisian intelligentsia." See letter from Debord to Jorn, July 11, 1959, in Debord, *Correspondence*, 244–45.

131. See Georges Bataille, *The Accursed Share: An Essay on General Economy* [1949], trans. Robert Hurley, 3 vols. (New York: Zone Books, 1988–91).

132. Jorn, *Critique de la politique économique*, 11.

133. Ibid., 21.

134. See ibid., 30.

135. Gallizio, "Manifesto of Industrial Painting," in *Laboratory of Writing*, 171, 176. [Here, as elsewhere, citation is made to the English version as a courtesy to the reader; nonetheless all the translations from the Italian are mine.—Trans.]

136. Ibid., 171; emphasis in the original. This part of the text is clarified by an undated manuscript, "Elementi per una *Teoria degli scambi*," conserved in the Fondo Gallizio, GAM, and reproduced in Bertolino, Comisso, and Roberto, *Pinot Gallizio*, 26–27; an English version may be found in *Laboratory of Writing*, 27–28.

137. Gallizio, "Manifesto of Industrial Painting," in *Laboratory of Writing*, 172, 171.

138. Bataille, *Accursed Share*, 1:12 (*luxury* italicized in the original).

139. Debord, *Correspondence*, 215. On the notion of "excess," see Henri Lefebvre, *The Production of Space* [1974], trans. Donald Nicholson-Smith (Oxford: Blackwell, 2009), 176–78; on the critique of the "asceticism" promoted by economists, ibid., 322–30.

140. Gallizio, "Manifesto of Industrial Painting," in *Laboratory of Writing*, 171–72.

141. See the discussion of this point by Nancy J. Troy, *The Afterlife of Piet Mondrian* (Chicago: University of Chicago Press, 2013), 178–81. Recall that T. J. Clark was himself a member of the Situationist International in the 1970s.

142. See Nancy J. Troy, *Couture Culture: A Study in Modern Art and Fashion* (Cambridge, Mass.: MIT Press, 2003).

143. On the condemnation of fashion by the Ulm School, see, among others, Tomás Maldonado, *Environnement et idéologie: Vers un écologie critique* [1970], trans. Giovanni Joppolo (Paris: Union générale d'éditions, 1972), 118, and Herbert Ohl, "Industrialized Building with Steel," *Ulm*, nos. 14–16 (December 1965): 22.

144. See Andrea Colli and Elisabetta Merlo, "Family Business and Luxury Business in Italy (1950–2000)," *Entreprise et histoire* 46, no. 1 (2007): 113–24. The only text, to my knowledge, that places Gallizio's work in this context is Anna Bondi, "Il lusso standard: Dalla creazione all'artigianato e viceversa," in *Pinot Gallizio e il suo tempo, 1953–1964*, ed. Andrea Busto, exh. cat. Palazzo mostre e congressi, Alba (Milan: Silvana Editoriale, 2007).

145. "Italy Gets Dressed Up," *Life*, August 20, 1951, p. 104.

146. Author's interview with Liliana Dematteis, director of the Galleria Martano, depository of the Archivio Gallizio, Turin, May 29, 2013.

147. Gallizio, "Manifesto of Industrial Painting," in *Laboratory of Writing*, 172.

148. "Pittura e moda," *Il Popolo nuovo*, June 1, 1958; press clipping, *Diario-registro*, Archivio Gallizio.

149. Ugo Pavia, "Curiosità per una mostra di 'pittura industriale,'" *Stampa sera*, June 2–3, 1958; press clipping, *Diario-registro*, Archivio Gallizio.

150. Ibid.

151. This quote and the ones preceding are found in Enzo di Calda, "Abiti d'autori," *Marie Claire* 10, no. 30 (September 8, 1958); press clipping, *Diario-registro*, Archivio Gallizio.

152. Bernstein, "Éloge de Pinot-Gallizio." [*Hand-sewn* refers here to anything of surpassing quality.—Trans.]

153. Asger Jorn, "Mouvement et forme: Sur le contenu progressif de la notion de dissymétrie," in *Pour la forme*, 97. The impression of artistic designs on fabrics is exactly the countermodel designated by Giorgio Gallizio in his 1958 report ("Relazione di Giors Melanotte") on the technique of industrial painting: "It is not a question of printing the same design over and over, on hundreds of meters of fabric, but of 'monotypes.'"

154. Calda, "Abiti d'autori."

155. Bernstein, "Éloge de Pinot Gallizio"; Asger Jorn, "L'état des passions au milieu du XXe siècle et Gallizio-le-Tatoué," in *Pinot-Gallizio*, 1960. Note that Jorn's animosity had a particular history: Dalí's habit of referring in lectures given in Italy to "nuclear painting" led to a suit being brought against him by Enrico Baj, with Jorn's support, in 1954; see Fréchuret, *Baj-Jorn*, 62–63. On the activities of the Surrealists (and Dalí, in particular) in the fields of design and fashion, see Ghislaine Wood, ed., *Surrealist Things: Surrealism and Design*, exh. cat. Victoria and Albert Museum, London (London: V and A Publications, 2007).

156. See *Diario-registro*, Archivio Gallizio, as well as the letter from Gallizio to his wife, Augusta, asking her to send the painting to the Maison Joséphine;

Archivio Gallizio, folder "Corrispondenza 1953–1960." Hans Platschek, a friend of Jorn, was expelled from the SI in February 1959; see Niggl, *Pinot Gallizio*, 43.

157. Christian Dior, *Christian Dior et moi* [1956], 2nd ed. (Paris: Vuibert, 2011), 28. On Dior's career as an art dealer and on his relations with artists, see Florence Müller, ed., *Dior: Le bal des artistes*, exh. cat. Musée Christian Dior, Granville (Versailles: Artlys, 2011).

158. Dior, *Christian Dior et moi*, 42.

159. Debord, "L'activité de la section italienne," 28.

160. "Situationisten per meter," *Haagse Post*, May 2, 1959, p. 13; "Die Produktion hängt meterweise im Treppenhaus," *Münchner Zeitung*, undated press clipping, *Diario-registro*, Archivio Gallizio.

161. Letters from Gallizio to Debord dated March 11, [1959], and March 25, [1959], Fondo Gallizio, GAM, folder XI ("1959").

162. Calda, "Abiti d'autori." See also "Ein Meter Kunst: 40 bis 70 Mark," *Münchner Illustrierte Presse*, May 3, 1959, p. 46; press clipping, *Diario-registro*, Archivio Gallizio.

163. Quoted in "Vende quadri dipinti su chilometri di tela."

164. Calda, "Abiti d'autori."

165. H. H., "Bilder-meterweise," *Madame* [Munich], June 1959, p. 29; press clipping, *Diario-registro*, Archivio Gallizio.

166. "There are women who can paint well, sculpt well," he goes on to say in his contribution to *Pinot-Gallizio*, "just as other women can make fine children. They have an acute sense of matter, they lack only mind. This hardly matters—Pinot-Gallizio supplies it"; see Jorn, "L'état des passions au milieu du XXe siècle et Gallizio-le-Tatoué." The same misogyny is evident in other writings as well, for example where Jorn ascribes the decay of functionalist industrial society to the domination of male by female (men will eventually disappear, for they will be considered superfluous once women are able to manage reproduction by themselves); see "Sortie: Pour en finir avec ces discours et entreprendre autre chose," in *Pour la forme*, 146.

167. Letter from Gallizio to Debord, March 25, [1959], Fondo Gallizio, GAM, folder XI ("1959").

168. Invitation card for the exhibit *Une caverne de l'antimatière*, Paris, Galerie René Drouin, May 1959. For a discussion of this show, see Sophie Cras, "Pinot Gallizio's *Cavern*: Re-Excavating Postwar Paris," in *France and the Visual Arts since 1945: Remapping European Postwar and Contemporary Art*, ed. Catherine Dossin (New York: Bloomsbury, 2018), 75–89.

169. "Problèmes préliminaires à la construction d'une situation," *Internationale situationniste*, no. 1 (June 1958): 11.

170. See Emmanuel Guy, "La dialectique de la *pin-up*," in *La fabrique du cinéma de Guy Debord*, ed. Fabien Danesi, Fabrice Flahutez, and Emmanuel Guy (Paris: Actes Sud, 2013), 9–21.

171. Georges Limbour, "Soleils, clowns, dragons et sages," *Les Lettres nouvelles* (May 27, 1959): 32.

172. Jorn, "L'état des passions au milieu du XXe siècle et Gallizio-le-Tatoué," in *Pinot-Gallizio*, 1960.

173. Lucien Goldmann, *Recherches dialectiques* [1959], 2nd ed. (Paris: Gallimard, 1980), 77; emphasis in the original.

CHAPTER 2
CURRENCY AS CONVENTION

1. Walter Benjamin, "One-Way Street" [1928], in *One-Way Street and Other Writings*, trans. Edmund Jephcott and Kingsley Shorter (London: NLB, 1979), 96.

2. See Lucy R. Lippard, *Pop Art* (New York: Praeger, 1966), 155–57; also Lawrence Alloway, ed., *American Pop Art*, exh. cat. Whitney Museum of American Art, New York (New York: Collier Books, 1974), 109.

3. See Jean-Baptiste Say, *A Treatise on Political Economy, or The Production, Distribution and Consumption of Wealth* [1803], reprint of 4th ed. [1819], trans. C.R. Princep (New York: A. M. Kelley, 1964), chaps. 15, 26, 30.

4. Georg Simmel, *The Philosophy of Money* [1900], ed. David Frisby, trans. Tom Bottomore and David Frisby, 2nd ed. (London: Routledge, 1990), 1.3.3, 272.

5. "Sur une cote," *Les Lettres françaises*, no. 847 (October 27–November 2, 1960): 11.

6. See Josh Lauer, "Money as Mass Communication: U.S. Paper Currency and the Iconography of Nationalism," *Communication Review* 11, no. 2 (2008): 109–32; and Eric Helleiner, "National Currencies and National Identities," *American Behavioral Scientist* 41, no. 10 (1998): 1409–36.

7. Andy Warhol and Pat Hackett, *The Philosophy of Andy Warhol (From A to B and Back Again)* (New York: Harcourt Brace Jovanovich, 1975), 92.

8. Glenn O'Brien, "Interview: Andy Warhol" [June 1977], in *I'll Be Your Mirror: The Selected Andy Warhol Interviews, 1962–1987*, ed. Kenneth Goldsmith (New York: Carroll and Graff, 2004), 253; Warhol and Hackett, *Philosophy of Andy Warhol*, 133–34.

9. In *The Andy Warhol Catalogue Raisonné*, eds. George Frei and Neil Printz, 4 vols. (New York: Phaidon, 2002–14), see vol. 1, *Paintings and Sculpture, 1961–1963*, entry 125; also James Panero, "The Art Market Explained: Why the Bubble Won't Pop for Pop," *New Criterion* 28, no. 4 (2009): 26. On the story of the initial price of *200 One Dollar Bills*, see especially "A Creative Interest in Cash: Art You Can Bank On," *Life*, September 19, 1969, p. 52.

10. Thomas Lawson, "Andy Warhol," *Artforum* 20, no. 8 (1982): 75.

11. The two exhibitions are *Fabulous Moolah: Andy Warhol and Money*, Andy Warhol Museum, Pittsburgh, 2001 (a small show without a catalogue organized by Matt Wrbican), and *Andy Warhol Enterprises*, accompanied by a catalogue of the same title.

12. Allison Unruh, "Signs of Desire: Warhol's Depictions of Dollars," in *Andy Warhol Enterprises*, ed. Sarah Urist Green and Allison Unruh, exh. cat. Indianapolis Museum of Art, Indianapolis (Ostfildern, Germany: Hatje Cantz, 2010), 137.

13. Tony Scherman and David Dalton, *Pop: The Genius of Andy Warhol* (New York: HarperCollins, 2009), 91.

14. This accounting is based on information contained in *The Andy Warhol Catalogue Raisonné*.

15. Paul Mattick has noted the tendency of certain historians to concentrate on Warhol's place in the history of art, studying the dialogue he instituted with other artists rather than analyzing the images drawn from popular culture to which he himself paid close attention; see Mattick, "The Andy Warhol of Philosophy and the Philosophy of Andy Warhol," in *Art in Its Time: Theories and Practices of Modern Aesthetics* (London: Routledge, 2003), 134–51. The catalogue *Warhol: Headlines*, edited by Molly Donovan for an exhibition at the National Gallery of Art in Washington, D.C. (New York: Delmonico Books, 2011), testifies by contrast to the renewed interest in recent years in

examining these source images. This approach makes it possible to escape the unproductive opposition between what Hal Foster characterized as "referential" interpretations (which hold that Warhol's images refer iconographically to real objects and situations) and "poststructuralist" interpretations (which hold that these images refer only to other images, deploying a discourse of signs, copies, and simulacra); see Foster, "Death in America," *October* 75 (Winter 1996): 36–40. In what follows, I consider money both as a pure sign—the history of the banknote is, after all, one of substituting an exchange value for an intrinsic value, metal giving way to a document having only institutional authority—and as a concrete object, massively reproduced and constantly changing hands, whose design is painstakingly conceived and historically changeable.

16. Very roughly, the debate involves three views of the artist, one that regards Warhol as a critical humanist during the 1960s; another that regards him as someone who was at best ambivalent and later, from the 1970s onward, reactionary and neoconservative; and, finally, one that regards him as a strictly neutral observer. See, respectively, Thomas Crow, "Saturday Disasters: Trace and Reference in Early Warhol" [1996], in *Andy Warhol*, ed. Annette Michelson (Cambridge, Mass.: MIT Press, 2001), 49–66; Benjamin H. D. Buchloh, "Andy Warhol's One-Dimensional Art: 1956–1966" [1989], in ibid., 1–46, and "The Andy Warhol Line," in *The Work of Andy Warhol*, ed. Gary Garrels (Seattle: Bay Press, 1989), 52–69; and John Coplans, *Andy Warhol* (Greenwich, Conn.: New York Graphic Society, 1970).

17. See John J. Curley, *A Conspiracy of Images: Andy Warhol, Gerhard Richter, and the Art of the Cold War* (New Haven: Yale University Press, 2013); also the recent exhibition *Andy Warhol: Pop, Power, and Politics*, Scottish Parliament, Edinburgh, October 5–November 3, 2013.

18. See Viviana Zelizer, "The Social Meaning of Money: 'Special Monies,'" *American Journal of Sociology* 95, no. 2 (1989): 342–77.

19. Typically, Warhol appears to lend credence to both versions of the story: see Andy Warhol and Pat Hackett, *POPism: The Warhol Sixties* (New York: Harcourt Brace Jovanovich, 1980), 18, 24. The first anecdote was initially related by Calvin Tomkins, "Raggedy Andy," in Coplans, *Andy Warhol*, 12, and subsequently confirmed by Ted Carey, who claimed to have witnessed the scene; see Patrick S. Smith, *Warhol: Conversations about the Artist* (Ann Arbor: UMI Research Press, 1988), 90–91. Scherman and Dalton consider a check for fifty dollars dated November 23, 1961, kept in Warhol's archives, to be a decisive piece of evidence; see *Pop*, 73. The date is problematic, however: all accounts agree that the exchange took place after the opening of Claes Oldenburg's exhibition *The Store*, and so after December 1 of that year. The second version of the story is recounted by several authors; see, for example, Victor Bockris, *The Life and Death of Andy Warhol* (New York: Bantam Books, 1989), 150. Yet it seems scarcely credible. Ward says that she offered Warhol a solo show in June 1962. By that point, the *Dollar Bill* paintings had been finished for some time. Moreover, in her first interview on the subject, Ward did not mention the story; see "Interview with Eleanor Ward by Paul Cummings," February 8, 1972, Archives of American Art, transcript, p. 10. And contrary to what Bockris implies, the *Dollar Bill* paintings were not included in Warhol's solo show at Stable Gallery; see the price list for the exhibition held there November 6–24, 1962, Stable Gallery Records, Archives of American Art, series 1, box 2.

20. O'Brien, "Interview: Andy Warhol," in Goldsmith, *I'll Be Your Mirror*, 242. For a survey of the techniques employed by Warhol, see Marco Livingstone, "Do It Yourself: Notes on Warhol's Techniques," in *Andy Warhol: A Retrospective*, ed. Kynaston McShine (New York: Museum of Modern Art, 1989), 63–78, and Rainer Crone, "Form and Ideology: Warhol's Techniques from Blotted Line to Film," in Garrels, *Work of Andy Warhol*, 70–92.

21. This according to Matt Wrbican, email to the author, August 19, 2011; see also *The Andy Warhol Catalogue Raisonné*, 1:131, 148.

22. Scherman and Dalton, *Pop*, 105. See also David Bourdon, *Warhol* (New York: Harry N. Abrams, 1989), 108. The transparent screens and Warhol's original drawings for his serigraphic designs are kept in the artist's archives at the Andy Warhol Museum, Pittsburgh.

23. Quoted in Scherman and Dalton, *Pop*, 105.

24. See Simmel, *Philosophy of Money*, 1.3.3, 272.

25. Warhol and Hackett, *Philosophy of Andy Warhol*, 129.

26. Andy Warhol, "New Talent USA," *Art in America* 50, no. 1 (1962): 40.

27. See Brian Burrell, *The Words We Live By: The Creeds, Mottoes and Pledges That Have Shaped America* (New York: Free Press, 1997), 191; also Elizabeth M. Fowler, "'In God We Trust': Biography of an Old American Motto," *New York Times*, July 28, 1956, pp. 21, 24.

28. See Stephen J. Whitfield, *The Culture of the Cold War* (Baltimore: Johns Hopkins University Press, 1991), 78–89. On Flag Day, June 14, 1954, President Eisenhower signed a joint resolution of Congress amending the Flag Code of 1942 to include the words "Under God" in the Pledge of Allegiance. This event led Jasper Johns to conceive his famous *Flag*; see Fred Orton, *Figuring Jasper Johns* (Cambridge, Mass.: Harvard University Press, 1994), 101–2.

29. Unruh, "Signs of Desire," 138.

30. Philip Warden, "New 'In God We Trust' $1 Bills Come Out Today," *Chicago Daily Tribune*, October 1, 1957, p. 1.

31. Centennial History Staff, Bureau of Engraving and Printing, *History of the Bureau of Engraving and Printing, 1862–1962* (Washington, D.C.: U.S. Treasury Department, 1964), 177.

32. "God and the Dollar: Mirror of World Opinion," *Christian Science Monitor*, April 9, 1963, p. 18.

33. "'In God We Trust' Will Be Printed on $1 Bills: Motto to Appear in December, Six Years after Congress Voted to Call for Its Use," *Los Angeles Times*, October 29, 1961, p. 2.

34. Ibid.

35. David Ovason, *The Secret Symbols of the Dollar Bill* (New York: HarperCollins, 2004), 90.

36. Herbert C. Bardes, "About the Motto: $1 Bills without 'In God We Trust' Are Not Irregular or Rare," *New York Times*, June 7, 1964, p. 22.

37. Ibid.

38. The phrase is due to the social psychologist Michael Billig, in *Banal Nationalism* (London: Sage, 1995); see also the discussion in Lauer, "Money as Mass Communication," 127.

39. See Centennial History Staff, *History*

of the Bureau of Engraving and Printing, 157–76.

40. Richard E. Mooney, "New Dollar Bill Makes Its Debut: 1957 Version Has Motto 'In God We Trust' on Back—Wet Paper Yields to Dry," *New York Times*, October 2, 1957, p. 35.

41. See Heinz Tschachler, *The Greenback: Paper Money and American Culture* (Jefferson, N.C.: McFarland, 2010), 31.

42. O'Brien, "Interview," in Goldsmith, *I'll Be Your Mirror*, 243.

43. Warhol and Hackett, *Philosophy of Andy Warhol*, 148.

44. "The Welcome Motto," *Wall Street Journal*, October 4, 1957, p. 8.

45. "Cuba Is Hit by Inflation, Communism Fails to Stop 'Capitalist Concept,'" *Baltimore Sun*, July 15, 1962, p. 8.

46. T. J. Clark, *Farewell to an Idea: Episodes from a History of Modernism* (New Haven: Yale University Press, 1999), 258.

47. "Inflation, Communism Equal Threats, Dworshak Tells C-C," *Lewiston Morning Tribune* [Lewiston, Idaho], October 12, 1961, p. 12.

48. "Yours Is the Choice," *Washington Observer* [Washington, Pa.], October 14, 1964, p. 15.

49. Henry Geldzahler, "Andy Warhol: Virginal Voyeur," in *Andy Warhol: Portraits of the Seventies and Eighties*, ed. Henry Geldzahler and Robert Rosenblum, exh. cat. Museum of Contemporary Art, Sydney, and Anthony d'Offay Gallery, London (London: Thames and Hudson, 1993), 21; essay reprinted in Henry Geldzahler, *Making It New: Essays, Interviews, and Talks* (New York: Harcourt Brace, 1994), 357–68.

50. Tschachler, *Greenback*, 182.

51. Interview with Andy Warhol concerning the "Art Cash" currency he designed for the Experiments in Art and Technology (EAT) benefit held at Automation House in New York, December 3–4, 1971; typescript document, "Experiments in Art and Technology Records, 1966–1993" (mostly covering the period 1966–73), The Getty Research Institute, series I, box 96, folders 1–16. The Bell Labs engineer Billy Klüver, a cofounder of EAT, asked six artists in addition to Warhol—Öyvind Fahlström, Tim Gormley, Red Grooms, Marisol, Robert Rauschenberg, and Robert Whitman—to imagine new versions of the one-dollar bill (Fahlström's design, directly attacking President Nixon, was rejected). In Warhol's version the bill is stripped down to bare essentials: the front is black monochrome; the back displays the word "ONES" on a green ground together with the artist's stamped signature. See Grace Glueck, "Artists' Designs for Currency Include a $12 Bill," *New York Times*, November 6, 1971, p. 33; Barbara Rose, "Venus, Adonis and Money," *New York Magazine*, December 13, 1971, p. 73; "Artists Dream Up Unusual 'Currency' to Raise Cash," *Coin World*, December 15, 1971, pp. 1–5.

52. Warhol and Hackett, *Philosophy of Andy Warhol*, 137.

53. Matt Wrbican, "Fabulous Moolah: Andy Warhol and Money," in Green and Unruh, *Andy Warhol Enterprises*, 120.

54. Warhol and Hackett, *Philosophy of Andy Warhol*, 130.

55. Zelizer, "Social Meaning of Money," 347–48.

56. Richard McPherren Cabeen, "$2 Bills Are Becoming Real Collectors' Items," *Chicago Tribune*, September 11, 1966, p. J8.

57. Maurice M. Gould, "Two Dollar Bills," *Baltimore Sun*, October 3, 1966, p. 19.

58. Tschachler, *Greenback*, 132–33.

59. David Fouquet, "Bad Reputation Leads to Decline in Usage of Two-Dollar Bills," *Washington Post*, November 1, 1965, p. D9.

60. "The No Longer Almighty Dollar," *Life*, April 6, 1962, p. 34.

61. Several authors have remarked on the tendency toward greater abstraction and metonymy in the evolution of Warhol's designs, from the early dollar bills to the later dollar signs. See Arthur C. Danto, "Andy Warhol and the Love of $$$$$," in *Andy Warhol: Dollar Signs*, exh. cat. Gagosian Gallery, Beverly Hills, 1997; Unruh, "Signs of Desire"; and Berkeley Reinhold, ed., *Andy Warhol: Making Money* (New York: Skira/Rizzoli, 2010).

62. Letter from Larry Rivers to Éric Meyer, April 28, 1971; Fales Library and Special Collections, New York University Libraries, Larry Rivers Papers, ms. 293, box 30, folder 18.

63. The absence of a catalogue raisonné makes it hard to establish the exact number of works in the series. Rivers estimated he made about fifteen of them; see Larry Rivers and Carol Brightman, *Drawings and Digressions* (New York: Clarkson N. Potter, 1979), 153. Documentation of at least a dozen that were sold between 1962 and 1965 (an indication of their success) can be found in Rivers's personal archives; see Larry Rivers Papers, box 26 ("Artwork Tracking"). The confusion caused by uncertainty as to the extent of the series is discussed in Phyllis Rosenzweig, ed., *Larry Rivers: The Hirshhorn Museum and Sculpture Garden, Smithsonian Institution* (Washington, D.C.: Smithsonian Institution Press, 1981), 28.

64. Doug McClellan, "Dealer's Choice: Dwan Gallery," *Artforum* 1, no. 9 (May 1963): 50.

65. Sam Hunter's early work on Rivers remains a standard reference; see, in particular, *Larry Rivers* (New York: Harry N. Abrams, 1969), as well as the catalogue edited by Barbara Rose and Jacquelyn Days Serwer, *Larry Rivers: Art and the Artist* (Boston: Little, Brown; Washington, D.C.: Corcoran Gallery of Art, 2002). Rivers has received attention more recently from scholars in the field of queer studies; see, especially, Gavin Butt, *Between You and Me: Queer Disclosures in the New York Art World, 1948–1963* (Durham, N.C.: Duke University Press, 2005) and Dong-Yeon Koh, *Larry Rivers and Frank O'Hara: Reframing Male Sexualities in Art, Literature and Culture of the 1950s* (Saarbrücken: Lambert Academic Publishing, 2010). On the relation of Rivers's painting to pop art and abstract expressionism, see Robert Rosenblum, "Pop Art and Non-Pop Art" [1963], in *On Modern American Art: Selected Essays* (New York: Harry N. Abrams, 1999), 187; and Pierre Restany, "Chelsea 1960," in *Paris–New York* (Paris: Centre national d'art moderne Georges Pompidou, 1977), 146. A revised edition of the 1977 exhibition catalogue was published by Gallimard in 1991 under the title *Paris–New York, 1908–1968*.

66. Thomas B. Hess argues that although Rivers's paintings have an identifiable subject, "[h]is pictures are abstractions because he uses the abstract assumptions of pictorial style to paint what he sees with the pressure and anxiety of a leader of the brilliant second generation of the School of New York"; in *Larry Rivers* (London: Gimpel Fils Gallery, 1962), 8. See also John Canaday, "Of Two Painters: Rivers and Roth," *New York Times*, December 9, 1962, p. 65.

67. Pierre Schneider, "Paris," *Art News* 61, no. 4 (1962): 43.

68. "A Statement Read to the International Association of Plastic Arts by Larry

Rivers at the Museum of Modern Art Symposium on 'Mass Culture and the Artist,'" New York, October 8, 1963; reprinted in the catalogue of a second exhibition titled *Larry Rivers* (London: Gimpel Fils Gallery, 1964), n.p.

69. Rivers and Brightman, *Drawings and Digressions*, 180.

70. See Larry Rivers and Arnold Weinstein, *What Did I Do?: The Unauthorized Autobiography* (New York: HarperCollins, 1992), 176–77; also Sam Hunter, ed., *Larry Rivers*, exh. cat. Rose Art Museum, Waltham (Waltham, Mass.: Brandeis University Press, 1965), 20.

71. Rivers and Weinstein, *What Did I Do?*, 376–95.

72. Rivers had showed Yves Klein and his wife around New York at the request of Georges Marci, owner of the Galerie Rive Droite, who feared Klein would be "depressed in the brave New World." In a letter to Rivers dated March 20, 1961, Marci hastened to emphasize, "You can be sure that when you come to Europe he will more than reciprocate, as he knows everybody." Klein subsequently acknowledged his debt in a letter dated July 27, 1961 (both letters in Larry Rivers Papers, box 26, folder 9), and kept up his end of the bargain. "[Klein] was helpful in getting me the Rive Droite exhibition," Rivers later recalled, "telling [Jean] Larcade I was an important American artist"; see Rivers and Weinstein, *What Did I Do?*, 382, and Larry Rivers, "Blues for Yves Klein," *Art News* 65, no. 10 (February 1967): 32–33, 75–76.

73. See Rivers's interview with Jean-François de Canchy, "Larry Rivers, février 1977," in *Paris–New York*, 590; also Pierre Restany's remembrance in *60/90: Trente ans de Nouveau Réalisme* (Paris: La Différence, 1990), 19, and Claude Laugier, "Impasse Ronsin," in *Paris, Paris: Créations en France, 1937–1957, arts plastiques, littérature, théâtre, cinéma, vie quotidienne et environnement, archives sonores et visuelles, photographie* (Paris: Centre Georges Pompidou, 1981; reissued by Gallimard in 1992 as *Paris 1937–Paris 1957*), 440–43. On the friendships and collaborations among American and Parisian artists of the time, see Amy Jo Dempsey, "The Friendship of America and France: A New Internationalism, 1961–1965" (PhD diss., Courtauld Institute of Art, University of London, 1999).

74. Letter from John Myers to Larry Rivers, December 30, 1961; Larry Rivers Papers, box 26, folder 9.

75. See, in particular, Barbara Rose, "Larry Rivers: Painter of Modern Life," in Rose and Serwer, *Larry Rivers*, 42.

76. Some *Dollar Bill* paintings were exhibited in New York at the Martha Jackson Gallery, beginning May 22, 1962, and subsequently at the Green Gallery and the Stable Gallery; see *Andy Warhol Catalogue Raisonné*, 146, 471. The first of the *Dollar Bill* paintings to have appeared in the press was *192 One Dollar Bills*, in "The Slice-of-Cake School," *Time*, May 11, 1962, p. 52. The first reproduction of a *French Money* painting was in an article by John Ashbery, "Paris Letter," *Art International* 6, no. 4 (1962): 61.

77. Letter from Myers to Rivers, December 30, 1961; emphasis in the original. Larry Rivers Papers, box 26, folder 9.

78. Letter from Myers to Rivers, May 29, 1962; Larry Rivers Papers, box 10, folder 12. See also Peter Gimpel's letter to Rivers, August 15, 1962; Larry Rivers Papers, box 5, folder 19. On the Paris art market crisis in 1962, see Julie Verlaine, *Les galeries d'art contemporain à Paris: Une histoire culturelle du marché de l'art, 1944–1970* (Paris: Publications de la Sorbonne, 2012), 421–35.

79. Undated letter from Rivers to Peter Gimpel (probably 1962); Larry Rivers Papers, box 5, folder 19.

80. "Don't Look behind You," *Newsweek*, December 17, 1962, p. 196.

81. "Art Finger: Turning Pictures into Gold," *Time*, June 25, 1973, pp. 45–47.

82. Letter from Myers to Rivers, December 10, 1962; Tibor de Nagy Gallery Records, 1950–1988, in the Archives of American Art, Smithsonian Institution, Washington, D.C.; box 16; folder 6. See also letter from Myers to Rivers, December 15, 1962; Tibor de Nagy Gallery Records, box 16, folder 6.

83. See, for example, Ashbery, "Paris Letter," 61; Schneider, "Paris," 43; and G.S. Whittet, "You Can't Write Off the British," *Studio International* 164, no. 832 (August 1962): 74–75.

84. Rivers made it clear on several occasions that the titles of the two paintings were mistakenly reversed in 1962: *French Money I* represents the back of the bill; *French Money II* represents the front, and should therefore be identified as the first of the pair, as the files relating to *French Money II* in the archives of the Hirshhorn Museum and Sculpture Garden confirm.

85. See Henry Ginigers, "A Franc Method to Change Money: Value of Currency Is Same, but Dropping of Zeros Brings a New Look," *New York Times*, January 12, 1960, p. 53.

86. The introduction of the new 100 francs notes occurred in three stages: the old 10,000 francs note was in circulation from 1955 to 1960; after this came a transitional design, with the number *100* displayed in red ink, that was eventually replaced by the new note Rivers depicted. This new 100 francs note was short-lived, being withdrawn from circulation in 1963. See Claude Fayette, *Les billets de la Banque de France, 1800–2000*, 5th ed. (Nice: Claude Fayette, 2000), 293, 299, 308.

87. Michel Ragon, "Larry Rivers," *Cimaise* 59 (May–June 1962): 91. Ragon was not alone in this; many people in France at the time were unsure of the correct number of zeros. The possibility of a printing error in the *Cimaise* article cannot be ruled out, however.

88. Rivers and Weinstein, *What Did I Do?*, 377.

89. Granger Blair, "Just Plain Franc Is Due to Return," *New York Times*, February 23, 1962, pp. 45, 48.

90. Rivers, "Statement Read to the International Association of Plastic Arts," n.p.

91. Ginigers, "Franc Method to Change Money," 53.

92. "New Franc Rate Mirrors Gold and French Pride," *New York Times*, December 30, 1958, p. 4.

93. Pierre Mendès-France, "Au Forum," *L'Express*, September 17, 1959, p. 13. Similar claims associating the new franc with the conduct of the Algerian war can be found in the left-wing press of the period. See, for example, Claude Bourdet, "Le franc léger et le général lourd," *France Observateur*, no. 452 (December 31, 1958), p. 3; also Jean Ecoche and Christian Hébert, "L'heure des économistes distingués," *France Observateur*, no. 452 (December 31, 1958), pp. 11–13.

94. Letter from Rivers to Myers, March 5, [1962]; Tibor de Nagy Gallery Records, box 16, folder 6.

95. See Hiroko Ikegami, *The Great Migrator: Robert Rauschenberg and the Global Rise of American Art* (Cambridge, Mass.: MIT Press, 2010), 29.

96. See Rivers and Brightman, *Drawings and Digressions*, 255; and Grace Glueck,

"Rivers Paints Himself into the Canvas," *New York Times*, February 13, 1966, pp. 220–23.

97. See Jill Carrick, "Phallic Victories?: Niki de Saint-Phalle's Tirs," *Art History* 26, no. 5 (December 2003): 700–29; also Kaira M. Cabañas, *The Myth of Nouveau Réalisme: Art and the Performative in Postwar France* (New Haven: Yale University Press, 2013), 62–95, and Sarah Wilson, "Tirs, Tears et Ricochets," in *Niki de Saint Phalle*, ed. Camille Morineau (Paris: Grand Palais, 2014), 99–100.

98. Fayette, *Les billets de la Banque de France*, 283–84.

99. These bonds are part of an extensive collection of military intelligence memorabilia assembled by Sergeant Major Herbert A. Friedman (U.S. Army, ret.). See his article "Cold War and Insurgency Propaganda Banknotes," portions of which were first published in nonconsecutive issues of *Whitman Numismatic Journal* (July and September 1967) and then some years later in *International Banknote Society Journal* 24, no. 1 (1985) and vol. 30, no. 1 (1991). The entire article is available online via www.psywar.org/coldwarcurrency.php.

100. Pierre Méallier, *OAS: La guerre d'Algérie vue de Bône à travers les tracts de l'OAS* (Nice: France Europe Éditions, 2004), 159–60.

101. Robert Escarpit, "BPNF," *France Observateur*, no. 505 (January 7, 1960), p. 24.

102. Alain Jouffroy, "Larry Rivers, réinventeur de la peinture d'histoire," *XXe siècle*, no. 49 (December 1977): 39–44.

103. Gérald Gassiot-Talabot, "Le sourire de Larry Rivers," *XXe siècle*, no. 41 (December 1973): 94.

104. Ibid., 99.

105. Annabelle Ténèze, "Pop George: Citation et art américain—Larry Rivers, Roy Lichtenstein . . . et George Washington," *Les Cahiers du Musée national d'art moderne*, no. 110 (Winter 2009–2010): 38–61.

106. Leutze's painting is now owned by the Metropolitan Museum of Art in New York. In his autobiography, Rivers says that it was his "patriotic ace in the hole" during the McCarthy years; see Rivers and Weinstein, *What Did I Do?*, 311–12.

107. Ibid., 310.

108. See the interview "Larry Rivers, février 1977," in *Paris–New York*, 590.

109. Letter from Bill Brooker to Rivers, December 10, 1961; Larry Rivers Papers, box 2, folder 25.

110. See, in particular, William Wilson, "Larry Rivers," *Artforum* 4, no. 2 (October 1965): 11; Hunter, *Larry Rivers*, 1965, 33; and Ashbery, "Paris Letter," 61.

111. "Don't Look behind You," *Newsweek*, p. 196.

112. James Schuyler, "Reviews and Previews: Larry Rivers," *Art News* 61, no. 8 (December 1962): 14.

113. On the importance in the art world of rumors concerning the sexual orientation of artists, particularly in the case of their presumed homosexuality, see Butt, *Between You and Me*, 1–16.

114. See ibid., 102–5.

115. Rivers and Weinstein, *What Did I Do?*, 375.

116. Louis-Ferdinand Céline, *Castle to Castle*, trans. Ralph Manheim (New York: Delacorte Press, 1968), 133–34.

117. Butt, *Between You and Me*, 102.

118. Paul Mirguet, a parliamentary deputy from Moselle, defended his proposed amendment before the National Assembly, insisting on the necessity of protecting French values menaced by the new world order of the day: "At a moment when our civilization, which to its peril finds itself in a minority in a rapidly changing world, has become so vulnerable, we must combat everything that threatens to diminish its prestige"; *Journal officiel*, no. 51, 2nd session, July 18, 1960, p. 1981. On the persecution of homosexuality in the United States during the Cold War, see Richard M. Fried, *Nightmare in Red: The McCarthy Era in Perspective* (New York: Oxford University Press, 1990), 167; also Whitfield, *Culture of the Cold War*, 43.

119. Typewritten letter from Charles Gimpel (Gimpel Fils) to Rivers, July 9, 1964, Larry Rivers Papers, box 5, folder 18; punctuation added by hand. Rivers refused to make any change, and Hirshhorn ended up purchasing the work with its original title.

120. Quoted in Rivers and Weinstein, *What Did I Do?*, 375.

121. André Orléan, *Le pouvoir de la finance* (Paris: Odile Jacob, 1999), 241.

CHAPTER 3
SPECULATION AS SPECTACLE

1. On the commercial success of pop art, see, in particular, Christin J. Mamiya, *Pop Art and Consumer Culture: American Super Market* (Austin: University of Texas Press, 1992).

2. Marvin Elkoff, "The American Painter as a Blue Chip," *Esquire*, January 1965, p. 37.

3. From a December 1969 interview with Ursula Meyer, reprinted as the preface to Lucy R. Lippard, ed., *Six Years: The Dematerialization of the Art Object from 1966 to 1972* (New York: Praeger, 1973), 7.

4. Thomas M. Messer, "Impossible Art—Why It Is," *Art in America* 57, no. 3 (1969): 30–31.

5. Catherine Millet, "Note sur Art-Language" [1971], in *Textes sur l'art conceptuel* (Paris: Daniel Templon, 1972), 31. On the success of conceptual art in Europe, see Sophie Richard, *Unconcealed: The International Network of Conceptual Artists, 1967–1977—Dealers, Exhibitions, and Public Collections* (London: Ridinghouse, 2009).

6. From Anne Seymour's introduction to her edition of *The New Art*, exh. cat. Hayward Gallery, London (London: Arts Council of Great Britain, 1972), 6. The commercial success of conceptual art is discussed in William Wood, "Still You Ask for More: Demand, Display and 'The New Art,'" in *Rewriting Conceptual Art*, ed. Michael Newman and Jon Bird (London: Reaktion Books, 1999), 69. Wood concludes that "the amount of money involved was small relative to the market for painting and sculpture."

7. See, in particular, Lucy Lippard's postface to the revised edition of *Six Years* (Berkeley: University of California Press, 1997), 263, as well as Gregory Battcock's introduction to his edited volume of writings on conceptual art, *Idea Art: A Critical Anthology* (New York: E. P. Dutton, 1973), 1–3. See also Blake Stimson's assessment, "The Promise of Conceptual Art," in *Conceptual Art: A Critical Anthology*, ed. Alexander Alberro and Blake Stimson (Cambridge, Mass.: MIT Press, 1999), xliii–xlvi.

8. Frances Colpitt, "The Formalist Connection and Originary Myths of Conceptual Art," in *Conceptual Art: Theory, Myth, and Practice*, ed. Michael Corris (Cambridge: Cambridge University Press, 2004), 39–40.

9. See Alexander Alberro, *Conceptual Art and the Politics of Publicity* (Cambridge, Mass.: MIT Press, 2003).

10. Quoted by Jack Burnham, "Alice's

Head: Reflections on Conceptual Art," *Artforum* 8, no. 6 (1970): 43. The historian Robert Hobbs argues that unprofitable art might even be considered the height of luxury in an economy of abundance; see his essay "Affluence, Taste, and the Brokering of Knowledge: Notes on the Social Context of Early Conceptual Art," in Corris, *Conceptual Art*, 201–10.

11. Barbara Rose, "Why Read Art Criticism?," *New York Magazine*, March 3, 1969, p. 45.

12. Ibid., p. 44.

13. It was widely noticed in the press. See particularly Jean Lipman, "Money for Money's Sake," *Art in America* 58, no. 1 (1970): 76–83.

14. Gerald Reitlinger, *The Economics of Taste*, 3 vols. (London: Barrie and Rockliff, 1961–70), 3:10, 15, 13.

15. Ron Grant, "The Art of Investment, or How to Make Money in Oils," *Montreal Gazette*, August 14, 1968, p. 25.

16. Leslie Judd Ahlander, "Art Becomes a Choice Investment," *Washington Post*, December 31, 1961, p. G6.

17. Eric Hodgins and Lesley Parker, "The Great International Art Market," *Fortune*, December 1955, p. 120.

18. Ibid., 150–52.

19. Ibid., 162.

20. "Sidelights: Of Art, Stocks and Inflation," *New York Times*, January 1, 1958, p. 36.

21. Zola describes the merchant Naudet as "a speculator, a dealer in stocks," who sells his canvases to "the rich dilettante who knows nothing about art, who buys a picture as he would a security on the stock exchange, out of vanity or in the hope that it will rise in value." Émile Zola, *L'Œuvre* [1886] (Paris: Gallimard, 1989), 186. The German art critic and novelist Julius Meier-Graefe, in a 1904 essay, noted that paintings were acquired and kept in the same way that shares were, and likened the great art exhibitions to stock exchanges; see "The Mediums of Art, Past and Present," in *Art in Theory, 1900–1990: An Anthology of Changing Ideas*, ed. Charles Harrison and Paul Wood (Oxford: Blackwell, 1993), 53–60.

22. Sylvia Porter, "Art Buying [a] Major Fad," *Sarasota Herald Tribune*, March 29, 1966, p. 8.

23. Sylvia Porter, "Far-Out Investments, Investors Eye Coins, Gems," *Milwaukee Sentinel*, March 17, 1969, p. 15.

24. Sylvia Porter, "Facts on Far-Out Investments: Part 1," *Lewiston Daily Sun* [Lewiston, Maine], December 22, 1969, p. 6.

25. Sylvia Porter, "Facts on Far-Out Investments: Part 3," *Youngstown Vindicator* [Youngstown, Ohio], December 24, 1969, p. 7.

26. Advertisement for *Art Market Guide and Forecaster* in the *New York Times*, January 7, 1962, p. 148; emphasis in the original.

27. See French and Company, *Taxes and Art* (Englewood Cliffs, N.J.: Prentice-Hall, 1961).

28. The trend was inaugurated with the appearance in 1963 of Enrique Mayer's *Annuaire international des ventes*, which became a standard reference for auction prices in the art market along with the Times-Sotheby's Index, first issued in England in 1967, and *Kunst-Kompass*, published in Germany from 1970 onward. Among periodicals, *La cote des peintres* in France and *Die Tat* in Switzerland specialized in artistic investment. Notable books of the period, typically translated into several or more languages, include Maurice Rheims, *La vie étrange des objets: Histoire de la curiosité* (Paris: Plon, 1959); Maurice Pariat, *Le tableau de peintre contemporain comme valeur de placement* (Paris: R. Pichon/R. Durand-Auzias, 1961); Richard H. Rush, *Art as an Investment* (Englewood Cliffs, N.J.: Prentice Hall, 1961); Horst Wagenführ, *Kunst als Kapitalanlage* (Stuttgart: Forkel, 1965); Willi Bongard, *Kunst und Kommerz: Zwischen Passion und Spekulation* (Oldenberg, Germany: Gerhard Stalling, 1967); Herbert Lust, *A Dozen Principles for Art Investment* (Chicago: Galerie le Chat Bernard, 1969); and Gilbert de Knyff, *Peinture et sculpture: Valeurs de placement, valeurs esthétiques et culturelles* (Paris: Guy Le Prat, 1971).

29. Pariat, *Le tableau de peintre contemporain*, 24.

30. Knyff, *Peinture et sculpture*, 9.

31. From Parinaud's preface to Enrique Mayer, *Annuaire international des ventes* (Paris: Publisol, 1965), v, vii.

32. Annie Verger, "L'art d'estimer l'art," *Actes de la recherche en sciences sociales* 66, no. 1 (1987): 107–12.

33. Advertisement for *Art Market Guide and Forecaster* in the *New York Times*, January 7, 1962, p. 148; emphasis in the original.

34. See Olav Velthuis and Erica Coslor, "The Financialization of Art," in *The Oxford Handbook of the Sociology of Finance*, ed. Karin Knorr Cetina and Alex Preda (Oxford: Oxford University Press, 2014), and Noah Horowitz, *Art of the Deal: Contemporary Art in a Global Financial Market* (Princeton: Princeton University Press, 2011), particularly the third chapter on art investment funds.

35. The two sources cited most frequently by commentators are Richard H. Rush's 1961 book *Art as an Investment* and the Times-Sotheby's Index of Fine Art, published each month in the *Times* of London since 1967; in the later connection, see Geraldine Keen, *The Sale of Works of Art: A Study Based on the Times-Sotheby Index* (London: Nelson, 1971). Similar charts and tables are nonetheless found in most of the publications referred to in this chapter.

36. Reitlinger, *Economics of Taste*, 3:11.

37. Keen, *Sale of Works of Art*, 243.

38. John Chamberlain, "Reading for Pleasure: The Market for Art," *Wall Street Journal*, November 24, 1961, p. 8.

39. Thomas B. Hess, "Impressionist Patterns in the Art Market," editorial in *Art News* 67, no. 9 (1969): 27.

40. "Market Letter," *Art in America* 48, no. 1 (1960): 4. See readers' reactions in the following issue, "Letters to the Editor," *Art in America* 48, no. 2 (1960): 9.

41. Most studies from the 1970s onward have shown that, over both the short and the long term, the rate of return on investment in art is lower than that of financial assets. See, in particular, Robert C. Anderson, "Painting as an Investment," *Economic Inquiry* 12, no. 1 (1974): 13–26; John P. Stein, "The Monetary Appreciation of Paintings," *Journal of Political Economy* 85, no. 5 (1977): 1021–35; William J. Baumol, "Unnatural Value: Or Art Investment as a Floating Crap Game," *American Economic Review* 76, no. 2 (1986): 10–14; Nathalie Buelens and Victor Ginsburgh, "Revisiting Baumol's 'Art as a Floating Crap Game,'" *European Economic Review* 37, no. 7 (1992): 1351–71; and Orley Ashenfelter and Kathryn Graddy, "Auctions and the Price of Art," *Journal of Economic Literature* 41, no. 3 (2003): 763–87. See also the survey of econometric studies on this topic in Horowitz, *Art of the Deal*, 165–70.

42. Scull confessed that when he assembled his collection of pop art works, "I felt as though I had bought all of AT&T";

quoted in "At Home with Henry," *Time*, February 21, 1964, p. 68. Kraushar, for his part, was emphatic: "These pictures are like IBM stocks, don't forget that, and this is the time to buy"; quoted in "You Bought It, Now Live with It: The Country's Leading Collectors of Pop Art Enthusiastically Fill Their Homes with It," *Life*, July 16, 1965, pp. 60–61. The comparison of General Motors to Cézanne and Renoir occurs in Hodgins and Parker, "Great International Art Market," p. 120.

43. Quoted in "Interview [with Allan Kaprow] Conducted by Susan Hapgood, Encinitas, California, August 12, 1992," in Susan Hapgood, *Neo-Dada: Redefining Art, 1958–1962* (New York: American Federation of Arts, 1994), 120. The *Fortune* article made a strong impression on members of the New York art scene. Serge Guilbaut notes, for example, that it led to a bitter exchange of letters between Clyfford Still and Mark Rothko; see Guilbaut, "Le marketing de l'expressivité à New York au cours des années cinquante," in *Le commerce de l'art de la Renaissance à nos jours*, ed. Laurence Bertrand Dorléac (Besançon: La manufacture, 1992), 280, 286.

44. Allan Kaprow, "The Artist as a Man of the World" [1964], in *Essays on the Blurring of Art and Life*, ed. Jeff Kelley (Berkeley: University of California Press, 1993), 54. The impact of this article may be measured, for example, by Thomas B. Hess's editorial, "The Artist as a Company-Man," *Art News* 63, no. 6 (1964): 19.

45. John Baldessari, "Information Paintings Never Completed," in *Konzeption/Conception*, ed. Konrad Fischer and Rolf Wedewer, exh. cat. Städtisches Museum, Leverkusen, Germany (Cologne: Westdeutscher Verlag, 1969), n.p.

46. See Donald H. Karshan, ed., *The Five Years of Bernar Venet: A Catalogue Raisonné* (New York: New York Cultural Center, 1971). The same columns of figures taken from the stock exchange listings in the *WSJ* appear in one of the date paintings (February 27, 1970) of the *Today* series created by the Japanese conceptual artist On Kawara.

47. *Number 7*, Paula Cooper Gallery, New York, May 18–June 17, 1969.

48. See Venet's contribution to Germano Celant, ed., *Conceptual Art, Arte Povera, Land Art*, exh. cat. Galleria civica d'arte moderna, Turin (Turin: Tipografia Impronta, 1970), n.p.

49. Letter from Venet to Lucy Lippard dated January 11, 1970; Lippard Papers, box 19, folders 30–31.

50. Catherine Millet, "Bernar Venet: La fonction didactique de l'art conceptuel" [October 1970], in *Textes sur l'art conceptuel*, 59.

51. Kynaston L. McShine, ed., *Information*, exh. cat. Museum of Modern Art, New York (New York: Museum of Modern Art, 1970), 129. Venet was disappointed to discover, on visiting the exhibit, that the television set had been removed, probably owing to ignorance of its supporting role in the installation. This detail is mentioned in an unpublished interview of Venet by Ken Allan, conducted by email between December 2001 and October 2002, pp. 6–7.

52. The photograph appeared in *Chroniques de l'art vivant*, no. 27 (February 1972): 7.

53. Jan van der Marck, *Bernar Venet* (Paris: La Différence, 1988), 14.

54. Author's interview with Bernar Venet, New York, September 28, 2010.

55. Quoted in Karshan, *Five Years of Bernar Venet*, 11.

56. From Venet's July 1967 statement, quoted in Celant, *Conceptual Art*, n.p.

57. From a 1971 interview with Ursula Meyer, quoted in her book *Conceptual Art* (New York: E. P. Dutton, 1972), 214.

58. From a 1970 interview with Catherine Millet, quoted in her essay "Bernar Venet," 25.

59. Ibid., 23.

60. Author's telephone interview with Venet, November 7, 2012.

61. Bernar Venet, "Bernar Venet," *Flash Art*, nos. 50–51 (December 1974–January 1975): 30–31; emphasis in the original. Venet elaborated this theoretical perspective in the mid-1970s, with the aid of the film theorist Thierry Kuntzel, when he took a break from his artistic activity. See Thierry Kuntzel and Bernar Venet, "Lecture de *Représentation graphique de la fonction* $y = -x^2/4$" [1975], and Bernar Venet, "Réponses récapitulatives à des questions de base" [1975], in Venet, *La conversion du regard: Textes et entretiens, 1975–2010* [2010], 2nd ed. (Dijon: Les presses du réel, 2011).

62. Lawrence Alloway, "American Stock Exchange Transactions," *Arts Magazine* 44, no. 5 (1970): 39–41. A year later Jean-Marc Poinsot expressed the same opinion: "It seems to me altogether improper to use ideas from linguistics and semiology to interpret such a work. . . . Venet's work makes us read a newspaper as [we would] a picture, abolishing the newspaper's distinctive content while at the same time incorporating it in a series of pictures from which its meaning is [now] derived." Poinsot, "Actualité," *Opus international*, no. 23 (March 1971): 46.

63. From Venet's unpublished interview with Allan (see n. 51 above), p. 5. Looking back, Venet recognized that his theoretical principles were debatable. "Experience," he explained in 1991, "has taught me that one's ideas change, that my thinking in 1976 could not have been the same as my thinking ten years earlier. To be sure, the visceral, the expressive did not suddenly take precedence over the rational, but from experience I learned that I had to challenge my own ideas, that theories become dogmas when one does not bring a critical faculty to bear, when one no longer doubts." See "Conversation avec Eddy Devolder" [1991], in Venet, *La conversion du regard*, 72.

64. Author's telephone conversation with Venet, November 7, 2012.

65. The critic Max Kozloff denounced this tendency as proof of the "bureaucratic tendencies" of conceptual art: "deliberately undigested accretions of data [resulting in] ever more extraneous, repetitive, and purposeless work [that] fills the air with crypto-efficiency." Kozloff, "The Trouble with Art-as-Idea" [1972], in Alberro and Stimson, *Conceptual Art*, 270, 276.

66. Chamberlain, "Reading for Pleasure," 8.

67. Barbara Rose, "Twilight of the Superstars" [1974], in *Readings in American Art, 1900–1975* [1968], ed. Barbara Rose, rev. ed. (New York: Praeger Publishers, 1975), 236.

68. Roselee Goldberg, Enrico Pedrini, and Damien Sausset, eds., *Bernar Venet: Performances, etc., 1961–2006* (Milan: Charta, 2006), 124.

69. Ibid.

70. Venet, "Conversation avec Eddy Devolder," 64.

71. Quoted in Alberto Toscano, "Seeing Socialism: On the Aesthetics of the Economy, Production and the Plan," in *Economy: Art, Production and the Subject in the 21st Century*, ed. Angela Dimitrakaki

and Kirsten Lloyd (Liverpool: Liverpool University Press, 2015), 103–19.

72. The quote from Morgello appears in Venet's work *In on the Ground Floor* (1969). See the entry for this work, and for *Why Some Stocks Go Up* and *Story of a Hot Stock* (both from the same year as well), in the catalogue raisonné edited by Karshan, *Five Years of Bernar Venet*, 26; for *Waiting for a Breakthrough or Two* (also 1969), see figure 43.

73. Joseph Masheck, "The Five Years of Bernar Venet," *Artforum* 10, no. 5 (1972): 86.

74. Christian Besson, "Transparence et opacité: L'œuvre de Bernar Venet de 1961 à 1976," in Venet, *La conversion du regard*, 268.

75. See Lorraine Daston and Peter Galison, *Objectivity* (New York: Zone Books, 2007).

76. See, for example, Theodore M. Porter, "Thin Description: Surface and Depth in Science and Science Studies," *Osiris* 27, no. 1 (2012): 209–26; also Porter, *Trust in Numbers: The Pursuit of Objectivity in Science and Public Life* (Princeton, N.J.: Princeton University Press, 1995).

77. Interview with Venet in Millet, "Bernar Venet," 18.

78. Author's telephone interview with Venet, November 7, 2012.

79. Milton Friedman, *Essays in Positive Economics* (Chicago: University of Chicago Press, 1953), 4.

80. See ibid., 135–42, 187–89.

81. See Susan Buck-Morss, "Envisioning Capital: Political Economy on Display," *Critical Inquiry* 21, no. 2 (1995): 434–67; also Loïc Charles and Yann Giraud, "Economics for the Masses: The Visual Display of Economic Knowledge in the United States (1910–1945)," *History of Political Economy* 45, no. 4 (2013): 567–612.

82. Interview with Bernar Venet, May 18, 1968, Archives of American Art; transcription available online via www.aaa.si.edu/collections/interviews/oral-history-interview-bernar-venet-13044. On the performance featuring Cornfield and Rosenfeld, staged on May 26, 1969, at The Theater in New York, see Goldberg, Pedrini, and Sausset, *Bernar Venet*, 144.

83. Jean Baudrillard, *For a Critique of the Political Economy of the Sign*, trans. Charles Levin (St. Louis, Mo.: Telos Press, 1981), 96. Thierry Kuntzel discusses Baudrillard's argument in relation to Venet in "Bernar Venet: Logique du neutre," in Venet, *La conversion du regard*, 17–18.

84. See Michel Foucault, *Archaeology of Knowledge* [1969], trans. A. M. Sheridan Smith (London: Routledge, 2002), 196–215. For a vigorous criticism of this phenomenon, see Deirdre N. McCloskey, *If You're So Smart: The Narrative of Economic Expertise* (Chicago: University of Chicago Press, 1990).

85. This was a topic of continuing debate, and one that holds a particular interest in connection with the work of Dan Graham, whom I discuss later in this chapter. In an unpublished fragment from the 1970s (translated into French under circumstances later forgotten by the author himself), Graham wrote: "I am in agreement with Lawrence Weiner's statement that an artist must accept the fact that society is organized into various specialized fields of knowledge. Art is therefore only one specialized field among others, such as physics; the artist is primarily a specialist in art—a professional manufacturer"; see Dan Graham, *Ma position: Écrits sur mes œuvres* (Villeurbanne: Nouveau Musée/Institut; Dijon: Les presses du réel, 1992), 11, 39. Subsequently, however, he distanced himself from this view, now regarding art not as a profession, but as a "passionate hobby"; see Bennett Simpson and Chrissie Iles, eds., *Dan Graham: Beyond*, exh. cat. Museum of Contemporary Art, Los Angeles (Los Angeles: Museum of Contemporary Art; Cambridge, Mass.: MIT Press, 2009), 99.

86. Seth Siegelaub, "Quelques observations à propos du soi-disant 'Art conceptuel': Extraits d'entretiens non publiés avec Robert Horvitz (1987) et Claude Gintz (1989)," in *L'Art conceptuel: Une perspective*, ed. Claude Gintz, exh. cat. Musée d'art moderne de la Ville de Paris (Paris: Paris-Musées, 1989), 86.

87. See Walter Benjamin, "The Work of Art in the Age of Mechanical Reproduction" [1935]; an English version of the revised and expanded version from 1935–36, by Edmund Jephcott and Harry Zohn, may be found in *The Work of Art in the Age of Its Technological Reproducibility, and Other Writings on Media*, ed. Michael W. Jennings, Brigid Doherty, and Thomas Y. Levin (Cambridge, Mass.: Belknap Press of Harvard University Press, 2008), 19–55. This phenomenon is an aspect of the more general enthusiasm in the late 1960s for what Buchloh called the "aesthetic of administration"—evidence of the strong influence that the capitalist ideal of technological and bureaucratic efficiency of the period exerted on even the most politically committed artists; see Benjamin H. D. Buchloh, "Conceptual Art 1962–1969: From the Aesthetic of Administration to the Critique of Institutions," *October* 55 (Winter 1990): 105–43.

88. See Grace Glueck, "Modules for the Millions," *New York Times*, June 22, 1969, p. D32.

89. Only three years later the very complete French catalogue of Oppenheim's work compiled by Mathias Fels noted different versions of this piece: the one subsequently preferred by the artist himself, and another with a shorter text, a quite different view of the interior of the Stock Exchange and of the rooftop, and geographical maps of New York; see Mathias Fels, ed., *Dennis Oppenheim, 1967–1971*, exh. cat. Galerie Mathias Fels, Paris (Paris: CEDIC, 1972), n.p.

90. I am grateful to Amy Plumb Oppenheim, the artist's widow and director of the Dennis Oppenheim Studio, and Pamela Seymour Smith Sharp, Willoughby Sharp's widow, for allowing me to view *Stock Exchange Transplant* (1969), black-and-white sound film, 15 minutes 25 seconds, directed by Douglas Collins and filmed by Ken Van Sichle.

91. It is true that Oppenheim himself acquired video equipment and began to film his own sequences in 1969, but this is quite beside the point. In an interview two years later with Willoughby Sharp, who had helped him produce *Removal Transplant—New York Stock Exchange* and who also played a role in the making of Collins's film, Oppenheim was at pains to emphasize that "[t]he fact that one of my pieces was presented as a film was a very incidental aspect of it. It had nothing to do with the *idea* of the piece." Documentation, he believed, whether photographic or cinemagraphic, violated the integrity of the work and closed off possible avenues of exploration: "[M]aking a film was permitting the work to be too accessible, removing one layer of accessibility." See Willoughby Sharp, "Interview with Dennis Oppenheim," *Studio International* (November 1971): 186–93; reprinted in Germano Celant, ed., *Dennis Oppenheim: Explorations* (Milan: Charta, 2001), 117.

92. See James E. Buck, ed., *The New York Stock Exchange: The First 200 Years* (Essex, Conn.: Greenwich Publishing, 1992), 140–41.

93. Dennis Oppenheim, voice-over in the film by Douglas Collins, *Stock Exchange Transplant*.

94. See the discussion of this event by Mignon Nixon, "Anatomic Explosion on Wall Street," *October* 142 (Fall 2012): 3–25.

95. Press release, "Naked Event outside the Stock Exchange," New York, July 14, 1968, reproduced in *Yayoi Kusama*, exh. cat. Le Consortium, Dijon (Dijon: Les presses du réel, 2001), 135.

96. Press release, "Naked Demonstration at Wall Street," New York, October 13, 1968, reproduced in ibid., 145. The two events jointly constitute the work entitled *The Anatomic Explosion Happening*.

97. See "Une autre entrée possible: Entretien avec Dennis Oppenheim," in *Dennis Oppenheim: And the Mind Grew Fingers*, ed. Alanna Heiss, exh. cat. Musée d'art moderne, Villeneuve d'Ascq, France, 1994, 31; also "Interview with Dennis Oppenheim" [1994], in Celant, *Dennis Oppenheim*, 333.

98. Oppenheim, voice-over in *Stock Exchange Transplant*. This work may therefore be seen as one of the first of the so-called gallery transplants, a project in which the artist reproduced the floor plan of an exhibition space outdoors, tracing it in snow, for example, or in grass or earth. See Jean-Louis Bourgeois, "Dennis Oppenheim: A Presence in the Countryside," *Artforum* 8, no. 2 (1969): 36; also Larisa Dryansky, *Cartophotographies: De l'art conceptuel au Land Art* (Paris: Éditions du Comité des travaux historiques et scientifiques/Institut national d'histoire de l'art, 2017), 273–93.

99. Like other artists associated with the land art movement, Oppenheim occasionally relied on private commissions as a source of funding. In one case, the wealthy California collector Rene di Rosa hired him to modify the contours of the hillsides and ravines of his property; see Howard Hunker, "The New Sculpture Getting down to the Nitty Gritty," *Saturday Evening Post*, November 2, 1968, p. 45. More generally in this connection, see Alberro, *Conceptual Art and the Politics of Publicity*, especially 72–74, 88–89.

100. Quoted by Roy Bongartz, "It's Called Earth Art—and Boulderdash," *New York Times*, February 1, 1970, p. 22.

101. Quoted in "A Creative Interest in Cash: Art You Can Bank On," *Life*, September 19, 1969, p. 56.

102. Quoted in Roy Bongartz, "Question: How Do You Buy a Work of Art like This?," *New York Times*, August 11, 1974, p. 19. The article wrongly states that Oppenheim himself lived in the building on Park Avenue South.

103. Les Levine, first press release for *Profit Systems I*, March 1969; artist's personal archives, New York.

104. Les Levine, second press release for *Profit Systems I*, November 1969; artist's personal archives, New York.

105. Les Levine, "Press Release," reprinted in *Toronto Star*, May 17, 1969, p. 3, and in *Artforum* 7, no. 10 (1969): 16.

106. Author's interview with Levine, September 28, 2010, New York.

107. Quoted in Jack Burnham, "Les Levine: Business as Usual," *Artforum* 8, no. 8 (1970): 41.

108. From interview with Thelma R. Newman, "The Artist Speaks: Les Levine," *Art in America* 57, no. 6 (1969): 91. See also Grace Glueck, "Mergers on the Rue Madison," *New York Times*, October 16, 1966, p. 135, and John Perreault, "Plastic Man Strikes," *Art News* 67, no. 1 (1968): 73, as well as Les Levine, "The Disposable Transient Environment," *0 to 9*, no. 5 (January 1969): 45; the contents of this short-lived journal have recently been reprinted in their entirety as Vito Acconci and Bernadette Mayer, eds., *0 to 9: The Complete Magazine, 1967–1969* (New York: Ugly Duckling Press, 2006).

109. Burnham, "Les Levine," 40. Looking back on this experiment a few years ago, Levine claimed not to mind that his disposable works were sold in supermarkets, but only because the extent of their commercial distribution was limited: "That it happened a little is a good thing, it was a good experience. But I don't want to be a manufacturer." Telephone interview with the author, September 16, 2010. A study of the archives of the Fischbach Gallery in New York, which represented Levine at the time, shows that the price of these *Disposables* rose over the course of a few years in proportion to his growing fame: sold for between three and seven dollars in 1966, they went for between twenty-five and thirty-five dollars in 1970; see "Invoices for Disposables" in 1966 and in 1970, Fischbach Gallery records, 1937–2015 (mostly covering the period 1963–77), in Archives of American Art, Smithsonian Institution (hereafter, "Fischbach Gallery Records"), box 21, folder 1.

110. David Bourdon, "Les Levine Bursts with Elusive Ideas—and Ego," *Life*, August 22, 1969, p. 65.

111. Jack Burnham, "Real Time Systems," *Artforum* 8, no. 1 (1969): 55.

112. Burnham, "Les Levine," 41.

113. Author's telephone interview with Levine, September 16, 2010.

114. Levine, second press release for *Profit Systems I*, November 1969.

115. Quoted in "Creative Interest in Cash," p. 58.

116. Levine deliberately chose a firm that was not listed on the New York Stock Exchange in order to reduce expenses and minimize paperwork. He nonetheless had to go through a broker, in compliance with securities regulations at the time. Author's telephone interview with Levine, September 16, 2010.

117. Burnham, "Les Levine," 43.

118. On this subject, see Ken Allan, "Business Interests, 1969–1972: N. E. Thing Co. Ltd., Les Levine, Bernar Venet, and John Latham," *Parachute*, no. 106 (April–June 2002): 106–22; Yann Toma, Stéphanie Jamet-Chavigny, and Laurent Deveze, eds., *Artistes et entreprises* (Dijon: Les presses du réel, 2012); and Marc-Olivier Wahler, "Rapports d'entreprises," *Art Press*, no. 230 (December 1997): 35–40.

119. Reproduced in Paul Grescoe, "Steady, Now: Is This Art?," *Canadian Magazine* (in *Calgary Herald*), January 25, 1969, p. 15.

120. Luc Boltanski and Ève Chiapello, *The New Spirit of Capitalism* [1999], trans. Gregory Elliott (New York: Verso, 2007), 18.

121. Ibid., 19.

122. Author's telephone interview with Levine, September 16, 2010. The name of the museum refers to the address of the artist's studio in New York, 181 Mott Street, but it is also unquestionably a punning allusion to the name "R. Mutt" used by Marcel Duchamp in his famous 1917 work, *Fountain*.

123. Les Levine, *The Museum of Mott Art, Inc.: Protetch-Rivkin Public Art Hearings* (New York: Museum of Mott Art, 1971),

1–4, 8. The brochure goes on to describe other services available to subscribers; see *Les Levine's Greatest Hits*, exh. cat. Galerie Gerald Piltzer, Paris, 1974, pp. 15–16.

124. Max Kozloff, "Junk Mail: An Affluent Art Movement," *Art Journal* 33, no. 1 (1973): 28.

125. For a description of one such hearing, and of subsequent exhibitions, see Henry Allen, "Art, Services Rendered: A Mottley Assortment," *Washington Post*, December 11, 1971, p. E8. A video record of various hearings in three parts was made by Levine: *Mott Art Hearings*, New York, 1970, black-and-white sound film, 5 hours; *Mott Art Hearings*, Rhode Island School of Design, Chicago Institute of Art, and the Corcoran Gallery in Washington, D.C., 1970, black-and-white sound film, 60 minutes; and *Mott Art Hearings*, Miami-Dade Community College, May 1974, black-and-white sound film, 60 minutes.

126. See the advertisement created by Calvin J. Goodman, reproduced in Julia Bryan-Wilson, *Art Workers: Radical Practice in the Vietnam War Era* (Berkeley: University of California Press, 2009), 39; also the ones that appeared in *Artforum* 7, no. 6 (1969): 12, and vol. 7, no. 7 (1969): 94.

127. Levine, *Museum of Mott Art, Inc.*, 1.

128. See, for example, Herbert Koshetz, "Ex-Broker Guides Art Investors," *New York Times*, February 2, 1967, pp. 31–32.

129. Author's telephone interview with Levine, September 16, 2010.

130. Levine, first press release for *Profit Systems I*, March 1969.

131. John Perreault, "Anything the Artist Spits Out," *Village Voice*, March 9, 1972, p. 25.

132. From the announcement created by Giorno for Levine's exhibit *18-Carat Solid Gold Chewing-Gum* at the Fischbach Gallery, February 19–March 9, 1972; Fischbach Gallery Records, box 12, folder 29.

133. Perreault, "Anything the Artist Spits Out," p. 25.

134. Peter Schjeldahl, "Les Levine: From Chewing Gum to Chou En-Lai," *New York Times*, December 22, 1974, p. C37.

135. Seven documents (dated 1969 and 1973) were added to the nine documents initially exhibited at the 1969 show. The complete work was displayed at a 1973 group exhibit in Australia, *Some Recent American Art*, National Gallery of Victoria, Melbourne.

136. Letter from Robert Morris to Howard Lipman, May 23, 1969, photocopy sent by Lipman to Leo Castelli; Leo Castelli Gallery Records, ca. 1880–2000 (mostly concerning the period 1957–1999), Archives of American Art, Smithsonian Institution (hereafter "Leo Castelli Gallery Records"), series 1, box 15, folder 6. The Whitney Museum still owes Morris his half-share of the profits ($168.38), for which he demanded payment in a letter of 1973 (included in the final version of *Money*) and again more recently; see *The Price of Everything . . . Perspectives on the Art Market*, exh. cat. Whitney Museum of American Art, New York (New York: Whitney Museum of American Art; New Haven: Yale University Press, 2007), 5.

137. Alfred Frankenstein, "The Great Rock on the Anti-Illusionists' Ramp," *San Francisco Sunday Examiner and Chronicle*, June 1, 1969. This press clipping (page number missing, as in many such cases), along with the others cited in this paragraph, are collected in a folder labeled "Press Releases and Reviews/Anti-Illusion: Procedures/Materials," in the archives of the Frances Mulhall Achilles Library, Whitney Museum of American Art, New York.

138. Margarita Dulac, "Exhibition of Placing, Not Art"; press clipping (source and date of publication unknown), in ibid.

139. Barbara Gold, "Invaluement Here to Stay," *Baltimore Evening Sun*, July 13, 1969, p. 90; press clipping, in ibid.

140. James Monte and Marcia Tucker, eds., *Anti-Illusion: Procedures/Materials*, exh. cat. Whitney Museum of American Art, New York (New York: Whitney Museum of American Art, 1969), 50–51.

141. Morris stated at the time that he had given the Whitney a free hand with regard to the exhibition of *Money*. It was therefore the museum's decision to display the documents relating to the transaction as it did, in plain frames without any accompanying commentary. See the transcript of Morris's May 16, 1969, interview with Patricia Norvell in Alexander Alberro and Patricia Norvell, eds., *Recording Conceptual Art: Early Interviews with Barry, Huebler, Kaltenbach, LeWitt, Morris, Oppenheim, Siegelaub, Smithson, Weiner* (Berkeley: University of California Press, 2001), 56. In a conversation two years later with Lucy Lippard, in October 1971, however, the artist seemed to regard Fiore's photographs as the true materialization of the work; quoted in Lippard, *Six Years*, 256–57.

142. Contact sheets of Fiore's photographs of Morris, conserved in the Whitney's archives pertaining to the *Anti-Illusion: Procedures/Materials* show (May 19–July 6, 1969), Frances Mulhall Achilles Library.

143. From the transcript of Morris's May 16, 1969, interview in Alberro and Norvell, *Recording Conceptual Art*, 63.

144. Author's interview by email with Robert Morris, March 27–29, 2011.

145. Quoted in Grace Glueck, "Now There Are Mutual Funds for Art," *New York Times*, November 7, 1969, p. 36.

146. For a chronological summary of the AWC's activities, see Lucy R. Lippard, "The Art Workers' Coalition: Not a History," *Studio International* 17, no. 6 (1970): 171–73. A more detailed account of the forms political activism assumed among American artists in the 1960s may be found in Francis Frascina, *Art, Politics, and Dissent: Aspects of the Art Left in Sixties America* (Manchester: Manchester University Press, 1999).

147. See, for example, Bryan-Wilson, *Art Workers*, 37.

148. See, for example, the statements by Carl Andre, David Lee, Sol LeWitt, Bruce Brown, Alex Gross, Bill Gordy, and Iain Whitecross, originally published in typescript by the AWC in the wake of the first public meeting held on April 10, 1969; the entire collection was digitally reissued in 2008 by the arts nonprofit organization Primary Information as *Open Hearing: Art Workers' Coalition*, available via www.primaryinformation.org/product/art-workers-coalition-open-hearing/.

149. Intervention at the April 10, 1969, hearing by Alex Gross, ibid., 109.

150. From the "Synthetic Report of the Public Hearing Held April 10, 1969," typescript, April 23, 1969, in ibid., 104.

151. Unsigned and undated typescript, in ibid., 113. It will be noted that Alternative A foreshadows the widely discussed "contract" drawn up by Seth Siegelaub; see, in particular, Alberro, *Conceptual Art and the Politics of Publicity*, 164–69, and Maria Eichhorn, *The Artist's Contract: Interviews with Carl Andre, Daniel Buren, Paula Cooper, Hans Haacke, Jenny Holzer, Adrian Piper, Robert Projansky, Robert*

Ryman, Seth Siegelaub, John Weber, Lawrence Weiner, Jackie Winsor, ed. Gerti Fietzek (Cologne: König, 2009).

152. Morris's and Lozano's involvement is now well documented; see Bryan-Wilson, *Art Workers*, 83–125, and Jo Applin, *Lee Lozano: Not Working* (New Haven: Yale University Press, 2018), 133–37, respectively. Graham and Lozano took part in the open hearing of April 10, 1969. Levine recalls having attended a few meetings of the AWC; he was also one of the signers of the open letter in support of the AWC published in *Studio International* 180, no. 928 (1970): 228. Indeed, it is possible that his *Mott Art Hearings* in 1970 deliberately echoed the famous AWC open hearing of the previous year.

153. Author's interview by email with Morris, March 27–29, 2011. Although the artist was not actively involved in the AWC's activities before 1970, he was surely familiar with the nature of the debates that took place in early 1969.

154. Dan Graham, "Income Piece: From a Talk to Students at the University of the State of New York at Oswego, New York—December 1973," published in *Dan Graham: Works and Collected Writings*, ed. Gloria Moure (Barcelona: Ediciones Polígrafa, 2009), 54–55.

155. Statement by Dan Graham, recorded in *Open Hearing*, 93.

156. Statement by Lee Lozano, recorded in ibid., 92.

157. Robert Morris, May 16, 1969, interview, transcribed in Alberro and Norvell, *Recording Conceptual Art*, 61, 64, 65.

158. Quoted in Gregoire Müller, "Points of View: A Taped Conversation with Robert C. Scull," *Arts Magazine* 45, no. 2 (1970): 37.

159. Lipman, "Money for Money's Sake," 76.

160. Author's interview with Dan Graham, October 7, 2010, New York. On the relationship between Lozano and Graham, see Sarah Lehrer-Graiwer, *Lee Lozano: Dropout Piece* (Cambridge, Mass.: MIT Press, 2014), 25–26.

161. The date that appears on the legal notice shown in fig. 52 is June 2, 1969. Now held by the Museum of Modern Art in New York, the work is sometimes erroneously referred to as "Income (Outgo) Piece." Graham corrected the title himself, changing *outgo* to *outflow* in a letter to Herman Daled; see Patrizia Dander and Ulrich Wilmes, eds., *Daled: A Bit of Matter and a Little Bit More: The Collection and Archives of Herman and Nicole Daled, 1966–1978* (Munich: Haus der Kunst; Cologne: König, 2010), 378. At about the same time, in an undated French text (the English original of which seems no longer to exist; see n. 85 above), Graham recorded for posterity the circumstances of its sale: "A Belgian collector, Herman Daled, . . . having 'discovered' one of my works at the Gibson Gallery in New York, suggested that I choose from among my works the three pieces I considered the most important, which he would add to his collection. Having decided that this part of my work was now 'ancient history' and that incorporating it in a [private] collection would not violate the original spirit, I accepted the offer. I was anxious that someone conserve these documents and perhaps be able to make them known to a part of the artistic world that was totally ignorant of my 'contribution.' The price of each work was $1,000, of which Gibson took half. The greatest advantage that Daled gave me by acquiring these works and exhibiting them in his home was to permit European artists such as Daniel Buren and Marcel Broodthaers (whose work and opinions I greatly respect) to see them and, I think, to appreciate them." Graham, *Ma position*, 26.

162. Text accompanying *Income (Outflow) Piece*, reproduced in Marianne Brouwer, ed., *Dan Graham, Works 1965–2000* (Düsseldorf: Richter, 2001), 118; emphasis in the original. In Emily Apter's view, this project represents "a play on the libertarian assumption (often attributed to Locke) that people can be the object of private property rules, and may alienate the property in their person if they so choose. . . . Portraying the risks attendant on expropriation of property in the person, *Income (Outflow) Piece* foretells anxieties around the right to self-ownership surfacing in the age of the genome." See her essay "Dan Graham Inc. and the Fetish of Self-Property," in *The Lure of the Object*, ed. Stephen Melville (Williamstown, Mass.: Sterling and Francine Clark Art Institute, 2005), 33.

163. Author's interview with Graham, October 7, 2010, New York. According to Graham, the artist Lawrence Weiner had expressed an interest in buying the work, but the sale fell through. See also Mike Metz and Dan Graham, "Dan Graham," *Bomb* 46 (Winter 1994): 26.

164. Graham, "Income Piece," in Moure, *Dan Graham*, 54.

165. Graham, *Income (Outflow) Piece*, reproduced in ibid., 52.

166. List of works exhibited in the *Language III* show, May 24–June 18 1969; Dwan Gallery Records, box 4, folder 1.

167. Author's interview with Graham, October 7, 2010, New York.

168. The Copley quote has no known source other than the work by Lozano itself. Mao's remark occurs in his essay "On Practice: On the Relation between Knowledge and Practice, between Knowing and Doing" [1937], in *Selected Works of Mao Tse-Tung*, 4 vols. (Peking: Foreign Languages Press, 1965), 1:296.

169. See Iris Müller-Westermann, "'Making Art Is Greatest Act of All': Lee Lozano's Investigations," in *Lee Lozano*, ed. Iris Müller-Westermann, exh. cat. Moderna Museet, Stockholm (Stockholm: Moderna Museet; Ostfildern, Germany: Hatje Cantz, 2010), 24–50.

170. "ALL WRITE-UPS ARE DRAWINGS." This and other such glosses are found in *Clarification Piece*, a work dated July 28, 1969, and reproduced in Ben Kinmont, *Project Series: Lee Lozano* (New York: Antinomian Press, 1998), 21.

171. A footnote added by Lozano herself explained that *lace* meant "bread, money." See photocopied page of the artist's notebook, dated January 1969, in Richard Bellamy Papers, series III.A, folder 55; Museum of Modern Art Archives, New York.

172. This placement is attested by a photograph of the *Language III* show at Dwan Gallery in the spring of 1969; Dwan Gallery Records, series 2, box 4, folder 1. See also Lozano's exhibition instructions for her *Infofiction* show at the Nova Scotia College of Art and Design in Halifax in early 1971; reproduced in Adam Szymczyk, ed., *Lee Lozano: Win First Don't Last, Win Last Don't Care*, exh. cat. Kunsthalle Basel (Basel: Schwabe, 2006), 146.

173. Notebook entry for May 13, 1969, reproduced in Lee Lozano, *Drawings*, ed. Barry Rosen and Jaap van Liere (New Haven: Yale University Press, 2006), n.p. This preoccupation had first asserted itself almost a year earlier: "Artists are unique because artists are autonomous. Everybody else has a boss," she wrote on July 17, 1968; later she added, "Most artists get a boss, though: their *dealer*."

See also her notebook entry for September 25, 1968, quoted in Müller-Westermann, "'Making Art Is Greatest Act of All,'" 42.

174. Jo Applin, "Hard Work: Lee Lozano's Dropouts," *October* 156 (Spring 2016): 75–99. Applin specifically connects this politics of "not working" to a form of "scandalous feminism"; see Applin, *Lee Lozano*, 129–51 and 158–59.

175. *Withdrawal Piece* is reproduced in Kinmont, *Project Series*, 7, and *General Strike Piece* in *0 to 9*, no. 6 (July 1969): 57, reprinted in Acconci and Mayer, *0 to 9*, 57.

176. See Lehrer-Graiwer, *Lee Lozano*, especially 47–61. Lozano's work did not really reappear on the art scene until a year before her death, in 1998, when the Wadsworth Atheneum Museum of Art in Hartford, Connecticut, organized an exhibition approved by the artist without any involvement on her part. She produced one final work (dated from August to October 1998 and titled *Questionnaire, with Jokes, concerning Purchases and Purchasers of My Art*), which analyzed the sociological profile of her collectors. After Lozano's death, in October 1999, several exhibitions allowed her work to be rediscovered by a wider audience. The Zurich gallery Hauser and Wirth acquired the Lee Lozano Estate in 2004 and in the years since has sought to promote her growing recognition. See also Helen Molesworth, "Turn In. Turn On. Drop Out: The Rejection of Lee Lozano," *Art Journal* 61, no. 4 (2002): 64–71; and Katie Siegel, "Market Index: Lee Lozano," *Artforum* 46, no. 8 (2008): 330–31.

177. See John Maynard Keynes, *The General Theory of Employment, Interest, and Money* (London: Macmillan, 1936), 4.12.5, 156.

CHAPTER 4
CIRCUITS OF COMMERCE

1. Montesquieu, *The Spirit of the Laws*, ed. and trans. Anne M. Cohler, Basia C. Miller, and Harold S. Stone (Cambridge: Cambridge University Press, 1989), 338.

2. See John Maynard Keynes, *The Economic Consequences of the Peace* [1919], vol. 2 of *The Collected Writings of John Maynard Keynes*, ed. Elizabeth Johnson and Donald Moggridge, 30 vols. (Cambridge: Cambridge University Press, 1971–89).

3. See David Long and Peter Wilson, eds., *Thinkers of the Twenty Years' Crisis: Inter-War Idealism Reassessed* (Oxford: Oxford University Press, 1995).

4. From a speech by Jean Monnet, president of the High Authority, at the Opening Session of the Common Assembly in Strasbourg, September 11, 1952; the quote occurs on p. 28 of the archival document available via http://ec.europa.eu/historical_archives/archisplus/files/MONNET_1952_09_11_EN.pdf.

5. Viviana A. Zelizer, "Circuits of Commerce," in *Self, Social Structure, and Beliefs: Explorations in Sociology*, ed. Alexander Jeffrey, Gary T. Marx, and Christine Williams (Berkeley: University of California Press, 2004), 123.

6. Letter from Ray Johnson to Richard Feigen, September 18, 1968; Richard L. Feigen and Co. Gallery Archives, New York (hereafter "Feigen Gallery Archives"), folder labeled "Ray Johnson to Richard Feigen."

7. See, for example, "A Creative Interest in Cash: Art You Can Bank On," *Life*, September 19, 1969, p. 56; "Greed," *New York Magazine*, April 28, 1969, p. 47; and "Happy Membership," *Christian Science Monitor*, July 14, 1969, p. 8.

8. *Who's Afraid of Virginia Woolf?* (1966), black-and-white sound film, 131 minutes, directed by Mike Nichols and produced by Ernest Lehman, with Elizabeth Taylor (Martha), Richard Burton (George), George Segal (Nick), and Sandy Dennis (Honey).

9. The same rhyme of *honey* and *money* is found in a famous passage of George Eliot's *Middlemarch* [1871]; see David Carroll's critical edition (Oxford: Clarendon Press, 1986), 592.

10. See Mary Emma Harris, ed., *Starting at Zero: Black Mountain College, 1933–1957*, exh. cat. Arnolfini Gallery, Bristol, and Kettle's Yard, Cambridge (Bristol: Arnolfini Gallery; Cambridge: Kettle's Yard, 2005); William S. Wilson, ed., *Ray Johnson*, exh. cat. Asheville Art Museum (Black Mountain, N.C.: Black Mountain College Arts Center, 1997); and Helen Molesworth, ed., *Leap before You Look: Black Mountain College, 1933–1957*, exh. cat. Institute of Contemporary Art, Boston (Boston: Institute of Contemporary Art; New Haven: Yale University Press, 2015).

11. Untitled exhibition, Mills College of Education Gallery, New York, April 2–30, 1957. See the corresponding entry in Frances F. L. Beatty, Jennifer Grossman, Muffet Jones, Clive Phillpot, Gillian Pistell, Michael von Uchtrup, and William Wilson, eds., *Ray Johnson Chronology*, Ray Johnson Estate and Archives, New York (hereafter, "Ray Johnson Archives"). Four of the five installments of this chronology (covering the periods 1954–64, 1965–75, 1976–82, and 1983–95) are at least partially available via www.rayjohnsonestate.com/timelines.

12. "Cover," *Art News* 56, no. 9 (1958): 5.

13. Donna De Salvo, "Correspondences," in *Ray Johnson: Correspondences*, ed. Donna De Salvo and Catherine Gudis, exh. cat. Whitney Museum of American Art, New York (New York: Flammarion, 1999), 20.

14. Grace Glueck, "What Happened? Nothing," *New York Times*, April 11, 1965, p. 18X.

15. Rosalind Constable, "The Mailaway Art of Ray Johnson," *New York Magazine*, March 2, 1970, p. 43. Johnson, who often wrote to journalists directly to express his satisfaction or displeasure with their work, congratulated Constable on her piece: "I write to say that I am delighted with the article *The Alloway Art of Ray Johnson* written by you in New York nagazine [*sic*]." His punning substitution of *Alloway* (a reference to the critic who coined the term *pop art*, Lawrence Alloway) for *Mailaway* points once more to his ambivalence at belonging to an artistic movement that had not advanced his own career. Letter from Ray Johnson to Rosalind Constable, February 25, 1970, published in Richard Craven, ed., *Correspondence: An Exhibition of the Letters of Ray Johnson*, exh. cat. North Carolina Museum of Art, Raleigh, 1976, n.p.

16. The term *New York Correspondence School* had been invented by Plunkett in 1962, echoing the famous New York School of abstract expressionist artists of the previous decade. According to his estate, Johnson himself used this term for a number of years (often playfully misspelling the third word as "Correspondance") before trying unsuccessfully to kill it off in 1973 with a letter to the obituary editor of the *New York Times*; see Edward M. Plunkett, "The New York Correspondence School," *Art Journal* 36, no. 3 (1977): 233–35.

17. "The Village Square," *Village Voice*, October 26, 1955, p. 3. The author evidently means to refer to Alfred H. Barr Jr., the museum's first director.

18. John Gruen, "Galleries and Museums," *New York Magazine*, March 9, 1970, p. 55.

19. Untitled, Undated Artist's Statement, Ray Johnson Archives. The document is partially quoted in Henry Martin, "Milan Letter," *Art International* 16, no. 6 (1972): 107.

20. David Bourdon, "Notes on a Letter Head," *Art International* 13, no. 9 (1969): 78.

21. See, for example, the undated letter to Dick Higgins signed "Picasso Gaglione" [possibly John Held], reproduced in John Held and Bill Gaglione, eds., *A Ray Johnson Miscellany: The Fake Picabia Bros.* (San Francisco: Snowman Publications, 1999), n.p. See also David Bourdon, "Cosmic Ray: An Open Letter to the Founder of the New York Correspondence School," *Art in America* 83, no. 10 (1995): 110.

22. Harvey Aronson, "What? You Never Heard from Ray Johnson?," *Newsday*, January 18, 1969, p. 12; Martin, "Milan Letter," 106; David Bourdon, "New York: Our Period Style," *Art and Artists* 1, no. 3 (1966): 57.

23. Jean-Marc Poinsot, *Mail art: Communication à distance, concept* (Paris: CEDIC, 1971), 25.

24. Held and Gaglione, *Ray Johnson Miscellany*, n.p.

25. See Ina Blom, "Ray Johnson's Postal Performance," in *The Name of the Game: Ray Johnson's Postal Performance*, exh. cat. National Museum of Contemporary Art, Oslo, 2003, pp. 11–14.

26. Aronson, "What? You Never Heard from Ray Johnson?," 10.

27. In addition to Christo and Jeanne-Claude, see the many other people interviewed in the 2002 documentary film about Johnson by John W. Walter, *How to Draw a Bunny*, color sound film, 90 minutes. See also the letters the artist exchanged with the Feigen Gallery regarding bookkeeping for the exhibitions between January and October 1971 of the *Dollar Bill* collages; Feigen Gallery Archives, folder labeled "Ray Johnson to Richard Feigen Gallery (1970–1981)."

28. Ray Johnson, solo exhibitions: *Dollar Bills*, at Richard Feigen Gallery, Chicago, September 16–October 17, 1970; and *Dollar Bills and Famous People Memorials*, Richard Feigen Gallery, New York, April 3–May 5, 1971.

29. Letter from Ray Johnson to Richard [Lippold], dated "Moon 2, 1970," reproduced in Craven, *Correspondence*, n.p.

30. Letter from Ray Johnson to Dana Atchley, June 27, 1970, reproduced in ibid., n.p.

31. See undated typescript, "Ray Johnson 'Dollar Bill Show,' Richard Feigen Gallery, Chicago"; Lucy Lippard Papers, box 10, folders 34–36.

32. Oral History Interview with Ray Johnson by Sevim Fesci, April 17, 1968, Archives of American Art, Smithsonian Institution, Washington, D.C.; available online via_www.aaa.si.edu/collections /interviews/oral-history-interview-ray -johnson-13236. Reproduced in Julie J. Thomson, ed., *That Was the Answer: Interviews with Ray Johnson* (Chicago: Soberscove Press, 2018), 49.

33. Author's interview with Michael Findlay, October 13, 2010, New York.

34. *Midnight Cowboy* (1969), color sound film, 113 minutes, directed by John Schlesinger, with Jon Voight (Joe Buck) and Dustin Hoffman (Enrico ["Ratso"] Rizzo).

35. Warhol and Johnson had known each other since the mid-1950s, and helped each other find work as commercial illustrators. They probably met through New Directions Press, for which they both designed book jackets. See Bourdon, "Cosmic Ray," 109.

36. See Walter Gutman, *The Gutman Letter* (New York: Something Else Press, 1969).

37. Letter from Ray Johnson to Richard Feigen and Michael Findlay, December 21, 1968; Feigen Gallery Archives, folder labeled "Ray Johnson to Richard Feigen Gallery (1966–1968)."

38. The collector Robert Scull had famously invited journalists to admire the works of pop art displayed in his home; see "You Bought It, Now Live with It: The Country's Leading Collectors of Pop Art Enthusiastically Fill Their Homes with It," *Life*, July 16, 1965, pp. 56–61.

39. Letter from Ray Johnson to Michael Findlay, December 18, 1970, signed "Babar Snodgress"; Feigen Gallery Archives, folder labeled "Ray Johnson to Richard Feigen Gallery (1970–1981)."

40. Letter from Ray Johnson to "B & E Productions," January 5, 1971; Feigen Gallery Archives, folder labeled "Ray Johnson to Richard Feigen."

41. Harriet Janis and Rudi Blesh, *Collage: Personalities, Concepts, Techniques* (Philadelphia: Chilton, 1962), 63. See also Curt Germundson, "Kurt Schwitters, *Hindenburg-Merzzeichnung 157*, 1920," in *Collecting Modernism: European Masterworks from the Munson-Williams-Proctor Arts Institute*, ed. Mary E. Murray, exh. cat. Munson-Williams-Proctor Arts Institute, Utica, N.Y., 2005, p. 60.

42. Letter from Ray Johnson to Richard Feigen, March 11, 1970; Feigen Gallery Archives, folder labeled "Ray Johnson to Richard Feigen Gallery (1970–1981)."

43. Barbon is quoted by Michel Foucault, *The Order of Things: An Archaeology of the Human Sciences* (New York: Pantheon, 1971), 192.

44. Aronson, "What? You Never Heard from Ray Johnson?," 10.

45. See, in particular, Michel Aglietta and André Orléan, eds., *La monnaie souveraine* (Paris: Odile Jacob, 1998); André Orléan, *The Empire of Value: A New Foundation for Economics* [2011], trans. M. B. DeBevoise (Cambridge, Mass.: MIT Press, 2014); and Jean-Pierre Dupuy, *Economy and the Future: A Crisis of Faith* [2012], trans. M. B. DeBevoise (East Lansing: Michigan State University Press, 2014). See also Luc Boltanski and Laurent Thévenot, *On Justification: Economies of Worth* [1996], trans. Catherine Porter (Princeton, N.J.: Princeton University Press, 2006); and Geoffrey Ingham, "Money Is a Social Relation," *Review of Social Economy* 54, no. 4 (1996): 507–29.

46. Ray Johnson, untitled mailing with envelope postmarked 1968; Lucy Lippard Papers, box 10, folders 33–37.

47. Jerry G. Bowles, "Out of the Gallery, into the Mailbox," *Art in America* 60, no. 2 (1972): 23.

48. Ace Space [Dana Atchley], untitled mailing, 1970; William Wilson Archives, New York (hereafter "William Wilson Archives").

49. Eleanor Antin, untitled mailing, photocopied document, October 31, 1969; William Wilson Archives.

50. See, for example, "The Image Bank Post Card Show," photocopied document, 1971; Lucy Lippard Papers, box 10, folders 7 and 34–36; also Michael Crane, "A Brief History," in *Correspondence Art: A Brief History*, ed. Michael Crane (Penryn, England: Uniart, 1979), 108.

51. See Jerry G. Bowles, ed., *Art Work, No Commercial Value* (New York: Grossman, 1972).

52. Image Bank, "Annual Report"; Lucy

Lippard Papers, box 10, folders 34–36, and box 10, folder 7, respectively.

53. Oral History Interview with Ray Johnson, April 17, 1968; reproduced in Thomson, *That Was the Answer*, 47.

54. See, in particular, Blom, "Ray Johnson's Postal Performance," 13–17.

55. Oral History Interview with Ray Johnson, April 17, 1968; reproduced in Thomson, *That Was the Answer*, 48.

56. See, for example, the untitled mailing dated October 27, 1969, in William Wilson Archives. *Midnight Cowboy* had been mentioned earlier by Johnson in a postcard of June 21, 1969, to Wilson, and then again in a letter of November 9 the same year.

57. Vincent Canby, "Midnight Cowboy," *New York Times*, May 26, 1969, p. 54.

58. "Viva was cast as the party's hostess," David Bourdon later recalled, "a filmmaker modeled upon Warhol himself. Shown at the party was a black-and-white 'underground' movie of Ultra Violet (actually filmed by Paul Morrissey)." Bourdon, *Warhol* (New York: Harry N. Abrams), 283. See also Steven Watson, *Factory Made: Warhol and the Sixties* (New York: Pantheon, 2003), 386–87.

59. Andy Warhol and Pat Hackett, *POPism: The Warhol Sixties* (New York: Harcourt Brace Jovanovich, 1980), 280–81.

60. Johnson had helped Warhol make one of his first films, *Jill Johnston Dancing*, in early 1964. See Debra Miller, *Billy Name: Stills from the Warhol Films* (New York: Prestel, 1994), 28.

61. See Jonathon Green, *Green's Dictionary of Slang*, 3 vols. (Edinburgh: Chambers, 2010), 1:754–56.

62. I am grateful to Frances Beatty, director of the Ray Johnson Estate at the Feigen Gallery, for having suggested this line of interpretation to me. See John Hope Franklin and Loren Schweninger, *Runaway Slaves: Rebels on the Plantation* (New York: Oxford University Press, 1999), 152, 170–76. Many examples may be found in Billy G. Smith and Richard Wojtowicz, eds., *Blacks Who Stole Themselves: Advertisements for Runaways in the "Pennsylvania Gazette," 1728–1790* (Philadelphia: University of Pennsylvania Press, 1989); see also Marcus Wood, *Blind Memory: Visual Representations of Slavery in England and America, 1780–1865* (Manchester: Manchester University Press, 2000). Michael O'Malley has studied the way in which monetary thought and racial prejudice are linked in U.S. history in *Face Value: The Entwined Histories of Money and Race in America* (Chicago: University of Chicago Press, 2012).

63. On this work, see especially Francis M. Naumann, *Marcel Duchamp: The Art of Making Art in the Age of Mechanical Reproduction* (New York: Harry N. Abrams, 1999), 90–91, 230–32. The image was borrowed and reworked by other artists at the time as well. See, in particular, the poster for Richard Pettibone's exhibition *Wanted: $2,000 Reward*, Ferus Gallery, Los Angeles, 1966; reproduced in Rebecca Peabody, ed., *Pacific Standard Time: Los Angeles Art, 1945–1980*, exh. cat. J. Paul Getty Museum, Los Angeles (Los Angeles: Getty Research Institute, 2011), 173.

64. Letter from Ray Johnson, addressed to "The Dead," April 5, 1973; Lucy Lippard Papers, box 10, folders 34–36.

65. Reproduced in De Salvo and Gudis, *Ray Johnson*, 136, and quoted by Bourdon, "Cosmic Ray," 111. For other examples, see Walter's film *How to Draw a Bunny*.

66. "Éloge du sujet," Kunstmuseum, Basel, October 5–November 3, 1974. On the history of the Basel fair, see Hans Furer, ed., *Looking Back at Art Basel: Photographs* (Basel: Schwabe, 2009).

67. Alfred Pacquement, preface to Catherine David, ed., *Marcel Broodthaers*, exh. cat. Galerie nationale du Jeu de paume, Paris (Paris: Éditions du Jeu de paume; Réunion des musées nationaux, 1991), 11. The other landmark exhibition shortly after the artist's death had been mounted two years earlier in the United States; see Marge Goldwater, ed., *Marcel Broodthaers*, exh. cat. Walker Art Center, Minneapolis, 1989 (New York: Rizzoli, 1989). A major touring exhibition followed some years later in Europe; see Manuel J. Borja-Villel, Michael Compton, and Maria Gilissen, eds., *Marcel Broodthaers: Cinéma*, exh. cat. Fundació Antoni Tàpies, Barcelona, 1997. Note also the recent exhibition *Marcel Broodthaers: A Retrospective*, February 14–May 15, 2016, Museum of Modern Art, New York, and its catalogue edited by Christophe Cherix and Manuel J. Borja-Villel, *Marcel Broodthaers* (New York: Museum of Modern Art, 2016).

68. Marcel Broodthaers, "To Be a Straight Thinker or Not to Be: To Be Blind" [1975], in Gloria Moure, ed., *Marcel Broodthaers: Collected Writings* (Barcelona: Ediciones Polígrafa, 2012), 469; original French text in Anna Hakkens, ed., *Marcel Broodthaers par lui-même* (Ghent: Ludion; Paris: Flammarion, 1998), 122.

69. To cite only a few: Rachel Haidu, *The Absence of Work: Marcel Broodthaers, 1964–1976* (Cambridge, Mass.: MIT Press, 2010); Rainer Borgemeister, *Marcel Broodthaers: Lessen und Sehen* (Bonn: Weidle, 2003); Deborah Schultz, *Marcel Broodthaers: Strategy and Dialogue* (Bern: Peter Lang, 2007); and Jean-Philippe Antoine, *Marcel Broodthaers: Moule, muse, méduse* (Dijon: Les presses du réel, 2006). Note also two important unpublished works: Tanya Angulo Alemán, "La utopia pervinguda: El model d'autoria de Marcel Broodthaers" (PhD diss., Universitat Politècnica de València, 2003); and Marie-Pascale Gildemyn, "Marcel Broodthaers (1924–1976): Les (noms de) personnes" (PhD diss., Université Rennes 2–Haute-Bretagne, 2006).

70. See, in particular, Susanne König, *Marcel Broodthaers: Musée d'art moderne, Département des aigles* (Berlin: Reimer, 2012), which retraces its political, artistic, and theoretical context; also Maria Gilissen and Benjamin Buckloh, eds., *Musée d'art moderne, Département des aigles, Section publicité, Marcel Broodthaers*, exh. cat. Marian Goodman Gallery, New York, 1995. A brief chronology of the various stages of this department of the museum may be found in David, *Marcel Broodthaers*, 190–91.

71. No doubt one of the most convincing attempts is Birgit Pelzer, "Les indices de l'échange," in David, *Marcel Broodthaers*, 24–33.

72. Marcel Broodthaers, *Projet pour un poisson (Projet pour un film)*, black-and-white 35 mm silent film, 9 minutes, 1971; opening credits by Jean Harlez. See Borja-Villel, Compton, and Gilissen, *Marcel Broodthaers: Cinéma*, 180–89.

73. This was first pointed out by Philippe Cuenat in the postface to his edition of Marcel Broodthaers, *Autour de "La Lorelei"* (Geneva: Musée d'art moderne et contemporain, 1997), 176. In an undated, handwritten draft titled "Projet pour un texte," however, Broodthaers wrote: "Fish have always seemed to me to belong to a secret society. Their viscosity and their strange mouths hardly lend themselves to metaphor." Manuscript reproduced (without accompanying English translation of this passage) in Moure, *Marcel Broodthaers*, 258–59.

74. Invitation for *Der Fisch/ein Film von Marcel Broodthaers*, Galerie Michael Werner, Cologne, shown there sometime in 1971. Reproduced in Borja-Villel, Compton, and Gilissen, *Marcel Broodthaers: Cinéma*, 187.

75. Marcel Broodthaers, *Jeter du poisson sur le marché de Cologne* (Cologne: Galerie Michael Werner, 1973). The book's publication coincided with Broodthaers's exhibition at the gallery during the fair that year, October 7–10.

76. Marcel Broodthaers, *Vingt fois sur le métier, remettez votre ouvrage*, ed. Maria Gilissen (Dijon: ADAC, 1988).

77. This project was exhibited and published in book form by Konrad Fischer Galerie after Broodthaers's death. Mention is made in the book's title of the "Finance Section, Department of Eagles," but this language seems to have been added by the editors; the "Contract" Broodthaers had drawn up speaks of a finance "department," not a "section." See Marcel Broodthaers, *Musée d'art moderne, Section financière, Département des aigles*, ed. Maria Gilissen and Konrad Fischer (Düsseldorf: Konrad Fischer Galerie, 1987).

78. The two met on the occasion of Manzoni's exhibit at Galerie Aujourd'hui in Brussels on February 17, 1962. A certificate of authenticity, numbered 071 and signed by Manzoni on February 23, declared Broodthaers to be "an authentic work of art for all intents and purposes." See Moure, *Marcel Broodthaers*, 220. Broodthaers later said that this meeting enabled him to appreciate "the distance separating poetry from a material artwork concerned with space (fine arts). In other words, the value of a message based only on the concept of merchandise as opposed to a message which identifies itself with merchandise." Quoted in Paul Martin, "Germany," *Studio International* 187, no. 965 (1974): 201.

79. Marcel Broodthaers, "Contract," reproduced in Moure, *Marcel Broodthaers*, 303.

80. Yves Klein, "Règles rituelles de cession des *Zones de sensibilité picturale immatérielle*" [1959], in *Le dépassement de la problématique de l'art et autres écrits*, ed. Marie-Anne Sichère and Didier Semin (Paris: École nationale supérieure des beaux arts, 2003), 278.

81. Author's interview with Maria Gilissen, April 13, 2013, Paris. The German curator Johannes Cladders recalls having seen the ingot during a visit to Broodthaers's home in the fall of 1971; see David, *Marcel Broodthaers*, 296.

82. See the map of booths in the Kölner Kunstmarkt catalogue of 1971. Galerie Michael Werner was located at this time at 14–18 Sankt-Apern-Straße in Cologne.

83. The historian Susanne König has very persuasively traced two lines of influence on this list of names: on the one hand, the genealogies constructed by the Surrealists (in accordance with a pseudo-objective method of evaluation based on a points system); and, on the other, the ranking (*Kunstkompass*) introduced by the critic Willi Bongard in 1970 in the magazine *Capital* of the "100 Größten" (the one hundred most important artists). In each case it is the presumptively scientific dimension of the ranking that is being attacked: "By incorporating imaginary, false, or incomplete names in his list, [Broodthaers] both mocks and criticizes the supposed objectivity [of these classifications] and calls attention to their random and unscientific character." König, *Marcel Broodthaers*, 118. This hypothesis is confirmed by the presence of a photograph of Bongard in the *Section des figures* exhibition in Düsseldorf, May 16–July 19, 1972; see Broodthaers, *Der Adler vom Oligozän bis heute: Marcel Broodthaers zeigt eine experimentelle Ausstellung seines "Musée d'art moderne, Département des aigles, section des figures,"* 2 vols., exh. cat. Städtische Kunsthalle, Düsseldorf (Düsseldorf: Städtische Kunsthalle, 1972), 1:17. The German artist Hans Haacke comments on this photograph, and on the meaning it held for Broodthaers, in *Symbolic Capital Management, or What to Do with the Good, the True and the Beautiful* [1997–99]; available online via www.societyofcontrol.com /research/haacke.htm.

84. These invitation cards are reproduced in David, *Marcel Broodthaers*, 212. Rachel Haidu speaks of the presence of posters and pamphlets at the fair as well; see *Absence of Work*, 150.

85. On this subject, see Haidu, *Absence of Work*, 142–43, and König, *Marcel Broodthaers*, 51–65.

86. Marcel Broodthaers, open letters from Antwerp ("J'ai trop à vous dire, chers amis. . . ."), October 11, 1968, and from Paris ("Chers amis, mes caisses sont vides. . . ."), November 29, 1968; both reproduced in Carel Blotkamp, ed., *Museum in Motion: Het museum voor moderne kunst ter diskussie* (The Hague: Staatsuitgeverij, 1979), 250. He had already made it clear, in an earlier open letter from Brussels ("À mes amis. . . .") dated June 7, of the same year, that "I have no material demands to make even though all I have to get drunk on is cabbage soup"; reproduced in ibid., 249.

87. Borja-Villel, Compton, and Gilissen, *Marcel Broodthaers: Cinéma*, 194.

88. Interview with Johannes Cladders, first published in the form of loose mimeographed sheets included in the catalogue of Documenta 5, the fifth edition of a quinquennial contemporary art exhibition held June 30–October 8, 1972, in Kassel, Germany; see David, *Marcel Broodthaers*, 229.

89. Marcel Broodthaers, "Projekt für den Kaufvertrag," *Heute Kunst*, no. 1 (April 1973): 20–23; translated into French in David, *Marcel Broodthaers*, 231, and into English in Moure, *Marcel Broodthaers*, 350.

90. Author's interview with Maria Gilissen, April 13, 2013, Paris. A photograph taken by Gilissen shows half of the bank counter sitting on the sidewalk before she and her husband carted it away; see Marie-Puck Broodthaers, ed., *Marcel Broodthaers: Livre d'images* (Paris: Flammarion, 2013), 68.

91. A photograph from 1965 shows Broodthaers seated in front of this version of *La Banque*; see David, *Marcel Broodthaers*, 64.

92. Ileana Sonnabend and Otto Hahn were identified by Amy De Decker and Bernd Lohaus during an interview with Marie-Pascale Gildemyn in 1978; see Gildemyn, "Marcel Broodthaers (1924–1976)," ABC 1041. Broodthaers emphasized his debt to Sonnabend on several occasions, notably in "À la Galerie Aujourd'hui: Marcel Broodthaers par Marcel Broodthaers" [1965], in Hakkens, *Marcel Broodthaers par lui-même*, 40–41. For Sonnabend's recollection of this episode, see Manuela Gandini, *Ileana Sonnabend: "The Queen of Art"* (Rome: Alberto Castelvecchi, 2008), 174–75.

93. This was, in any case, the form in which it was exhibited at the *L'Angelus de Daumier* show sponsored by the Centre national d'art contemporain at the Hôtel de Rothschild in Paris, October 2–November 10, 1975. The photographic record of this exhibition by Jacques

Faujour is conserved in the photography collection maintained by the documentation department of the Musée national d'art moderne–Centre de création industrielle, Paris.

94. The memory of these earlier incarnations of *La Banque* was preserved by Broodthaers in a work titled *100/100% Ordres de Bourse, La Banque* (1967); photographic canvas print cut into pieces, mounted on panel and painted, 41¼ × 42⅞ × ¾ in. (106 × 110 × 2 cm), private collection. See Marie-Puck Broodthaers, *Marcel Broodthaers*, 69.

95. "[J]ust as a gold bank, the public backing of the Bank of France, is necessary in order that the circulation of capital and private speculation be organized," Baudrillard says, "so the fixed reserve of the museum is necessary for the functioning of the sign exchange of paintings. Museums play the role of banks in the political economy of paintings." Jean Baudrillard, "The Art Auction: Sign Exchange and Sumptuary Value" [1972], in *For a Critique of the Political Economy of the Sign*, trans. Charles Levin (St. Louis, Mo.: Telos Press, 1981), 121–22.

96. Typed document titled "Ma collection," reproduced in Rosalind E. Krauss, *"A Voyage on the North Sea": Art in the Age of the Post-Medium Condition* (London: Thames and Hudson, 2000), 40. [Krauss's English version (p. 62) slightly modified.—Trans.]

97. The German art market underwent very rapid expansion in the six years following the recession of 1966–67; see Christine Mehring, "The Art of a Miracle: Toward a History of German Pop, 1955–1972," in *Art of the Two Germanys: Cold War Culture*, ed. Stephanie Barron and Sabine Eckmann, exh. cat. Los Angeles County Museum of Art, Los Angeles (New York: Harry N. Abrams, 2009), 154, 162. On the reception of pop art in Germany and the role of the Cologne Art Fair, see Catherine Dossin, "Pop begeistert: American Pop Art and the German People," *American Art* 25, no. 3 (2011): 100–111.

98. Jean-Marc Poinsot, "La crise du marché de l'art," *Chroniques de l'art vivant*, no. 24 (October 1971): 14. [Poinsot uses the term *speculative* here in its philosophical, not its financial, sense.—Trans.] It is interesting to note that Robert Filliou was attacked at the inaugural Art Basel for having offered his *35 m² of the International Art Fair* (3⅞ × 3⅞ in. [10 × 10 cm]), squares of white paper on which the title is printed in black, priced by the square meter, for sale at the gallerist Ingo Kümmel's booth; see Sylvie Jouval, ed., *Robert Filliou: Éditions et multiples* (Dijon: Les presses du réel, 2003), 48.

99. See Günter Herzog, "A History of the First Modern Art Fair, 1967–1969: 'Kunstmarkt Köln' "; available online via www.artcologne.com/ART-COLOGNE/Trade-fair/History-of-ART-COLOGNE/index.php.

100. Joseph Beuys, Erwin Heerich, and Klaus Staeck, "A Call to Action," February 10, 1971; Seth Siegelaub Papers (donated by Seth Siegelaub and the Stichting Egress Foundation, Amsterdam), series I. A, folder 97, in Museum of Modern Art Archives, New York (hereafter "Siegelaub Papers"). See also Sevim Riedinger, "République Fédérale: Un manifeste signé Beuys, Staeck et Heerich," *Opus international*, no. 26 (June 1971): 58–60.

101. Letter from Klaus Staeck to Seth Siegelaub, August 8, 1971. See also the list of signers of the appeal that was sent to him; Siegelaub Papers, series I. A, folder 97.

102. Poinsot, "La crise du marché de l'art," 14.

103. Press release (in German, English, French, and Italian); Siegelaub Papers, series I. A, folder 97.

104. Günter Wirth, "International Free Art Market in Heidelberg" (English translation by Klaus Staeck from an article in *Stuttgarter Zeitung*, September 9, 1971); and letter from Klaus Staeck to Seth Siegelaub, September 13, 1971, Siegelaub Papers, series I. A, folder 97.

105. "Several times during the discussions," Staeck noted, "mention was made of your artist's agreement, as our activities are closely connected." Letter from Klaus Staeck to Seth Siegelaub, September 13, 1971, ibid.

106. "Entretien de Freddy de Vree avec Marcel Broodthaers" [October 1971], in Hakkens, *Marcel Broodthaers par lui-même*, 76.

107. Ibid., 78.

108. Interview by Achille Bonito Oliva, October 12, 1971. From "A Score of Joseph Beuys: We Are the Revolution," p. 5 of a typescript in file labeled "*Ronald Feldman Fine Arts, Inc.*"; Lucy Lippard Papers, box 3, folder 33.

109. These opposite positions hardened in the months that followed, as may be seen from a handwritten letter from Broodthaers to Beuys dated September 25, 1972, and published in German under the title "Politik der Magie?," *Rheinische Post*, October 3, 1972; reproduced in both French and English in Marcel Broodthaers, *Magie: Art et politique* (Paris: Multiplicata, 1973), n.p. Many scholars have studied the origins and implications of the disagreement between the two artists. See, for example, Stefan Germer, "Haacke, Broodthaers, Beuys," *October* 45 (1988): 63–75; Dorothea Zwirner, "Beuys und Broodthaers: Dialektik der Moderne zwischen 'Analytischer Geometrie und dem Glauben an einen unglaublichen Gott,' " in Rainer Borgemeister, Birgit Pelzer, Julia Schmidt, and Dorothea Zwirner, eds., *Vorträge zum filmischen Werk von Marcel Broodthaers* (Cologne: Verlag der Buchhandlung, 2001), 93–127; and Schultz, *Marcel Broodthaers*, 257–58.

110. Letter from Michael Werner to Herman Daled, November 13, 1971; reproduced in Patrizia Dander and Ulrich Wilmes, eds., *Daled: A Bit of Matter and a Little More: The Collection and Archives of Herman and Nicole Daled, 1966–1978* (Munich: Haus der Kunst; Cologne: König, 2010), 333.

111. In 1975, Staeck put the number of self-financed posters, postcards, and pamphlets he had distributed at two million. See *Klaus Staeck: Politieke Affiches*, exh. cat. Van Abbemuseum, Eindhoven, 1975, n.p. These postcards and posters may still be obtained today from Edition Staeck for a few euros each via www.edition-staeck.de/.

112. Handwritten certificate, reproduced as entry no. 18 in *Marcel Broodthaers: The Complete Prints*, exh. cat. Michael Werner Gallery, New York, n.p. The exhibition took place from May 24 to June 29, 1991. Two copies of the edition were set aside, one for the artist and the other for the publisher.

113. See the list of editions in vol. 2 of the catalogue that Broodthaers assembled for his exhibition *L'Angelus de Daumier*, October 2–November 10, 1975; *L'Angelus de Daumier* (Paris: Centre national d'art contemporain, 1975), n.p.

114. Marcel Broodthaers, open letter from Kassel, June 27, 1968, reproduced in Blotkamp, *Museum in Motion*, 249. This text was inspired by an earlier poem that

associated the fish, a "ferocious" creature, with the cube, ball, pyramid, and cylinder. A set of four drawings from the same year directly identifies the fish, symbol of art as a commodity bought and sold on the market, with these same geometric volumes: *Un cube–une sphère–une pyramide–un cylindre (Poissons)*, 1968; pencil and felt-tip pen on paper, 11⅝ × 16⅜ in. (29.7 × 42 cm) each. See Marie-Puck Broodthaers, *Marcel Broodthaers*, 126–27. On Broodthaers's rejection of "primary structures" and "academic forms," see Dirk Snauwaert and Kaatje Cusse, "The Figures," *October* 42 (1987): 131; Michael Compton, "In Praise of the Subject," in Goldwater, *Marcel Broodthaers*, 43; and Benjamin H. D. Buchloh, Christophe Cherix, Rachel Haidu, Rosalind Krauss, and Trevor Stark, "The Moment of Marcel Broodthaers?: A Conversation," *October* 155 (2016): 141–43.

115. See Herzog, "History of the First Modern Art Fair." Two years later, writing about the crisis of the art market, Broodthaers extended the symbolism of the fish-as-commodity: "And if it were the sea that had collapsed / and the cod with their paint brushes combing [the] glory [of the prince]." Marcel Broodthaers, "A Book by Marcel Broodthaers," *Studio International* 189, no. 974 (1975): 109. (The bracketed addition was added by hand to the original text.)

116. Marcel Broodthaers, *Rendez-vous mit Jacques Offenbach*, 1972; 16 mm sound film in black-and-white and in color, 18 minutes, 30 seconds. Combining very short films and scenes from longer films by the artist, it was shown for the first time at the Palais des Beaux-Arts in Brussels, December 7, 1972. See Borja-Villel, Compton, and Gilissen, *Marcel Broodthaers: Cinéma*, 208–21.

117. Nixon's speech was published in its entirety by many American newspapers. The highlights were translated by French journalists; see, for example, Jacques Amalric, "Les mesures économiques et monétaires prises par le président des États-Unis," *Le Monde*, August 17, 1971, pp. 1–5.

118. Some of these coins were shown as part of the *Section des figures* exhibition in Düsseldorf in 1972, identified as loans from "the collection of the Department of Eagles": see entry no. 75 in Broodthaers, *Der Adler vom Oligozän bis heute*, 22. Eight original drawings of these coins, employing the technique of frottage, were published posthumously by the artist's widow in 1992. Like the "Contract" of 1971, they bear the imprint of the "Finance Department." It would appear, then, that they are not part of the Finance Section in the strict sense (the Cologne exhibits), but that they are related to it. See *Catalogue des monnaies (collection privée), Service financier*, exh. cat. Galerie Ronny Van de Velde, Antwerp (September 1972). On the artist's interest in gold, see also "Interview with Marcel Broodthaers by Michael Oppitz and Benjamin Buchloh," in Moure, *Marcel Broodthaers*, 399. Broodthaers was also interested, though to a lesser degree, in banknotes featuring the figure of the eagle. One thinks, for example, of the series of *Cahiers* produced in 1972, twelve (perhaps more) children's school exercise books (about 8 × 5¾ in. [20.5 × 14.5 cm]), labeled, each with a blue envelope (often addressed to the Deutsche Bundesbank) containing a 100 deutsche mark bill inside. The eagle appearing on the face of the bill has been cut out and used as a seal to close the flap of the envelope. The labels are inscribed with warnings such as "Counterfeiters shall be sentenced to hard labor in perpetuity." See Jos. Jamar, ed., *Marcel Broodthaers: Het Volledig Grafisch Werk en de Boeken*, exh. cat. Galerie Jamar, Antwerp, 2001, pp. 90–93. On the hoarding of money in France, see, for example, Michel Tardieu, "Les Français et leur argent," *L'Express*, January 17–23, 1972, p. 77.

119. Author's interview with Maria Gilissen, April 13, 2013, Paris.

120. Pol Bury, "L'art à bicyclette et la révolution à cheval," *Chroniques de l'art vivant*, no. 34 (November 1972): 21.

121. Otto Hahn, "L'avant-garde choisit le mark," *L'Express*, January 3–9, 1972, p. 50.

122. Michel Ragon, "Exécution pour une avant-garde," *Chroniques de l'art vivant*, no. 27 (February 1972): 5.

123. Michael Compton, "Les éditions de Marcel Broodthaers," in *Marcel Broodthaers: L'œuvre graphique*, exh. cat. Centre genevois de gravure contemporaine, Geneva, 1991, p. 32. Most commentators on this work take the same view: see Martin Mosebach, "Die Beschwörung des toten Museums: Marcel Broodthaers's "L'entrée de l'exposition,'" and S. D. Sauerbier, "Rebus sic stantibus," in *Marcel Broodthaers: "L'entrée de l'exposition,"* exh. cat. Galerie Michael Werner, Cologne (September 27–October 31, 1984), n.p.; and Rainer Borgemeister, "La signature, l'artiste," in *Marcel Broodthaers: L'œuvre graphique*, 47. One finds a similar reading more recently in Schultz, *Marcel Broodthaers*, 87. The most complete and the best interpretation of this work is given by Philippe Cuenat, "L'œuvre graphique dans le décor: 'L'entrée de l'exposition'," in *Marcel Broodthaers: L'œuvre graphique*, 74–75; nonetheless, it is marred by errors of observation, noted below.

124. The third "stanza" of the last column, "Poème," contains an omission: it lacks an "M. B." in the fourth "verse," reducing the total to forty-four, not forty-five as indicated there.

125. This is also the case in the film *Figures of Wax*. See Borja-Villel, Compton, and Gilissen, *Marcel Broodthaers: Cinéma*, 268–75.

126. One counts 198 signatures for "1,650 F.F." and 246 signatures for "50 $."

127. Pierre Bourgeois, "Un *happening*: 'Au pied de la lettre,'" *Le journal des poètes*, no. 10 (December 1966): 11.

128. Author's interview with Maria Gilissen, April 13, 2013, Paris.

129. Broodthaers walked around the room, a packet of detergent slung over his shoulder, and recited a poem suggesting the futility of cleansing books ("Must we still go on writing Persil? Books will never be white enough"), while another man "sawed off large letters after having washed them in a bathtub." See Bourgeois, "Un *happening*," 11.

130. Ibid.

131. This is only one of many examples of Broodthaers's "cartographic" works. On this subject, see Schultz, *Marcel Broodthaers*, 193–235.

132. Marcel Broodthaers, "Denk ich an Deutschland–La Lorelei–Die Lorelei," draft preface to *En lisant "La Lorelei"* (1975). Two pages, typescript and fountain pen on watermarked paper, reproduced in Broodthaers, *Autour de "La Lorelei,"* ed. Cuenat, 84. Another version of the text (without this formula) is translated as "The Lorelei," in Moure, *Marcel Broodthaers*, 465.

133. Stéphane Mallarmé, "Or," in *Œuvres complètes*, ed. Bertrand Marchal, 2 vols. (Paris: Gallimard, 1998–2003), 2:245.

134. Filliou and Broodthaers met in Düsseldorf in 1968. On their relationship, see Heike Van den Valentyn, "L'Allemagne est un bon endroit pour dormir: Robert Filliou à Düsseldorf de 1968 à 1974," in *Robert Filliou: Génie sans talent*, exh. cat. of an exhibition that traveled to Barcelona, Düsseldorf, and Villeneuve d'Ascq, December 6, 2003–March 28, 2004 (Villeneuve d'Ascq: Musée d'art moderne Lille Métropole, 2003), 22–23; and Hans-Werner Schmidt, ed., *Robert Filliou, 1926–1987*, exh. cat. Städtische Kunsthalle, Düsseldorf (August 6–September 11, 1988), 126. Filliou also had known Ray Johnson since the 1960s through the Fluxus group and received NYCS mailings. In a telephone conversation with Michael Morris of Image Bank in 1973, he said: "I haven't seen [Ray] for a very long time myself, since the last time I was in New York in 1967. But I hear from him often." Telephone conversation published on audiocassette by Voicespondence Audio Art Publishing and subsequently transcribed in Scott Watson, ed., *Robert Filliou: From Political to Poetical Economy*, exh. cat. Morris and Helen Belkin Art Gallery, Vancouver (Vancouver, B.C.: Belkin Art Gallery, University of British Columbia, 1995), 72.

135. Robert Filliou, "Transcript: The 'Gong Show' Tape," *Centerfold* 2, no. 4 (1978): 29.

136. Luis Camnitzer, "Contemporary Colonial Art" [1969], in *Conceptual Art: A Critical Anthology*, ed. Alexander Alberro and Blake Stimson (Cambridge, Mass.: MIT Press, 1999), 225–26.

137. One thinks also of the work of the Swedish artist Öyvind Fahlström, who used displays of economic statistics to draw attention to the mechanisms of systematic capitalist exploitation of the countries of the Third World, as well as the Brazilian artist Cildo Meireles's Coca-Cola project, *Insertions into Ideological Circuits* [1970]. On Fahlström, see in particular *Öyvind Fahlström*, exh. cat. Centre Georges Pompidou, Paris (Paris: Éditions du Centre Pompidou, 1980); Öyvind Fahlström, *Essais choisis* (Dijon: Les presses du réel, 2002); and *Öyvind Fahlström*, exh. cat. Institut d'art contemporain, Villeurbanne, 2002. On Meireles, see Okwui Enwezor, "On the Politics of Disaggregation: Notes on Cildo Meireles's 'Insertions into Ideological Circuits,'" in Guy Brett, ed., *Cildo Meireles*, exh. cat. Tate Modern, London (London: Tate Publishing, 2008), 68–73; and Paulo Herkenhoff, Gerardo Mosquera, and Dan Cameron, *Cildo Meireles* (London: Phaidon, 1999), 108–16.

CONCLUSION

1. Robert Filliou, *Teaching and Learning as Performing Arts* (Cologne: König, 1970), 51.

2. "Petit dictionnaire Filliou (extraits)," *Chroniques de l'art vivant*, no. 18 (March 1971): 20.

3. Robert Filliou, "The Propositions and Principles of ROBERT FILLIOU," *Centerfold* 2, nos. 2–3 (1978), n.p.

4. Interview with Robert Filliou by Jean-Pierre Van Tieghem [January 1972], reprinted in *Robert Filliou*, exh. cat. Musée national d'art moderne, Paris (Paris: Éditions du Centre Georges Pompidou, 1991), 72–74.

5. Robert Filliou, "A Proposition, a Problem, a Danger, and a Hunch," in *Manifestos* (New York: Something Else Press, 1966), 14.

6. Robert Filliou, "From Robert Filliou's Work-in-Progress, *Principles of Poetical Economy*," in George Brecht and Robert Filliou, *Games at the Cedilla; or, The Cedilla Takes Off* (New York: Something Else Press, 1967), n.p.

7. Interview with Jean-Pierre Van Tieghem [January 1972], reprinted in *Robert Filliou*, exh. cat. 1991, 75.

8. Irmeline Lebeer, "Musées Personnes–Filliou," *Chroniques de l'art vivant*, no. 35 (December 1972): 19.

9. See Natilee Harren, "*La cédille qui ne finit pas*: Robert Filliou, George Brecht, and Fluxus in Villefranche," *Getty Research Journal*, no. 4 (2012): 130–34; also Brecht and Filliou, *Games at the Cedilla*, n.p.

10. Undated text, late 1960s, conserved in the Sohm Archives, Staatsgalerie, Stuttgart; quoted in *Robert Filliou*, exh. cat. 1991, 37.

11. Filliou, "Propositions and Principles of ROBERT FILLIOU," n.p.

12. Robert Filliou, "Filliou," *Opus International*, no. 22 (January 1971): 20.

13. Robert Filliou, "Transcript: The 'Gong Show' Tape," *Centerfold* 2, no. 4 (1978): 30; Filliou quoted in Irmeline Lebeer, "Le Petit Robert Filliou," *Chroniques de l'art vivant*, no. 18 (March 1971): 20; and Filliou, "Filliou," 20.

14. One finds traces of these chapters in several published texts: initially in *Manifestos* (1966), and then *Games at the Cedilla* (1967); the first substantial development occurs in *Teaching and Learning as Performing Arts* (1970), followed by an oblique mention in the January 1971 article "Filliou." The most important source remains the corpus of lectures and video films produced in the second half of the 1970s, notably *Porta Filliou*, 1977 (black-and-white sound film, 43 minutes 35 seconds) and *The Gong Show*, 1977 (filmed lecture at the University of Calgary, Alberta, Canada), the text of which was reproduced as "Transcript: The 'Gong Show' Tape." More generally, see the three-volume DVD set of Filliou's work issued posthumously in 1997 by The Western Front, an artist-run contemporary art center in Vancouver, B.C., under the title *From Political to Poetical Economy*.

15. Sharla Sava, "Les bandes Filliou: De l'économie politique à l'économie poétique," in *Robert Filliou: From Political to Poetical Economy*, ed. Scott Watson, exh. cat. Morris and Helen Belkin Art Gallery, Vancouver (Vancouver, B.C.: Belkin Art Gallery, University of British Columbia, 1995), 19.

16. Allan Kaprow, "The Artist as a Man of the World" [1964], in *Essays on the Blurring of Art and Life*, ed. Jeff Kelley (Berkeley: University of California Press, 1993), 53.

17. Loïc Charles and Christine Théré, "The Writing Workshop of François Quesnay and the Making of Physiocracy (1757–1764)," *History of Political Economy* 40, no. 1 (2008): 1–42.

18. Craufurd Goodwin, "Art and Culture in the History of Economic Thought," in *Handbook of the Economics of Art and Culture*, ed. Victor A. Ginsburgh and David Throsby (Amsterdam: Elsevier North-Holland, 2006), 37.

19. For a selection of Fry's writings on the economics of art, see Craufurd Goodwin, ed., *Art and the Market: Roger Fry on Commerce in Art* (Ann Arbor: University of Michigan Press, 1999). See also Craufurd Goodwin, "Economics Meets Aesthetics in the Bloomsbury Group," in *Sublime Economy: On the Intersection of Art and Economics*, ed. Jack Amariglio, Joseph W. Childers, and Stephen E. Cullenberg (New York: Routledge, 2009), 137–51.

20. Georges Bataille, *The Accursed Share:*

An Essay on General Economy [1949], 3 vols., trans. Robert Hurley (New York: Zone Books, 1988–91), 1:9–10.

21. Exhibitions treating the theme of financial crisis have done much to sharpen this militant perspective on both sides of the Atlantic. See, in particular, two published catalogues: Gregory Sholette and Oliver Ressler, eds., *It's the Political Economy, Stupid: The Global Financial Crisis in Art and Theory* (London: Pluto Press, 2013), and Tatiana Bazzichelli and Geoff Cox, eds., *Disrupting Business: Art and Activism in Times of Financial Crisis* (New York: Autonomedia, 2013).

22. Walter Benjamin, *One-Way Street and Other Writings*, trans. Edmund Jephcott and Kingsley Shorter (London: NLF, 1979), 96. In this connection see the entire second chapter as well.

23. *Robert Filliou: Das Immerwährende Ereignis Zeigt/The Eternal Network Presents/La Fête permanente présente*, exh. cat. Sprengel-Museum, Hannover (Hannover: Sprengel-Museum; Paris: Musée d'art moderne de la Ville de Paris; Berne: Kunsthalle, 1984), 35.

24. See, for example, Isabelle Graw, *High Price: Art between the Market and Celebrity*, trans. Nicholas Grindell (Berlin: Sternberg Press, 2009).

25. Robert Filliou, *Sans titre–Sans tête*, 1983; color sound film, 11 minutes 32 seconds, camera J.-H. Martin; conserved in the archives of the executor of Filliou's estate, Galerie Nelson-Freeman, Paris.

Index

Illustration Credits

Fig. 1. Courtesy Estate Robert Filliou.
Fig. 3. © ADAGP, Paris, 2018.
Figs. 4–6, 8. © Yves Klein/ADAGP, Paris, 2018.
Figs. 9, 11. © Kienholz. Courtesy of L.A. Louver, Venice, CA.
Fig. 10. © Kienholz. Courtesy of L.A. Louver, Venice, CA. © Photo: Malcolm Lubliner.
Figs. 15–18. Courtesy Archivio Gallizio, Turin.
Fig. 19. © Andy Warhol Foundation for the Visual Arts/ADAGP, Paris, 2018. © Photo: Courtesy of Sotheby's, Inc., 2018.
Figs. 20, 50. © Yayoi Kusama.
Figs. 21–24, 27–28. © Andy Warhol Foundation for the Visual Arts/ADAGP, Paris, 2018.
Fig. 30. © ADAGP, Paris, 2018.
Figs. 31, 37. © Photo by Lee Stalsworth, Hirshhorn Museum and Sculpture Garden, Smithsonian Institution, 2018. © ADAGP, Paris, 2018.
Figs. 32–35. Courtesy Banque de France, Paris.
Fig. 38. Photo © RMN–Grand Palais (musée du Louvre)/Franck Raux.
Figs. 43–46. Courtesy Archives Bernar Venet, New York.
Figs. 47–49. Courtesy Dennis Oppenheim Estate, New York.
Fig. 51. © The Estate of Lee Lozano. Courtesy Hauser & Wirth.
Fig. 52. Courtesy Dan Graham Studio.
Figs. 53, 55. © Les Levine / ADAGP, Paris, 2018.
Fig. 54. Courtesy Robert Morris. © ADAGP, Paris, 2018.
Fig. 56. © ADAGP, Paris, 2018.
Fig. 57. Courtesy of Primary Information.
Fig. 58. © The Estate of Lee Lozano. Courtesy Hauser & Wirth. Photo: © Allen Phillips/ Wadsworth Atheneum.
Figs. 59–62, 66, 68. © The Ray Johnson Estate.
Fig. 63. Photo © BPK, Berlin, Dist. RMN–Grand Palais/Michael Herling/Aline Gwose.
Figs. 64–65. © The Ray Johnson Estate. Photo: Archives of American Art, Smithsonian Institution.
Figs. 69–70, 72. © The Estate of Marcel Broodthaers/ADAGP, Paris, 2018. Photo: © Museu d'Art Contemporani de Barcelona.
Figs. 71, 74–77. © The Estate of Marcel Broodthaers/ADAGP, Paris, 2018.
Fig. 73. © The Estate of Marcel Broodthaers/ADAGP, Paris, 2018. Photo: © Raussmüller Collection, Basel.
Fig. 78. Courtesy Estate Robert Filliou & Peter Freeman, Inc. New York/Paris © Estate Robert Filliou.